SY

ACP-1359

Troubleshooting PC

M. David Stone & Alfred Poor

PUBLISHED BY
Microsoft Press
A Division of Microsoft Corporation
One Microsoft Way
Redmond, Washington 98052-6399

Copyright © 2001 by M. David Stone and Alfred Poor

Library of Congress Cataloging-in-Publication Data
Stone, M. David.
    Troubleshooting Your PC / M. David Stone, Alfred Poor.
        p. cm.
    Includes index.
    ISBN 0-7356-1163-7
    1. Microcomputers--Maintenance and repair.   I. Poor, Alfred E. II. Title.

  TK7887.S78   2000
  621.39'16--cd21

                                                                    00-048722

Printed and bound in the United States of America.

1 2 3 4 5 6 7 8 9   QWT   6 5 4 3 2 1

Distributed in Canada by Penguin Books Canada Limited.

A CIP catalogue record for this book is available from the British Library.

Microsoft Press books are available through booksellers and distributors worldwide. For further information about international editions, contact your local Microsoft Corporation office or contact Microsoft Press International directly at fax (425) 936-7329. Visit our Web site at mspress.microsoft.com. Send comments to *mspinput@microsoft.com*.

Acquisitions Editors: Christey Bahn and Alex Blanton
Project Editor: Wendy Zucker
Technical Editor: Jim Fuchs

Acknowledgments

Writing may be a solitary business, but putting a book together requires the cooperation and contribution of many more people than just the author or authors. With this book we've been struck by how much help those other people have been—even more so than with other books we've written. Our editor, Wendy Zucker, has demonstrated endless good humor and support at all stages of this project. Our two technical editors, Jim Fuchs and Marc Young, were impressively perceptive in picking up on our approach and tone, and making suggestions where needed. We'd also like to thank Christey Bahn, who brought us to Microsoft Press for this book.

Also high on our list is our agent, Claudette Moore, who shepherded this project through to its successful conclusion. We hope that she'll have the time for a few more Plum Island picnics in the future.

We would like to give special thanks to Reena Spektor, who arranged for the loan from Epson America of the digital cameras we used to create the reference pictures for the artwork in this book.

Alfred would like to thank Michael Goldman for his work organizing materials from Alfred's *PC Magazine* and *Computer Shopper* question-and-answer columns. Michael's efforts turned that mass of information into a valuable resource that helped us create this book. (David, alas, had to organize his columns and articles himself, but will be happy to accept volunteers for future editions.)

Finally, in keeping with the troubleshooting spirit of this book, and recognizing that one corollary to Murphy's law is that no one ever reads acknowledgments except the people that the writers should have mentioned, but didn't, we'd like to thank those we never dealt with directly at Microsoft Press, but who were responsible for such things as copyediting our manuscript, translating our reference pictures into finished artwork, and otherwise improving the quality of the finished work.

Quick contents

Contents

Appendix
When you have to reinstall Windows   337

Index   341

About this book

Troubleshooting Your PC presents a new way to diagnose and solve problems you've encountered with your computer hardware, even if you don't know anything beyond the basics of how your system works. Chances are that you bought this book because you want to fix those problems as quickly and easily as possible, without having to read pages of technical background information. Because we know that you don't want to waste a lot of time searching for answers, we wrote this book with three goals in mind: ease, simplicity, and speed. We'll show you how to identify your problem, describe what might be causing it without going into too many specifics, and then lead you right to the solution so that you can get back to what you were doing.

How to use this book

This book isn't meant to be read by following the chapters in any particular order, or even from cover to cover. It's designed so that you can jump in, quickly diagnose your problem, and then get the information you need to fix it, whether you've just begun to learn about computers or whether you're knowledgeable enough to get right to the source of the problem. We've grouped the problems you're most likely to encounter into chapters, listed alphabetically, with short, straightforward titles that let you see at a glance what kinds of topics the chapter covers. Each chapter is broken down into two specific elements: the flowchart and the solution spreads.

Flowcharts

The first thing you'll see when you go to a chapter is a dynamic, easy-to-use flowchart. It starts by asking you a broad question about a common problem and then, as you answer a series of yes-or-no questions, guides you toward a diagnosis of your problem. If the solution to the problem is a simple one that requires only a few steps, you'll find a quick fix right there on the flowchart. Take a few minutes to work your way through the steps, and presto—your problem is solved and you're back to work (or play) with a minimum of down time. If the solution to your problem requires a little more explanation and a few more steps, you'll find a statement that describes the problem, along with the page number of the solution spread you need to go to. And if you can't find your specific problem in the series of questions on the flowchart, look through the list of related chapters for another area where your problem might be addressed.

Solution spreads

The solution spreads are where the real troubleshooting takes place. We provide you with the source of the problem you're experiencing and then, with clear, step-by-step instructions, tell you how to fix it. The solution spreads contain plenty of screen shots and illustrations that show you what you should be seeing as you move through the steps. Although our goal is to give you just the facts so that you can quickly get back to what you were doing, in some cases we've provided more detailed background information that you might or might not want to read, depending on whether you're looking for a deeper understanding of what caused your problem. Also scattered throughout the solution spreads are tips that contain related material or advice that you might find helpful, and a few warnings that tell you what you should or shouldn't do in a given situation.

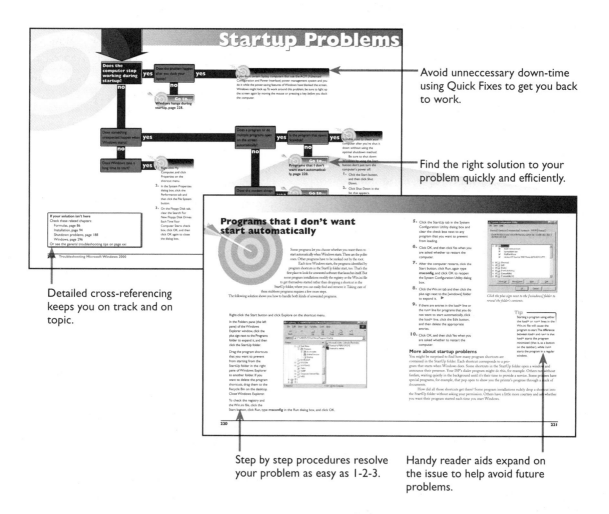

Avoid unneccessary down-time using Quick Fixes to get you back to work.

Find the right solution to your problem quickly and efficiently.

Detailed cross-referencing keeps you on track and on topic.

Step by step procedures resolve your problem as easy as 1-2-3.

Handy reader aids expand on the issue to help avoid future problems.

Troubleshooting tips

The truth about troubleshooting

There's a dirty little secret about trouble-shooting hardware. And it's a secret you won't hear from the guys who charge you $75 an hour and up for fixing your computer (unless, maybe, you take them out, get them drunk, and start them bragging about it).

Finding hardware problems and fixing them is *easy*. One of us, whose first computer was an all-in-one design, with keyboard, computer, and monitor in one case, found this out the hard way. It seems he had a habit of banging the desk with his fist when something went wrong on the computer. (Read: When he hit the wrong key.) Then one day, the computer stopped working. This was in the days when entry-level computers cost $5,000 and came with on-site technical support, so he waited two days for a technician to show up. The technician opened the case, saw that the cable to the keyboard had been jarred loose, and reconnected it. Problem fixed. In about 10 minutes. After waiting two days.

That was the last time the unnamed writer (OK—it was David) waited two days for a technician to open the case.

Tracking down the problem may not always be as easy as spotting a loose connector (although you may be surprised how often the connection is the problem), and when the cause isn't obvious, it won't always be the first thing you'll think of. But pinpointing the source of most problems is easy, if you go about it the right way. It certainly doesn't take a genius or even someone who knows a lot about computers. What it takes is some detective work, a methodical approach, and patience.

There are, in fact, just six rules you need to know to be able to troubleshoot not just computers, but almost anything. (With computers, we'd add the seventh rule of using this book.) If you take a careful look at our solutions in this book, you'll see that we use these six rules repeatedly. Unfortunately, we can't cover the specifics for every possible problem. If you run into a problem that isn't covered here, one place you might look is *www.mspress.microsoft.com/troubleshooting*, which is described in more detail at the end of this introduction. However, we can't cover everything online either, so sometimes you'll be on your own. When that happens, these rules will help you immeasurably when you need to find and fix a problem.

The six golden rules

First, do no harm

No doubt you've heard the medical credo to first do no harm. What you may not have realized is that same rule applies to computer problems. You've probably never thought about it this way, but when you try to diagnose a computer problem you're doing much the same thing as a doctor diagnosing a disease. The particulars are different, but the strategies are similar.

Suppose, for example, that your system just crashed. You're working hard against a deadline, trying to get a report finished, and you haven't saved your file for at least half an hour. You're in a rush, so the first thing you want to do is reboot, right? Wrong. The first thing you want to do is nothing. Sit on your hands and think a bit. In this particular case, the smartest thing to do is to grab a pen and write down anything that shows on the screen, so you won't have to recreate that information from scratch. Then think about the best way to retrieve the rest of the information, most of which is probably sitting in a temporary file on the disk. Details, of course, will vary depending on the problem, but the strategy should always be the same: Avoid rushing headlong into doing something, even if you have an immediate thought about what to do. Stop and think about it for a moment. Then do whatever you decide to do.

This rule applies on all sorts of levels. If you need to open your computer case to work on the hardware, for instance, don't just rush in and start messing around inside the computer. Make sure you take the time to read "Working inside your computer" on page xxv—or reread it if you haven't read it recently—so you know how to avoid doing damage to your computer with static electricity. When something goes wrong, in short: Stop. Think. See if you can find the answer in this book. If you can't find it, plan what you're going to do before you do it. Above all else, don't rush in without thinking and risk making matters worse.

Don't overlook the obvious

We use a second medical rule also, because there is at least one other similarity between a doctor diagnosing a medical problem and you diagnosing a computer problem. In both cases, you've got to pinpoint the problem before you can do anything to fix it.

We bring this up because doctors have a relevant saying: *When you hear hoof beats, think horses, not zebras.* It's a way of reminding medical students and new doctors that when a patient presents with a set of symptoms, the symptoms are most likely due to the most common causes of those symptoms, rather than some exotic disease they just read about in a medical journal. More to the point, the spirit behind that saying is also why the first question you'll usually get from almost any hardware company's tech support line is, "Is it plugged in?"

It's not because they think you're stupid (at least not most of the time), and it's not because (or at least not *just* because) the people on the first level of the tech support lines don't generally know a lot and are limited to the easy fixes. It's because most people don't think to check the obvious causes of a problem before they give up. We've seen highly competent reviewers in magazine testing labs grousing about a piece of hardware not working, until they discover—usually with some embarrassment—that they forgot to plug in some critical cable or power connector. (Neither of *us*, of course, has ever done such a thing.)

In real life, as in a testing lab, this is most likely to happen when you first set something up, but cables can get jarred loose—as with the keyboard connector in the (true) story at the beginning of this discussion. Someone may have tripped over a power cord or data cable, or bumped into it and dislodged it. If the computer is set up in a home office with dogs, cats, or small children running around, the odds of that happening go way up.

The point is, whether your system is brand new, or it's been working without problems for months, when something goes wrong, check the obvious things first: Do you see a power light? Is the switch turned on? If the computer is plugged into a power strip, is the switch on the power strip on? Are the cables all connected? Is the fan turning? Are all the adapter cards solidly seated in their slots? And so on.

Keep in mind too that what's obvious in some situations is not obvious in others. If you leave your system on during a thunderstorm—with or without a surge protector—and come back to find that it doesn't work, the obvious possibility is that some components got zapped. Or, if you prefer: *When you're in Africa, you probably should think zebras when you hear hoof beats, after all.*

Do any part you can

If *First, do no harm* and *Don't overlook the obvious* are our medical rules, this must be the science fiction rule, since we cribbed it from Robert A. Heinlein's *The Moon Is a Harsh Mistress.* The first person narrator—who happens to be a computer technician, among other things—points out that the best problem solving advice he ever got was this: *When faced with a problem you don't understand, do any part of it you do understand, then step back and look at the problem again.*

We can't think of a better approach to troubleshooting a problem when you're not sure what to do. Even if all you can think of is to open the case, the answer may be revealed to you—like that loose keyboard connector we mentioned earlier. And in the more likely event that you don't solve the problem immediately from doing the parts you understand, the results of whatever you do may give you an idea about what to do next. If not, at least you'll know that you've done what you can, before giving up and handing the job over to someone else.

Simplify, bracket, and swap out

We like to call this trio the *troubleshooting for poets* rules, largely because they don't depend on having very much technical knowledge. Even though these rules represent three different tactics for troubleshooting, they overlap with each other in practice so much that sometimes it's hard to tell which one you're following. Don't let that bother you. It doesn't matter how you decide whether a given step is worth taking. What matters is that you take it.

Simplify

No one has ever said it better than Thoreau: *Simplify, simplify.* The simpler you can make your system, the fewer things you need to look at when you're tracking down a problem.

If you can test for the problem without Microsoft Windows running, for example, you don't have to consider a software conflict in Windows as the source of the problem. If you can't test without Windows running, you can at least close all programs that aren't absolutely necessary, which eliminates those programs from the equation. If you can remove other hardware plugged into your system's ports, you can eliminate that hardware as the source of the problem. And if you can remove some adapter cards from your computer, you have that many fewer adapter cards to consider as possible sources of the problem. The point is that the more you can simplify the system you're testing, the fewer things you have to look at to find the problem.

Bracket

There's enough overlap between simplifying and bracketing that it's hard to draw a sharp distinction between them. Bracketing is most easily understood in context of a game we'll call *Guess the Number*. Consider a game in which a computer randomly picks a number between 0 and 100. Your job is to guess the number. With each guess, the computer will answer *Higher* or *Lower*, to indicate that its chosen number is higher or lower than the one you guessed. What's the best strategy for finding the number with the fewest possible guesses on average? Bracketing. The trick is to always bracket the number by picking one that's midway between the current possibilities. Always start with 50, and you guarantee that you've bracketed the number between 0 and 50 or 50 and 100, depending on the answer. If the answer is *Lower*, your next guess is 25, which brackets the number between 0 and 25 or 25 and 50, and so on.

Bracketing a computer problem works pretty much the same way. Suppose you have a problem printing, for example. At the risk of oversimplifying, there are five possible sources of the problem: The software you're printing from, the printer driver (the software that tells Windows how to print with the particular printer), the computer hardware, the cable, and the printer.

Run the printer's self test. If the printer works, the problem lies somewhere between the application program and the connector on the printer. If it doesn't work, the problem is in the printer itself, and you can look at things like whether it has any ink or toner left. (Or paper. Remember Rule 2: Don't overlook the obvious.) Either way, you've bracketed the problem and have fewer things to look at.

Bracketing overlaps with simplifying, because one of the ways to bracket a problem is to simplify your system. With a printing problem, for example, if the printer is plugged into some other hardware, one bracketing step you'll want to try is to remove the other device, which also simplifies the system. In much the same way, when you simplify your system, you may find that a problem disappears—in which case you've effectively bracketed the problem by showing it's related to whatever you eliminated. You can then add things back to help pinpoint the item that's causing the problem. Whether you get to this point by thinking about simplifying your system or thinking about bracketing the problem, however, doesn't matter. What matters is that you get there.

Swap out

Swapping out doesn't overlap with simplifying, but it certainly overlaps with bracketing a problem. The idea behind swapping out is simple. Suppose you have two flashlights. One works; the other doesn't. The problem with the one that doesn't work could be bad batteries or a bad bulb. Swap the batteries and see what happens. If the problem goes with the batteries to the second flashlight, you need new batteries. If the problem stays with the same flashlight only, you need a new bulb. If both flashlights now have a problem, you need new batteries and a new bulb.

Swapping out overlaps with bracketing because sometimes the only way to bracket a problem is to swap out some pieces. Returning to printer problems, for example, swapping printers will tell you if the problem goes with the printer or with the rest of the system, which in turn helps you bracket the problem. And swapping cables is the easiest way to decide whether you have a problem with the cable. Whether you think of what you're doing as swapping out or as bracketing doesn't matter, as long as you get around to swapping the cables.

There is a warning that goes with swapping out. In rare circumstances, hardware can fail in a way that will also damage other hardware that's plugged into it or that it's plugged into—call the two pieces *Item A* and *Item B*. Swap out Item A for a working version, and you can damage the replacement. Then swap out Item B, and the newly damaged replacement for Item A can damage the replacement for B. Worse, if you take the newly damaged replacement for Item A and plug it back into the system that it came from, it can damage the equivalent to Item B in the second system. This scenario happens rarely enough that we feel comfortable ignoring it, but you need to be aware that it's a possibility and that you are taking a chance,

however small, when you swap a piece of hardware that you know is working with one that you're not sure of. More important, if things that were working suddenly stop working during your troubleshooting tests, it's a good idea to stop and let a professional repair service take over. (And it's not a bad idea to check the warranties on parts that you're swapping before you start swapping them.)

The troubleshooter's strategy

The idea of a strategy for troubleshooting may sound a little grand, but that's exactly what you need when you go on a troubleshooting expedition. Once you get past doing no harm and checking the obvious, think about the specific steps you need to take, but keep in mind that the grand strategy is almost always the same: Do whatever you can to simplify your system. Then approach the problem as a bracketing problem if you can, and swap out items if you can, particularly if that's the only way to confirm that a particular item is or is not working properly.

Steps you can take to prevent or minimize problems

There are a number of steps you can take to help minimize the problems you might otherwise have to troubleshoot. Some of these steps will prevent problems altogether. Others will make it easier to recover from problems when (not if) they happen.

Your troubleshooting swap out kit

Before you can swap out anything, you need things to swap out. And that means keeping extras around so they'll be available for swapping. High on the list is anything you'll eventually need anyway; you might buy it sooner than you would otherwise, but it won't cost you extra to have it in the long run. Items in this category include

- Extra toner or ink cartridges
- Extra blank floppy disks
- Extra CD-R discs if you have a CD-R or CD-RW drive
- Extra CD-RW discs if you have a CD-RW drive
- Extras of any other removable disks or discs, to match the drives you have (Zip, Jaz, DVD-RAM, and so forth)

The second key category is items you can cannibalize from older equipment when you upgrade. An old computer may be so out of date that the only thing it's useful for is a doorstop, but odds are that some, if not all, of the parts inside can serve as troubleshooting tools to swap out parts. The hard disk, for example, may offer a laughingly low capacity, but if it's the same kind of drive as in your current system, you can swap it out when you think you may have a problem with your current disk drive. Other key parts would include

- Any other drive
- Adapter cards (particularly graphics cards)
- Cables

Also in this category are old external devices, including

- Printers
- Older modems, even if limited to slow speeds
- Zip drives and other external drives
- Speakers
- Headsets

You may never expect to use any of these items again, but they can be invaluable when you need to troubleshoot a problem.

Finally, there are some things that are very much worth investing in just to have handy. In particular, many cables—including printer cables and ribbon cables for hard disks—are inexpensive enough that you my decide they are worth keeping around, just in case.

Back up your system on schedule

Everybody knows they should back up their system on a regular basis. Not enough people do it. We know all the reasons why not: Hard disks today have such large storage capacities that getting an appropriate backup tool can be expensive; nobody wants to pay for a tape drive or a removable disk drive with a high enough capacity to back up the entire hard disk; backing up a 10-gigabyte drive on 100-MB Zip disks is way too time consuming, and backing up to floppy disks is a joke. Besides, hard disks are highly reliable today, so why bother?

All of these are terrific excuses for not backing up, right up to the point when your hard disk crashes or a critical data file gets corrupted, and you don't have a backup available.

We can't emphasize this enough: Make a backup plan and stick to it. Whether your problem is a power surge scrambling your hard disk, or a complete hardware failure, having recent backups can make the difference between dealing with a catastrophe and a minor inconvenience. There's no backup plan that's right for everyone. If you're in a large office connected to a network, your system administrator has (hopefully) designed a backup plan. Follow it.

If you're in an office and responsible for your own backups, put all your data folders in one place—as subfolders inside a main data folder (My Documents, for example), so you can easily back up your data. Then backup just the data folders regularly. How often? Wait just as long between backups as it takes to create the amount of work you're willing to waste time recreating if the disk dies. We each have our systems set to backup all our changed data every time we close our word processing programs.

Cheap and easy backup

You can setup your system to back up files incrementally with most commercial backup programs, but you can also do it for free with an MS-DOS-level batch file.

For simplicity's sake, we'll assume that you have a My Documents folder on Drive C that holds all your data folders, and that you want to back up to Drive E, which could be a hard disk, a Zip disk drive, or any other disk drive that you care to use. If your data files or backup disks require a different drive or directory, make the appropriate substitutions in these instructions.

Load Windows Notepad (by choosing Start, Programs, Accessories, Notepad). Type the line

xcopy c:\"My documents"*.* e:\ /c/h/e/k/r/m

Then choose File, Save and save the file in an appropriate folder, using a name like *DataBackup.bat*. The first part of the name doesn't matter, but the extension (after the period) must be *bat*, which identifies the file as a batch file and tells Windows there are commands in the file that Windows should run.

Next, right-click on the Windows desktop and choose New, Shortcut. In the Create Shortcut dialog box, choose the Browse button, navigate to the file you just created, and then select it to enter it in the Command Line text box. Choose Next, type an appropriate name for the shortcut, choose Next again, pick an icon to go with the shortcut, and then choose Finish.

The payoff for all this is that you'll be able to back up your data files by choosing the shortcut. The first time you run the batch file, it will back up all your data files. From then on, it will back up only those files that have been modified since the last time you backed up. Depending on what programs you use, you may be able to set them to run the batch file automatically when you close the program. (Look for a macro feature that includes Auto macros with names like AutoExit.)

If you're responsible for buying hardware as well as backing up data, we strongly recommend making sure you have an appropriate backup tool, whether it's a tape drive, a high-capacity removable disk drive or disc drive (a CD-RW drive for example), or a second hard disk, just for backing up.

Create and store a backup of your entire system whenever you made major changes, like adding a new program.

Create and store a full backup of your data as often as necessary to keep the amount of time you would have to spend to recreate your work down to an acceptable level.

Back up your system before installing or uninstalling any new hardware (or software)

Backing up on a regular basis is not enough. The most likely time for tying the Windows Registry in knots or trashing a critical file in the Windows folders is when you're installing or uninstalling a new piece of hardware (or software for that matter). We strongly recommend backing up your entire system before installing, uninstalling, or updating any hardware or software, so you can easily return to a known working state by restoring the backup. At the very least, back up your entire Windows folder structure and, for upgrades or uninstalls, the folders related to the hardware or software you're upgrading or uninstalling. Make sure you have a backup solution that can easily restore a Windows installation without making you first reinstall Windows from scratch before you can restore the backed up version of the installation.

Organize your distribution disks and back up the floppy disks

Too many people take the distribution disks they get with their computers, hardware upgrades, and software, throw them in a box, throw the box in a closet or in the basement, and forget about them. This works OK until they need a disk and can't find it.

The distribution disks are valuable property; they are often the only way to fix problems. If trying to install a new piece of hardware leads you to conclude that your Windows Registry is tied up in knots, and you have to reinstall everything from scratch, you'll want those disks well organized and where you can find them. If a driver—the software that tells Windows how to control a particular piece of hardware—gets trashed, or you accidentally delete it, you'll want to be able to put your hands on that driver quickly and easily. And don't count on being able to download the most recent version from a Web site. What if the trashed driver keeps your system from booting, so you can't get to the Web site?

Organizing your disks means keeping them all together. If you have only a few CDs, you can get notebook-style disk holders that will serve your purposes, with plastic sleeves for the CDs. If you have more than one computer, you might want to get a separate notebook for each one. Alternatively, you might want to get a CD rack, which you can find in most places that sell CDs. If you mix CD-ROMs from different computers, make sure each one is clearly labeled so that you know which discs go with which computers.

You probably also have some distribution disks that are floppy disks, particularly for drivers, which tend to be small files.

Floppy disks are more susceptible to losing data than CDs, so be sure to back up the floppy disks and label them. It's a good idea to keep the backups separate from the originals. That way, if you do something like spill coffee on the originals, you won't spill it on the backups at the same time. If you have a reasonably large hard disk, you may also want to create a Drivers folder on your hard disk and create subfolders under the Drivers folders, with each subfolder backing up one floppy disk. You should be able to find floppy disk drawers and cases easily, as well as plastic sleeves for floppy disks so you can store them in the same notebook as your CDs.

Labeling becomes particularly important when you get upgrades—whether you receive a new disk or download an upgrade from a Web site. Make sure you mark the old disk as superceded, and also indicate which disk it's superceded by. That way, if you have several generations of upgrades, you'll be able to pick out the most recent—or back up one generation, if an upgrade seems to be the source of the problem.

Treat your installation keys like the valuables they are

This actually comes under the category of organizing your distribution disks, but it's an important enough point to deserve its own section. All those disks are of no use if you don't have the installation keys. So make sure that part of your labeling includes the installation key. Or keep a master list identifying each disk and installation key. Better yet, do both. If you keep the disks in their jewel cases, label each case with the key *and the name of the disk that belongs in the case*. If you keep them in plastic sleeves, label each sleeve

with the key and the name of the disk. Create the master list on your computer. Update it when you get a new disk, and print it out each time. Then keep the list with your disks—in the notebook, if you use one.

If you keep your disks in their jewel cases in a CD rack, get an extra case, tape the list to the *inside* of the case, so you can read it through the plastic, and keep the list in the CD rack also. If the list is too long to fit the size of the case, fold the paper so it fits in the case and store it there.

Protect your hardware from untamed power

Electricity, like fire, only pretends to be a tame companion. When it's behaving well, it lets you run your computer, among other things. But when it starts acting up—if you get too much or too little coming down the power lines, particularly too much in the form of sudden surges—it can zap your system.

A surge protector is the minimum you should have on your system, but there are much more capable choices, ranging from a line filter to an uninterruptible power supply (UPS). We cover these in the section "My computer may be crashing due to power problems" on page 18. But don't think you don't need protection just because your system isn't crashing regularly due to power problems. These devices can also protect your system from sudden, once-in-a-decade surges from, for example, a nearby lightning strike. The lightning doesn't even have to hit anything connected to the power lines to create problems. It only needs to be close to the lines to cause a surge.

Your telephone line provides another pathway for electric surges to find their way into your system and fry expensive components. Don't ignore this back door to your system. Many surge protectors, UPSs, and similar devices provide telephone line protection as well as power line protection. You can also find surge protectors specifically for phone lines. One way or the other, make sure your phone line is protected.

Turn off your computer during thunderstorms—or better yet unplug it (assuming you're near the computer, of course). Power surges from lightning get into your computer by following the electrical circuit up through the power lines, through the power cord connecting your computer, and through the switch that turns the computer on. Turn off the computer, and you create a gap in the line. For the rampaging electrons to get into your computer, they have to jump across the gap—which can happen with a strong enough power surge. (Read: a close enough lightning strike.) Unplug the computer, and the lightning would just about have to hit your computer to get into it, so unplugging the computer during a severe thunderstorm is a smart precaution. If the storm is extreme enough to make you think about unplugging the power cords, don't forget to unplug the telephone cord too.

Keep a notepad near your computer

We strongly recommend keeping notepad near your computer—either a notebook or something similar to a steno pad, with the pages permanently attached. There are several kinds of information you'll want to keep in the notepad.

First, keep a list of technical support phone numbers and the hours available for each piece of hardware. When you first get the hardware, check out the technical support information immediately and write it down. You might want to start with the last page of the notebook for this, and work your way backwards, one page for each piece of equipment. If you need to call technical support at any time, you should also document the calls for future reference, both because you may need to follow up on a given problem, and because you may have the same problem again in the future, in which case we guarantee that you will be highly frustrated if you can't remember the fix.

Keep a list of Web sites for your hardware. You might want to add this information on the same page as the phone information. Note that you can often find such information as the correct jumper settings for a disk drive on the Web site much more quickly than you can get the information over the phone. Make sure also that when you visit the Web site you save it as a Favorites, or bookmark it (depending on what your browser calls it). You might want to create a folder called Tech Support to store all the tech support information in one place.

Finally, use the pad to write down error messages word for word when they occur and are still on the screen. Whether you find a database of error messages on a Web site to search through yourself or you call technical support for help, you'll find it much easier to track down the error message if you have the exact wording, spelling, and punctuation. Without the exact error message as it shows on your computer, finding it in a database is strictly a hit or miss proposition.

If you're still stuck

We've worked hard to address the most common problems you're likely to run into as you use your computer, but, obviously, we can't address every problem. There's even a possibility that one of our solutions won't solve your specific problem. If we haven't addressed your problem, make sure that what you've encountered is a real problem rather than your not knowing exactly how to do something.

If you do run into a dead end, you can turn to your company's help desk, the manufacturer of your computer or hardware device, or Microsoft product support. Be cautious, however, about turning to your co-workers for help, unless you're certain they know what they're doing.

If you want to try to search out the information you need yourself, there are some Web sites worth trying. One excellent place to start is the Microsoft Knowledge Base, at *search.support.microsoft.com/kb/c.asp?ln=en-us*. You'll find lots of detailed information that can help with hardware problems. Try *www.driverguide.com* and *www.windrivers.com* if you're looking for a driver for a hardware component. Also, the PC Guide at *www.pcguide.com* has a number of useful references and links.

Troubleshooting Web site

With the purchase of this book, you now have access to the Microsoft Press Troubleshooting Web site at *www.mspress.microsoft.com/troubleshooting*, which complements the book series by offering additional trouble-shooting information that's updated monthly. You'll find that some of the flowcharts have been expanded to cover additional problems, and that entirely new flowcharts with accompanying solutions have been created to address some important but perhaps slightly less common problems than those addressed in this book.

You'll find the Troubleshooting Web site as easy to navigate as this book, and it furthers our goal of helping you locate your problem and its solution quickly and easily. To access the Web site, you need this code: TSP0901.

Working inside your computer

Rearranging the innards of a computer does not require any great skill or technical knowledge. The most important attributes are caution and attention to detail, and it doesn't hurt to be a bit tidy. Aside from that, most of the tasks are no more difficult than repairing a flashlight.

The first concern to dispense with is getting an electrical shock. This is a reasonable concern if you don't know much about computers or other electrical devices, but you need not worry about it. There are only two areas where you could get a dangerous shock from a system that is turned off—inside the computer's power supply case and inside a monitor's case—which is why we do not recommend that most people ever open up those particular cases.

You can get an annoying shock from static electricity (which we address in more detail in "My computer crashes when I touch it" on page 4), and static electricity shocks can also damage your computer's components. That's why grounding is an important concept. You need to discharge any built up charge *before* you start handling sensitive semiconductor components.

A conservative approach is always to use a grounding wrist strap when working with computers and components. There's nothing wrong with this approach, even though it can be a bit inconvenient, but it's not necessary in most cases. In the past dozen years, each of us has disassembled and reassembled hundreds of computers and peripherals, and never once had a problem due to static electricity damage (a dangerous boast to make, but true nonetheless).

Instead, we take a slightly less conservative approach, which starts off with a step that contradicts the instructions offered by many other sources. We recommend that you do *not* unplug a computer or other device before you start working on it. Why? Because the device relies on the three-pronged power cable to tie it to the electrical ground. If you then touch a part of the grounded device—typically any part of the metal case will do—then you are also grounded. So long as you don't scuff your rubber-soled shoes on a wool carpet while you're working on the computer, you are not likely to build up any significant static charge. You can work without a grounding strap and not have to worry about causing damage to the components.

Now, in order for this approach to work, we assume two important points. First, we assume that you're going to turn off the power to the device before you stick your hands in it. This would fall under the "caution" and "attention to detail" attributes mentioned earlier. The other assumption is that your electrical outlet is properly grounded. As we describe in "My computer crashes when I touch it" on page 4, you can buy an inexpensive outlet tester that has indicator lights that will show whether or not your outlets are wired correctly.

So, whenever you need to work inside your computer, follow these steps:

1. Shut down Windows (if it's running).

2. Turn off the power.

3. Do not unplug the power cord.

4. Open the case.

5. Touch the power supply case or some other grounded metal component before you start touching expansion cards or other parts.

Here are some other tips to keep in mind when working inside your computer.

Be firm but gentle. There is rarely any need for great force or strength when working on computers. If you push or pull too hard, bad things can happen. It can be easy to bend or damage connectors, some of which cannot be replaced easily or at a reasonable cost. If your hand should slip, you risk grating your knuckles on the tiny points of soldered wires on the backs of printed circuit cards, and trust us when we say that this is an experience you can live without. On the other hand, an incomplete connection won't work correctly, and it's possible to short out connections that can cause other types of damage.

So how do you know how hard to push or pull? This is another place where paying attention to detail pays off. If you're replacing an expansion card, look carefully before you remove the first one, so that you can tell when you've pushed the replacement into the slot as far as the original. If you're unplugging a connector, look carefully to see if there are any locking tabs—such as those on the sides of memory modules—that need to be released before you can remove the device.

Remove connectors and cards with care. When you can't pull out a connector or card easily, you may have to rock it back and forth a bit. If you do, make sure you rock it along its long side. You should rock an adapter card, for example, in the plane of the card. If you rock it in an angle perpendicular to the plane of the card, you risk flexing the card and breaking a lead on the card. Similarly, if you rock a connector at an angle perpendicular to the long edge of the connector, you risk flexing a card or the motherboard, and breaking a connector.

Don't rush. If you hurry, you're more apt to make mistakes. It's entirely too easy to connect some cables backwards, and if you hurry, you may not take the time to note how a cable was connected before you removed it. When it comes time to reconnect that cable, you may end up with a troubleshooting problem that will take far longer to solve than the few moments you "saved" with your haste.

Be thorough. The time to make sure you've completed every step comes before you turn the power back on, because afterwards may be too late for everything but regrets. A single machine screw lost while trying to snug down an expansion card bracket may seem like a small enough detail that it could be ignored. However, that little metal screw may find itself

bridging two traces on the motherboard and causing an electrical short that at best may make the system run unreliably, and at worst could cook your computer's processor or some other expensive component. This is where tidiness can be an asset; keep track of all the loose parts as you work—an empty 35-mm film canister is a useful aid—and then make sure that all are accounted for when you close up the patient at the end of the procedure.

Most will admit that this advice is largely a matter of common sense, and we'd agree. There's nothing mystical or deeply technical about working with computers and their parts. Once you have the confidence to dive in and emerge with a graphics adapter or hard disk in your grasp, you will be well on your way to troubleshooting a wide range of PC hardware problems all on your own.

Assumptions about operating system versions

In spite of this being a book about hardware problems, software plays an important part in the diagnosis and solution of many of the problems. As a result, you'll find that we have different instructions for you to follow, depending on whether you are running Windows 98 or Windows 2000. We decided not to try to cover any earlier versions of the Windows operating system, but you will find that most of the instructions for Windows 98 will also apply to Windows 95.

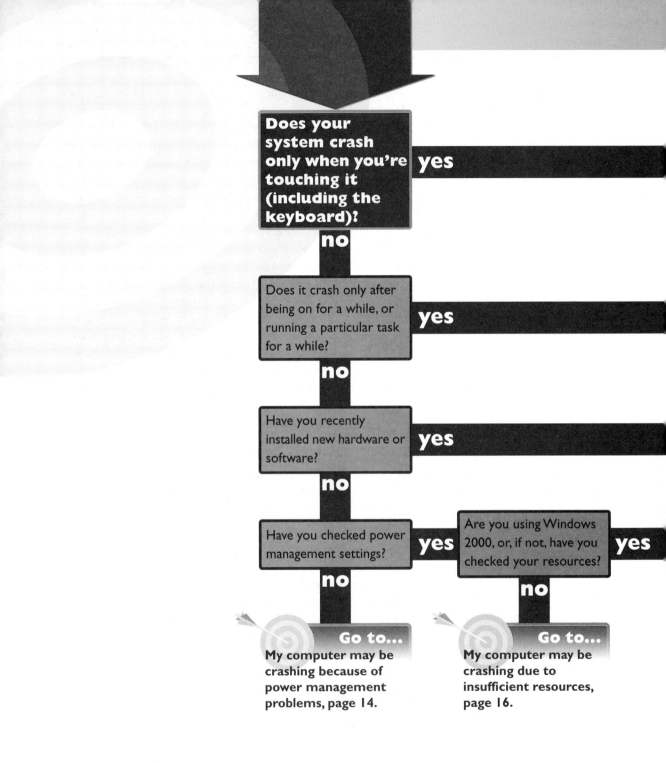

Does your system crash only when you're touching it (including the keyboard)? yes

no

Does it crash only after being on for a while, or running a particular task for a while? yes

no

Have you recently installed new hardware or software? yes

no

Have you checked power management settings? yes

Are you using Windows 2000, or, if not, have you checked your resources? yes

no

no

Go to...
My computer may be crashing because of power management problems, page 14.

Go to...
My computer may be crashing due to insufficient resources, page 16.

Computer crashes

Go to...
My computer crashes
when I touch it, page 4.

Go to...
My computer crashes
after it has been
working for a while,
page 6.

Go to...
My system started
crashing after I installed
some hardware or
software, page 10.

Have you checked your
power source?

Go to...
I don't have any good
clues about what's
making my computer
crash, page 20.

no

Go to...
My computer may be
crashing due to power
problems, page 18.

If your solution isn't here
Check these related chapters:
Computer hardware and Windows, page 22
Computer startup: won't boot, page 74
Or see the general troubleshooting tips on page xv.

My computer crashes when I touch it

Source of the problem

You walk across the thick carpet, reach out to touch the light switch on the wall, and…OUCH! A spark jumps between your finger and the switch. You've just been jolted by static electricity. You can get a 30,000-volt shock from such an incident—which is a bit scary compared with the 110 volts you get from a household electrical outlet, or the meager 1.5 volts you get from a penlight battery. The reason the static electricity doesn't do more harm is that it has very little current—which means there aren't that many electrons involved. But they have a lot of force behind them, which translates into a high voltage.

A shock that's painful to your finger can be a fatal jolt for a sensitive electronic component. Shooting electrons through your keyboard or computer can temporarily wipe out the information they need to work or even cause permanent damage. So if static electricity is a problem where you work with your computer, you need to address the problem.

How to fix it

Is it caused by static electricity?

1. The first step in solving problems with static electricity is to determine whether it's the likely cause of your crashes. Static electricity can be difficult to diagnose, because you can't see it. You don't need a spark to cause problems; just transferring a large charge from your hand to the computer can be enough. You don't even need to touch the computer, because passing within a few inches of the system can cause problems. So be on the lookout for conditions that are ripe for static electricity:

   - Air loses humidity when you heat it, so the problem tends to be worse in winter.

   - Insulated shoes, such as those with rubber soles, are likely to build up charges.

   - Susceptible flooring, such as thick carpets and rubber tile flooring, can also cause static electricity build-up.

   If you are wearing synthetic clothing and you notice that the material tends to cling to itself or to your legs, you probably have a problem with static build-up. And, believe it or not, that could be the cause of your system crashes.

Solving problems caused by static electricity

1. The most important step for curing problems caused by static electricity is to make sure your computer is properly grounded. This provides a safe path to channel the static electricity away from the computer's sensitive innards. Always plug your computer into a three-prong outlet, and make sure that the outlet is wired correctly. You can use an inexpensive outlet tester—available at hardware and electronic stores—to make sure the outlet is properly grounded. Plug one of these into the wall outlet, and the pattern of lights will tell you whether there is a problem with the wiring. If there is, get a professional electrician to fix it. ▶

2. If you're in an area where humidity tends to be low during all or part of the year, consider a humidifier, or something more decorative, like an aquarium.

3. If you can't avoid working in an environment that encourages static electricity, ground yourself before touching the computer. You can get mouse pads and wrist rests that include grounding straps for connecting to an electrical ground. You can connect the grounding strap to your computer, if it's properly grounded, using a screw on the computer case, or to the center screw on the cover plate of an electrical outlet that's properly grounded. You can then touch the mouse pad or wrist rest each time you reach for the mouse or keyboard to ground yourself.

4. Get an anti-static chair mat or carpet to put under your chair.

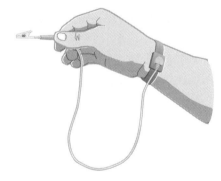

5. If you want to be particularly cautious, you can wear a grounding strap. This is a device used by people who assemble electronic components. You attach one end to a good electrical ground and slip the other end over your wrist. This is more than you'll need in all but the most extreme situations, but it will guarantee that you won't have problems with static electricity while you're using the computer. ▶

My computer crashes after it has been working for a while

Source of the problem

One of the most serious enemies of your computer is heat. When components get too hot, they behave erratically, which can cause strange things to happen—right up to and including your system coming to a halt. The essential problem is that when electricity moves through wires, it generates heat (which is why light bulbs get hot). The faster semiconductors run, the hotter they get. Computers have to get rid of the heat—using fans, for example. Computers that don't get rid of the excess heat well enough crash and burn, both metaphorically and literally. (Literally for the *crash* part at least. What can happen to the components is better described as cooked than burned, but that doesn't leave them any more useable than if they did burn.)

The most important clue that overheating is causing crashes is that the crashes show up only after the computer's been on for a while and has had a chance to warm up. Another giveaway is that the crash happens only when the computer performs a specific function for a long time. If it can print 5 pages without problems, for example, but consistently starts printing gibberish on print jobs longer than 10 pages, odds are that some chip, somewhere is getting overheated from constant use during printing, and is...well...losing it. Here's how to cool down a hot situation.

How to fix it

Before you open the computer case

1. Before you do anything else, make sure that there's nothing blocking any of the air vents, louvers, or anything that looks like it might let air flow through the computer. There should be at least a few inches of clear space around any air vent or fan.

2. If you have computer furniture or a computer cabinet that includes an enclosed space for the computer itself, try taking the computer out of its cubbyhole and see whether the computer still crashes. If the crashing stops, you need look no further for the cause. Either add cooling fans to the furniture, or consider using the furniture for something else, and find a better way to set up your computer.

Tip

Make sure the room isn't too hot. The rule of thumb is that the computer will be as comfortable as the person working on it. Once you get into the 90-degree room temperature range, the computer may not be able to shed excess heat well enough; consider turning on the air conditioning.

3. Make sure that you don't have your equipment set up so the hot air coming from one piece of equipment—like your printer—is aimed at an air vent in another piece of equipment—like your computer.

4. If your power supply has a cooling fan, make sure the fan is turning. If it isn't turning, you may need to replace the fan or the power supply (for details about how to replace the power supply, see "My power supply is making a noise" on page 53).

5. Check all louvers and air vents in the computer case, including the vent for the fan, for dust or debris that may be clogging the openings and impeding air flow.

6. If you see a buildup of dust or debris in a vent, do *not* try to clean it with a dust rag. This may push a clump of dust into the computer innards and create additional problems, including the possibility of shorting out an electrical connection. The fact that the vents are clogged with dust suggests that the inside of the case also needs cleaning.

Removing dust from inside the computer

1. Before you open the computer case, make sure you've read "Working inside your computer" at the beginning of this book, which explains how to handle computer components safely. Then turn off the computer and open the case.

2. No matter what else may be causing or contributing to the overheating problem, your first step once you open the case should be to clean out any dust that may have accumulated. *Do not* use a vacuum cleaner, which can build up static charges. And do not even *think* of using a specially treated dust rag anywhere inside the computer, unless you know absolutely, for sure, beyond any possible doubt and then some, that 1) it doesn't have anything on it that can do damage to delicate electronic components, and 2) whatever ability it has to pick up dust like magic doesn't have anything to do with static electricity.

3. The only safe way to remove dust is to blow it away with a can of compressed air, which you can buy almost any place that offers photo or electronics supplies. Blowing away dust can be messy—particularly if you haven't done it in awhile—so you might want to do this outdoors.

Tip

If you have an overheating problem, don't assume you can solve it—even temporarily while you're waiting for a new fan, say—by taking the cover off your computer. The cooling system for many computers requires the air to flow past the components on its way from the air vents to the fan. If you take off the cover, you may eliminate the airflow, which can make the problem worse. All of this means that it's best not to run your system with the cover off. But if you choose to ignore this recommendation, you should at least aim a desk fan at your computer's innards to help keep it cool.

Tip

In dusty environments, you may need to clean out your computer's insides every two or three months, especially if someone smokes in the vicinity of the computer. Under normal conditions, you should clean it at least once a year.

If this solution didn't solve your problem, go to the next page.

My computer crashes after it has been working for a while

(continued from page 7)

4. The can of compressed air should come with a hollow extension, like a thin straw. Use the extension, so you can easily direct the stream of air. Blow out all the dust, working consistently in one direction. Make sure you reach between adaptor cards and under the motherboard to blow out the dust, but don't force the tube between parts.

5. If your computer has enough dust in it that you notice a lot of dust floating around the computer as you're working, remove the extension from the can and blow a few short bursts around the computer or over its top (depending on how it's oriented), to keep the dust from settling in the computer. You might want to repeat this step when you finish working as well.

6. While you are removing dust, pay special attention to any fans in the computer, including the power supply fan. Check the leading edges of the fan blades. These are carefully designed to do their job. Dust that accumulates on the leading edge can disrupt the airflow on the blades. That, in turn, would make the fan less efficient at moving air, so it may not cool the computer effectively.

7. Finally, to remove dust, blow the dust from the vents from the inside of the case. Unfortunately, you won't be able to follow this advice for the fans built into most power supplies, or for the vents on power supplies. You would have to open the power supply to get inside it and blow the dust out, which we can't recommend doing. Instead, use a clean, dry, untreated cloth to wipe the dust off the power supply's fans and vents.

Other reasons for overheating

1. There are several other things you should check, in case something other than dust is causing the overheating. With the case still open, make sure the power switch is set to off, plug in the power cord if necessary, and turn the computer on, being careful not to touch anything inside. Look carefully at any other cooling fans on the case, motherboard, and expansion cards to make sure they're turning when the computer is running. Some fans may be controlled by a

TIP

You can keep dust out of your computer, or at least minimize the amount of dust that gets past the air vents, and make it much easier to keep both the air vents and the inside of your computer clean, which will also help your computer run cooler.

Take air conditioner filter material, which you can get at a hardware store, and cut it to fit inside the case next to any air vents that you can reach conveniently. You may not be able to add a filter to all the air vents, but for those that you can add the filter to, any dust that gets pulled into the air vent will be trapped in the filter, before it gets to the motherboard and other components. Be sure to clean or replace the filter material when it gets dusty. If you don't, the dust will slow down the air flow in the case and can contribute to overheating problems, rather than help prevent them.

thermostat, so make sure you give the computer a chance to warm up thoroughly before you decide that a fan isn't working. If you find one that's not working, you'll need to replace it. Unfortunately, there are too many variations on the details of replacing fans for us to cover them here.

2. Look for heat sinks on the motherboard and expansion cards. Make sure they're not blocked by ribbon cables or other obstructions that would restrict air flow. ▶

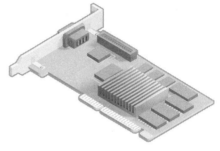

3. If an expansion card has a heat sink or a large chip—such as a graphics adapter—on it, try to arrange the other expansion cards in such a way that there is as much space as possible on both sides of the card. This may mean relocating the card or the neighboring cards. If the card with the heat sink or large chip is an AGP graphics card, then it can go only in one slot, so you'll have to move the other cards to give it more space.

4. If you have an expansion card with a heat sink, and you suspect that it may be overheating even after moving other cards to make more space available around the heat sink, you can add a cooling fan. There are products made specifically for graphics cards, but you can also use a fan designed for a square CPU chip. You can mount it right onto the heat sink using self-tapping screws—which you'll have to purchase separately. The screws will thread themselves into the spaces in the heat sink. The added airflow from the fan will keep the chip cooler. ▶

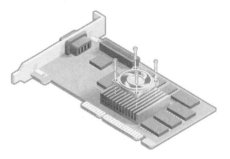

5. If you have the free bays to allow it, move your drives to provide space around hard disks and CD-R and CD-RW drives, since these can get hotter than other disk drives. If you can place these drives so there are open bays on one or both sides of each hard disk, CD-R, and CD-RW drive, the drives should run cooler and more reliably.

6. If you are still concerned that your hard disk or CD-R or CD-RW drive is running too hot, and you have an empty disk drive bay adjacent to it, consider adding a drive bay cooling fan. These use the same power connector as a disk drive and move additional cooling air near the drive. You can get these fans from electronics parts suppliers, such as Dalco Electronics (*www.dalco.com*) or Altex Computers & Electronics (*www.altex.com*). ▶

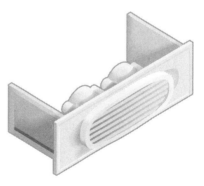

My system started crashing after I installed some hardware or software

Source of the problem

New York will be a great city someday, once they finish working on it. The same can be said about most computer systems; none of them ever seem to come with everything you'll ever want. Sooner or later—and probably sooner—you'll need to upgrade some feature, add a new piece of hardware, or install some software that wasn't included in the original bundle. It's part of the normal life of any computer.

While these new arrivals, whether hardware or software, may coexist peacefully with the prior residents—much like the multiple generations of immigrants to New York—there will also be instances where the different parts don't get along. And if the operating system isn't able to arbitrate successfully between the squabbling parties, it may give up trying, in which case the system will crash.

How to fix it

If you just added new hardware

1. Choose Start, Settings, Control Panel, and then System.

2. Choose the Device Manager tab. (In Microsoft Windows 2000, choose the Hardware tab and then the Device Manager button.)

3. Find the category entry for the type of hardware you just added, and expand it if necessary. Then select the entry for the specific hardware you just added,

4. Choose the Remove button, then close the System Properties dialog box. (In Windows 2000, choose Action, Uninstall, close Device Manager, and then close the System Properties dialog box.)

Tip

If you're already dealing with a crash that may be related to the addition of new hardware or software, don't read this tip. We'd hate to have you think that we're saying we told you so.

If you are fortunate enough to read this *before* you encounter a problem, however, we urge you to make a backup of your system before you add any new hardware or software. At the very least, backup your Windows folder and all subfolders. Not all installations can be undone completely and reliably. A backup can make it easier to restore your system to the condition it was in before the new hardware or software was added.

5. Choose Start, Programs, and look for any programs installed with the new hardware. Look for an Uninstall option in the program's entry on the Start menu; if you find one, run it.

6. If there is no Uninstall option for the hardware's programs, choose Start, Settings, Control Panel, and then Add/Remove Programs. Check for an entry relating to the new hardware. If you find one, select it and choose the Add/Remove button. (In Windows 2000, choose the Change/Remove button.) Follow the prompts to remove the software. Then close the Add/Remove Programs dialog box.

7. Exit Windows and shut down the system.

8. Remove the new hardware device.

9. Restart the system, and see whether the problem still shows up. If it does, the new hardware is probably not involved. Try to resolve the problem before reinstalling the hardware.

10. If the system does not crash with the new hardware removed, try reinstalling it. (Before you do, this would be a really good time to make a backup of your system, if you didn't create one before originally installing the new hardware.)

11. After you install the hardware again, choose Start, Settings, Control Panel, and then System.

12. Choose the Device Manager tab. (In Windows 2000, choose the Hardware tab, and then the Device Manager button.) All the device type headings should be listed with a plus sign next to them, with none of them expanded to show the items below them. If any of the first-level items are expanded, look for a yellow circle with an exclamation mark that indicates that the device is not working properly. If you see such a mark next to the item, go to "Computer hardware and Windows," on page 22. ▶

13. Make sure that you have the latest driver for the new hardware. Contact the hardware vendor, or check the vendor's Web site to determine the latest version.

14. You can check the version you have on your system by selecting the hardware item in the Device Manager window and choosing the Properties button to open the Properties dialog box for that hardware. (In Windows 2000, choose Action, then Properties.)

> *If this solution didn't solve your problem, go to the next page.*

My system started crashing after I installed some hardware or software

(continued from page 11)

15. In the Properties dialog box for the hardware, choose the Driver tab. The window will show some information about the driver. Choose the Driver File Details button for more information. (In Windows 2000, choose the Driver Details button.)

16. The Driver File Details window will list the provider, file version, and copyright for each driver used by that device. Select each line in the Driver Files to view the information for that line. ▶

17. If the manufacturer has a later driver version than the one you have installed, download the driver from the company's Web site and follow the installation instructions that come with it. If there are no instructions, save the new driver to a floppy disk or a temporary folder on your hard disk, and choose the Update Driver button on the Driver tab in the device's Properties window.

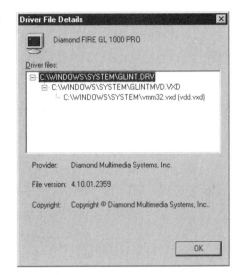

If that didn't solve the problem

1. If the hardware you installed is an expansion card, shut down the computer, and try placing the card in a different slot. (This will not be possible for an AGP graphics adapter, since there is only one AGP slot in a computer.)

> **Tip**
>
> Graphics card drivers are notorious for causing conflicts with other hardware and software in computers. If nothing else helps, check to see that you have the latest driver for your graphics adapter, and upgrade your driver if you don't.

2. If the hardware that's causing the problem attaches to a parallel port and is sharing the port with another device, consider exchanging it for a different version that can use a port that's designed to be shared, such as a USB port. If you must use a parallel port, consider adding a second parallel port to your system so each device can have its own port; an expansion card with a parallel port can cost $10 to $50 depending on features and type of expansion slot.

If you just added new software

1. Conflicts caused by new software may take a while to appear, because the problem may occur only when a certain combination of programs is used at the same time. It may also show up when you're running programs other than the one you installed, because the installation changed something in the Windows Registry that another program needs entered in the registry in a different way, or because the new program has added a utility that automatically loads when Windows starts and that runs at all times. In this book, which is concerned with *hardware* troubleshooting, we mainly want to help you establish that the problem is indeed a software problem rather than a hardware problem.

2. **If the problem shows up when you run a different program,** without running the program you recently installed, try reinstalling the program that was already installed, and see if that eliminates the problem. If it does, then even if another problem shows up with the newly installed software, you'll know you don't have a hardware problem.

3. **If the problem shows up only when running the new program** at the same time as another specific program, check for updates for both the newly installed program and the older program. The updates may prevent the problem.

4. **If the problem was not related to running a different program** or neither of the two steps before this one solved the problem, back up any data files you created with the new program, and then try uninstalling it. First look for an Uninstall option in the program's entry on the Start menu. If you can't find an option there, choose Start, Settings, Control Panel, then Add/Remove Programs, and look for the program in the list of programs available to uninstall.

5. After you uninstall the program, restart Windows. If uninstalling does not help, it may be that the new program is not involved in the crashes. It's also possible that the uninstall process did not remove all of the program's parts. Contact the software publisher for details on how to completely remove the program.

6. Some programs overwrite Windows files with new versions, and in some cases, the uninstall process does not reverse this process. In these cases, you have to reinstall the original versions—and it may be difficult to determine which ones have been changed.

7. Start by running the Windows System File Checker if it's available on your system. Choose Start, Programs, Accessories, System Tools. If there's a System Information menu item available, choose it.

8. If your version of System Information includes a Tools menu, choose Tools, and then System File Checker. This will check the Windows files and restore any that are damaged or missing. Note that you can also use this program to restore individual files if necessary. ▶

9. If this fails to resolve the problem (or if you don't have System Information on your system, or your version of System Information does not include System File Checker), you should restore your system from a recent backup. If you don't have one available, consider reinstalling Windows.

My computer may be crashing because of power management problems

Source of the problem

During the past few decades, interest in conserving energy and other resources has waxed and waned. Along the way, the Energy Department, the Environmental Protection Agency, manufacturers, retailers, and utility companies got together to create the Energy Star program, which identifies energy-efficient products from computers to washing machines to roofing material.

One by-product of these efforts has been power management. Originally developed to conserve battery power in notebook computers, these features now show up on desktop systems as well, on the grounds that cutting electricity use not only saves on electric bills, but also can reduce the need for air conditioning and extend the life of the hardware.

Unfortunately, power management can cause problems with software running on the computer and may cause crashes. The good news is that you can turn off the feature and possibly eliminate crashes.

How to fix it

1. If you're running Windows 2000, go to step 8. Otherwise start by disabling the Advanced Power Management feature for your computer. Right-click on My Computer, and choose Properties to open the System Properties window.

2. Choose the Device Manager tab. ▶

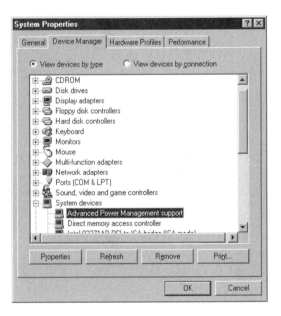

3. Click on the plus sign next to System Devices, and select the Advanced Power Management Support item. (If there is no Advanced Power Management Support item, close the System Properties window and skip to step 8.

4. Choose the Properties button to open the Advanced Power Management Support Properties window. ▶

5. Check the Disable In This Hardware Profile check box to disable power management.

6. Choose OK, then OK again, and then restart Windows.

7. If the problem is fixed, you can stop here. If this procedure did not solve the problem, repeat the steps and remove the check from the Disable In This Hardware Profile check box. Then continue with the next step.

8. Choose Start, Settings, Control Panel, and then Display to open the Display Properties dialog box.

9. In the Display Properties window, choose the Screen Saver tab. In the Screen Saver drop down list, choose (None).

10. Choose the Settings button in the Energy-Saving Features Of Monitor box. (In Windows 2000, choose the Power button.)

11. In the Power Management Properties window, in the Power Schemes drop-down list, choose Always On. (In Windows 2000, the Window is named Power Option Properties.)

12. Choose OK on each open window to return to the Windows desktop, then restart Windows. If this does not resolve the problem, power management is not the cause of your crashes.

Advanced Power Management support Properties	?	X

General | Settings | Driver

Advanced Power Management support

Device type: System devices
Manufacturer: (Standard system devices)
Hardware version: Not available

Device status
This device is working properly.

Device usage
☐ Disable in this hardware profile

OK   Cancel

Tip

If you're running Windows 98, and find in step 6 that disabling power management stops your crashes, you still may be able to use the feature. In the Advanced Power Management Support Properties window, choose the Settings tab. First, try checking the Force APM 1.0 Mode check box, then choosing OK, and then restarting Windows. If that doesn't work, remove the check from the check box, and try checking the Disable Power Status Polling check box. One of these two settings may provide crash-free power management.

My computer may be crashing due to insufficient resources

Source of the problem

One of the great features of Windows is that it lets you run many programs at once. While you're browsing the Web, you can cut and paste text right into your word processing program, and then save a file that will show up in a Windows Explorer window, from which you can drag and drop the file onto your e-mail program so you can send it to someone else. And while all this is going on, your scanner is ready to activate its software when you click a button, a utility watches the clock until it's time to automatically back up your data files, and an anti-virus program is watching all files as they're opened to make sure that they aren't infected. That's a lot of stuff going on inside one computer.

However, there are limits to how much a computer can do at once. Most people are all too familiar with the idea of the hard disk getting too full to hold another program. They are less familiar with the idea of the computer running out of memory—partly because Windows covers this by using free space on your hard disk as virtual memory—but most people know that adding more memory can improve system performance.

What many people don't realize that is that there are some types of memory that cannot be increased by adding more memory chips. And when you run low on these resources, your computer can crash—often without warning. The only way to solve the problem is to have fewer programs running at once. Here's how to know if your system is crashing because of insufficient resources.

Warning

This problem and solution do not apply to Windows 2000.

How to fix it

1. Choose Start, Programs, Accessories, System Tools, and then Resource Meter.

2. When you run the program, it will open a window warning you that your system may run more slowly while it is running. Choose OK.

3. Resource Meter will add an icon to your Windows System Tray with room for four green bars. Each bar represents 25 percent of your available resources. Green is good; if you see two or

Tip

The Resource Meter does not install in Windows by default. If you don't see it, choose Start, Settings, Control Panel, and then Add/Remove Programs. Choose the Windows Setup tab, find System Tools in the Components list, make sure the check box is checked and has a white, rather than gray, background, choose OK, and follow any directions on screen to insert a Windows CD-ROM.

more green bars, your system is fine. If you get below that—as shown here—you should start thinking about closing some programs. If you see a yellow bar, close some programs immediately. If you put the mouse pointer over the Resource Meter icon, a Tool Tips box will pop up to show the percentage of resources available in each of three categories. ▶

4. For a more detailed look at the resource levels, double-click on the icon in the System Tray to open the Resource Meter window. This window will display a report of System, User, and GDI (Graphical Device Interface) resources. ▶

5. If you get below 25 percent in any single category, you are at high risk for a system crash. The lower the number, the more likely that the crash will come without warning. Your system may simply halt the next time a program requires additional resources.

6. Running out of resources is not a hardware issue, and is not something you can solve by adding more memory, even though you may see an error message that indicates the computer is out of memory. Troubleshooting the problem is really a software issue, but in general terms, the way to solve it is to reduce the number of programs that are automatically loaded, and thus free up resources.

Tip

Resources aren't used just by programs. Every font that you install in Windows consumes part of the GDI resources. If you have hundreds of fonts installed, and you are low on resources, consider uninstalling some of the ones you use infrequently. There are shareware and commercial font management utilities available that make it easy to install and remove fonts from Windows as needed and still have them readily available on your hard drive. Among the choices are MyFonts Windows Font Manager from Unitech ($35 shareware registration fee) and Printer's Apprentice from Lose Your Mind Development ($25 shareware registration fee). You can download these files from the ZDNet Software Library at *www.hotfiles.com*.

Finding memory leaks

A memory leak doesn't mean that your computer is becoming forgetful, or that data is spilling out of its chips all over the motherboard. In fact, it's not really a hardware problem at all. Some programs take control of system resources, and then fail to release them when you exit the program. This can cause more resources to be tied up each time you open the program, and if you open and close the program often enough, your system will crash.

You can check for a memory leak by opening Resource Meter, and noting the levels of various resources. Then open the suspect program, check the resources, close the program, and check the levels once more. If the levels return to the same amount as before you opened the program, you don't have a memory leak problem with that program. If the levels remain the same as when the program was running, however, you do have a problem. Check with the program publisher to see if the program has been fixed.

My computer may be crashing due to power problems

Source of the problem

Electricity is often referred to as "clean" energy—it has no smell, it can't be spilled, and it doesn't make smoke when you use it (at least, it doesn't make smoke unless something goes wrong).

But electricity—meaning the electrical power itself—can be dirty. Interference from other sources, your power utility switching lines, lightning strikes miles away, or a power line swaying in a wind can all cause problems for your computer. Improper wiring can cause the electricity to flow in ways that it shouldn't. Other electrical devices on the same circuit can lower the voltage to levels that cause problems. And your local utility may choose to treat you to a brownout or blackout at peak periods. Here are some of the most common power problems you might encounter.

How to fix it

You get a shock from the case

1. If you feel a tingling, continuous shock when you touch metal parts of the computer—especially the case itself—then you may have an electrical short in the computer or a problem with the electrical wiring. Use an outlet tester to make sure that your computer is plugged into an outlet that is grounded correctly. If there's a problem with the outlet, have an electrician fix it. If there is no problem with the outlet, or if fixing it doesn't resolve the problem, get your computer checked by a repair service. ▶

2. If you feel a sharp shock that ends right away, it's probably caused by static electricity. See "My computer crashes when I touch it" on page 4.

The lights dim sometimes

1. Sometimes as you work on the computer, you may notice the sound of the fan changing. This can be a sign of the voltage dropping in your electrical supply. If the voltage drops too far, your computer can reboot spontaneously. Plug a light into the same outlet to see whether it dims from time to time. In particular, keep an eye out to see whether it dims when devices with large electrical motors—such as air conditioners, refrigerators, or elevators—start.

There are also some hidden electrical problems that can cause problems for your computer. The voltage can increase to many times the correct levels, so you need to protect your computer. The simplest solution is to use a surge protector, which will block the majority of these problems. In the event of a major power spike, the surge protector may be permanently damaged but will still protect your system.

Protect yourself

The best overall protection you can get is to give your computer system a source of electrical power that is isolated from the rest of the electrical supply. There are three basic designs, though you may find that people (and vendors) use the terms interchangeably.

- A Standby Power Supply (SPS) has a circuit that monitors the incoming electricity. If the voltage drops below a certain level or cuts off entirely, the SPS will switch almost instantly to its battery backup to power your computer, and your computer won't know that the power was interrupted.

- An Uninterruptible Power Supply (UPS) provides electricity to the computer through its battery all the time. If the electricity goes out, it is already on. UPS units usually cost more than SPS units, because the battery and power conversion components must be designed for continuous use.

- If you get an SPS, consider getting one with line monitoring This lets it operate much like a line conditioner, providing voltage regulation to protect against brownouts, and surge protection to guard against power spikes. A UPS doesn't need these additional capabilities, because your computer is always connected to the battery, and thus always gets the correct voltage.

2. If you find that the voltage is dropping, you may want to put the computer on a separate circuit from the device that's causing the problem. This may mean getting an electrician to rewire the outlet or add a new line. If your building's electrical service doesn't have sufficient capacity for all the devices you have installed, however, this won't solve the problem.

3. A more effective cure may be to add a power conditioner, also called a line conditioner. This is a device that maintains the electrical voltage within a narrow range. If the voltage drops below a given level, the device will cut the power to your computer to avoid possible damage. An even better choice is a standby power supply with line monitoring or an uninterruptible power supply.

The power sometimes goes out

1. If you notice flickering lights, you're probably having micro-blackouts. These often happen when power companies switch power sources. Unfortunately, even the shortest blackout can cause your computer to hang or reboot. The best solution is to get a standby power supply or uninterruptible power supply. Both have batteries that can provide power when the electricity goes off, and both will automatically reconnect the computer to the electrical supply when the power comes back on.

I don't have any good clues about what's making my computer crash

Source of the problem

Sometimes, you can't tell what's causing a problem. If you've eliminated all of the obvious answers, then you have to break the puzzle down into the smallest pieces possible, and go from there.

It's not too surprising that it can be difficult to identify the cause of a computer crash. There are dozens of different processors and hundreds of different motherboards on the market. These can be combined with a nearly endless range of choices for hard disks, CD drives, printers, network adapters, and other devices. Many of these require drivers to work. There are also what feels like an infinite number of combinations of programs and configurations to add to the chaos. It is not surprising that computers crash. Rather, it is a tribute to the hard work of many engineers and programmers that computers work at all.

The range of permutations and combinations are bound to result in sets of products that don't coexist peacefully. There is also the possibility that a component has quietly failed, either in part or completely. To find the cause of the problem, you need to play detective. Note that the steps here require a bootable floppy disk. If the version of Windows you're using won't let you create a bootable disk, you'll need to create it using Windows 98, Windows 95, or even MS-DOS.

How to fix it

1. Before you do anything else, make a total backup of your system. You are going to be changing hardware and software configurations, and you will want an easy way to get back to the starting point.

2. In Windows 95 and Windows 98, create a boot floppy disk: Open My Computer, select the floppy disk drive, place a disk in the floppy disk drive, then choose File, Format. (If your computer is not working at all, create the boot floppy on another computer.) Be sure to select Full and check the Copy System Files check box at the bottom of the dialog box. When the format finishes, test the floppy disk by rebooting the computer, and see whether it boots from the floppy and displays an MS-DOS prompt. (If the computer boots from a different disk drive, go to "The computer is booting from the wrong disk drive" on page 82.) ▶

3. Once you have confirmed that the boot floppy disk works, you will disconnect or remove all hardware from your system that isn't absolutely necessary. Be sure to check our recommendations in "Working inside your computer" at the beginning of this book before you continue.

4. Start by opening the computer case and disconnecting the power to all disk drives other than your floppy drive. ▶

5. Remove any expansion cards aside from your graphics adapter and hard disk controller.

6. Reboot your computer with the boot floppy disk in place. If the computer crashes after booting this way, the problem must lie in either the motherboard or the graphics adapter, and you should consider replacing them or sending them for repair.

7. If the computer didn't crash, turn off the computer and reconnect the power to your hard disk. Turn the computer back on; ignore any messages you may get about missing hardware. If the system crashes at this point, then the problem most likely involves your hard disk; take a look at the chapters "Drives: hard drives booting" and "Drives: after installation," as appropriate.

8. If the computer works with the hard disk, add the other hardware components back, one at a time. Remember to turn off the computer each time before making a change, and then test each addition before going on to the next one. This single-step approach takes a lot of time, but it is the only way to be certain you have eliminated a component as a possible cause of the problem.

9. If you can pinpoint a piece of hardware as the cause of the problem, it may or may not be obvious whether the hardware itself is causing the problem, or whether it is some interaction between the hardware and a piece of software. If you can't determine whether the problem is with hardware or software, reformat the drive and reinstall Windows. (Before you do, make sure you have a complete backup of the hard disk, as we suggested earlier. Also make sure that you have a bootable floppy that lets you boot and access your CD-ROM drive; see the Appendix, "When you have to reinstall Windows" on page 337.)

10. To reformat the drive, find the file Format.com on your hard disk (normally in the Windows \Command folder), and copy it to your boot floppy disk. Then boot from the floppy disk and type the command **format c: /s**.

11. After you reformat the drive, reinstall Windows, and install the minimum number of applications you need to do your work for a day or two. If the crashes no longer show up, you've proven that the problem was almost certainly related to software. If they still show up, confirm that the crashing is related to the hardware you pinpointed earlier by removing everything but the hard disk, floppy disk drive, and graphics adaptor. Then add each component back, one at a time. Once you've pinpointed the culprit, you can decide whether to replace it or send it for repair.

Tip

If you're working inside your computer, it's easy to lose track of what goes where. There are two simple things you can do that will help when it comes time to put the pieces back together. You can use an instant film, digital, or video camera to take pictures of the pieces as you take them apart, or you can label cables and the devices they connect to with small stickers.

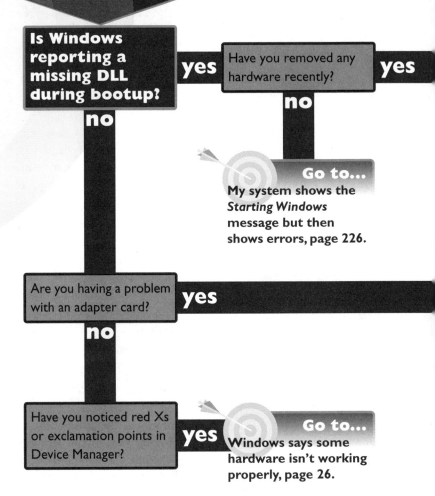

Is Windows reporting a missing DLL during bootup?

yes → Have you removed any hardware recently? **yes**

no

Go to...
My system shows the *Starting Windows* message but then shows errors, page 226.

Are you having a problem with an adapter card? **yes**

no

Have you noticed red Xs or exclamation points in Device Manager? **yes**

Go to...
Windows says some hardware isn't working properly, page 26.

Go to...
Windows reports a
missing DLL file during
bootup, page 24.

Have you checked to see
if Windows sees the card
as installed properly, and
have you tried reinstalling
the card?

yes

Does the card support
Plug and Play?

yes

Go to...
My computer isn't
recognizing a Plug and
Play adaptor card
properly, page 38.

no

no

Go to...
I may need to reinstall
an adapter card,
page 28.

Go to...
My computer isn't
recognizing a non–Plug
and Play adapter card
properly, page 34.

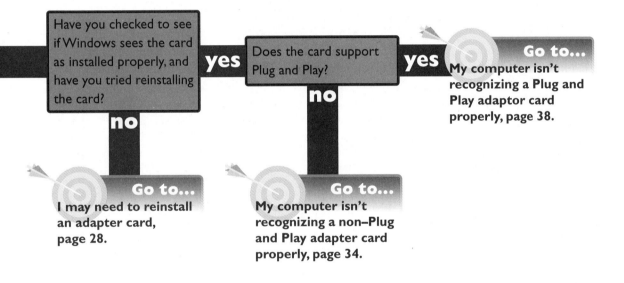

If your solution isn't here
Check these related chapters:
   Computer crashes, page 2
   Computer startup: won't boot, page 74
Or see the general troubleshooting tips on page xv.

Windows reports a missing DLL file during bootup

Source of the problem

If Microsoft Windows stops while loading to display an error message on a full, blue screen (widely known as the *blue screen of death*), it can be unnerving. The typical error message refers to a missing DLL file, as in *A required .DLL file, ABCD.DLL, was not found.* But if you press a key, Windows will continue to load. And once loaded, Windows will work normally. *What*, you may ask, *is going on here?*

This is more of a Windows problem than a hardware problem, but it may show up after you've made a hardware change. A DLL file is a *dynamic link library*—actually a library of programming code that other programs can dip into and use. The error message indicates that Windows has been instructed to load one of these files, but can't find it.

The cause is often that you deleted a program, which may have been associated with a piece of hardware that you removed from your system. If you did everything the way Windows likes it done, you used an Uninstall utility or the Windows built-in Add/Remove Programs feature. Unfortunately, these choices will sometimes fail to remove every mention of the DLLs in the files Windows looks to when it loads. That leaves Windows looking for a file that isn't there, and you see an error message. Since you don't actually need the file, the fact that it's missing doesn't really matter. However, having to skip over the error each time you boot is an annoyance that you can get rid of. (If the fix here doesn't work, see "Drives: hard disk booting" on page 220.)

How to fix it

1. Boot your system. When you reach the error message on the blue screen, write down the name of the file.

2. Choose Start, Run, and then type **sysedit** in the Open text box. Press Enter.

3. Choose the System.ini window.

4. Choose Search, Find, and then enter the name of the missing DLL file in the Find text box. Press Enter.

5. If the search locates a match, make a record of the line it's in. The easiest way may be to print the System.ini file by choosing File, Print.

> **Tip**
>
> It's easy to make changes to the files Windows uses when it loads, but if you make the wrong changes, they can make your system unusable. Before making changes to these files, you may want to back up your hard disk, just in case. And be sure to keep a careful record of anything you change or delete, so you can easily change it back.

6. Delete the entire line.

7. It's unlikely that the DLL filename will appear twice, but repeat the search, just to be sure.

8. If you made any changes, choose File, Save.

9. Close the Sysedit program

10. Choose Start, Run, and then type **regedit** in the Open text box. Press Enter.

11. You should see both left and right panes in the Registry Editor. If you don't, choose View, Split, and then move the mouse left or right to see both panes. The left pane shows what are known as *keys*. The right pane shows values (in the Name column) and data (in the Data column).

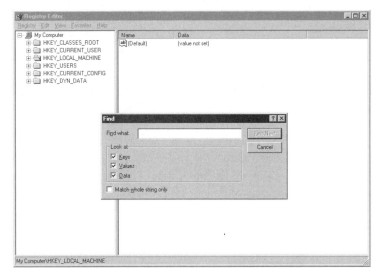

12. Choose Edit, Find, and then enter the name of the missing DLL file in the Find text box. Make sure the Keys, Values, and Data check boxes are all checked. Press Enter. ▶

13. If the search finds a match in the left pane, first record the exact entry for the key and for each value and data entry for that key, so you can re-create them if you need to. The key's location in the Registry tree should show in the status bar at the bottom of the Registry Editor window. If you don't see the status bar, choose View, Status Bar. Then delete the key, which will also delete all the value and data entries associated with that key.

14. If the search finds a match in the right pane, record the exact entry for the value and data of the found item, and record the exact entry for the key the value is associated with. Then delete the value entry for the matched item. This will not delete the associated key or other values for that key.

15. Press F3 to find the next match and repeat these steps. When the Find feature reports that there are no more matches, choose Registry, Exit. Your system should now boot without looking for the missing DLL file.

Windows says some hardware isn't working properly

Source of the problem

Windows tries hard to let you know when there are certain kinds of hardware problems. Unfortunately, sometimes it sees problems that aren't there. If you open the System Properties window—by right-clicking on My Computer and choosing Properties—and then choose the Device Manager tab (or, in Windows 2000, choose the Hardware tab, and then choose the Device Manager button), you may see one or more lines marked with a red X or with a yellow circle with an exclamation point. These icons indicate that there is something wrong with these devices.

And here you were thinking that everything was working.

So what do you do now? If you're not aware of a problem, you may have a nonproblem that you can safely ignore. On the other hand, the icon may be pointing out a real problem that can cause crashes, and that you ought to do something about. Here's how to tell the difference.

How to fix it

1. In the Device Manager window, select the device that shows a warning icon. Right-click on the Device line and choose Properties.

2. If the icon is a red X, check the Device Usage area, and clear the Disable In This Hardware Profile check box if there is a check in it.

3. If the icon is an exclamation point in a yellow circle, check the Device Status message area on the General tab of the device's Properties window for a description of the problem. If the device is working properly and the problem is reported as a missing driver, you can almost certainly ignore the message.

4. If the reported problem is an IRQ or DMA conflict, and you haven't noticed any problems, you can probably ignore it. Check the Resources tab to find out which resource has a conflict and what other device is also trying to use the resource. In most cases, if the two devices aren't things you'll use at the same time—like a modem and a dedicated label printer—you won't have any problems. If the two devices could be used at the same time—like a modem and a mouse—you should try to correct the conflict. See "I may need to reinstall an adapter card" on page 28.

> **Tip**
> If you see an icon in Device Manager that's a blue circle with a white, lowercase *i*, it means you've made a resource setting manually. It is not reporting a problem.

I may need to reinstall an adapter card

Source of the problem

Ben Franklin wrote that there's many a slip twixt cup and lip, which is a good aphorism for expansion cards. Just because a card fits into a slot in your computer's motherboard doesn't mean that it will work correctly. It doesn't even mean that you put in the slot correctly.

There are any number of factors that can cause a card not to work correctly. There may be errors in the way the system's BIOS is configured, required software may not be installed, or the card may be trying to use the same resources as another device. That means there is a long list of things you may have to check if a card isn't working properly. If you reach a point where the card is functioning correctly, you can stop without completing the rest of the steps.

How to fix it

Check Device Manager

1. Check to see if Windows recognizes the card. Right-click on My Computer, then choose Properties from the shortcut menu that pops up.

2. Choose the Device Manager tab. (In Windows 2000, choose the Hardware tab, and then choose the Device Manager button.) ▶

3. Look for the device in the Device Manager window. If you don't see it in the list, expand the category of device that best describes the type of device. (From this point on, we will refer to *the device* rather than *the card*, since these same steps will work for troubleshooting problems with all sorts of devices besides adapter cards.)

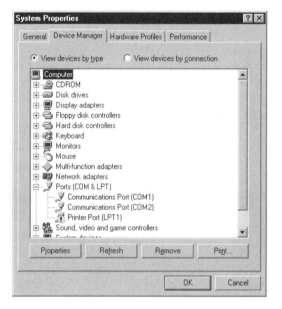

If Device Manager lists the card

1. Look for a red X or a filled-in yellow circle with an exclamation point next to any of the lines in the Device Manager window. If either icon is next to the card you're concerned about, you may be able to find out more details about the problem. If one of the icons is next to a different device, it's possible that the problem with that device is also causing the problem you're currently trying to track down.

2. Select the device that has the exclamation mark or X. Choose the Properties button.

3. If the device had a red X in the Device Manager window, check the Device Usage box. If there is a check in the Disable In This Hardware Profile check box, remove the check. (In Windows 2000, choose Use This Device (Enable) in the Device Usage drop-down list.)

4. Check the Device Status message box on the General tab of the Properties window for the device. This may give some indication of the problem with the device. ▶

5. Choose the Resources tab. You may see a message indicating that the device isn't using any resources because it isn't enabled or has a problem. If you see this message, you can be fairly sure that the problem is not a resource conflict. If you see a table of Resource Types and Settings, check the Conflicting Device List message area at the bottom of the page. If there is a conflict, the resource will be marked with a barred red circle in the Resource Type column, and the message area will name the conflicting device. Note the details of the conflict. ▶

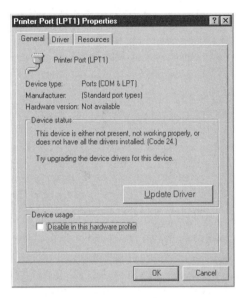

If this solution didn't solve your problem, go to the next page.

I may need to reinstall an adapter card

(continued from page 29)

If Device Manager reports a driver problem

1. If the General tab of the device properties window indicates that there is a problem with the driver, try upgrading the driver. Go to the Driver tab of the device properties window and choose the Update Driver button.

2. At the opening window of the Update Device Driver Wizard, choose the Next button.

3. Choose the default action for Windows, which is to search for a better driver than the one your device is using now. Then choose the Next button.

4. If the device you're having a problem with came with a driver or other software on a floppy disk drive, put the driver disk in the floppy disk drive, and then check the Floppy Disk Drives check box. ▶

5. If your copy of Windows was installed from a CD-ROM and you don't have a copy of the installation files on your hard drive, place the disc in the CD-ROM drive and select the CD-ROM Drive check box.

6. If Windows was preinstalled on your system, and the Windows installation files are stored on your hard drive, check the Specify A Location check box and type the name of the folder where the files are stored. In many cases, this will be the *C:\windows\options\cabs* folder. (In Windows 2000, check the Specify A Location check box, choose Next, and type the name of the folder where the files are stored.)

7. Choose the Next button.

> **Tip**
>
> If you have a new driver for a device and want to update Windows to use it, open the device properties window, and then choose the Driver tab. Choose the Update Driver button to start the Update Device Drivers Wizard, and tell the Wizard where to find the new driver.

8. Windows will report on the file it finds for the device. If it finds a new driver for the device, Windows will install the new driver when you choose the Next button. If it fails to find a new driver, it will offer to use the same one, or let you back up (using the Back button) to pick a different one. If you choose the Next button at this point, Windows will continue using the existing driver.

9. Choose the Finish button to close the Update Device Driver Wizard, close the device's Properties window and then close the System Properties window.

10. Choose Start, Shut Down to open the Shut Down Windows dialog box.

11. Choose the Restart option, and then choose the OK button.

12. After Windows reboots, choose the Device Manager tab in the System Properties window and see if the driver problem has been fixed. (In Windows 2000, choose the Hardware tab in the System Properties window, and then choose the Device Manager button.) If it hasn't been fixed, check with the device manufacturer to see if there is an updated driver available. The manufacturer's Web site is usually the best place to start looking for one.

13. If there is an updated driver, make a folder for it on your hard disk and download or copy the driver to the folder. Follow the manufacturer's instructions for installing the driver. If there are no instructions, use the Update Device Driver Wizard as described above. When you reach the Specify A Location text box, enter the folder where you put the driver.

If your card has a resource conflict with another device

1. If the Resources tab in the device's Properties window indicates that you have an Interrupt Request (IRQ), Direct Memory Access (DMA), Input/Output, or memory range conflict, note which other device is trying to use the same channel.

2. If the Use Automatic Settings check box on the Resources tab is not checked, put a check in it, and then see if that resolves the conflict. If it does, you're done. Choose OK, and then close the device's Properties window and System Properties window.

3. If the Use Automatic Settings check box on the Resources tab has a check in it, remove the check.

4. In the Setting Based On drop-down list, start with the first option, and see if its settings result in a conflict. If so, try each of the other settings (if there are any) in turn.

5. If none of the predefined configurations resolve the conflict, select the resource that's in conflict and choose the Change Setting button. (Note that you must remove the check, if any, from the Use Automatic Settings check box before this button will be available.)

If this solution didn't solve your problem, go to the next page.

I may need to reinstall an adapter card

(continued from page 31)

6. Choose a new setting for this resource if you can. (In some cases, you'll get a message that the resource setting cannot be modified.) The Conflict Information message box will indicate whether there is a conflict with another device at that setting. Choose a setting that does not have a conflict. ▶

7. Check the documentation for the device to see how to change its resource configuration. Some older cards may have switches or pins that you connect with rectangular plastic jumpers (that fit over a pair of pins to tie them together) to change settings. Some cards come with a utility program for changing settings. Some cards may not need any special treatment; the Windows Plug and Play feature can adjust their settings as needed. In any case, make sure the resource settings you choose are supported by the card.

8. Choose OK to accept the new setting. Then close the device Properties window and the System Properties window.

9. Turn off the computer, and make any appropriate jumper or switch changes. (Make sure you've read our advice in "Working inside your computer" at the beginning of this book.) ▶

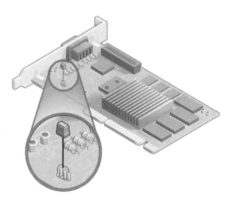

10. Turn the computer back on and check to see if the resource conflict has been resolved.

If your card doesn't show in Device Manager

1. First, make sure you've read our advice in "Working inside your computer" at the beginning of this book. Then turn the computer off, take the card out of its slot, and reinsert it. Turn the computer on and see if the card shows up in Device Manager. Repeat this step at least three times before you move on to step 2.

2. Exit Windows and turn off the computer

3. Move the card to a different slot. If no slots are available, swap slots with another card.

4. Turn the computer back on. Check the Device Manager window. If the card still doesn't show in Device Manager, you need to make sure that the card is functioning.

5. Turn off the computer and remove the card.

6. Install the card in another computer system. If it still fails to work, it's probably defective.

7. If the card functions properly in the other computer, take a card that you know works, and install it in the slot you've been using for the card that isn't working.

8. If a second card doesn't work, there may be a problem with the slot.

9. If the second card does work, you may need to upgrade the problem card to work with your computer, or you may need to upgrade your computer's BIOS to work with the card. Check with the card's manufacturer to see if any upgrades are required. If not, go to the question "Does the card support Plug and Play?" on the decision flowchart for this chapter.

My computer isn't recognizing a non-Plug and Play adapter card properly

Source of the problem

Plug and Play is a feature that lets Windows recognize and configure expansion cards and other devices automatically—just plug 'em in and they'll play (or work, if you want to be stuffy about it). Older cards and other devices—often called *legacy* devices—don't know about Plug and Play. Windows is designed to work with those cards too, but sometimes it won't recognize them without a little help from you.

There are ways to force the system to recognize a legacy device. Here's how to get the card working in your system. (Note that this section assumes you've already worked through the section "I may need to reinstall an adapter card" on page 28, which applies to both legacy and Plug and Play devices.)

How to fix it

1. The Add New Hardware Wizard in Windows is designed to find not only Plug and Play devices, but also legacy devices. Start by closing any open programs, and then choosing Start, Settings, Control Panel.

2. Choose Add New Hardware. (In Windows 2000, choose Add/Remove Hardware.)

3. Choose Next to pass the opening screen, and then choose Next again to make the computer search for Plug and Play devices. On the next screen, choose Yes to let Windows automatically search for legacy devices, and then choose Next. (With Windows 2000, first choose Add A New Device, and then choose Next.) ▶

4. Choose Next once again, to start the search.

5. When Windows 98 finishes scanning your system, you can see the items it found by choosing the Details button on the final window. (Windows 2000 does not provide this list.) Choose Finish to install the detected devices. You may be prompted to insert the Windows CD-ROM. If your system came with the Windows distribution files on your hard disk, you can enter that location instead. Most often they will be located in the *C:\windows\options\cabs* folder.

6. When Windows finishes, reboot your system and see if the card works. If it does, you can stop here. Otherwise, proceed to the next heading.

Finding the available resources

1. Check your card's documentation to see if it requires one or more Interrupt Request (IRQ) channels, Direct Memory Access (DMA) channels, or both. If it does, note which choices it supports and how to configure the card for the different settings. You may have to set switches, move jumpers (small plastic rectangles that fit over a pair of pins to tie them together), or run a utility program.

2. Right-click on the My Computer icon on your Desktop.

3. Choose Properties from the shortcut menu to open the System Properties window. In Windows 98, choose the Device Manager tab. In Windows 2000, choose the Hardware tab, then the Device Manager button.)

4. Look for the card in the list. If the card isn't working, you should see it in the list with some indication that there is a resource conflict.

5. Turn off the computer and remove the card. (Be sure you've read "Working inside your computer" at the beginning of this book before you open the case.)

6. Start the computer, and open the Device Manager window again (steps 2 and 3 above).

7. Select Computer at the top of the Device Manager window, and choose the Properties button. (In Windows 2000, choose View, Resources By Connection.)

Tip

If your system doesn't have any available IRQs, you may be able to free one up. First, check to see if you have both COM1 and COM2 listed in the Ports section of the Device Manager window. If you don't have any devices attached to your serial ports and you have a single internal modem, then you may be able to disable a COM port to free up an IRQ. Determine which port your modem uses—either COM1 or COM2—and then go into the CMOS configuration settings for your system (see "The computer is booting from the wrong disk drive" on page 82 for details about using the CMOS setup) and disable the one that your modem isn't using.

If you're using both COM ports, or one has already been disabled, you may be able to eliminate the IRQ assigned to your printer port, LPT1. This is not needed by Windows in most cases. It's needed only if you plan to print directly from MS-DOS programs.

> *If this solution didn't solve your problem, go to the next page.*

My computer isn't recognizing a non-Plug and Play adapter card

(continued from page 35)

If the card needs one or more IRQ channels

1. Choose Interrupt Request (IRQ) at the top left of the View Resources tab. (In Windows 2000, expand the Interrupt Request (IRQ) category.) ▶

2. The IRQs are numbered from 0 through 15. Look to see if any IRQ that the card supports is missing from the list. The list will skip any that are not in use.

3. If a supported IRQ is available, configure the card to use that IRQ. Reinstall the card in the computer. If Windows recognizes it, you can stop. If Windows does not recognize the card, go on to the next heading.

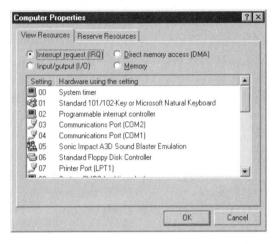

4. If there is no supported IRQ available, identify the device that conflicts with the card's current setting.

5. Exit Windows and turn off your computer.

6. Remove the card that conflicts with the non–Plug and Play card.

7. Install the non–Plug and Play card. Turn on the computer. The computer should now recognize the card without showing a conflict. Exit Windows and turn off the computer.

8. Insert the card that was conflicting earlier. If it's a Plug and Play card, it should find another available IRQ automatically when you turn on the system. If it isn't a Plug and Play card, you may have to reconfigure it to use an available IRQ.

If the card needs one or more DMA channels

1. Choose the Direct Memory Access (DMA) option at the top of the View Resources tab to see the list of DMA channels currently assigned to devices. (In Windows 2000, choose View, Resources By Connection, and then expand the Direct Memory Access (DMA) category.) ▶

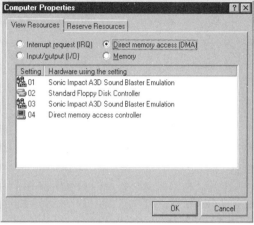

2. The DMA channels are numbered from 0 through 7. Look to see if any of the channels the card supports are missing from the list. If a channel isn't listed, it should be available.

3. If a DMA channel that the card supports is available, configure the card to use it. Reinstall the card in the computer. If Windows recognizes it, you can stop. Otherwise go on to the next step.

4. If there is no supported DMA available, identify the device that conflicts with the current setting for your card.

5. Exit Windows and turn off your computer.

6. Remove the card that conflicts with the non–Plug and Play card.

7. Install the non–Plug and Play card. Turn on the computer. The computer should now recognize the card without showing a conflict. Exit Windows and turn off the computer.

8. Insert the card that was conflicting earlier. If it's a Plug and Play card, it should find another available IRQ automatically. If it isn't, you will have to reconfigure it manually to use an available IRQ.

Check for available Input/ Output or Memory Ranges

1. Most cards do not have options for their input/output or memory ranges, but some do. If the card that you're having problems with supports different settings for these resources, use the View Resources window to find out if any of the supported settings are available. If they are, configure the card to use them. If not, see if you can reassign any of the conflicting devices. ▶

My computer isn't recognizing a Plug and Play adapter card properly

Source of the problem

Plug and Play is meant to make computers easier to work with. Just plug in a new adapter card or other device and it will *play*—a term engineers like to use to say that something works. Early incarnations of Plug and Play were flaky enough that some people who used them (we both plead guilty) started referring to the feature as *plug and pray*. Some people still do (we take the fifth), but the fact is that much of the promise of Plug and Play has been fulfilled, and when you're adding new hardware to your system, Plug and Play generally makes life much easier than it was in the early days of personal computers. Alas, *generally* is not synonymous with *always*. There are times when Windows assigns resources to some devices in ways that create problems instead of solving them. The good news is that if your computer isn't recognizing a Plug and Play adapter card, there are some steps you can take to get it working. (Note that this section assumes you've already worked through the section "I may need to reinstall an adapter card" on page 28, which applies to both Plug and Play and non–Plug and Play devices. It also assumes you're familiar with the section "Working inside your computer" at the beginning of this book.)

How to fix it

1. Install the card in a different slot if one's available, since there may be a problem with that slot. Turn the computer off, move the card to the other slot, and turn the computer back on. If that solves the problem, stop here.

2. Next, make sure that Plug and Play support is enabled for your computer. Reboot, and start the CMOS configuration utility. In most cases, your computer will show a message telling you which key you have to press for the utility during bootup—F2 and Del being the most common choices. If it doesn't show you which key to press, and neither of these work, see "The computer is booting from the wrong disk drive" on page 82 for more details about starting the CMOS utility.

3. Check the menus for an option that mentions *PNP Setup* or something similar. (See the graphic on the following page.)

4. Make sure that support for a Plug and Play operating system is enabled—this may be labeled *PNP OS Installed* or something similar—and then exit the CMOS utility. Be sure to save the changes when you exit.

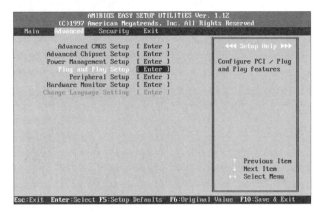

5. After Windows loads, see if the card shows up in Device Manager. (To open Device Manager, right click on My Computer, and choose Properties. Then choose the Device Manager tab in Windows 98, or, in Windows 2000, choose the Hardware tab, then the Device Manager button.) If the card shows up, it should work at this point.

6. Sometimes, the sequence in which cards are installed can make a difference in whether Plug and Play cards install correctly. To see whether installing the cards in a different order solves your problem, start by exiting Windows and turning off the computer.

7. Remove all expansion cards except the graphics adapter and—if it's on a separate card—the hard disk controller.

8. Start the computer, and make sure that it works in this minimal configuration. If it doesn't, you have some problem other than just recognizing the card; solve that problem first. If the computer works in this stripped-down arrangement, proceed.

9. Exit Windows, turn off the computer, and reinsert the problem card.

10. Turn on the computer and boot Windows. If Windows recognizes the problem card, exit Windows, turn off the computer, and add the remaining cards one at a time, restarting the computer after each one to make sure that the system sees all the installed cards. If at any point in the process the computer doesn't work after installing a card, proceed to the next step.

11. The BIOS on your motherboard may have a problem recognizing your card. Check with the manufacturer to see if you have the latest version of the BIOS installed. If not, you may need to download the latest version and transfer it to the BIOS chips on your motherboard. This process is called *flashing the BIOS*, because the information is stored in flash memory chips. Follow the motherboard manufacturer's instructions for updating the BIOS.

Tip

There are 16 IRQs available in a personal computer; sometimes this isn't enough to give every device its own IRQ. However, Windows allows newer computers to use a technology called *IRQ Holder for PCI Steering,* which lets two devices use the same IRQ.

As long as both devices are not active at the same time, they can share an IRQ. For example, if a mouse and a modem share the same IRQ, you risk a system crash if you move the mouse while the modem is on line. On the other hand, a network card and a USB controller may be able to coexist successfully.

So if you see two items in Device Manager that have the same IRQ assignment, it shouldn't be a problem, as long as they also share it with IRQ Holder for PCI Steering.

If your computer suddenly stops making the noise you're used to hearing, check to make sure that the power supply cooling fan is still turning. If it's not, turn off your computer and re-place the power supply as soon as possible. Without the cooling fan, your computer can over-heat and perform erratically; you can even damage some components permanently. The same advice applies to any oth-er cooling fan that stops run-ning when it should be on continuously.

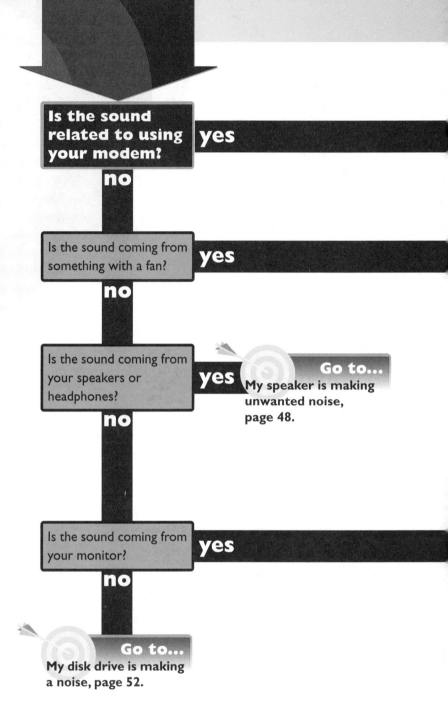

Is the sound related to using your modem?

yes

no

Is the sound coming from something with a fan?

yes

no

Is the sound coming from your speakers or headphones?

yes

Go to...
My speaker is making unwanted noise, page 48.

no

Is the sound coming from your monitor?

yes

no

Go to...
My disk drive is making a noise, page 52.

Computer noises

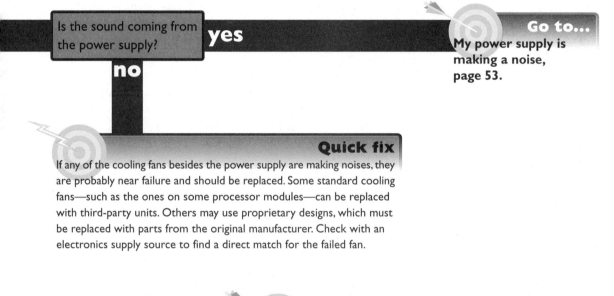

Go to...
My modem is making noise when it shouldn't, page 42.

Is the sound coming from the power supply? **yes**

Go to...
My power supply is making a noise, page 53.

no

Quick fix
If any of the cooling fans besides the power supply are making noises, they are probably near failure and should be replaced. Some standard cooling fans—such as the ones on some processor modules—can be replaced with third-party units. Others may use proprietary designs, which must be replaced with parts from the original manufacturer. Check with an electronics supply source to find a direct match for the failed fan.

Go to...
My monitor is making funny noises, page 50.

If your solution isn't here
Check these related chapters:
Drives: CD, CD-R, CD-RW, DVD, page 196
Drives: floppy disk drives, page 212
Drives: hard disk booting, page 220
Or see the general troubleshooting tips on page xv.

My modem is making noise when it shouldn't

Source of the problem

Problems with modem noises are not usually that the modem is making a noise, but that it's making a noise that bothers you. Modems are designed to make noise. That's how a modem talks with another modem at the other end of the phone line. (We're talking about real modems here, not the boxes for DSL, cable, or ISDN that lots of people call modems, even though they aren't.)

When a modem makes a connection, it goes through two key steps. First, it dials the phone number. Next, if a modem answers, the two have to handshake—chatting back and forth to agree on the speed to use and other details. Typically, modems let you eavesdrop on both steps; you get to hear the dial tone, dialing, and the start of the conversation, which consists of some combination of humming, screeching, and static. Sometimes you might not want to hear this. Sometimes you might want to hear it, but not so loud. And sometimes the modem may answer the phone and start screeching when you don't want it to. Here's how to tell it—ever so politely—to shut up.

How to fix it

If you don't want to hear the modem dial the phone and start a connection

1. The sounds of dialing and making a connection are normal, and they can be useful for troubleshooting a call that's not getting through, but you can turn them off if you like.

2. First choose Start, Settings, and then Control Panel to open the Control Panel.

If you use Windows 98	If you use Windows 2000
3. Choose Modems.	Choose Phone And Modem Options.
4. Select the entry for your modem, and choose the Properties button to open the Modem Properties dialog box.	Choose the Modems tab, select the entry for your modem, and then choose the Properties button.
5. Choose the Connection tab, and then the Advanced button to open the Advanced Connection Settings dialog box.	Choose the Advanced tab of the modem's Properties dialog box.

6. The Extra Settings text box in the dialog box may already have some text in it. (In Windows 2000, the dialog box will look somewhat different from the Windows 98 version shown here. The equivalent text box is labeled Extra Initialization Commands.) This text is actually a set of commands for the modem. Modem commands vary from one modem to the next, but most use the command M0—that's a zero, not a capital O—to tell the modem to keep the speaker off at all times. First make sure that the text box doesn't already have a command beginning with M. (And note that an M with a symbol before it is not the same as an M alone. &M0, /M0, and M0 are three different commands.) If there is an M command already, replace it with an M0 command. If there isn't an existing M command, simply type **M0** in the text box. (It's okay to add it at the end of other commands that are already there.) Choose OK, and Windows will send the command to the modem every time it dials a connection. If this doesn't work, you'll need to check your modem manual to see if the modem has an oddball command for controlling the speaker. ▶

If you want to hear the dialing and the connection, but not so loud

1. Some modems have a physical volume control—often on the back of the modem—to crank the volume up or turn it down.

2. Those modems that don't have a physical volume control usually let you set the volume through a command, typically the L command. For these modems, the choices are usually L, L1, or L0 (that's a zero again, not a capital O) for the lowest volume; L2 for medium volume; and L3 for high volume. To set the volume, follow the same steps we just described for turning the speaker off, but enter one of the L commands instead.

Tip

If you can't hear your modem while it's dialing and hand-shaking, type **M1L3** in the Extra Settings text box. M1, which turns off the speaker after the connection is established, is typically the default setting. If you still can't hear the modem with both M1 and L3, and you've checked that the modem follows these commands rather than some unusual alternative, the modem may simply lack a speaker. Or, as with some internal modems, the speaker may be so wimpy that it's almost impossible to hear at any setting.

If this solution didn't solve your problem, go to the next page.

My modem is making noise when it shouldn't

(continued from page 43)

(continued from page 43)

3. Try all three to find a comfortable volume, making a test call each time you change the setting. If you don't notice any difference in volume between one setting and the next, check your modem manual. The modem may be designed to ignore the volume command, or it may use a different command for volume control.

Tip
Two other speaker commands worth knowing about for troubleshooting purposes are: M2, which leaves the speaker on all the time for most modems, and M3, which typically turns the speaker on only during the handshake, so you don't hear the dial tone or dialing.

If your modem answers the phone when you don't want it to

1. If your modem is plugged into the same phone line you use for voice calls, you may find that it answers the phone when any call comes in, and then screeches in your caller's ear—and yours too if you pick up the phone. This doesn't mean there's anything wrong with the modem. It simply means the modem has been set to answer the phone automatically. You need to track down what's setting the modem to auto answer, and find out how to stop it.

2. If you have an external modem with a bank of status lights, look for one that indicates the current modem setting for auto answer; it's usually labeled *AA*, and it lights up to show when auto answer is on. ▶

```
●  ○  ○  ○  ○  ○  ○  ○
AA RX TX CD OH HS TR MR
```

AA (or RI) light:
If the light is on without blinking, the modem is set to automatically answer the phone.

3. Some modems label the light *RI* instead, because it typically leads a double life. When the auto answer feature is off, the light stays off except that it turns on when the modem detects the ringing of an incoming call. That makes it a ring indicator light as well as an auto answer light.

Tip
For most modems the command for setting auto answer will be S1=n, where *n* is a number. S1=0 (the number zero) turns off auto answer. Any other number tells the modem which ring to wait for before answering the phone.

4. If you don't see either an AA or RI light, check your modem manual to see if it has a status light for the auto answer setting.

5. Once you've identified the auto answer light, turn your computer and modem off, wait a few seconds, and then turn them back on. After the computer finishes booting up, see if the auto answer light is on.

6. If you have an internal modem, it may come with a utility that creates a set of onscreen status indicators. If not, the easiest way to find out if the system boots up with the modem set to auto answer is to call a friend immediately after booting up, and ask him or her to call back. Turn off anything like an answering machine that may answer the phone before the modem. Then let the phone ring at least ten times before picking up. A modem can be set to pick up only after a specific number of rings, so if it doesn't pick up right away, that doesn't tell you anything. If it still doesn't pick up after the tenth ring, you can assume that the system does not set the modem to auto answer.

If your modem is *not* set to auto answer immediately after booting

1. If you've proven that the system does not set the modem to auto answer immediately after booting, it means that some program sets the modem that way when you use the program. If the program turns auto answer off when you leave the program, tracking down the culprit will be easy. Wait till the next time the problem occurs, then close each program that's running, one at a time, and check after closing each one to see whether auto answer is still on.

2. If the culprit does not turn auto answer back off when you finish using it, tracking it down will take a little more detective work.

3. First check your modem manual for the setting that turns on auto answer. Then check for that setting in the Advanced Connection Settings dialog box (or, in Windows 2000, the Advanced tab of the Modem Properties dialog box) that we mentioned earlier. Briefly:

    In Windows 98, to open the dialog box, choose Start, Settings, Control Panel; then choose Modems. Select the entry for your modem and choose Properties, then the Connection tab, and then the Advanced button. Make sure the command for auto answer is not included in the Extra Settings text box.

    In Windows 2000, choose Start, Settings, Control Panel; then Phone And Modem Options, and then the Modems tab. Select the entry for your modem and choose Properties, and then the Advanced tab. Make sure the command for auto answer is not included in the Extra Initialization Commands text box.

4. If the command to turn on auto answer is in the text box, Windows will send the command to your modem every time you use the modem and will then leave the modem set that way. You can simply delete the command, but be aware that a program may have added this setting. If you delete the setting, then some program that has properly answered the phone in the past may suddenly stop answering. If that happens, you can then decide whether it's more important to have that program working or to stop the modem from picking up the phone when you don't want it to.

If this solution didn't solve your problem, go to the next page.

My modem is making noise when it shouldn't

(continued from page 45)

If your modem *is* set to auto answer immediately after booting

1. If you found that the modem is set for auto answer immediately after booting, it means you are either loading a program that's setting the modem to answer the phone, or the modem itself is set to wake up with auto answer on. Either possibility requires some detective work to track down.

2. Start with any application that loads each time you boot up and that shows in the Taskbar at the bottom of the Windows screen, including programs that show as icons in the Windows System Tray, at the extreme right side of the Taskbar. Fax programs are a common culprit, and so are remote control communications programs. If you find a suspect program, check to see whether it is set to automatically answer the phone. If so, change the setting to turn off auto answer. ▶

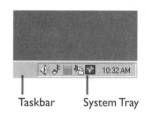

Taskbar System Tray

3. If you don't find the culprit in applications that show in the Taskbar, odds are that the modem is set to wake up to answer the phone every time you turn it on. Most modems will let you change the default setting, but before you take that route, be aware that the modem may have been set that way by a particular program that you use. If so, the program expects the modem to have those settings. If you change the setting, the program may not work properly anymore.

4. The particular setting you want to change will vary depending on the modem. So will the command for saving the changed setting as the new default. In most cases, however, the setting will be S1=0 (the number zero) and the command for saving it as the new default will be some variation of &W. You'll need to get this information from the modem manual or modem vendor, along with details explaining how to send these commands to the modem.

My speaker is making unwanted noise

Source of the problem

The music goes 'round and 'round and 'round… and it comes out here. But sometimes other stuff comes out here, too—sounds that you don't want.

The problem is that electrons are whizzing around all over the place inside the average computer, and in spite of engineers' best efforts, these little bundles of energy sometimes stray from the straight and narrow. And sometimes they can find their way into the computer's sound system, making sounds that you don't want to hear.

How to fix it

1. Start by making sure that all the speaker cables are firmly plugged in.

2. Next, make sure that the speakers are plugged into the correct jack on your sound card. Some sound cards offer separate jacks labeled (with text or icons) for speakers and for line out. If your sound card offers both, and the speakers are self-powered—meaning that they have batteries or plug into an electrical outlet on their own—they should be connected to the line out jack. If the speakers are not self-powered, they should be plugged into the speaker jack. ▶

3. Try rerouting your speaker cables. If you have a mare's nest of wires tangled in the back of your computer, sort out the speaker cables and run them as directly as possible from device to device. Also try to route the speaker cables separately from any other cables to reduce the chances of picking up interference. Do *not* tie them together in neat bundles with other wires—particularly power cords.

4. Try relocating the speakers. For example, some monitors are poorly shielded and give off a lot of electromagnetic interference, which can affect the speakers. Move the speakers a foot or more from any other electronic device—including, in particular, cordless telephones—and devices that have motors, such as printers or fans. ▶

5. Make sure that your computer and speakers are plugged into the same electrical circuit. The easiest way to do this is to plug them into the same outlet or into the same surge protection strip.

6. You may notice that the sound changes depending on what is displayed on the monitor, even though the sounds are clearly coming from the speakers. In that case, the graphics adapter may be the source of the interference. If you've already tried rerouting the cables (as described in step 3), shut down the computer, open the case, and make sure the sound card and graphics card are not next to each other. If possible, put the sound card in the left-most slot, and leave the adjacent slot empty. (Be sure you've read "Working inside your computer" at the beginning of this book.)

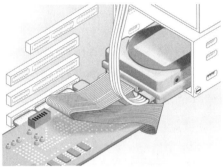

7. If the sound appears to change with disk drive activity, shut down the computer, open the case and check to see whether the sound card is immediately adjacent to the hard disk controller. If it is, relocate it as described in the previous step. Also make sure that no disk drive ribbon data cables are routed next to or across the sound card. ▶

8. Noise can also occur when you print. If rerouting the speaker cables (described in step 3 on the previous page) didn't help, make sure that the printer cable is solidly grounded. This shouldn't be an issue with a USB cable, but with a parallel cable; check that you're using both connector clips at the printer end to make a good connection to ground on the printer side, and both screws at the computer end to make a good connection there.

9. Many computers come with inexpensive speakers. One way to keep costs down on these speakers is to use inexpensive cables that may not be adequately shielded. Try replacing them with good quality stereo cables, available at most electronics and music stores. And if your problem seems related to your printer, try replacing the printer cable as well, using a better-quality cable with better shielding.

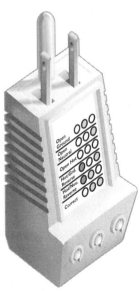

10. If you hear a low hum from the speakers, make sure that your electrical outlet is properly grounded. Use an outlet tester to make sure that the outlet is wired correctly. If it isn't, get an electrician to fix it. You can get an outlet tester at Radio Shack or most electronic supply stores and even many hardware stores. ▶

My monitor is making funny noises

Source of the problem

Monitors are meant to be seen and not heard—unless they have speakers built into them—but some make sounds anyway. Some of these sounds are cause for concern. Others are more or less benign.

In any case, you won't be able to fix the problem yourself. The best you can hope for is to identify whether the sound requires attention or is safe to ignore. But that in itself is important. Not only can it help your peace of mind, it can make the difference between fixing or replacing a monitor before it dies, and waking up one day to find that you don't have a working monitor when you need one.

How to fix it

If you hear a high-pitched whine

1. If you hear a high-pitched whine, you may notice that it changes as the image on the screen changes or that it comes and goes. Either way, the sound is typically the result of a loose part or a failing part, and it needs a professional to repair it. You can get it repaired right away, or wait until the monitor fails completely (which may never happen).

2. If the monitor is under warranty, get the work done right away, while it's free. If it's not under warranty, fixing it immediately lets *you* decide when you'll be without the monitor, rather than letting fate decide for you.

If you hear a low-pitched hum

1. If you hear a low-pitched hum for a second or two when you turn on the monitor, it's most likely nothing to worry about. This sound, which is more noticeable on monitors with larger screen sizes, is caused by something called degaussing. Briefly, degaussing eliminates the effects of unwanted magnetic fields on the display (a subject we cover in "I see discolored splotches on my screen," on page 116).

2. Many, if not most, monitors today automatically degauss when you turn them on. Many also offer a manual degauss button or menu command. If your monitor offers a manual degauss feature, try it to confirm that the sound you hear with manual degaussing is similar to what you hear when you turn on the monitor. If it is, then the sound you hear when you turn on the monitor is almost certainly the degaussing. (See the figure on the next page.)

3. If your monitor doesn't have a manual degaussing command or button, or you've used the manual degaussing and still have doubts whether the degaussing feature explains the sound you hear when you turn the monitor on, check your manual or check with the manufacturer to make sure the monitor does, in fact, offer automatic degaussing when you turn it on. If it does, it is almost certainly responsible for the sound you hear.

If you hear clicking

1. You might also hear a loud clicking when the monitor changes from one resolution to another—for example, when switching from the clouds screen that Windows shows while loading to the higher-resolution screen that Windows uses after loading. The clicking may be accompanied by the image growing and shrinking in size during the switch. If you hear clicks, you can run a quick test to confirm the cause, although there isn't much you can do about it.

2. Start by opening an MS-DOS window. In most versions of Windows, you can find the MS-DOS Prompt shortcut on the Start menu. Depending on the version of Windows, and assuming you haven't moved the shortcut elsewhere, choose Start, then Programs, then the MS-DOS Prompt shortcut, or choose Start, Programs, Accessories, and then the Command Prompt shortcut to open the window.

3. The MS-DOS window may open as a partial-screen window or a full-screen window. If it opens as a partial-screen window, press Alt-Enter to make it full-screen. This will switch the monitor to the MS-DOS–level resolution on your computer, which is usually VGA.

4. Finally, use Alt-Tab to switch between the MS-DOS window and a Windows screen that shows the Windows desktop or a Windows application. Switch back and forth several times, waiting a few seconds each time. If you hear the clicking as it switches, you've got positive proof of what's causing the sound. As we already pointed out, however, there's isn't much you can do about it. Basically you've noticed a design flaw that often shows up in inexpensive monitors. The only fix is to replace the monitor with a better model. On the other hand, at least you know that the sound is nothing you have to worry about.

Tip

Look on the back of your monitor, and you'll likely see a statement along the lines of *No User Serviceable Parts, Do Not Open This Cover*, or *Trained Service Personnel Only*. These are polite ways of telling you to keep your hands off the monitor's innards. Take them seriously. Monitors include components (specifically, capacitors) that store a significant electric charge long after the power has been turned off. You do not want to find out what a capacitor discharge feels like.

My disk drive is making a noise

Source of the problem

There are remarkably few moving parts in a typical computer, and most of them are related to disk drives of one type or another. When pieces spin around or move back and forth—often at astonishing speeds—it's no surprise that some of these parts make noises. Some sounds warn of impending breakdowns; others are just part of normal operation. Here's how to tell the difference.

How to fix it

If you hear noise during bootup or when reading or writing data

1. Humming and grinding during boot up are noises you should expect. You may hear them when the system tests the drive during bootup and a second time for a given drive—typically a CD-ROM or floppy drive—if the system is set up to try to boot from that drive.

2. A whining noise or a sound like a low-volume siren that rises and falls in pitch is normal when your CD-ROM drive is reading data. As long as the drive can read the CD reliably, don't worry about this type of sound.

3. When your computer's hard disk drive is active—as indicated by a hard disk access light or similar indicator—you may hear a chirping noise. This is typically caused by the mechanism that positions the read/write heads within the drive. It's perfectly normal.

If your hard disk makes noise when it's not reading or writing data

1. If you hear sounds from your hard disk when it's not reading or writing data, it's time to get concerned. The most common sounds are a low rumble or a rattling, grinding sound. Either one suggests that the hard disk drive bearings or motor may be wearing out. If you hear a sound like this, there's nothing you can do to fix the problem. However, you can guard against disaster: **back up all your data at least once a day.**

2. If the drive is under warranty, return it immediately for repair or exchange. If it's not under warranty, consider replacing it right away. If you choose not to replace it, be sure to keep all your important working files backed up elsewhere—use floppy disks if necessary—so you don't lose anything if the hard disk fails completely.

My power supply is making a noise

Source of the problem

Your computer's power supply serves two main functions. It contains electrical components that convert the standard electricity that comes out of a power outlet into the kind of power the electronics inside your computer needs. In most cases, it also includes a cooling fan. The fan is essential for keeping the temperature inside your computer's case low enough for the electronics to operate reliably, not to mention letting them live a long (for electronics), healthy life. If the power supply falls down on either function, your computer will operate erratically, if at all. And often, the best early warning is when the fan or the power supply itself starts making noise.

How to fix it

If you hear a high pitched whine or rumbling, grinding, rattling, or screeching

1. If the sound is a high-pitched whine, then the problem is in one of the electrical components in the power supply. The safest course of action is to replace the power supply as soon as possible. (See "I need to replace my power supply" on page 72.)

2. If the sound is a low, rumbling sound, a grinding, rattling sound, or a screeching sound, the chances are good that the bearings on the cooling fan are wearing out, even if the sound comes and goes. Plan on replacing the power supply as soon as possible. Until you do, be sure to check the fan every hour or two to make sure it's still turning.

> **Tip**
> You may be able to extend the useful life of a fan by squirting some light oil—such as WD-40—on the fan shaft. This may quiet the sound, but it's only a temporary fix. The sound will return sooner or later. If you try this, be careful not to get any oil on the computer innards.

If the fan noise changes

1. If the fan noise pitch changes from time to time, it may simply be that the cooling fan is responding to temperature changes in the computer. This is particularly common in notebooks—but also happens in some desktop systems—and is normal.

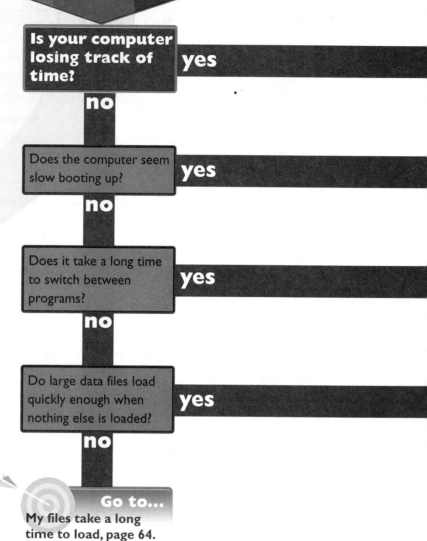

While there are indeed some problems and other factors that can slow down a computer, slow performance is more often a case of cotton candy syndrome—a little taste only makes you want more.

A process that took one minute with your last computer may now take only 40 seconds, and that may have seemed fast when you first got the computer. But now it seems slow, and you want it done in 20 seconds.

If none of the solutions in this chapter bring your computer up to speed, it may be time to think about upgrading. If you can get an improvement with one new component, then go ahead. If you need to replace two or more parts, however, a completely new system may give you a better return on your upgrade investment.

Computer s

Is your computer losing track of time?   **yes**

no

Does the computer seem slow booting up?   **yes**

no

Does it take a long time to switch between programs?   **yes**

no

Do large data files load quickly enough when nothing else is loaded?   **yes**

no

Go to...
My files take a long time to load, page 64.

Go to...
My computer is losing track of the time, page 56.

Go to...
My computer seems slow at startup, page 58.

Go to...
My computer takes a long time to switch between programs, page 60.

Do graphics (such as the cards flying at the end of Solitaire) seem slow?

yes

Go to...
My computer's graphics seem slow, page 66.

no

Quick fix
If you've gotten this far in this flow chart, you've eliminated everything but the CPU and motherboard. Your system may accept a faster CPU, but in most cases, you will get more for your money with a CPU and motherboard upgrade or an entirely new system, so you get supporting components that are able to make the most of the increased performance.

If your solution isn't here
Check these related chapters:
Connections, page 84
Computer startup: won't boot, page 74
Or see the general troubleshooting tips on page xv.

My computer is losing track of the time

Source of the problem

The original IBM PC couldn't remember what time it was when you turned it off; you had to reenter the date and time whenever you turned it on. Some companies came up with products that solved this problem. IBM sidestepped it in the IBM AT by including a tiny battery that let the onboard clock keep time until the computer was turned on again. This battery is now a nearly universal feature for computer systems, and it also provides power to the CMOS memory that stores the Basic Input/Output System (BIOS) configuration settings.

If the battery power runs down, however, the clock can run slower than designed and lose time. This is the most common cause for a computer's clock falling behind. There are other possible causes, however, such as software problems. Diagnosing whether it's a hardware or software problem is easy; if the system loses time while it is shut down, it's a hardware problem. If it loses time while it's running, it's a software problem.

How to fix it

1. Before you do anything else, open the CMOS configuration utility for your computer and record all the settings. If you lose them during the battery replacement process, having a record of them will make it much easier to get your computer running again. Your system may give you an on-screen prompt as it boots to tell you what key to press to start this setup program—often it is either the Delete key or the F2 key—but some systems have a separate program. Check your system documentation for details, or contact the system manufacturer. If you have an MS-DOS–compatible printer attached to your computer, you may be able to print the screens by pressing the PrintScrn key; if not, you'll have to record the data by hand.

2. If your computer is running Windows 98, start Windows and create a floppy boot disk: open the My Computer window, right-click on the floppy disk, choose Format, choose the Full Format Type option, and then check the Copy System Files check box. Note that this will erase any data that's on the floppy. (If your computer is running Windows 2000, you'll need to create the floppy boot disk using another computer that is running Windows 98.)

3. Exit Windows and turn off the computer. Restart the computer and enter the CMOS configuration utility. Set the correct time and date in the CMOS settings, and then exit the utility. Boot using the floppy disk, and then turn off the computer and leave it off for an extended period; overnight is ideal.

4. Turn the computer on, and before it can boot from the floppy or hard disks, enter the CMOS configuration utility again. Check the time. If the time is accurate, then you have a software problem and should check for programs or drivers that may be causing the slowdown. Try disabling them all and then adding them back one at a time to find the offending party. See "My computer seems slow at startup," on page 58 in this chapter, for detailed information on how to disable programs and drivers at startup.

5. If the computer lost time overnight, you have a hardware problem. Make sure you've read our warnings about working safely in "Working inside your computer," at the beginning of this book. Then shut down the computer and open the case.

6. Look for a battery on your motherboard. Different motherboards use different types of batteries, but they are typically either shaped like a coin or a barrel. If the battery is mounted in a holder, remove it and get an exact replacement. Be sure to match the voltage carefully, since different motherboards have different requirements. ▶

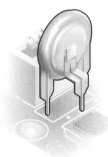

7. If the battery is soldered in place, look around the motherboard for a set of pins that are labeled *BATTERY* or something similar. If you don't see such a label, consult the motherboard documentation or the manufacturer's technical support to find out if the pins are labeled with a code, such as *JP6* or something similar. Also find out the voltage required by the motherboard. You may be able to buy a battery with a connector that will match the pins and provide the correct voltage. ▶

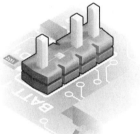

8. If you can't locate anything that looks like a battery, look for a chip made by either Dallas Semiconductor or Benchmarq. These are chips that contain the clock and CMOS memory, as well as a battery. The battery is rated for up to 10 years of use, but it is possible for one to give out in less time than that. If the chip is mounted in a socket, you can get a replacement—for about $30 or less—and insert it yourself. If the chip is soldered directly onto the motherboard, you'll need to find a professional repair service to make the replacement. ▶

My computer seems slow at startup

Source of the problem

You boot your computer, and then you wait… and wait… and wait… until finally Microsoft Windows loads and is ready to run. But you don't have to twiddle your thumbs waiting for it to load—there are some things you can do that may speed it up. They all relate to the same cause: you may be loading more than you need to.

How to fix it

1. Choose Start, Programs, Accessories, System Tools, and then choose System Information, if this option is available. (System Information is not available in all versions of Windows, but some other Microsoft programs also install it.)

2. In the Microsoft System Information program, choose Tools and then choose System Configuration Utility, if that option is available. (Depending on your version of System Information, you may not have a Tools menu.)

If you have the System Configuration Utility

1. Choose the Startup tab, and clear the check boxes for any programs you don't want to load every time Windows loads. ▶

2. Choose the Win.ini tab, and click the plus sign next to the *[windows]* section. Look for lines that begin with *load=* or *run=,* and clear the check boxes for any items you don't want to load.

3. Choose OK, and then exit the System Information program and restart Windows.

If you don't have the System Configuration Utility

1. Anything that you can do through the System Configuration Utility you can do manually as well. Start by finding out what programs are loading along with Windows. Immediately after starting Windows, and before running any programs, open the Close Program dialog box—in Windows 95 or 98, do this by pressing Ctrl+Alt+Delete. (In Windows 2000, press Ctrl+Alt+Delete, and then choose Task Manager.)

2. On a freshly installed system, with nothing but Windows loading, the only entries you will see in the Close Program dialog box are Explorer and Systray. Anything else is extra and is slowing down the time it takes Windows to finish loading. You need to track down each program, figure out what it is, and decide whether you really need it to load every time you start Windows. (For more details on how to do this, see "I need to install my printer driver with nothing else running," on page 298.)

Tip
Two other things that can slow down Windows during startup are having to load lots of fonts or read through a long Registry. Try deleting any fonts you don't need, using the Windows font utility, and consider trying a utility to clean out unused entries in your Windows Registry. Be sure to make a backup of the Registry first.

3. Open Windows Explorer and find the Windows\Start Menu\Programs\Startup folder. The program shortcuts in this folder will load automatically every time you start Windows. Delete any shortcuts you don't want, or move them to a different folder in case you want to move them back.

4. Other programs load based on command lines in the WIN.INI file. To edit the file, choose Start, Run, type **sysedit** in the Open text box, and then choose OK. Then choose the window for WIN.INI.

5. Look for the part of the file that begins with *[windows]*, and under this header look for a line that starts with *load=* and another that starts with *run=*. Either or both of these lines can include the names of programs for Windows to run. Delete any that you don't want to run. ▶

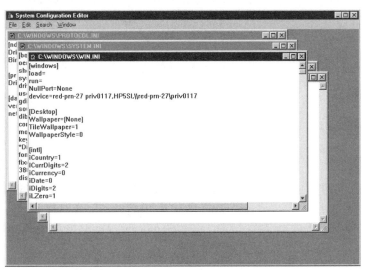

6. If you made any changes in WIN.INI choose File, Save, and then close the System Configuration Editor by choosing File, Exit.

My computer takes a long time to switch between programs

Source of the problem

Windows lets you open more than one program at once, which can be very convenient; it's like having more than one book or file folder or pad of paper on your real desk. Just like your real desk, however, there are limits to how much will fit on it at one time. At some point you'll need to bring over an extra table to hold everything that you're working with. Windows is no different. Windows uses the memory in your computer to hold programs and data that it's using. When you ask it to use more than the memory can hold, it uses the Windows swap file as something called *virtual memory*. That means programs and data are written to temporary storage on the hard drive to free up the real memory for the current task. When you switch tasks and want to work with something that has been parked on the hard disk, Windows writes part of the current memory contents to the swap file, and retrieves information you need. Unfortunately, as fast as hard drives are, they are much slower than memory, and it can take a considerable length of time to move all this information back and forth. And the slower the hard disk, the more time it will take.

One way to address this problem is to speed up the hard drive, as discussed in "My files take a long time to load," on page 64. The most effective approach, however, is to come at this issue from the memory side of the problem.

How to fix it (in Windows 98)

1. Watch your computer's disk drive activity light—if it has one—or listen for hard drive activity when you switch between applications. If the light comes on or you hear hard drive activity, you need more memory in your system.

2. To find out how much more memory you need, start by booting your system and starting Windows.

3. Before you open any programs, choose Start, Programs, Accessories, System Tools, and then choose the System Monitor application.

> **Tip**
>
> When you have more than one program open in Windows, you can choose the Task Bar at the bottom of your desktop to switch between them. If you'd rather keep your hands on the keyboard, just hold down Alt and press Tab. This will open a window showing all your open applications, and you can press Tab—while still holding the Alt key—to move between them and select the one that you want.

4. If System Monitor is not available, you'll need to install it. Choose Start, Settings, Control Panel, and then choose Add/Remove Programs. Choose the Windows Setup tab, and then make sure the System Tools check box is checked with a white background in the check box. Choose OK, and then follow any prompts, such as instructions to insert the Windows disk.

5. Load System Monitor. If there are any graphs showing, choose Edit, Remove Item, and then remove all the items.

6. Choose Edit, Add Item to open the Add Item window.

7. Select the Memory Manager item in the Category list. ▶

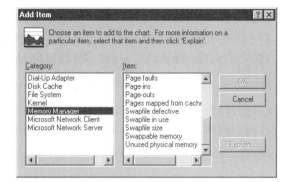

8. In the Item list, select Swapfile in Use, and then choose OK.

9. Chose Edit, Add Item, Memory Manager, and then select Unused Physical Memory.

10. System Monitor will show two graphs in its Window. The Swapfile In Use graph shows how much information, if any, has been parked on your hard disk. The Unused Physical Memory graph shows how much memory is available. ▶

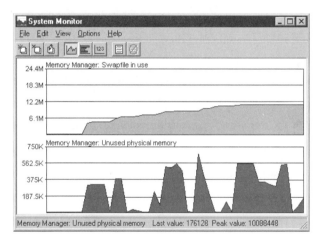

11. Now open all the programs that you typically use at one time. The Unused Physical Memory count will drop, and the Swapfile In Use count will rise as you open each program. When you're finished, look at the count for Swapfile In Use; for best performance, you'll want to add at least this much more memory.

12. Consult your system documentation to find out whether the motherboard can accept that much additional memory. Also find out what combinations of memory module capacities you can install at one time, and what other specifications you must match: rated speed, type of memory, parity, and size of the modules. Note that you may need to remove some smaller capacity modules in order to make room for larger capacity modules and reach the total you need.

My computer takes a long time to switch between programs

(continued from page 61)

How to fix it (in Windows 2000)

1. To find out whether you need to add memory to your computer, start by booting your system and starting Windows.

2. Choose Start, Run, type **perfmon** in the Open text box, and then choose OK.

3. Choose the System Monitor node.

4. Choose Add (the + icon on the toolbar).

5. From the Performance Object drop-down list, choose Memory.

6. From the Select Counters From List list, choose Available Bytes.

7. Choose Add, and then choose Close.

8. Now open all the programs you typically use at one time. System Monitor will graph how much memory is available in your computer. A value less than 4 MB indicates that you need to add memory to your computer.

9. Consult your system documentation to find out whether the motherboard can accept more additional memory. Also find out what combinations of memory module capacities you can install at one time, and what other specifications you must match: rated speed, type of memory, parity, and size of the modules. Note that you may need to remove some smaller capacity modules in order to make room for larger capacity modules.

My files take a long time to load

Source of the problem

If you think that your hard disk is slower than it used to be, you may be right. The more you use it, the more likely each new file is to be broken into pieces scattered around the disk, instead of having all the pieces stored together, where the drive can retrieve them more quickly. Also, a hard disk can develop problems areas, so it has to re-read data from a particular spot several times to get the information right.

Issues like these can slow down a hard disk, but you're not necessarily stuck with the slow performance. There are some things you can do with your hard disk to make it go faster. If these steps don't work, the hard drive may have a problem you can't fix. If all else fails, you can consider getting a faster hard disk drive.

How to fix it

1. The first step is to make a backup of your hard disk. If it has a problem, then you might be about to lose your data. Even if there isn't a problem, it's still a good idea to make a copy in case something goes awry.

2. If there is a particular file that seems to take a long time to load, listen carefully to the hard disk while it loads. If you hear a repetitive sound that doesn't occur when loading other files, the drive may be having a problem reading a portion of the disk. Even if you don't hear any indication of a problem, however, it's worth confirming that there is none.

3. Open My Computer, and right-click on the drive that seems slow.

4. Choose Properties from the shortcut menu that pops up.

5. Choose the Tools tab.

6. The top area is marked Error-Checking Status (Error Checking in Windows 2000). This area will display a message indicating how long it has been since you last checked the drive for errors. Choose the Check Now button.

Tip

If there's anything in computing that's as certain as death and taxes, it's that next year's programs will be bigger and create larger data files than this year's programs. One result is that when you upgrade your software, you'll often spend significantly more time waiting for files to load from your hard drive, or, once you've finished working with them, waiting for them to be saved. Keep this in mind when you're considering upgrading. If the version you've got makes your computer a tad slow, odds are that the upgrade will make it downright lethargic. And you may want to hold off the software upgrade until you move to a new computer.

7. In the ScanDisk window, make sure that the drive you want to check is selected in the Select the Drive(s) You Want To Check For Errors list. In the Type Of Test section, choose the Thorough option. Clear the Automatically Fix Errors check box if it has a check in it. (Windows 2000 simply asks whether you want to automatically fix errors and whether you want to attempt to recover bad sectors. Don't select either option; simply click OK and let the tool scan your drive.) ▶

8. Choose the Start button.

9. ScanDisk will check the file system for errors and then scan the surface of the disk to test for errors or weak spots. This can take a half hour or more, depending on the capacity and speed of the hard disk. If the program finds any surface errors, you may want to get a third-party disk utility program—such as Symantec's Norton Utilities or Gibson Research's SpinRite—that can provide more rigorous testing and help you recover and move any files that have been damaged by the defects.

10. If your hard disk passes the ScanDisk test, the next step is to defragment the files on the drive. Files get fragmented when a file is deleted and a larger one is written in its place, with part of the file placed elsewhere on the disk. Hard disk performance decreases when the heads have to jump all over searching for the different pieces of the file being loaded. Defragmentation writes all the parts of each file in contiguous parts of the disk, making access faster. Windows has a disk defragmenting utility. Close the ScanDisk window (or the summary window in Windows 2000), and return to the Tools tab in the hard disk Properties window. The Defragmentation Status section of the Tools tab will indicate how long it has been since you last defragmented the hard disk. To defragment it, choose the Defragment Now button. (In Windows 2000, you'll then need to select the drive and choose Defragment.)

11. The program will proceed to defragment your files. If you choose the Show Details button (not available in Windows 2000), it will display a map of the files on the hard disk as it relocates and consolidates them. When it is finished, you should note that files open more rapidly. If the hard disk still seems slow, you may want to consider purchasing one with faster performance specifications.

My computer's graphics seem slow

Source of the problem

Moving graphic images across the screen takes a lot of work, for several reasons. Chances are good that you are running your display at XGA resolution—1024 by 768 pixels—and at least 64 thousand colors (also known as *high color* or 16-bit color depth). With high color, there are two bytes of information required for every dot on the screen. Run that through a handy calculator and you'll see that it translates to more than 1.5 million bytes of data. That's a lot of information.

Now think about the work your graphics adaptor has to do, whether you're scrolling through a word processing document or playing a game and moving through a 3-D scene being rendered on screen as your character moves though the 3-D world. Almost all of those 1.5 million bytes of data gets changed as you move—and almost instantly. Maybe you shouldn't be so surprised when graphics performance seems slow, because it's a small miracle that it's as fast as it is. The simple truth is that older cards have slower memory than current cards and offer poorer graphics acceleration—a name for features that speed graphics movement. However, there are a few things you can do to make sure you're getting the best performance you can from your graphics adapter card, short of throwing it out and buying a new, high performance card.

How to fix it

1. As a first step, you should confirm that the problem is really a slow graphics card and not that some other part of the system is feeding information to the graphics card too slowly. It's easy to find a benchmarking program on the Web that will isolate your graphics card for testing and report the results. (A quick search on Yahoo! for *graphics* and *benchmark* and *program* turned up a variety of programs to choose from.) You can use one of these to get a measure of how fast (or slow) your graphics adapter really is, and you can compare it to results for other cards to help put the benchmark results in context.

2. When you look at the results from benchmarking programs, keep in mind that there is a vast difference between 2-D and 3-D graphics. Business applications and most older games typically deal with 2-D graphics only. Windows Solitaire is a good example, with cards that move only in two dimensions. Many newer games, and some graphics and design programs, use 3-D

> **Tip**
>
> If you're running movie or animation clips—such as .AVI files—and you get herky-jerky motion on the screen, the graphics adapter may not be at fault. Make certain that the source device, such as a CD-ROM drive, is capable of reading the data at the full speed. If the data stream is too large for the device, you'll get breaks in the playback, and you'll get a stuttering motion.

graphics, with objects moving through a 3-D space—rotating and changing appearance based on rules of perspective, shadow, and so on. If you don't use programs that take advantage of 3-D effects, it doesn't matter if your graphics adapter scores poorly on a 3-D benchmark. Only the 2-D score matters.

3. If the graphics score is lower than you'd like, check out the vendor's Web page for a newer driver. More than any other category of hardware, graphics adapters are notorious for early production units shipping with drivers that aren't really ready. If you bought your system when the card was still relatively new, it may have come with a driver that simply doesn't take full advantage of the card's capabilities.

4. If you find a newer driver on the vendor's Web site, download it. Then back up at least your Windows directory, and preferably your entire system, so you can return to a working state if something goes wrong. Then install the driver.

5. If the new driver doesn't improve the graphics performance noticeably, or even if it does, but the improvement isn't enough, consider setting your driver to use fewer colors. First find out your current settings: right-click on your desktop and choose the Settings tab.

6. Look in the Colors box to see your current color depth setting. If it says *True Color (32 bit)* or *True Color (24 bit)*, consider changing it to *High Color (16 bit)*. In many cases, you won't notice the difference even for graphics and photographs. And you'll cut down the amount of information your graphics adapter has to move around by a third (going from 24-bit to 16-bit color) or half (going from 32-bit to 16-bit color). ▶

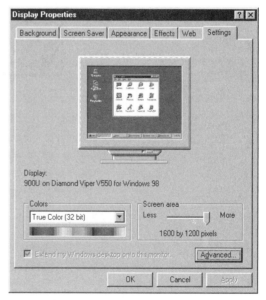

7. To change the color depth, open the Colors pull-down menu, choose the new setting, choose OK, and then follow the instructions on screen. (Windows may tell you that it has to restart the computer, or it may give you a warning that some programs could operate improperly if you don't restart the computer.)

8. If you're still not satisfied with the boost in performance, and you don't mind if photos and graphics have a banding effect, consider changing the color depth to 256 colors.

9. If you're still not satisfied with the graphics performance, consider getting a new, higher performing graphics adapter card.

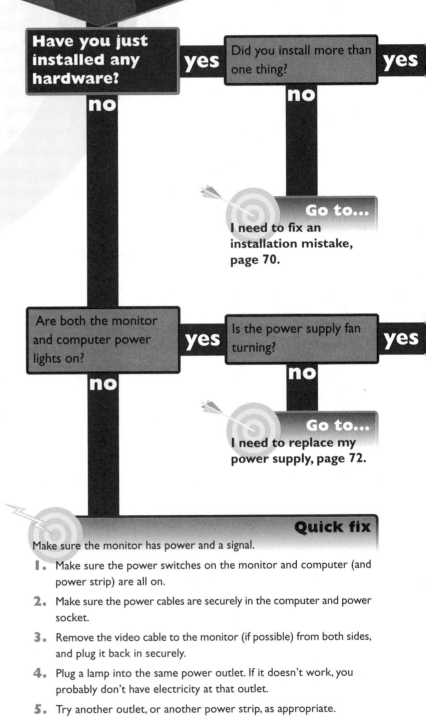

Have you just installed any hardware?

yes → **Did you install more than one thing?** **yes** →

no

no

Go to...
I need to fix an installation mistake, page 70.

Are both the monitor and computer power lights on?

yes → **Is the power supply fan turning?** **yes** →

no

no

Go to...
I need to replace my power supply, page 72.

Quick fix

Make sure the monitor has power and a signal.

1. Make sure the power switches on the monitor and computer (and power strip) are all on.

2. Make sure the power cables are securely in the computer and power socket.

3. Remove the video cable to the monitor (if possible) from both sides, and plug it back in securely.

4. Plug a lamp into the same power outlet. If it doesn't work, you probably don't have electricity at that outlet.

5. Try another outlet, or another power strip, as appropriate.

tup: blank screen

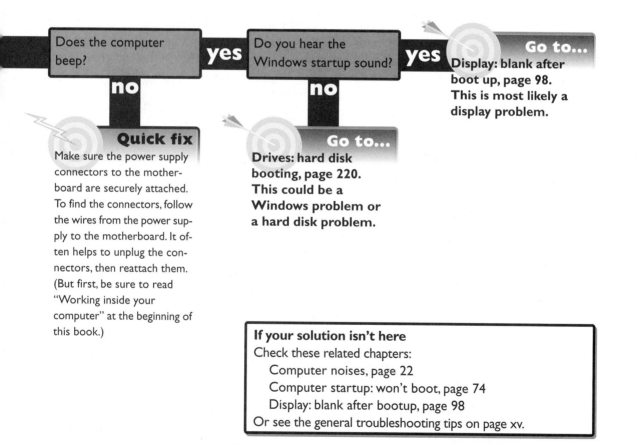

Quick fix

Simplify your system.
First remove anything you've
just installed, make sure the
system is set up the way it was
the last time it worked, and
confirm that it will start correctly. Then add adapter cards
or other new items one at a
time, until you find one that
causes a problem—if, indeed,
you find one. Simply removing
the items and reinstalling them
may solve the problem.

Does the computer beep?	**yes**	Do you hear the Windows startup sound?	**yes**

no

no

Go to...

Display: **blank after
boot up, page 98.
This is most likely a
display problem.**

Quick fix

Make sure the power supply
connectors to the mother-
board are securely attached.
To find the connectors, follow
the wires from the power supply to the motherboard. It often helps to unplug the connectors, then reattach them.
(But first, be sure to read
"Working inside your
computer" at the beginning of
this book.)

Go to...

**Drives: hard disk
booting, page 220.
This could be a
Windows problem or
a hard disk problem.**

If your solution isn't here
Check these related chapters:
Computer noises, page 22
Computer startup: won't boot, page 74
Display: blank after bootup, page 98
Or see the general troubleshooting tips on page xv.

I need to fix an installation mistake

Source of the problem

There are many good reasons to add new parts inside your computer. You might want to add a network card so you can connect with other computers. Or you might want to replace a sound card or display adaptor with a new and improved model. Or you may need more storage space and want to replace your hard disk or add another one. Adding a card isn't much harder than changing a light bulb. OK, maybe it's as hard as changing the light bulb in a car's headlight, but it's still not all that hard.

Most people with normal intelligence and coordination can handle these tasks without problems most of the time—the key phrase being *most of the time*. Even an experienced technician can make a mistake that will keep a computer from booting. The good news is that most mistakes are reversible; they are a simple matter of having plugged something in the wrong way, or having plugged it in so it's not making good electrical contact. The rare cases that aren't reversible are pretty easy to spot. They're usually accompanied by sparks, smoke, or both. But don't let that scare you. It takes real talent to trash hardware. We've been amazed through the years at how forgiving computers have been when we've plugged things in the wrong way.

Here are the steps to correct any mistakes you might have made while installing new parts. (And be sure to see "Working inside your computer," at the beginning of this book, for our advice about working inside your computer's case, including things like when to turn the power off.)

How to fix it

If you added a new expansion card

1. Check that the card is securely seated in its socket. PCI and AGP slots are notorious for letting you put cards in partially without making good contact all around.

2. The edge bracket should rest on the case when the card is inserted properly; don't try to force it into place with the screw on the end bracket. Make sure it's in place, and then use the screw to *hold* it in place. Also be sure to always use the screw; without it, the card can come loose while the computer's running and possibly cause a damaging electrical short. You may have to repeat this step several times, particularly with PCI or AGP slots, before the card is seated properly. ▶

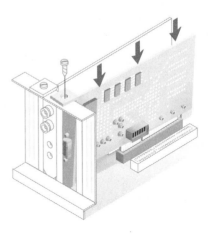

3. If the system still won't boot after trying the first two steps several times, check the cards close to the one you just added, in case you put pressure on them and moved them slightly while plugging in or removing the expansion card. Push down on each in turn to make sure they are well seated.

If you moved or installed memory modules

1. Take the modules out and then put them back to make sure that they are seated properly.

2. Also check your computer or motherboard manual to make sure you have the right memory modules in the right slots.

If you added a floppy disk drive

1. If you've just added a floppy disk drive, or you disconnected and reconnected the ribbon cable to a floppy disk drive, check to make sure the cables are oriented correctly. Almost all ribbon cables have a colored stripe along one edge; this gets connected to pin I of the connectors on your motherboard (or disk controller if it's a separate card) and on the floppy drive itself. The connector on the motherboard will usually have a *I* marked near one end. On the drive end, there are two types of connectors. 3.5-inch floppy drives use a connector that mates with two rows of pins. 5.25-inch drives use a slot connector that mates with the edge of a circuit board. The connectors are often keyed with a bump on the outside edge or a plugged hole, to prevent connecting them the wrong way. If the cable isn't keyed, look for an arrow or a *I* next to the connector on the drive case or circuit board. ▶

If you disconnected the power connectors on the motherboard

1. Make certain the power connectors were reconnected properly. On motherboards that have two power connectors coming from the power supply, the black wires go next to each other in the middle. If they are connected in the right orientation, make sure they are making a good connection. Remove the connectors and reconnect them.

I need to replace my power supply

Source of the problem

If the processor is the brains of your computer, the power supply is its heart. It takes electricity from your wall outlet and converts it into the different voltages that the various parts of your computer need in order to work. The power supply usually contains a fan also, which plays an essential role in keeping your computer cool.

If the power supply stops performing either of these tasks, your computer will not run dependably, and may not run at all. Rather than throw out the whole system, however, you can replace the power supply. Be aware that you can replace just the fan in many, if not most, power supplies, but this is a more complicated procedure, and we don't recommend it for most users.

How to fix it

1. If the fan has stopped working, turn off your computer and don't turn it on again until you have replaced the power supply. The heat that builds up without a fan can cause permanent and far more expensive damage.

2. Determine what type of power supply you need. Some major manufacturers use proprietary case and motherboard designs, and you may not be able to find a suitable third-party replacement for the power supply. For those systems, you'll have to contact the manufacturer to get a replacement part. One easy way to find out is to call the manufacturer's technical support line (use the toll free number if it has one) and ask whether your particular model uses a standard power supply. You can also try calling a vendor that sells power supplies, and ask if they have one for your make and model of computer.

3. If your computer uses a standard case, you should be able to find a replacement easily. There are a number of standard case and motherboard designs, but the two most common are AT and ATX. They are easy to tell apart, even without opening your system. An AT motherboard doesn't have any connectors on the board itself, other than a keyboard port. ▶

4. An ATX motherboard has other connectors on the left side of the back edge (viewed from the back). If you look at the back of a computer and see some combination of parallel, serial, graphics, sound, and USB connectors lined up vertically, on the left side near the top of the case, you almost certainly have an ATX motherboard. If the connectors are elsewhere, you almost certainly have an AT motherboard. ▶

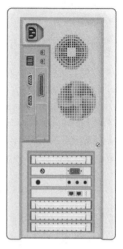

5. When picking a replacement power supply, be sure to get one that's rated at the same wattage as the one you're replacing, or higher. Getting one with a lower rating than you need can cause you grief. To check the rating of your current power supply, take a look at the label on top of the power supply itself. You may be able to see this simply by removing the cover to your computer.

6. In some systems—particularly those with tower cases—you may have to remove the power supply from the computer before you can see the label with the ratings. The power supply is typically mounted with four screws. Just look for screws where the corners of the power supply meet the case. The label should show the power supply's AC input rating, DC output rating, and maximum power output. You need to match all three ratings, but the first two are standard, so they shouldn't be an issue. The maximum power output is the rating that needs to be met or exceeded by the replacement power supply.

7. Different motherboards and power supplies use different power connectors. Make sure that the connectors match on your replacement. AT motherboards use a pair of connectors, and most of these use connectors made by Bundy. These connectors have pins that are rectangular when viewed from above. A few AT motherboards use similar connectors made by Molex, which have square pins. It is possible to mate dissimilar connectors, but it's better to get the correct type from the outset. ATX motherboards also vary; some have a single 20-pin connector, while others also have an optional 6-pin secondary connector. You can leave the secondary connector unplugged if your motherboard doesn't need it, so a power supply with both connectors should work with any ATX motherboard.

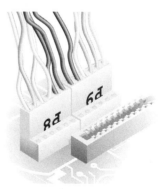

8. When you get the replacement power supply, remove the old one and install the new one in its place. If you have a single-piece connector to attach to the motherboard, simply plug it in; you won't be able to plug it in backwards. If you have two connectors, attach them so that the colored wires are arranged with the black wires next to each other in the middle. ▶

Computer st

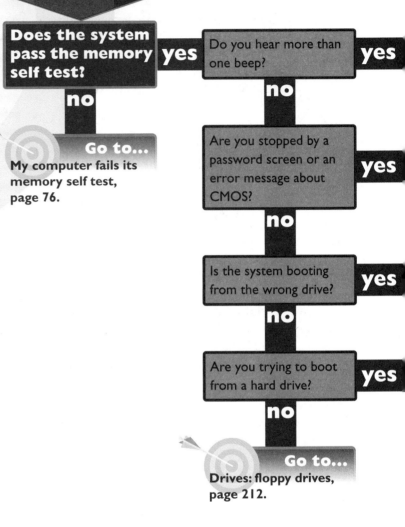

If your computer displays a company logo when you first turn it on, you will not be able to see the power-on self-test information, such as the memory test. You can clear the logo by pressing the Escape key. This also works to clear the Windows "clouds" screen while Windows is loading.

Does the system pass the memory self test? **yes**

no

Go to...
My computer fails its memory self test, page 76.

Do you hear more than one beep? **yes**

no

Are you stopped by a password screen or an error message about CMOS? **yes**

no

Is the system booting from the wrong drive? **yes**

no

Are you trying to boot from a hard drive? **yes**

no

Go to...
Drives: floppy drives, page 212.

Go to...
My computer is beeping instead of booting up, page 78.

Go to...
My computer says it has a **CMOS** error or is asking for a password, page 80.

Go to...
The computer is booting from the wrong disk drive, page 82.

Do you get an error message before "Starting Windows" appears?

yes

Go to...
I see an error message before my system shows the *Starting Windows* message, page 224.

no

Go to...
My system shows the *Starting Windows* message, but then shows errors, page 226.

If your solution isn't here
Check these related chapters:
Computer hardware and Windows, page 22
Computer startup: blank screen, page 68
Drives: hard disk booting, page 220
Or see the general troubleshooting tips on page xv.

My computer fails its memory self test

Source of the problem

People tend to have problems remembering the odd bit of information here and there as they get older, even though they can still remember most things. With computers, memory is more likely to go at a young age rather than old age, and it's more often an all-or-nothing proposition. If your computer's memory isn't working correctly, it can cause all sorts of frustrating, hard-to-track-down problems, but the most likely result is a memory error when you start your system, leaving you with a computer that won't boot.

There are some fairly straightforward steps that will help you find and fix a memory problem. But don't…well…forget that that memory modules are potentially sensitive to static. Be sure to follow our suggestions in "Working inside your computer," at the beginning of this book, about handling sensitive equipment when you're working inside a computer. After each of the potential fixes in the steps that follow, you should turn your system on and try booting to see if you've solved the problem. If not, turn it off and continue with the next step.

How to fix it

1. The first step is to make sure that the memory modules are correctly seated in their slots. Start by pushing down firmly with one finger on each memory module in turn and rocking it back and forth to make sure each module is firmly in its slot.

2. If that doesn't solve the problem, try removing the memory modules. There are little tabs at the sides of the slots that hold the modules in place; use a small screwdriver to bend the tabs back, one side at a time, and tilt the modules past them. Be careful not to break them off in the process. ▶

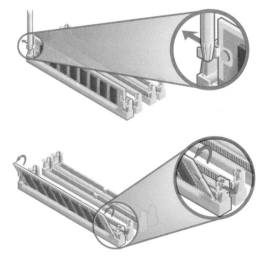

3. When both sides are released, tilt the module forward and pull it out of the slot. ▶

4. Check for dust or debris that may have fallen in the slot where it can block the electrical connection to the module. A blast from a can of compressed air—which you should be able to get at any good photo supply store—is a handy way to dislodge anything from the slot. Do not try to clean the slot by blowing air from your mouth. Human saliva is one of the more corrosive substances you can get on your computer's innards. You don't want to risk getting any on the connectors.

5. Reinsert each module in its slot. Insert each one at an angle, and make sure it is firmly inserted to the bottom of the slot before you start to tilt it upright. When it reaches a vertical position, you should hear two clicks as the tabs at the ends pop into place. Visually check the tabs to make sure they are holding the module correctly. ▶

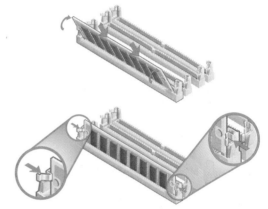

6. If the system still fails the memory test on startup, and you have more modules in the system than the minimum required, try removing some modules. (You'll need to check your system or motherboard manual to find out what combinations of modules it can take—how many, and which slots they should go in.) If you have four identical modules, for example, and the system can take a minimum of two, you may find that one combination of two modules works, but the other doesn't. That implies that at least one of the modules in the second pair has a problem. You can swap each of those modules with one of the working modules to pinpoint which one is bad. You'll then have to buy a replacement.

7. If you don't have more memory modules in the system than the minimum, you can run the same sort of swapping test with any additional modules that will work in the system. If you don't have additional suitable modules available for testing, however, it's time to consider taking or sending the system in for repair.

My computer is beeping instead of booting up

Source of the problem

Before it boots, a computer is a lot like an infant—it doesn't have any way to tell you where it hurts. So it does what any healthy baby would do; it makes noises and hopes that you can understand what it is trying to say. Most of the time you get one happy little chirp before it goes about its business, but sometimes you'll hear a series of decidedly unhappy noises, better known as beep codes. When you hear them, be assured that your computer is trying to tell you something.

How to fix it

Unfortunately, there is no standard for beep codes. The information for your system should be in the owner's manual or available from the manufacturer's technical support sources, but it is often well hidden. If you can't find a list of beep codes, however, it may be enough to know what brand of BIOS (Basic Input/Output System) you have. If you don't already know, open the case and look for large chips on the motherboard. You're looking for a chip from American Megatrends, Incorporated (AMI), Phoenix, or IBM, the three most popular brands of BIOS. If you find the chip, you can look up the codes in the lists we've put together here. We can't guarantee these codes apply to every version of each brand of BIOS. In fact, Phoenix specifically warns that its codes may vary because of individual manufacturer's requirements. However, most manufacturers use the standard codes presented here.

If your computer has an AMI BIOS...

and you hear...	then...
1, 2, or 3 beeps	Try reseating or replacing memory (see "My computer fails its memory self test," on page 76).
4, 5, 7, 9, or 10 beeps	The motherboard, main processor chip, or other components have problems. The least expensive and easiest solution may be to replace the entire motherboard.
6 beeps	There's a problem with the keyboard. Turn off the computer, unplug the keyboard, plug it back in, and then try again. If the problem persists, try a new keyboard. If a new keyboard doesn't work, you may need to replace the motherboard.
8 beeps	The graphics adapter has a problem. Turn off the computer, reseat the card, and try again. If you still get this error, you may need to replace the graphics adapter.

If your computer has a Phoenix BIOS...

and you hear ...	then...
1-1 followed by more beeps, 1-2 followed by more beeps, 1-3 followed by more beeps, or 3-1 followed by more beeps	The motherboard, main processor chip, or other components have problems. The least expensive and easiest solution may be to replace the entire motherboard.
1-4-1, 1-4-2, or 2 beeps followed by two sets of 1-4 beeps	Try reseating or replacing memory (see "My computer fails its memory self test," on page 76).
3-2-4 beeps	There's a problem with the keyboard. Turn off the computer, unplug the keyboard, plug it back in, and then try again. If the problem persists, try a new keyboard. If a new keyboard doesn't work, you may need to replace the motherboard.
3-3-4 or 3-4 beeps followed by more beeps	The graphics adapter has a problem. Turn off the computer, reseat the card, and try again. If you still get this error, you may need to replace the graphics adapter.

If your computer has an IBM BIOS...

and you hear ...	then...
1 continuous beep or repeating short beeps	The power supply or motherboard has problems. Check the power supply first (see "I need to replace my power supply," on page 72), since it is the less expensive component. If a new power supply doesn't solve the problem, you may need to replace the entire motherboard.
1 long beep followed by 1 short beep	There's a problem with the motherboard, and it may need to be replaced.
1 long beep followed by 3 short beeps	There's a problem with the keyboard. Turn off the computer, unplug it, and plug it back in. Then try again. If the problem persists, try a new keyboard. If a new keyboard doesn't work, you may need to replace the motherboard.
1 long beep followed by 2 or 3 short beeps	The graphics adapter has a problem. Turn off the computer, reseat the card, and try again. If you still get this error, you may need to replace the graphics adapter.

My computer says it has a CMOS error or is asking for a password

Source of the problem

Computers are basically dumb. Turn on your system, and it remembers less than the proverbial drunken sailor remembers in the morning after a hard night's shore leave. In particular, it barely knows how to read a disk and handle other basic tasks. (For you programmers out there who think *basic* is spelled all in capitals, we mean basic as in *fundamental*, not the programming language.)

What little your computer knows how to do when you turn it on comes from a program called the BIOS (Basic Input/Output System). The BIOS is permanently stored on the motherboard in a special chip that retains its contents even when the power is off. This program, in turn, needs to get some configuration settings, such as the essential information it needs about your hard disk, before it can do anything. The configuration information is stored in CMOS memory—memory that uses a battery to maintain its contents when the power is turned off. If the CMOS settings are wrong, or they include a password you can't remember, your computer may not boot properly or at all.

Here's how to bring your computer back under control if you get a CMOS error or you've forgotten your password.

How to fix it

If you've forgotten your password

1. Not all BIOS versions can store a password in the CMOS settings. But for those that can, once you take advantage of this feature, you have to enter the password before the computer will boot. This can be a useful security feature, but it can disable the computer if you lose the password or inherit a computer from a co-worker or friend, or if someone adds a password without telling you about it. Fortunately, most motherboards have a way to reset the CMOS configuration settings, which will clear the password.

2. You may need to consult your system manual or contact the computer manufacturer for details on the procedure. In general, however, you need to clear the CMOS contents by turning off the computer and locating a pair of pins on the motherboard—typically near the BIOS or CMOS chips—and then connecting them with a jumper (a small connector that's plastic on the outside, has an electrical conductor on the inside, and fits over the pins). ▶

3. If you can't locate the pins, look for a battery mounted on the motherboard; remove the battery and leave the computer turned off for an hour, which should also clear the CMOS settings. It is relatively rare, but some motherboards have batteries that are permanently soldered in place. We don't recommend removing a battery that's soldered onto the motherboard, unless you are confident you know how to do it without damaging other components. ▶

If you get a CMOS error message

1. If you get some other error about CMOS settings or configuration, the boot process will usually halt and you will be prompted to press a specific key to enter the CMOS configuration utility. (You can also start the configuration utility on most computers by pressing the same key during the boot-up process. The key will vary depending on the type of BIOS and brand of computer, but common choices are Delete, F2, F1, and F10. Most systems will show a message on screen during bootup specifying the key.)

2. When the configuration utility opens, check that the basic settings are correct: time, date, size and capacity of floppy disk drives, and so forth. In most cases, the system will automatically set the installed memory size, and even hard disk size, but check the memory size to make sure that it is correct for your system.

3. In many cases, simply opening the CMOS configuration utility, saving the settings, and closing the utility again to reboot will be sufficient to clear a CMOS error.

4. After you make your changes, save the settings and exit the configuration utility to reboot your computer.

The computer is booting from the wrong disk drive

Source of the problem

You turn on your computer, and it tries to boot from a different drive than you had in mind. So what's going on? And why the surprise?

There are a number of possible causes for this problem, but they all are connected by one simple fact: your computer will look at specific drives in a specific sequence, searching for the information it needs in order to boot successfully. Older computers have a single sequence—floppy drive A first, and then hard disk C second—and you can't change it. Newer computers add CD drives and even Zip drives and other removable media drives to the list of possibilities. They also let you define what order to use to check the drives, so you can preferentially boot from whichever drive you like. This additional flexibility can be useful if you want to take advantage of it. It can also be confusing if it's not working the way you expect it to. Either way, the information you need to change is stored in the CMOS settings.

How to fix it

1. If you are trying to boot from the hard disk and the system seems to be ignoring the hard disk, remove any disks from floppy, CD, and other removable media drives, and try again. If the system fails to boot, you may have a problem with your hard disk: check "Drives: hard disk booting," on page 220. If the system boots with the other disks removed, you may want to change the boot sequence. We'll describe how in the following steps.

Common keys to get into CMOS Setup

Some of these keys and key combinations are more widely used than others to get into CMOS Setup, but all are used widely enough to be worth trying if you can't get the information from your computer manufacturer.

Delete	Ctrl+S	Ctrl+Alt+Enter
F1	Ctrl+Alt+Esc	Ctrl+Alt+I
F2	Ctrl+Alt+Ins	Ctrl+Alt+R
F10	Ctrl+Alt+"+"	Ctrl+Alt+F1
Esc	Ctrl+Alt+"-"	Ctrl+Alt+Q

2. If you are trying to boot from a floppy disk and the system insists on booting from the hard drive instead, open the CMOS configuration utility. Most computers let you press a key during power-up to open the utility. Typically the system will provide an onscreen prompt during bootup, usually at the bottom of the screen, saying which key to press. If the system is covering the boot up messages with a logo, press Escape to clear the logo as soon as it shows. If you still don't see a message telling you to press a specified key to enter CMOS Setup, try Delete, F2, and any of the other key combinations listed in the sidebar "Common keys to get into CMOS Setup," on page 82.

3. If none of the key combinations listed in the sidebar gets you into CMOS Setup during bootup, your system may use a particularly unusual key combination, or it may not include a feature to let you launch the CMOS Setup during booting. Some systems require instead that you run a separate program from an MS-DOS prompt. Check your system manual for details, or call the manufacturer's technical support line.

4. If all else fails, you should be able to force your system into a CMOS error on bootup that will result in a message along the lines of *Press <F1> to resume, <F2> to Setup*. Try rebooting while holding down the Spacebar. Once you see a message about a stuck key, or hear repeated beeping, you can release the Spacebar. If the system ignores that error, turn it off, remove the case, remove the cable from your floppy disk or hard disk, and then turn the system on again. (See "Working inside your computer," at the beginning of this book, for advice about working inside the computer.)

> **Tip**
>
> Setting the hard disk as the first boot choice speeds the boot process, because the computer does not have to check the floppy disk drive first. This also serves as a mild security measure against viruses, since you won't accidentally boot up from a floppy disk that may have a virus, even if you leave the floppy disk in your A drive.

5. When you are in the CMOS Setup program, be careful not to change any settings accidentally, since the wrong settings can keep your system from booting. Details for changing the boot sequence will vary, depending on the BIOS, but you can browse through the choices, looking for an option for boot priority or boot sequence. If the feature exists at all, you may be able to pick a specific drive as first, another as second, another as third, and so on. In other cases, you may be limited to cycling through such choices as Hard Drive Only, Diskette Then Hard Drive, and Hard Drive Then Diskette. Pick the appropriate setting from the possible choices, and then look for the option to exit and save your changes. ▶

Are you having a problem with a USB connection? **yes**

no

Are you having a problem with a game port, or is your system not seeing a joystick that's plugged into the game port? **yes** Does your joystick attach to a game port? **yes**

no

no

 Go to...

The considerations for SCSI are identical for any SCSI device. If you have a problem with a SCSI port go to "My new SCSI hard disk isn't working," page 176. Parallel ports are used primarily for printers and are covered in the chapter "Printer hardware basics," page 260.

Quick fix

If your joystick connects to a USB port, and you're having a problem with the USB port itself, follow the flowchart from the beginning, answering yes to the lead-off question, "Are you having a problem with a USB connection?" If your USB port is working correctly, go to "My game port or joystick isn't working," page 92.

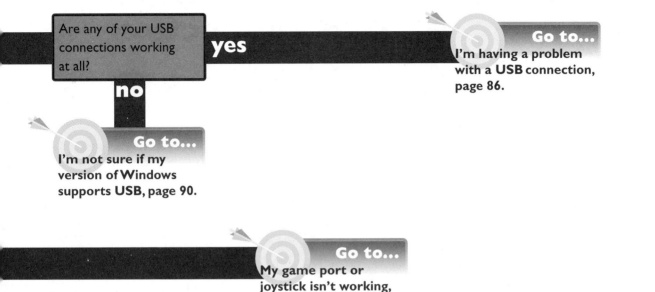

Are any of your USB connections working at all?

yes

Go to...
I'm having a problem with a **USB** connection, page 86.

no

Go to...
I'm not sure if my version of Windows supports **USB**, page 90.

Go to...
My game port or joystick isn't working, page 92.

If your solution isn't here

Check these related chapters:

Drives: after installation, page 170

Keyboard and mouse, page 250

Printer hardware basics, page 260

Or see the general troubleshooting tips on page xv.

I'm having a problem with a USB connection

Source of the problem

The Universal Serial Bus—better known as USB—is a huge improvement over the serial port, which dates back before the first IBM PC. USB ports can connect as many as 127 devices at once rather than just one device; they move data around roughly 100 times faster than a standard serial port; and they offer *hot swapping*, which lets you add or remove devices without having to turn your computer off. All of which helps explain why manufacturers are using USB ports to connect modems, mice, keyboards, printers, scanners, speakers, cameras, and more. Some newer systems even come with nothing but USB ports—no parallel ports, no serial ports, not even a standard keyboard or mouse connector. Just USB ports (and plenty of them).

Unfortunately, USB does not always work as promised. If you have too many devices, if the cables are too long, if you mix different devices, or if you have a fast CPU, you may find that you've thrown a monkey wrench into what's supposed to be a simple process. Here's how to track down a problem if one shows up. These steps assume that you're using Microsoft Windows 98, with variations noted for Windows 2000. Details may vary with other versions of Windows.

How to fix it

Things to check first

1. A USB hub is any device outside your system unit that provides multiple USB ports for plugging in other USB devices. Keyboards and monitors, for example, sometimes include built-in USB hubs. Make sure that you have no more than 5 external hubs in a chain.

2. Make sure you have not exceeded the design specifications for USB connections. The cables should not be longer than 16 feet for full-speed USB devices and 9 feet for low-speed devices.

3. If you can't determine from a device's documentation whether it is a full-speed or low-speed device, assume you need the shorter cable length until you prove otherwise. (And note that you can get this information yourself, at least if you're using Windows 98. In the section "If you're using Windows 98" on page 88, we describe the Windows USB View utility. If USB View detects the device, it will tell you whether it's a full-speed or low-speed device.)

> **Tip**
>
> There are two types of USB hubs: self-powered and bus-powered. Self-powered hubs require connection to an external power supply—typically a block transformer that plugs into an electrical outlet. A bus-powered hub—also called a *passive* hub—relies on the bus for its power. As you might suppose, a self-powered hub can provide more power for devices than a bus-powered hub without getting overloaded.
>
> If you are using the USB ports in a keyboard or monitor, check the documentation to find out whether they are self-powered or bus-powered ports. When in doubt, use external power for your USB devices, if possible, to make sure that all devices get sufficient power.

4. When you're checking cable length, keep in mind that each device that includes a second connector is a hub, so if you have one device plugged into your system and a second device plugged into the first, you need to look at each cable separately. The cable between your system and the first unit has to meet the 9-foot or 16-foot limit. So does the cable between the first device and the second device. However, you are also limited to connecting a maximum of 5 hubs one to the other in a daisy chain.

5. One advantage of USB is that devices can get their power from the port, which provides a 5-volt power connection. The port can provide a total of only 500 milliamps (mA), however, so it is possible that one device might work if it's the only device on the line, but it won't work if a second device is connected. Disconnect all devices but one, and then add them back one at a time. If the problem shows up after you've added a device, connect one or more of the devices to an external power source and see if that solves the problem.

6. If your system has a problem booting up with a USB device attached, try removing the device before booting up. Then reconnect it after Windows has booted successfully.

7. If one specific device is not working, and it is connected to a hub, disconnect it and plug it directly into one of the USB ports on the computer to see if it works at all. If it does, the problem may be with the hub, the cable to the hub, or the combination of other devices plugged into the hub. Add each element back, one at a time, until the problem shows up again. Depending on which component goes with the problem, you may need to replace the cable, bypass or replace the hub, or plug some of the devices in using other connectors.

If you're using Windows 98

1. If you have a USB mouse or other pointer or controlling device, and its performance becomes erratic during hard disk activity, right-click on My Computer on your Desktop, choose Properties to open the System Properties window, and choose the Device Manger tab. Make sure the View Devices By Type option is selected.

2. Click on the plus sign next to the Disk Drives line, select the hard drive that is causing the problem, and choose Properties.

3. Choose the Settings tab. Look in the Options section for a check box labeled DMA. If the check box is available, but cleared, try selecting it to add a check to the check box. Then follow the onscreen instructions, rebooting the system if necessary. ▶

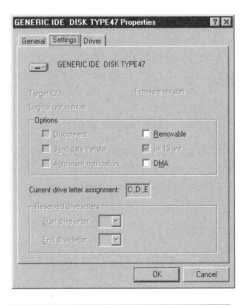

If this solution didn't solve your problem, go to the next page.

I'm having a problem with a USB connection

(continued from page 87)

4. If you're using Windows 98 or earlier, you have a mouse and a printer connected to USB ports, and your print jobs abort if the mouse is moved while they are printing, you may need to upgrade to Window 98 Second Edition or later to resolve the problem.

5. If none of the previous suggestions solves the problem, and you are using Windows 98, run the USB View utility to verify that Windows sees your USB devices. The utility is on the Windows 98 CD.

6. Put the disc in the CD-ROM drive.

7. If your system opens the Windows 98 startup window, choose Browse This CD. Otherwise, start Windows Explorer.

8. Navigate to the *\tools\reskit\diagnose* folder. Find the program usbview.exe.

9. Double-click on the file name or icon to run the program.

10. The program will show a tree arrangement with all the devices that it recognizes. You can follow the tree from My Computer, through the hubs to the individual ports. If a device is detected at a port, you can highlight the port in the tree to see details about the device on the right side. The details will include the vendor and the device bus speed used for the device. ▶

11. If the device does not appear in USB View, exit USB View, and then reinstall the device following the manufacturer's instructions.

> **Tip**
>
> USB devices rely on Plug and Play to recognize them, but the installation procedures are not standardized. Some let the Plug and Play feature prompt you for any required drivers, while others require that you install the drivers *before* you connect the device for the first time. You can save yourself time and frustration by reading the installation instructions and following them carefully.

If the device appears in USB View

1. Exit USB View. Right-click on My Computer, and choose Properties.

2. Choose the Device Manager tab. Choose the View Devices By Connection option.

3. Click on the plus sign next to the Plug and Play BIOS line to show the Plug and Play BIOS items. ▶

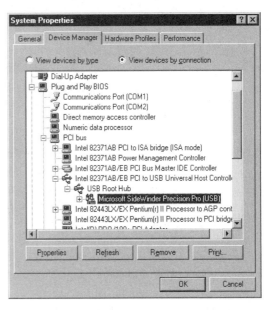

4. Click on the plus sign next to the PCI Bus icon to expand that line to see the PCI Bus items.

5. Look for a line similar to *PCI to USB Universal Host Controller* (which may have a different name on your system). Click on the plus sign next to the line see the items under that line.

6. Click on the plus sign next to the USB Root Hub icon to expand that line to show the USB Root Hub items.

7. If you have additional hubs plugged into your USB ports, click on the plus sign next to them as appropriate to expand them to locate the device you are trying to find.

8. If you find your device in the list, check for conflicts and driver problems by selecting the device, choosing Properties, and then viewing the properties. If you find a problem, go to "I may need to reinstall an adapter card," on page 28. The techniques in that section for tracking down and eliminating resource conflicts for adapter cards work just as well for USB devices.

9. If you can't find your device in the list, close Device Manager, check the manufacturer's installation instructions, and repeat the installation.

10. If the device still doesn't install properly, it may need to be repaired or replaced, or there may be a compatibility problem between it (or its driver) and your computer. Contact the device vendor to see if there is a known problem or a driver upgrade. Also contact your computer vendor to check for known problems.

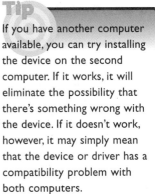

Tip

If you have another computer available, you can try installing the device on the second computer. If it works, it will eliminate the possibility that there's something wrong with the device. If it doesn't work, however, it may simply mean that the device or driver has a compatibility problem with both computers.

I'm not sure if my version of Windows supports USB

Source of the problem

USB is still relatively new. It's new enough, at least, that if you're not the sort of person who upgrades your operating system if you don't have to, you may still have a version of Windows that doesn't support it.

Or, it may support USB but not very well.

Microsoft introduced USB support with the OEM Service Release (OSR) 2.1 of Windows 95. It was not included in the retail versions of Windows 95, and there is no free upgrade path from earlier versions to one that does provide USB support.

And that's not the whole story. Although Windows 95 OSR 2.1 and 2.5 support USB devices, both versions have some problems with some USB devices under some circumstances. Windows 98 does a much better job. And Windows 98 Second Edition (SE) does better still. Later versions of Windows—namely, Windows Millennium Edition (Me) and the various flavors of Windows 2000—should handle USB at least as well as Windows 98 SE. Although, as we write this, that's only an assumption, not a field-tested fact.

How to fix it

If you have Windows 95 or 98

1. You need to find out which version of Windows you have. Right-click on the My Computer icon on your Desktop, and choose Properties from the shortcut menu to open the System Properties window.

2. Choose the General tab.

3. The first line on the tab should read *System:*, followed by the name of the Windows version (Microsoft Windows 95 or Microsoft Windows 98) on the second line. The third line is a version number, which indicates the version installed. ▶

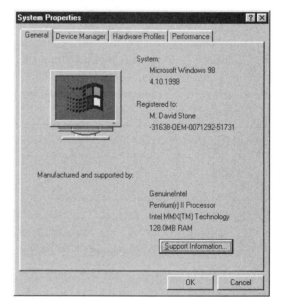

4. Check the version number you see against the lists in steps 5, 6, and 7.

5.

Version Number	Version
4.00.950	Windows 95 retail or OEM
4.00.950 0A	Windows 95 retail Service Pack 1
4.00.950A	OEM Service Release 1
4.00.1111	OEM Service Release 2

If your version is on this list, you don't have USB support. Your best bet is to upgrade to Windows 98 Second Edition or a still later version of Windows.

6.

Version Number	Version
4.03.1212-1214	OEM Service Release 2.1
4.03.1214	OEM Service Release 2.5
4.10.1998	Windows 98 retail or OEM

If your version is one of these, you have USB support. If you have problems with USB devices, consider upgrading to Windows 98 Second Edition or a later version of Windows.

7.

Version Number	Version
4.10.2222A	Windows 98 Second Edition

If your version is Windows 98 Second Edition, or any later version of Windows, you can be confident that you have robust support for USB devices.

If you have another version of Windows

1. Windows NT 4 and earlier versions of Windows NT do not support USB. Microsoft has said there are no plans to add support to Windows NT 4. If Windows NT is your preferred version of Windows, you can upgrade to Windows 2000.

2. All versions of Windows 2000 provide USB support.

3. Windows Me provides USB support.

Tip

If your version of Windows supports USB, but that support doesn't seem to be working at all, check your CMOS configuration settings to make sure that your computer's BIOS has been set to support USB.

You can start the CMOS configuration utility on most computers during boot up. In most cases, the system will show a message on the screen telling you which key to press to enter setup—typically Del or F2. If your system doesn't show which key to press, and neither of these work, see "The computer is booting from the wrong disk drive," on page 82, for more details about starting the CMOS utility.

Look for an item related to USB connections. It is often part of the "Plug and Play and PCI" sections of most BIOS configurations. The item may be labeled *USB Controller* or *USB Function*. If you find such an item, make sure it's enabled. If you don't find an item like this, contact your manufacturer to make sure that your system supports USB.

My game port or joystick isn't working

Source of the problem

If you're gonna play games, you gotta get serious. Even though many games give you the option of playing using the keyboard or mouse, you'll put yourself at a major disadvantage when you've redlined your engine or the bad guys start swarming out of the alien mother ship. Success and survival depend on having the right tools. And for most games, that means a joystick.

If your hardware and operating system support USB, consider getting a USB joystick; it's much easier to connect and configure than one that plugs into the game port. If you have a traditional game port—as found on most sound adapter cards—you need to make sure that the game port and joystick are working, that Windows recognizes both of them, and that the joystick is properly calibrated before you can set out to make the galaxy safe for free enterprise.

How to fix it

If you are using Windows 98

1. Create a bootable floppy disk: Open My Computer, select the floppy disk drive, place a disk in the floppy disk drive, and then choose File, Format. Select Full, and then select the Copy System Files check box to put a check in the box. ▶

2. Put your Windows CD in your CD-ROM drive and the boot floppy disk in the floppy disk drive.

3. Open Windows Explorer, and navigate to the Windows CD \tools\oldmsdos\ folder.

4. Copy the MSD.EXE file from the Windows CD to the bootable floppy disk.

5. Exit Windows Explorer, shut down Windows, and boot from the floppy disk. (If the computer boots from a different drive, see "The computer is booting from the wrong disk drive," on page 82.)

6. Make sure your joystick is plugged into the game port. At the MS-DOS prompt, type **MSD** and press Enter.

7. This will start the Microsoft Diagnostic (MSD) program. Look at the next to last block in the left text column. Game Port should be listed. If it isn't there, the game port may be defective or disabled. Check with the manufacturer for further information.

8. If Game Port is listed, choose the Other Adapters block; a window should open with a screen showing that the joystick has been detected. ▶

```
 File  Utilities  Help
┌─────────────────────────────────────────────────────────┐
│  Computer...    American Megatrend      LPT Ports...   1 │
│              ┌──── Other Adapters ────┐                  │
│  Memory...   640│ Game Adapter: Detected │rts...      2 │
│              │ Joystick A - X: 44     │                 │
│              │            Y: 92       │                 │
│  Video...    VGA│    Button 1: On     │us...     4.00    │
│              │    Button 2: On        │       Not Active │
│              │ Joystick B - X: 0      │                 │
│  Network...  Not│            Y: 141    │atus...          │
│              │    Button 1: On        │                 │
│  Mouse...    PS/│    Button 2: On      │rams...          │
│              │      ┌──────┐          │                 │
│ Other Adapters... Gam│  OK  │         │rivers...        │
│              │      └──────┘          │                 │
│  Disk Drives... A: B: C: D:                             │
│                 E: F: G: H:                             │
├─────────────────────────────────────────────────────────┤
│Other Adapters: Displays game adapter information.       │
└─────────────────────────────────────────────────────────┘
```

If MSD does not recognize the joystick

1. If MSD does not detect the joystick, the joystick connector may not be firmly seated in the game port, or the pins in the connector may be bent.

2. Turn off your computer. Then remove the joystick cable from the connector and check for bent pins. If there are any bent pins, you may be able to straighten them.

3. You can use needle-nose pliers or tweezers to straighten a bent pin. However, be aware that the pins are made of thin metal and will break off if you bend them back and forth too often, so don't be too surprised if you break the pin while trying to straighten it. This isn't much of a loss, however, since the joystick is useless with the pin bent. (For a detailed discussion of how to straighten bent pins, see "If the pins in the connector are bent," on page 102 in the section "I need to make sure my monitor's video cable works.")

4. After you straighten the bent pins, plug the connector back into the game port. If you feel any resistance, don't force it. Remove the connector again, and look carefully at the pins to make sure they're aligned properly. Adjust them if necessary.

5. If there aren't any bent pins, the connector may simply not have been seated properly. Plug the connector back in (but don't force it), reboot from your floppy disk, load MSD again, and see if MSD recognizes the joystick.

Tip

We mention this elsewhere in this book, but this is a tip that can't be repeated too often. If you feel any resistance when you try to plug in a connector, don't force it in. The resistance is almost certainly caused by a pin not fitting precisely into the hole it's supposed to mate with. Force the connection, and you'll likely bend the pin.

If you feel any resistance, pull out the connector and take a careful look at the pins. If you're lucky, they will be bent only a little, and you'll find it easy to bend them back to the right position.

If this solution didn't solve your problem, go to the next page.

My game port or joystick isn't working

(continued from page 93)

6. If MSD recognizes the joystick after rebooting, the problem was almost certainly an issue of the connector not being properly seated. Use the screws on each side of the connector to connect the cable connector solidly to the game port.

7. If you didn't find any bent pins, and reseating the joystick connector doesn't make any difference, the joystick may be defective. Try it on another computer to see if the other computer recognizes it.

8. If the second computer doesn't recognize the joystick, it's almost certainly defective and needs to be replaced. If the second computer recognizes the joystick, you should suspect that your game port has a problem.

If MSD recognizes the joystick

1. If MSD recognizes the joystick, note the X and Y values for Joystick A. Choose OK to close the Other Adapters window.

2. Move the joystick to the upper left corner of its range of movement. Hold it in this position, and choose the Other Adapters block again. This time, the X and Y values for Joystick A should be lower. If not, the joystick may be defective or it may not be plugged into the port securely.

3. Turn off your computer.

4. Remove the joystick connector from the game port.

5. Turn your computer back on, reboot from the floppy disk, and load MSD again. Confirm that MSD shows no joystick attached. (If it still shows a joystick attached, you'll need to track down why; the most likely cause is a defective port and the card may need to be replaced.)

6. Turn off your computer.

7. Plug the joystick back in (but don't force it), reboot from your floppy disk, and load MSD again.

8. Confirm that MSD recognizes the joystick, and note the X and Y values for the joystick. Choose OK to close the Other Adapters window.

9. Repeat step 2 above: move the joystick to the upper left corner of its range of movement, choose the Other Adapters block again, and note the X and Y values.

10. If the X and Y values are still not changed, the joystick may be defective. Try it in another computer to confirm this. If it fails in the other computer also, the joystick probably needs to be replaced. If it works in another computer, suspect the game port as the source of the problem, and consider replacing it.

If the joystick and game port pass the MSD test (or if you're using Windows 2000)

1. If the joystick and game port pass the Microsoft Diagnostic test, exit the program, remove the floppy disk from the drive, and reboot your computer to restart Windows.

2. Right-click on My Computer, and choose Properties to open the System Properties window.

3. Choose the Device Manager tab. (In Windows 2000, choose the Hardware tab, and then the Device Manager button.)

4. Click on the plus sign next to the Sound, Video and Game Controllers category. You should see a line for Gameport Joystick. (In Windows 2000, it's called Standard Game Port.) If the line is there, select it, choose the Remove button, and choose OK to remove the device. ▶

5. Chose OK to exit System Properties. Close Windows, and then restart Windows.

6. Choose Start, Settings, Control Panel, and then choose Add New Hardware. (In Windows 2000, it's called Add/Remove Hardware.)

7. When the Add New Hardware Wizard opens, choose the Next button on the first screen.

8. Choose the Next button again, to let the system search for Plug and Play devices.

9. If Windows finds the joystick, select it from the list of devices, choose the Next button, and skip to step 15 on the next page.

10. If the joystick is not on the list of devices, choose the option No, The Device Isn't On The List, and then choose the Next button. (In Windows 2000, select the Add A New Device option, and then choose Next.)

11. Choose the option No, I Want To Select The Hardware From A List, and then choose Next. ▶

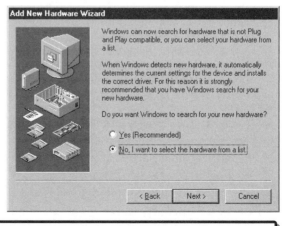

If this solution didn't solve your problem, go to the next page.

My game port or joystick isn't working

(continued from page 93)

12. Select Sound, Video And Game Controllers from the Hardware Types list, and then choose Next.

13. Scroll down the list of manufacturers and select Microsoft. Then scroll down the list of models and select Gameport Joystick. (In Windows 2000, select Standard System Devices under Manufacturers, and Standard Game Port under Models.) ▶

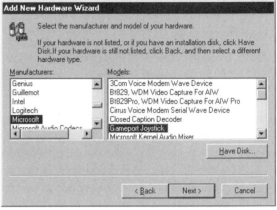

14. Choose the Next button.

15. On the next screen, choose Next again to install the device.

16. Choose the Finish button to close the Add New Hardware Wizard.

17. Choose Start, Settings, and then Control Panel to open the Control Panel.

18. In the Control Panel, choose Game Controllers. If there is a joystick listed in the Controller list, and the status is displayed as Connected (OK in Windows 2000), choose the Properties button to open the Game Controller Properties window, and skip to step 22 (choose the Test tab). If there is no controller, or there is one but the status is shown as Not Connected, continue to the next step.

19. Select the joystick in the Controller list, and choose the Remove button on the Game Controller Properties window. Then choose the Add button. Find the joystick model or a configuration that most closely matches your joystick. Choose OK. ▶

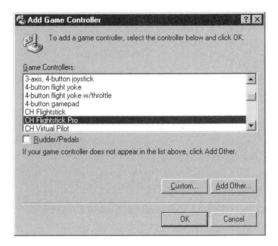

20. Choose the Properties button in the Game Controller Properties window.

21. If you have rudder pedals connected to the game port, or if the joystick has a fourth axis, make sure that there is a check mark in the Rudder/Pedals check box in the Rudder section of the Settings tab. If you don't have rudder pedals, be sure that the check box is cleared.

22. Choose the Test tab.

23. The Test tab on the Game Controller Properties window lets you test the controller functions and buttons. Test each axis for the full range of motion, and test each button. ▶

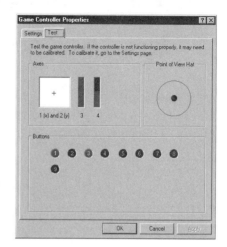

24. You may find that the controller does not move to the full limits of the test range, and that the X and Y axes are not centered on the test area when the joystick is centered. You also may find that the buttons don't work. If this is the case, you need to calibrate the joystick.

25. Choose the Settings tab, and then the Calibrate button.

26. This will open the Controller 1 Calibration screen. ▶

27. Read the directions in the window carefully, and perform each step as instructed. If you make a mistake, you can choose the Back button to go back to the last step.

28. If your joystick fails to calibrate correctly, or if the buttons fail to activate the Test screen buttons correctly, your joystick may be defective. Try the joystick on another computer. If it fails there in the same way, replace it.

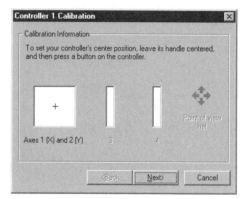

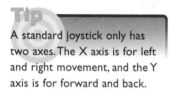

A standard joystick only has two axes. The X axis is for left and right movement, and the Y axis is for forward and back.

A game port is capable of much more, however. It can have two joysticks at once, or the second joystick's axes can be used for other functions. Typically, the third axis—the second joystick's X axis—is assigned to throttle control. And the fourth axis—the second joystick's Y axis—is used for rudder pedals in flying games or for accelerator and brake pedal signals in driving games.

Display: l

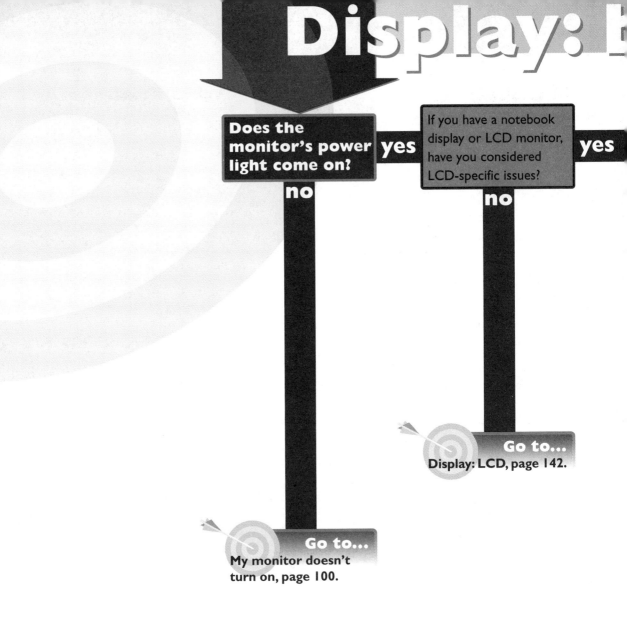

Does the monitor's power light come on? yes

If you have a notebook display or LCD monitor, have you considered LCD-specific issues? yes

no

no

Go to...
Display: LCD, page 142.

Go to...
My monitor doesn't turn on, page 100.

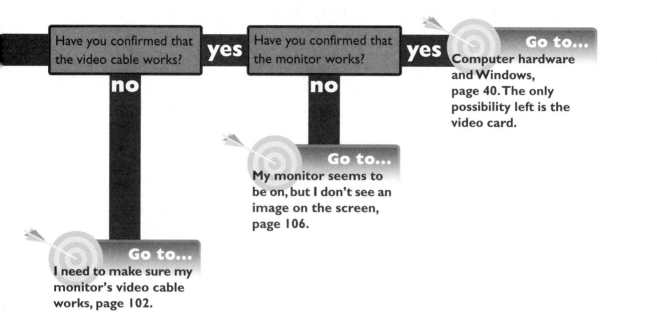

Have you confirmed that the video cable works? **yes** Have you confirmed that the monitor works? **yes**

no

no

Go to...
Computer hardware and Windows, page 40. The only possibility left is the video card.

Go to...
My monitor seems to be on, but I don't see an image on the screen, page 106.

Go to...
I need to make sure my monitor's video cable works, page 102.

If your solution isn't here
Check these related chapters:
Computer hardware and Windows, page 40
Computer startup: won't boot, page 74
Display: LCD, page 142
Or see the general troubleshooting tips on page xv.

My monitor doesn't turn on

Source of the problem

Electricity. We depend on it in so many ways, but—since it's invisible and so reliable—we often take it for granted. Turn a switch, and things happen. There's no need to think about it. Just remember to pay your bills on time, and there it is.

But what if you turn a switch on your computer and nothing happens? Has the electricity abandoned you, or is it just having trouble getting where it needs to go? Very often the issue is as simple as a loose power cord: somebody walks by your desk, brushes against the power cord, and it comes out of the socket just enough to break the electrical connection. Which is why, if you call most tech support lines about a hardware problem, the first question you'll get is whether your hardware is plugged in.

Here's how to find out whether your monitor simply isn't getting the power it needs, or has forgotten what to do with it once it gets there.

How to fix it

Check the obvious first

1. Turn off the monitor's power switch.

2. Make sure the power cord is plugged in—both to the power outlet and the monitor. Don't just look at the connections; get a good grip on the connector and push it in firmly at both the monitor and power outlet. Then turn on the monitor to see if that solved the problem.

3. Some monitors have what's called a *captive* or *captured cord*—meaning they are permanently attached. In those cases, you won't be able to check the actual electrical connection on the monitor side, but you can check to see if the cord is held firmly in place at the point where it enters the case. If it isn't, be careful with it. A tug on the cord can easily dislodge the electrical connection inside. And that may be what has happened. Before you assume that's the problem, however, there are a few more things to try. ▶

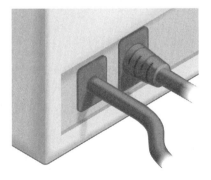

4. Turn off the monitor's power switch again.

5. Unplug the power cord from the power outlet, and from the monitor if it's not a captured cord.

6. Plug the cord back into the wall outlet and the monitor.

7. Turn on the monitor power switch.

8. If the monitor still doesn't work, make sure the outlet has power. Turn off the monitor and unplug the monitor from the outlet.

9. Plug a table lamp into the same outlet. If it lights up, there's power coming from the outlet. If it doesn't light up, don't draw any conclusions yet. Plug the lamp into another outlet that you know is working so you can prove that the lamp works. If the lamp works, the power outlet is the problem. You need to have an electrician fix it, plug the monitor into another outlet, or both.

If the monitor has a captured cord

1. If there is power in the outlet, the problem must be in either the monitor power cord or the monitor itself. Either way, this is not something you should pursue unless you're a competent, trained technician. The monitor needs to be repaired or replaced.

If the monitor doesn't have a captured cord

1. If the power cord can be detached from the monitor, it's probably a standard cord. Find another cord like it that you know is working correctly; chances are good that your computer uses the same type of cord. ▶

2. Unplug the original cord from the monitor, and plug the replacement cord into the monitor and power outlet.

3. Turn on the monitor. If the monitor is now receiving power, as indicated by the power light, you need to replace the power cord. If it isn't, the monitor needs to be repaired or replaced.

Tip

If your monitor has a captured cord, and someone has managed to trip over the cord or otherwise yank on it so that it's loose, but the monitor is still working, you should still get it repaired. It won't take much of a tug to yank the cord from its electrical connection inside the monitor. Until you get it repaired, however, you can minimize the chances of accidentally pulling the cord from its connection by taping it to the monitor case with a high-quality tape. Be careful not to cover any of the monitor vents, however.

Tip

An extra power cord is a highly useful thing to have around. Next time you upgrade to a new computer, monitor, or anything else that uses a standard power cord, hang on to the power cord if you can. You may not be able to if you are selling or giving away a working unit, but if you're throwing out a broken or obsolete device, you can certainly hold on to the cord.

I need to make sure my monitor's video cable works

Source of the problem

A computer is a powerful tool for handling information, but it's essentially useless if you don't know what information it's handling. Your monitor is the window to the world inside your system. In order to see through this window, the computer has to tell the monitor what images to display. And the way the computer communicates with your monitor is through the cable. If the cable isn't connected properly, if it has the wrong wiring or connectors, or if it isn't making a good electrical connection, it won't carry the signal from the computer to the monitor. Here's how to find out if the cable is working.

How to fix it

Make sure you have the right cable

1. If you've been using the monitor for a while before the problem occurred, and you haven't changed the cable, you must have the right cable, even if it turns out to have a problem. In that case, skip to the next section, on page 103. However, if you haven't used the monitor previously on the computer it's currently plugged into, the first thing you should check is that you have the right cable and connectors.

2. Most monitors and graphics adapters use a cable in the style of the standard Video Graphics Adapter (VGA), with a high-density 15-pin connector on each end, but this is far from the only possibility. ▶

3. Older monitors (and obsolete video cards) may use 9-pin connectors. Some new monitors use new Digital Visual Interface (DVI) connectors, which come in different configurations for digital signals, analog signals, or both. Other monitors use still other types of connectors on the monitor side. And some monitors come with cables that use less common connectors for the graphics card side of the cable, but many of these will work with the most common graphics connectors on computers by way of an adapter. If the connector on the computer end of the cable doesn't match the graphics connector on your computer, first confirm from the manual or directly from the monitor or

graphics card vendor that the monitor is designed to work with the kind of graphics card (or motherboard graphics connector) on your system. Then get the appropriate adapter. ▶

4. If your monitor has a captive graphics cable—one that's permanently attached to the monitor—it's obviously the right one. However, monitors with captive cables often come with a variety of adapters so they can plug into a variety of computers. Here again, if the connector on the computer end of the cable doesn't match the graphics connector on your computer, first confirm from the manual or directly from the vendor that the monitor is designed to work with the kind of graphics card or motherboard graphics connector on your system. Then get the appropriate adapter.

5. Your monitor may offer two (or more) connectors for connecting to the monitor. One special case worth mentioning is that some monitors come with both a VGA-style connector and a standard 15-pin connector like the video connector on the Apple Macintosh. These usually come with a single cable for PCs or Macs. Simply plug the appropriate end of the connector into the PC or Mac, and then plug the remaining end into the appropriate connector on the monitor.

6. Keep in mind too that it's not enough that the cable has the right connectors; they also have to be wired the right way. If you have any doubts about the cable, you may have to hunt up—or order—another one, even if you need to pay for a custom cable. Be prepared to specify both the monitor and graphics card when you order the cable.

If you have the right cable

1. Before you do anything else, if your monitor was working and has suddenly stopped working, check to make sure the cable is plugged in at both the monitor and computer sides. This may sound almost too basic to bother with, but it's not unusual for someone to brush against a cable and pull it halfway out. If your computer is set up as a home computer or in a home office, and you have pets or small children, the odds that the cable was pulled out rise dramatically.

2. Make sure your computer and monitor are both off.

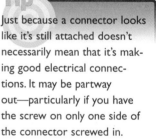

Tip

Just because a connector looks like it's still attached doesn't necessarily mean that it's making good electrical connections. It may be partway out—particularly if you have the screw on only one side of the connector screwed in.

The standard VGA connector, and most other connectors on monitor cables, include a screw on each side of the connector. You should screw these in firmly on both sides. The screws ensure that the cable is grounded properly, that the pins are making good electrical contact, and that the connectors won't accidentally be pulled out.

If this solution didn't solve your problem, go to the next page.

I need to make sure my monitor's video cable works

(continued from page 103)

3. Check both connections—at the computer and at the monitor. If the connectors are firmly screwed in on both sides, with the screws all the way in, you can safely assume that the cable is connected properly. However, if the screws are only partway in, or a connector is screwed in on only one side, or not screwed in at all, consider the connection suspicious. Reseating the cable may clear up the problem.

4. Unplug the cable from both pieces of equipment. If the connectors are screwed in on one side or partly screwed in, you may need a small screwdriver to unscrew them. More often, the connectors will have thumbscrews that you can unscrew by hand, although they too may have slots in their ends so that you can use a screwdriver to undo them if they're tight.

5. Check the connectors at both ends of the cable for bent pins. All the pins should be parallel and evenly spaced.

6. Plug the cable back in. Be careful not to force the cable into its connector. If it doesn't insert with just a gentle push, take it out and examine it carefully for pins that are even slightly bent.

7. Turn the monitor and computer on again to see if the problem is solved.

> **Tip**
>
> There are 15 pins in the standard VGA analog cable connectors, yet only 10 are needed to transfer the required signals between the computer and the monitor. As a result, one or more pins may be missing from your monitor cable's connector; this is not cause for concern. As long as none of the pins the monitor actually needs is missing, the cable will work as intended.

If the pins in the connector are bent

1. If you see a bent pin in a connector, you may be able to straighten it and save the cable. The pins are made of thin metal, however, and if you subject one to too much bending back and forth, it's likely to snap off, rendering the cable useless. So approach this task carefully: don't bend the pins any more than is required to get the cable connected again. And don't be too surprised if the pin breaks when you try to straighten it. At least you'll be no worse off than if you didn't try to salvage the cable at all.

2. If the pin is merely bent at the base, take a small pair of tweezers or needle-nose pliers and try to grab the pin as close to its base as possible. Gently pull the pin back to its approximate original position. ▶

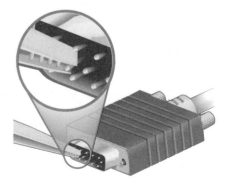

3. If the pin itself is bent in the middle, unbending it is more of a challenge, but you can often straighten even a severely bent pin. Here again, use tweezers or needle-nose pliers to grab the base of the pin. Hold the base firmly, and use a small, flat-bladed screwdriver to open up the bend and straighten the pin enough for needle-nose pliers to fit on either side of it. Then use the pliers to gently squeeze the pin to straighten it out. You may need to do this several times, rotating the needle-nose pliers so they squeeze the pin from different directions each time. ▶

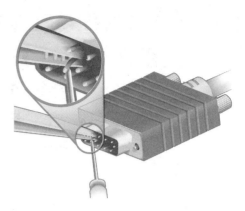

4. Whether the pin started out slightly misaligned or seriously bent, once it's back in roughly the right alignment, position the pliers or tweezers to hold the misaligned pin and the adjacent pins on either side in the same row, then gently squeeze all three to align them. Repeat this in both diagonal directions. Then look carefully at the connector; if the pins are not in evenly spaced rows, try to align them again.

5. Some people find it easier to align the pins using a small, flat-bladed screwdriver. Place the edge of the blade at the base of the pin, and pivot it to apply slight pressure to the pin in the direction you want it to move. Then release the pressure and look carefully at the connector to see if the pins are aligned.

6. Once the pin is straight, carefully plug in the cable. If you feel any resistance, don't push; you may only bend the pin again. Instead, remove the connector and try aligning the pins again.

7. With the cable plugged in, turn on the monitor and computer to see if the problem is solved. If it is, make sure the screws on both sides of the connector are inserted in the screw holes and tightened. Try to avoid disconnecting and reconnecting the cable if at all possible. Once a pin has been bent it's much more likely to be bent again.

Testing the cable

1. If you still have a problem, try using another cable that you know to be working correctly. Borrow one from a working monitor that uses the same cable. Turn the monitor off and unplug the original cable. Plug the borrowed cable into the graphics adapter and monitor.

2. Turn on the monitor. If this works, you need a new cable. You can get standard ones at most computer or electronics stores. If you need a special cable, you may have to contact the graphics adapter or monitor manufacturer to find a source for a replacement, or you may have to have one custom built for you. Be prepared to specify both the monitor and graphics card when you order the cable.

3. If the borrowed cable doesn't work, you need to find out if the problem is in the graphics adapter or the monitor. You can test them in either order.

My monitor seems to be on, but I don't see an image on the screen

Source of the problem

You turn your monitor on; you know it's on because the power light says so; you know you've got the right cable, because it's the same cable you've been using for months without problems. And the cable is plugged in. So why isn't the monitor working?

One possibility is that the monitor is dead. Monitors last a long time—long enough to make it worth investing in a relatively expensive monitor for one computer, so you can move it to your next computer, and maybe the one after that. But nothing lasts forever. The electronics die, the picture tube loses brightness, and mechanical switches break. On the other hand, someone may have simply set the controls so you can't see a picture, or the problem may lie in your graphics card. Here's how to check out the monitor.

How to fix it

Check the monitor settings

1. Start by turning on the computer and the monitor, and making sure the computer has booted properly. For example, you should hear the sound that indicates that Microsoft Windows has loaded successfully.

2. If your monitor has an onscreen display (OSD), press the front panel control that brings it up; check the monitor manual for the specifics for your model. If you can see the OSD, it means that the monitor is capable of producing an image. ▶

3. Some monitors can accept input from two or more computers. A common choice, for example, is between BNC (a type of connector that was once popular for high-end monitors) and D-Sub (a name for the D-shaped connector that the typical monitor or graphics card uses). If your monitor has two or more inputs, make sure you have the correct signal source selected. There may be a dedicated button or switch for signal source on the monitor panel, or you may have to make a selection using the OSD.

4. Some monitors with OSDs will let you turn brightness and contrast all the way down so the screen is black, but will not apply those settings to the OSD, so you can still see the OSD, even though you can't see anything else. Whether you could see the OSD in step 1 or not, adjust the monitor's brightness control to maximum brightness and adjust the contrast control to maximum contrast.

5. Different monitors have different controls for these settings, but most monitors, even those with OSDs, offer dedicated controls for both. The brightness control is usually indicated by an icon that resembles a sun with light radiating from it (a circle with short lines on the outside pointing away from the circle). The contrast control is usually indicated by a circle or by a circle that's dark on one side and light on the other (or some variation of that if the icon is stamped into the case). Consult your monitor's manual for the operating instructions. Make sure that you are setting both to their maximum setting rather than their minimum settings. ▶

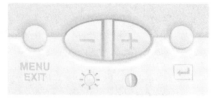

6. If the brightness and contrast controls are available only through the OSD, and you can't see the OSD, you'll have to try to change these settings through dead reckoning (which is a navigator's term that means you can't see what you're doing). The manual should tell you which buttons to press, and how many times, to reach the contrast controls and then set them both to maximum.

7. If your monitor can accept input from two or more computers, and the button for choosing between them simply toggles the setting without indicating which input the monitor is set for, try the toggle again at this point. If you still don't see an image on screen, your monitor settings are not responsible for the problem.

Determine whether the monitor works

1. If the monitor still shows no signs of life, plug the monitor into a graphics adapter that you know is working. The preferred choice is to use a notebook computer that offers a connector for an external monitor and an easy way to switch between the notebook's screen and the external monitor. Most do. (And you'll find it much easier to carry a notebook computer to the monitor than carry the monitor to another computer.) If you don't have a notebook computer and can't persuade anyone to bring one by, you can move the monitor to a nearby computer. Failing that, consider taking the monitor to a friend's or neighbor's computer.

2. To eliminate possible problems with Windows graphics and display drivers, you will want the system to boot up to an MS-DOS prompt. This will provide your monitor with a VGA-resolution signal, which will demonstrate whether your monitor is working. The easiest way to do this is with a notebook computer.

> *If this solution didn't solve your problem, go to the next page.*

My monitor seems to be on, but I don't see an image on the screen

(continued from page 107)

If you have a notebook computer to test with

1. Make sure you know the keystrokes for switching between an external monitor and the notebook's screen. (Most often, this involves holding down the notebook's Function key while pressing another key on the keyboard. This is a hardware-based command that should work no matter what's running on the computer.) Connect the monitor to the notebook, using a cable that you know works. Boot up in Windows, choose Start, Shut Down, select the option Restart in MS-DOS mode, and then choose OK. (If you are using Windows 2000, you will have to boot from a floppy disk that has the Windows 98 or earlier operating system on it.)

2. The notebook should boot into MS-DOS mode. When it does, press the keys that switch from the notebook screen to the external LCD.

3. Give the monitor a moment to warm up. If the MS-DOS screen doesn't show on the monitor, make sure the brightness and contrast controls are still set to maximum as described earlier, in the section "Check the monitor settings," on page 106. If the MS-DOS screen still doesn't show, you almost certainly need to replace the monitor or get it repaired professionally.

If you have only a desktop computer to test with

1. With a desktop system, you may not be able to see the computer's prompts on your monitor if it's not working, so the easiest way to boot up to an MS-DOS screen is to boot from a floppy disk. If you don't have a bootable floppy disk for the computer, you'll have to create one. (If you're running Windows 2000, you'll need to make the boot disk using a computer running Windows 98 or an earlier version of the operating system.)

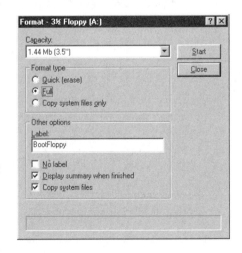

2. Choose a disk that doesn't contain any information you want to save, since you will be erasing the contents of the disk. Run Windows on the second computer, and put the floppy disk in the floppy disk drive.

3. Open Windows Explorer, and open the shortcut menu either by right-clicking on the floppy disk drive icon in the left window or by selecting it and pressing Shift+F10.

4. Choose Format from the menu to open the Format dialog box. ▶

5. Choose Full for the Format Type, and make sure a check is in the Copy System Files check box. Then choose Start.

6. After the format is complete, remove the floppy disk from the drive and shut down the computer.

7. If the computer is configured to boot from the hard disk first, you will have to reconfigure it to boot from the floppy disk drive first. See "The computer is booting from the wrong disk drive," on page 82.

8. Place the floppy disk in the floppy drive, and restart the computer to make sure that it works correctly. If it boots to the MS-DOS prompt, proceed to the next step. If it doesn't boot to the MS-DOS prompt, the floppy disk might be faulty; repeat steps 2 through 8 with a different floppy disk.

9. Turn off the computer and the monitor. Disconnect the computer's monitor.

10. Connect your monitor and plug it into the electrical outlet. Turn on the computer and your monitor, and boot to an MS-DOS prompt. If you don't get an image on the monitor, you almost certainly need to replace the monitor or get it repaired professionally.

If the monitor works on a different computer

1. If you've just proven that the monitor works on a different computer and you've previously proven that the cable works too, the only thing left to suspect is your computer, most likely the graphics adapter. (If you haven't already proven that the cable works, rerun the test for your monitor using the same cable you normally use on your computer, to confirm that the cable is OK.)

2. Before you settle on the video card as the guilty party, it's best to run a quick test to confirm it.

3. Bring a monitor that you know is working correctly to your computer (or take your computer to the monitor).

4. Turn off your computer and monitor. Disconnect your monitor. Connect the working monitor, and plug it into the electrical outlet.

5. Turn on your computer and the monitor. If you don't get an image, you've pretty well confirmed that the problem is most likely caused by your graphics adapter, which you can absolutely confirm by removing it and installing another graphics adapter. (Also see "Computer hardware and Windows," on page 22.)

6. If you get an image with the second monitor, turn everything off, plug in your original monitor, and turn everything back on again.

7. If the original monitor now shows an image, it may mean the problem has mysteriously disappeared. (Stranger things have happened with computers.) However, it could also mean that you have an intermittent problem that will reoccur.

8. The more likely result is that the original monitor will not show an image. This indicates an incompatibility of some kind between the monitor and the graphics card. You may need to call the manufacturers to find out what adapter card to get for the monitor, or what monitor to get for the adapter card.

If you care about color, don't get sucked into buying a designer color monitor. The color of the bezel—the portion of the case that surrounds the screen—affects your perception of the colors on screen. The neutral beige is there for a reason. You can see how the surrounding color affects the screen colors by putting a colored matte around your screen, closing your eyes while removing the matte, and then opening your eyes.

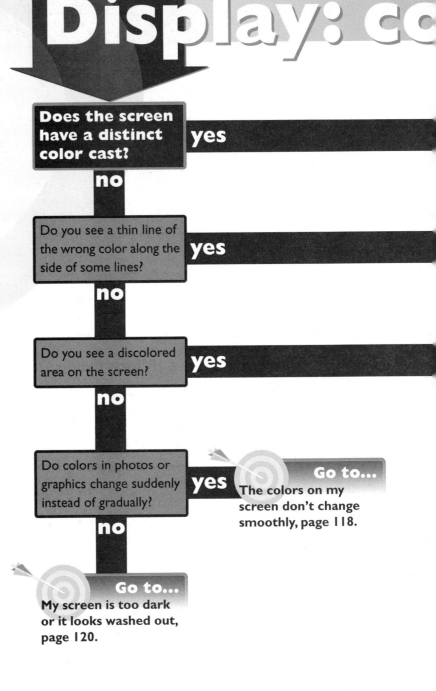

Does the screen have a distinct color cast?

yes

no

Do you see a thin line of the wrong color along the side of some lines?

yes

no

Do you see a discolored area on the screen?

yes

no

Do colors in photos or graphics change suddenly instead of gradually?

yes

Go to...
The colors on my screen don't change smoothly, page 118.

no

Go to...
My screen is too dark or it looks washed out, page 120.

Go to...
My screen colors all look shifted toward a specific color, page 112.

Quick fix
This problem is called misconvergence and is caused by the electron beams not being aligned correctly. Some expensive monitors provide limited controls to correct this problem, but in large part, it's a permanent part of the display. It may be more pronounced at some resolutions than at others, and you may be able to have a professional repair service make some adjustments, but if the problem is bothersome, you should consider replacing the monitor.

Go to...
I see discolored splotches on my screen, page 116.

If your solution isn't here
Check these related chapters:
Display: color and brightness, page 110
Display: quality flaws, page 156
Or see the general troubleshooting tips on page xv.

My screen colors all look shifted toward a specific color

Source of the problem

The world may look better through rose-colored glasses, but not when you're trying to work with your computer. If your display has a color problem that uniformly affects the entire screen, the problem most likely stems from one of two things: The first likely cause is that a signal is not getting to the screen correctly. If that's the case, the problem may lie in the monitor's cable or connectors, or deep inside the monitor itself. The second possibility is that the display is doing exactly what it is supposed to do, but the color settings aren't the way you want them. In either case, here's how identify and fix the problem.

How to fix it

1. Choose Start, Programs, Accessories, and then Paint to open the Microsoft Windows Paint program.

2. Look at the color blocks in the lower left corner of the window. If you don't see the blocks of color, choose View, Color Box to turn on the Color Box feature. ▶

3. On the bottom row of colors, the first block should be white, and the next should be light gray, followed by blocks of red, yellow, green, cyan, blue, and magenta. If any two of these blocks appear to be the same color, continue on to the next section, "A color signal is missing." If they all appear different—but not the right shades or colors—skip to "The screen colors are off" on page 114.

A color signal is missing

1. If any pair of the six color blocks in the previous step appear to be the same color, one of the color signals isn't getting through to the screen. The most likely source of the problem is the monitor cable, which is where you should start.

2. Turn off the monitor, and unplug the cable from the display adapter and the monitor. (Note that some monitors have *captive* cables that are permanently attached; do not attempt to disconnect a captive cable.)

3. Examine the cable connectors for bent pins. If you find any, see "I need to make sure my monitor's video cable works" on page 102 for instructions on how to fix them.

4. Reconnect the cable to the display and monitor. Insert the connectors carefully to avoid bending any pins. Do not force them if you meet any resistance.

5. Use the screws on each side of the connectors to secure the cable to the adapter card and monitor.

6. Turn your system and monitor back on. If the problem is resolved, stop here.

7. If the problem is not resolved, there may be a problem with the cable itself, an internal failure in the monitor, or a problem with the graphics adapter.

8. If you have a spare cable that you know is good or you can borrow one—and assuming the monitor doesn't have a captive cable—replace the cable on your system to see if the problem goes away. If it does, you have a faulty cable and need to replace it.

9. If the cable isn't the problem, and you have a spare monitor or can borrow one, replace the monitor on your system to see if that solves the problem. If it does, you probably have a broken monitor that you need to repair or replace. If it doesn't solve the problem, and you've already eliminated the cable as the cause of the problem, your video card becomes the primary suspect, and you may need to repair or replace it.

10. If you don't have a second monitor, but you have access to a second computer, try moving your monitor to the second system. The easiest option is often to plug it into a notebook. (And if you don't have one, you may have a friend who you can persuade to bring one over to help you.)

11. For a notebook, you'll need to know the keystrokes for switching between the notebook's own screen and an external monitor. This is often a combination keystroke using the notebook's Function key with another key on the keyboard, which is often marked with a self-explanatory icon. If you can't determine the right key from looking at the keyboard, check the notebook system's manual. If the command for your notebook isn't obvious, and you can't find it in the notebook's manual, check *www.infocus.com/service/tech_library/laptop_chart.asp*. This site lists the right keystrokes for hundreds of popular laptops.

Tip

A spare monitor cable is a worthwhile investment for your personal troubleshooting toolkit. If you don't have one, you may want to get one the next time you stop by a computer store or order something else from a catalog or Web site that also sells monitor cables. The cable shouldn't cost much, and it's certainly handy to have around for troubleshooting a variety of monitor problems. Be sure you get one with the right connectors and wiring for your computer and monitor.

If this solution didn't solve your problem, go to the next page.

My screen colors all look shifted toward a specific color

(continued from page 113)

12. Connect the monitor to the second system and turn on the monitor and the system. If the second system is a notebook, press the keys that switch from the notebook screen to the external display.

13. Open Windows Paint on the notebook, and check the color blocks in the lower left corner as described in step 3 on page 112. If they're correct, the problem probably lies in the graphics adapter on your computer. If they're not correct, and you've eliminated the cable as the source of the problem, you probably need to repair or replace the monitor.

The screen colors are off

1. If the color blocks in Windows Paint are all different, but they're the wrong colors, the most likely cause of the problem is that your monitor's control for adjusting colors isn't set correctly. Someone may have changed the settings without telling you, or you may have accidentally changed them yourself.

2. Depending on your monitor, the color controls may be available through dedicated buttons, buttons that serve multiple functions, or through an onscreen display (OSD). You should be able to find out which by checking the monitor's manual or looking for a color or color temperature control.

3. If your monitor changes color settings through buttons, it probably has some predefined settings as well as a custom option. Try the predefined settings—which might be accessed by pressing a button labeled Memory Recall or Reset—to see if they solve the problem.

4. If your monitor has a color temperature setting, it probably lets you choose the temperature through an onscreen menu. Call up the menu if there is one (usually by pressing a button labeled Menu), and then find the Color Temperature option. (On some monitors, this may be under an Advanced Setting menu option.) Note the current settings, and then try all the color temperature choices to see if any of them fixes the problem. If not, try adjusting the custom settings if custom settings are available. (But be sure to note the settings you started with, so you can return to them easily if necessary.) ▶

Tip

Your monitor may offer color controls, a color temperature control, both, or neither.

Color controls let you adjust the balance of red, green, and blue individually. A color temperature control lets you set all three as a single option, with the balance of red, green and blue determined by the color temperature.

Because of a perverse relationship between physics and psychology, a hotter temperature, like 9300 degrees Kelvin (K), yields cooler colors psychologically than a cooler temperature, like a 6500 degrees K setting. A warmer color temperature means colder, bluer whites. A cooler temperature yields warmer, pinker whites.

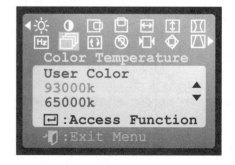

I see discolored splotches on my screen

Source of the problem

Psychedelic hues are great if you're designing a Hendrix album cover, but they're probably not what you want to see on the screen when you're trying to work. Unfortunately, sometimes strange things can happen to your screen colors in certain areas of the display. They stem from the fact that the image is painted by beams of electrons striking chemicals that then glow different colors. A weak magnetic field is all it takes to pull the electron beam off its proper path, so it lights up the wrong dots. How weak are these fields? They can be caused by the magnets found in small speakers, or by fields generated from a small electric motor. For some large monitors, even the earth's magnetic fields can cause discoloration. Sometimes the effects of these fields can be easily reversed, while other cases may result in permanent damage. Here's how to do what you can to fix a monitor with this problem.

How to fix it

1. Make sure that there are no sources of magnetic fields within at least a foot of your monitor. This is farther than necessary, but it's a good place to start. After you solve the problem, you can move the devices back one by one to see which, if any, cause the problem.

2. If the discoloration persists, turn your monitor off and on two or three times, waiting a moment each time you press the switch. Most monitors automatically *degauss* when you turn them on, a process designed to eliminate stray magnetic fields from the innards of the display.

3. If the discoloration remains, check your monitor's controls for a manual degauss feature, and try using it if you find one.

4. If you still don't see any improvement, take the monitor to a repair service. The monitor may require a stronger degauss treatment, or—if the damage is permanent—replacement. It's also possible to degauss a monitor with a hand-held magnet, but we advise against trying it, since you're likely to make the problem worse instead of better.

Playing keep-away

Here's a partial list of devices that can cause the discoloration problem in monitors:

- speakers
- telephones
- fans
- sub-woofers
- cassette players
- answering machines
- "boom box" stereos
- magnetic paper clip dispensers
- other monitors
- printers
- scanners

The colors on my screen don't change smoothly

Source of the problem

The sky may be blue, but it's not just one blue. It's many shades of blue that blend imperceptibly from one to the next. The same can be said of skin tones, expanses of water, stone, and almost anything else that can take up a large portion of an image but isn't all one shade of a color. Graphics can have the same kind of smooth variation, in what's called a *gradient*, since the colors change gradually, one into another.

Unfortunately, displays don't always portray these changing shades accurately. Instead of a smooth transition from one shade to another, the image may show bands of shades that change abruptly. This effect is sometimes called *posterization* and is caused by the graphics adapter not generating enough different shades to cover all the colors in the image. ▶

The solution is to provide more color information for each dot on the screen, which is known as increasing the *color depth*. Eight bits of information per pixel provides only enough information to define 256 colors, which isn't enough to portray a photographic image realistically. In contrast, 24 bits per pixel defines more than 16 million colors, which is roughly twice as many colors as the

24-bit image (16 million colors)   8-bit image (256 colors)

human eye can see, and allows smooth shading even if the shades aren't distributed to match the same variations the human eye can see. Still higher color depths can be of interest to professional graphic artists (and yes, in this case it makes sense to talk about a "higher" depth).

How to fix it

1. To change the color depth on your display, right-click on an open space on your desktop.

2. Choose Properties from the shortcut menu that pops up.

3. In the Display Properties dialog box, choose the Settings tab. ▶

4. In the Colors drop-down list box, choose at least High Color (16 Bit), and then choose OK.

5. Windows may warn you that the settings you have chosen may cause some programs to operate improperly if you do not restart your computer. Choose Apply The New Color Settings Without Restarting, and then choose OK. You can restart your computer later.

6. Using the appropriate program, load an image that you've previously noticed shows images with colors that don't change smoothly, but should. If the problem is gone, you can stop. If you still see the problem, open the Display Properties dialog box again by right-clicking on the desktop and choosing Properties, and then return to the Settings tab.

7. You'll need to change the Colors setting to a higher color depth, which will usually be identified as True Color. Depending on your graphics card and driver, the True Color setting may provide 24 bits or 32 bits of information per pixel and will likely be listed as either True Color (24-bit) or True Color (32-bit). These are equivalent for your purposes.

8. After you change the Colors setting to True Color, choose OK. Windows may again warn you about the possible need to restart your computer. Choose Apply The New Color Settings Without Restarting, and choose OK. If the colors still don't change smoothly, the problem may lie in the image itself.

My screen is too dark or it looks washed out

Source of the problem

If you're like the majority of people with computers, you've never adjusted any of the settings on your computer monitor. And for the most part, if you're trying to read black text on a white background, it doesn't make a whole lot of difference how the monitor's set.

The situation changes when you start viewing more demanding images, however. If you work with photographic images—such as from a digital camera or a DVD movie—you may notice problems. Bright areas—such as images of sky or beach or snowfields—may wash out and lose detail. Dark areas, like the trees around a lake, may merge into a mass of solid black. Colors may look dusty and flat. It's possible you have a monitor problem—displays tend to get dimmer as they grow older—but if your display is less than four or five years old, chances are good that you can improve the image quality with some simple adjustments.

How to fix it

1. Start by locating the brightness control on your monitor. Different monitors have different controls; some have dedicated buttons on their control panel, while others rely on an onscreen menu for this adjustment. If the monitor has a button, it will generally be marked by an icon showing a circle with short radiating lines. ▶

2. The brightness control has its greatest effect on the dark shades and the black level of an image. To adjust it correctly, you need an image with a black background covered by objects in assorted dark grays. DisplayMate from DisplayMate Technologies (*www.displaymate.com*) has a Black-Level Adjustment screen that is well suited for this task. If you have a reasonably sophisticated graphics program, you can create a similar image of your own. ▶

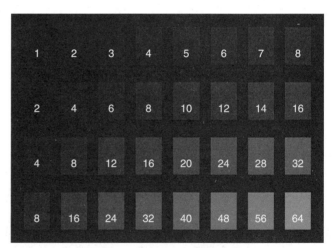

Maximize the visibility of the darkest grays while maintaining a black background.

3. The settings you'll wind up with will depend on the lighting conditions. Make sure the room lighting is set the way it most often is when you use the computer.

4. Turn the brightness control down to its minimum level.

5. Next, increase the brightness until you see the black background barely begin to get lighter. Then turn the brightness control down just enough so the background is its darkest again. You may have to try this several times to find the setting that gives you the highest possible brightness without making the black background lighter—particularly if the only way to set the brightness is with an onscreen menu that covers part of the test image and washes it out.

6. Next locate the contrast control on your monitor. As with the brightness control, it may be available only through an onscreen menu. It will typically be marked by an icon showing a circle with one half shaded. ▶

7. The contrast control has its greatest effect on the light shades of gray, so you need a test image with a white background covered by objects in assorted light grays. Again, DisplayMate has a White-Level Saturation image that is ideal for this step. And again, you can create a similar image in a graphics program if you prefer. ▶

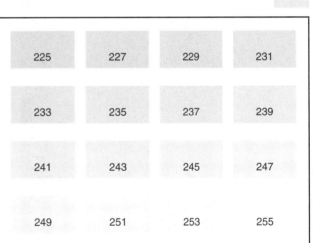

225	227	229	231
233	235	237	239
241	243	245	247
249	251	253	255

8. Lower the contrast setting until you reach the point that you can see as many light gray shades as the monitor allows.

9. On some displays, changing the contrast setting may affect the dark shades significantly also. Repeat steps 2 through 8 to make sure that both the brightness and contrast settings are correct. Following these instructions should give you the best detail that you can get from this monitor in both light and dark areas of an image.

10. If the display is still too dim after making these adjustments, you can increase the brightness. But keep in mind that raising brightness will tend to make dark shades merge into each other. Similarly, raising the contrast will tend to make light shades merge into each other. Either way, you lose details. If you can't get brightness to a satisfactory level, it may be because the monitor has aged and lost the ability to be bright enough. If so, you should consider replacing it.

Tip

If you have a digital LCD monitor, you may find that it has a brightness control but no contrast control, or a contrast control but no brightness control. Either way, the control may have limited effectiveness, and may not behave the way controls of the same name behave in standard desktop monitors. This is normal. The brightness control on a digital LCD monitor typically controls only the brightness of the backlight that illuminates the LCD panel.

Do circles look round and straight lines look straight?

yes

When you switch resolutions, does the screen switch without sudden jumps in size and without showing garbage on the screen?

yes

no

no

Quick fix

Better monitors blank the screen briefly when changing resolutions so that you don't see the momentary confusion as the signal switches. Less sophisticated designs handle this task less smoothly, resulting in image bounce, size changes, or scrambled images during the changeover. In general, this is normal, and while it can be distracting or even annoying, it doesn't indicate that there's anything wrong with the display.

Go to...

Circles on my screen aren't round, or lines are bent, page 138.

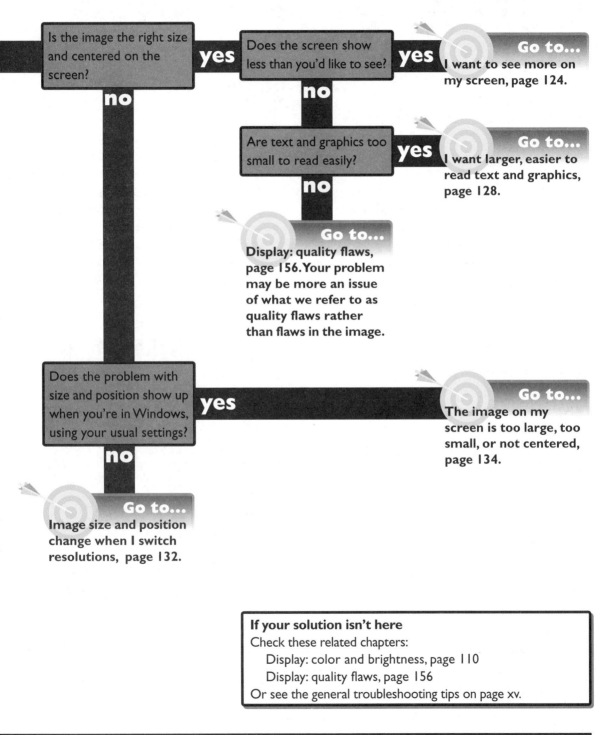

Is the image the right size and centered on the screen?

yes → Does the screen show less than you'd like to see?

yes → **Go to...**
I want to see more on my screen, page 124.

no ↓

Are text and graphics too small to read easily?

yes → **Go to...**
I want larger, easier to read text and graphics, page 128.

no ↓

Go to...
Display: quality flaws, page 156. Your problem may be more an issue of what we refer to as quality flaws rather than flaws in the image.

no ↓

Does the problem with size and position show up when you're in Windows, using your usual settings?

yes → **Go to...**
The image on my screen is too large, too small, or not centered, page 134.

no ↓

Go to...
Image size and position change when I switch resolutions, page 132.

If your solution isn't here
Check these related chapters:
Display: color and brightness, page 110
Display: quality flaws, page 156
Or see the general troubleshooting tips on page xv.

I want to see more on my screen

Source of the problem

Microsoft Windows lets you have more than one program open at a time, and there are good reasons to take advantage of this feature. Many programs let you drag text or images from one program to another. Even if you don't move content from one window to another, however, it can be helpful to have a Web browser in one window as you write a report in another, while keeping a To Do list open in another. That's a lot of information to have on one screen, and you may find it doesn't all fit on the screen at once—in which case, you'll need to shrink everything down. Ultimately, it's a matter of resolution, with a lower resolution translating into less information on screen, and a higher resolution translating into more information.

How to fix it

1. Right-click on an open area of your desktop.

2. On the shortcut menu, choose Properties to open the Display Properties dialog box.

3. In the Display Properties dialog box, choose the Settings tab. ▶

4. Look at the area of the window marked Screen Area. The slider ranges from Less to More. If you want to increase the resolution for your display, and the slider isn't already pegged at the extreme right side, move the slider to the right, toward More. The resolution for each available step will show below the slider as you move to the right.

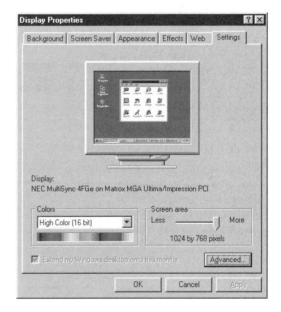

5. Choose OK. You may be prompted to restart Windows before the changes take effect, or the screen may change and a window will appear asking you to confirm the change. If the image size is pretty much the way you want it, accept the change. (You may then need to adjust the image size or position. See "The image on my screen is too large, too small, or not centered" on page 136.)

If the slider is already all the way to the right at the More end of the scale

1. If you can't increase the resolution, make sure you have the correct settings in Windows for the current graphics adapter and monitor.

Tip

If you're a bargain hunter, you may find 20-inch and larger monitors available for sale for astoundingly low prices. If you try to plug one into your computer, however, you may find that it's not such a bargain.

Many of these monitors are *fixed frequency* monitors, which means that they are designed to work at one specific resolution. Originally designed for use with engineering workstations, they cannot display the standard VGA resolutions produced by personal computers when they first power up or start in MS-DOS mode.

Fortunately, there are graphics cards available that can translate the lower VGA resolutions to the higher resolutions required by these monitors and display the image legibly. These cards used to be much more expensive than standard multi-frequency graphics adapters, but the prices are now competitive, and you can find models with 3D acceleration and video support. Two vendors that produce these cards are Software Integrators (*www.si87.com*) and Photon(*www.photonweb.com*).

2. Check the specifications for both pieces of hardware. For both graphics card and monitor, check the manuals, or check with the vendor, to find the maximum *noninterlaced* resolution that it supports. (There's no need to know what *noninterlaced resolution* means. Just make sure that the number you get is for the maximum noninterlaced resolution, rather than the maximum *interlaced* resolution. From this point on we'll talk about maximum resolution as shorthand for maximum noninterlaced resolution.)

3. Once you've found the maximum resolution for both monitor and video card, compare them. The maximum resolution you can actually use will be the lower of the two numbers—or, more precisely, the highest resolution that both the monitor and video card support. In other words, if the graphics adapter can support both 1024-by-768 and 1600-by-1200 resolution, but the monitor maxes out at 1024-by-768, you'll be limited to 1024-by-768 maximum. If this is the case and you want to use a higher resolution, you'll need to replace whichever device is limiting the other. If both devices claim to support a higher resolution than you can set with the slider in the Display Properties dialog box, continue to the next step.

Tip

When you switch to a higher resolution, you may find that Windows automatically adjusts the number of colors (in the Colors drop-down list box to the left of the Screen Area box) to a lower number. That's because both higher resolution and the ability to define more colors require additional memory. If your graphics card doesn't have enough memory to handle the maximum number of colors it allows at its highest resolution, Windows will adjust one of these settings downwards whenever you set the other to a higher setting than the amount of memory allows.

Keep in mind too that when you increase either the resolution or the number of colors, you increase the amount of data that your computer has to move around with each screen of information. So you may notice slower performance when you increase the resolution or color setting. Short of investing in an upgrade, your only solution may be to compromise between resolution, number of colors, and speed.

> *If this solution didn't solve your problem, go to the next page.*

I want to see more on my screen

(continued from page 125)

4. On the Settings tab of the Display Properties window, choose the Advanced button to open the graphic adapter's Properties dialog box.

5. Choose the Adapter tab. This screen will tell you the graphics adapter, accelerator chip, and current driver version, among other details. Check with your graphics card manufacturer to make sure that you have the current driver. If there is a new driver, follow the manufacturer's instructions to obtain and install the updated version. ▶

6. Choose the Monitor tab, and look to see if Windows indicates that the right monitor is installed. If Windows shows the correct monitor name near the top of the dialog box, or shows the monitor as *Plug and Play Monitor*, it should have the correct information about the resolution the monitor can handle. If Windows shows the wrong name for the monitor, you may need to update the installation, but first you'll need to investigate further. ▶

7. Windows will allow only those resolutions appropriate for the installed monitor, so if the maximum resolution for the installed monitor is lower than the maximum resolution for the monitor you actually have, it won't let you use your monitor's higher resolution. If Windows shows the wrong name for the monitor, check with your monitor manufacturer to find out if there is a configuration file available for the monitor. The file would have an .INF extension; you may have gotten one on a disk that came with the monitor, there may be an appropriate file that ships with your version of Windows, or the file may be available from the manufacturer's Web site.

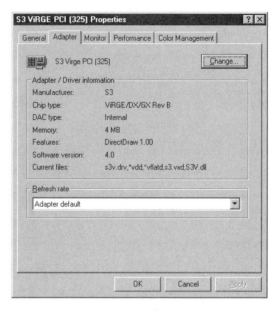

8. If there is no configuration file available for your model of monitor, find out from the manufacturer if there is another monitor with specifications similar enough to yours that you can use its configuration file. (If there is, and it's the same model Windows shows as the installed monitor, then the correct configuration file is already installed.) If you can't find someone to answer the question directly, you should be able to ferret out the answer yourself with some research at vendors' Web sites, looking for a monitor with specifications that match the monitor you have.

9. Once you know which configuration file to use and have it in hand, you can install it. Right-click on the desktop to open the Display Properties dialog box. Choose the Settings tab, then the Advanced button to open the display adaptor's dialog box. Next choose the Monitor tab and then the Change button to open the Update Device Driver Wizard. (For Windows 2000, choose the Properties button on the Monitor tab, then the Driver tab, and finally the Update Driver button.) Even though the Wizard's name indicates that it updates a driver, you will actually be updating the configuration file.

10. On the first Wizard screen, choose Next. Then choose Display A List Of All The Drivers In A Specific Location, So That You Can Select The Driver You Want, and choose Next again.

11. If you have an INF file on disk, chose Have Disk, navigate to the file, select it, and follow the rest of the instructions in the Wizard to install the configuration file.

12. If you're using a file that ships with Windows, choose Show All Hardware, select the appropriate manufacturer in the list on the left, then the appropriate model in the list on the right, choose Next, and again, follow the rest of the instructions in the wizard to install the configuration file. ▶

I want larger, easier to read text and graphics

Source of the problem

Elsewhere in this chapter, we explain how to set windows to let you see more on screen at once. But sometimes you may have too much on screen already. Perhaps your forty-something (or even twenty-something, but not 20-20) eyes have started to balk at deciphering fine print. Making everything a little larger would minimize the eyestrain and let you postpone that trip to the optometrist.

What you need to do is simple: make things on the screen bigger.

There are several ways to do that—including buying a bigger (and more expensive) monitor. Here are some of the less expensive options.

How to fix it

1. First decide exactly what you need to change. Do you only need to change the size of text in menus and Windows utilities like Windows Explorer? Do you only need to change the size of text in documents? Or do you need to make everything on the screen bigger across the board? Then pick the solution that matches your needs.

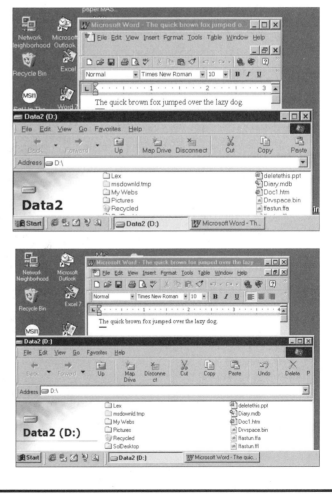

If you want to change text size overall without changing the size of graphic elements

1. Windows offers an option to let you change the size of fonts throughout Windows without changing the size of graphic elements like toolbar buttons or icons on the desktop.

Compare the two screen captures at the beginning of this section to see the difference. The setting affects text in menus, icons descriptions on the desktop, file lists, and even text in documents. Desktop and toolbar icons remain the same size.

2. To change the Windows font size, right click on the desktop and choose Properties to open the Display Properties dialog box.

3. Choose the Settings tab, and then choose the Advanced button to open the Properties dialog box for your graphics card. The dialog box should open to the General tab. If not, choose it. ▶

4. In the Display area near the top of the dialog box, look at the entry for Font Size. Most often, this will read Small Fonts. Open the drop-down list and change it to Large Fonts. (There's also an Other setting that will let you choose other sizes, but Large Fonts increases font size by 25 percent over Small Fonts, which is enough to make a noticeable difference.)

5. Choose OK, Close, and then Yes when Windows asks if you want to restart your computer. (Windows 2000 will simply notify you that you have to restart the computer in order for the change to take effect.) When the computer restarts, Windows will be using the new font size. Work with this for a while and see if it serves your purposes.

If you need to enlarge only the text in programs

1. If you're comfortable with the size of the icons on your desktop and toolbars, as well as the text in title bars, menu bars, and menus, your best solution may lie in the programs you use.

2. Many programs offer a zoom feature that lets you zoom in to magnify text or graphics, or zoom out so you can see more at once. Most people tend to ignore this kind of zoom in word processors, spreadsheets and the like, but the feature can be quite useful. For example, If you work mostly with a word processor, Instead of switching to a lower resolution and leaving your word processor set at 100 percent zoom, you can stay at the higher resolution and set the word processor's zoom to, say, 125 percent. This can also give you better formed characters, which are less tiring for your eyes; you wind up with both larger text and the additional smoothness to the text that comes from the higher resolution.

If this solution didn't solve your problem, go to the next page.

I want larger, easier to read text and graphics

(continued from page 129)

If you want to make everything on the screen bigger

1. Lowering your resolution will make everything bigger.

2. Start by right-clicking on an open area of your desktop, then choosing Properties to open the Display Properties dialog box.

3. In the Display Properties dialog box, choose the Settings tab. ▶

4. Look at the area of the window marked Screen Area. The slider ranges from Less to More. If you want to decrease the resolution for your display, move the slider further to the left, toward Less. The actual resolution for each available step in resolution will show below the slider as you move it.

5. Choose the next lowest resolution available, and then chose OK.

6. You may be prompted to restart Windows before the changes will take effect, or you may see a warning that the screen is about to change, with instructions that you can either accept the change or wait 15 seconds to have it reversed. Follow the instructions on screen, and, if the screen is the way you want it, accept the change. You may then need to adjust the image size or position. (See "The image on my screen is too large, too small, or not centered" on page 134.)

If you want to experiment a bit

1. There's still another way to get larger text and icons while keeping your monitor at a higher resolution. As with setting Windows to Large Fonts or using the zoom feature in a program, this has the advantage of providing smoother text, because Windows uses more dots to create the characters—much like the difference between looking at page from an old dot matrix

Tip

We don't recommend changing resolution for Liquid Crystal Display (LCD) monitors. Unlike cathode ray tubes (CRTs), LCDs have a native resolution that provides one set of red, green, and blue cells for each pixel, or picture element, in the image. Images look best on LCDs when the resolution you're using matches the native resolution of the LCD. However, the other techniques described here work just as well for LCDs as for CRTs.

printer compared to one printed on a laser printer. The disadvantage is that this only works on the elements that Windows controls directly, such as menu text size, scroll bar size, and window titles. Icons such as toolbars in applications won't be affected by the changes you make, and may still be too small to view comfortably.

2. To try this approach, start by right-clicking on an open area of your desktop, then choosing Properties to open the Display Properties dialog box.

3. Choose the Appearance tab, and experiment with changing the size of the different elements. To change them, select an item, such as Menu, in the Item drop-down list box, and then set the size and font size for that item. ▶

4. Windows also comes with a number of predefined choices that you might want to try. You'll find them listed in the drop-down Scheme list. Try some of the choices with names that include the words Large or Extra Large. The two examples below show the difference between the settings for Windows Standard and Windows Standard (Extra Large).

Image size and position change when I switch resolutions

Source of the problem

Most desktop displays rely on an analog signal, which leaves a lot of guesswork for the monitor's electronics. Even though the signal's resolution may be defined clearly, the monitor still has to make all sorts of decisions. For example, what part of the signal contains the first dot of the first line? How far across the screen should the image go before stopping and going back to the left edge for the next line? How high on the screen does the first line go? Most of the time, the monitor will make good guesses about these choices. Other times it may need some help.

The big problem comes when you change resolutions, because all these decisions have to be made all over again. Most monitors have factory presets that are designed to work pretty well with the most common signal formats for the standard resolutions. Many also have a feature that remembers settings for a specific resolution if you make adjustments for that resolution, and will automatically use those settings when you use that same resolution again later. Some don't store custom settings for more than one resolution, which can lead to images that are the wrong size or off center. Some of these problems can be fixed. Others can't. Here's how to fix the ones that are fixable.

How to fix it

1. First check to see if your monitor is storing customized size and position settings. Adjust the Windows desktop so that the size and position is correct, using your monitor's horizontal and vertical size and position controls. These may be dedicated buttons or multi-function buttons on a front panel, or they may be available through an onscreen menu. (For more details on how to adjust the size and position, see "The image on my screen is too large, too small, or not centered" on page 134.)

2. Choose Start, Programs, and then MS-DOS Prompt. (In Windows 2000 choose Start, Programs, Accessories, and then Command Prompt.)

3. If this opens the MS-DOS screen as a window on your desktop, press Alt+Enter to make it full screen, which will force the monitor to display the image at VGA resolution.

4. Run an MS-DOS program that will fill the screen. The MS-DOS–level program EDIT should be in the Windows\Command folder, and it will serve for this purpose. (In Windows 2000, EDIT is in the Winnt\System32 folder.)

5. Adjust the size and position of the image using the monitor's controls.

6. Press Alt+Enter to switch the MS-DOS session from full screen to window mode, and then wait a moment and press Alt+Enter again to switch back to full screen mode. If the position and size are now correct in both modes, they have been stored by the monitor. If not, your monitor might not store the custom settings. However, you might still be able to fix the problem.

If your monitor cannot store position and size settings

1. You may be able to get the monitor to display a given resolution at the proper size by adjusting the refresh rate your system uses for that resolution. If it is the Windows resolution that does not maintain the correct size, you can adjust the refresh rate in the Display Properties window. Right-click on an open area of your desktop, choose Properties from the shortcut menu, and then choose the Settings tab.

2. On the Settings tab, choose the Advanced button.

3. Choose the Adapter tab. ▶

4. In the Refresh Rate drop-down box, choose a different refresh rate—if one is available— and choose OK, and then follow the instructions on screen. (These can vary, and may include a requirement to restart your system.) In Windows 2000, choose the List All Modes button and choose a resolution and refresh rate combination.

5. See if this change causes your Windows screen to be the right size.

6. If this does not work, or if it is the VGA settings that are not correct, check your graphics adapter documentation and see if the card comes with a utility you can use to set the refresh rate for the card at different resolutions. If so, experiment with different refresh rates for the problem resolution. Check your monitor's documentation for the rates the monitor supports as factory settings.

The image on my screen is too large, too small, or not centered

Source of the problem

You paid for you whole monitor; why not use the whole screen?

Many people never adjust their monitors, even to fix the position and size of the image. Yet the process is simple in the extreme, and it can help you get the most from your monitor. In general, there are four controls that almost all monitors have that will let you adjust size and position: vertical size, vertical position, horizontal size, and horizontal position (sometimes called horizontal phase, for reasons best known to engineers). And if you've never used this to adjust your monitor, you don't know what you're missing.

How to fix it

1. Check your monitor documentation to find out where the size and position controls are. Some monitors will have dedicated buttons on a front panel, others will have multi-function buttons, and still others will rely on prompts from an onscreen menu.

Size and position icons

Here are the common icons used to indicate the size and position controls:

⬜	Horizontal position
⬜	Vertical position
↔	Horizontal size
↕	Vertical size

2. Display a full-screen image. The Windows desktop or a maximized Windows application window will do.

If you have a CRT monitor

1. Adjust the horizontal position until the image is roughly centered on the screen.

2. Adjust the horizontal size until you have about a quarter-inch or larger border on the left and right of the image.

---

3. If the image is off-center after resizing, repeat steps 1 and 2 until the image is the right size and centered on the monitor screen.

4. Adjust the vertical position until the image is roughly centered on the screen.

5. Adjust the vertical size until you have a border of a quarter-inch or so at the top and bottom of the image.

6. If the image is off-center after resizing, repeat steps 4 and 5 until the image is the right size and centered on the screen.

7. If the largest size that the vertical and horizontal size and position controls allow still doesn't fill the screen, look for an overscan control, which you'll find in relatively few monitors. If a monitor has this control—usually as a switch that is either on or off—it will adjust vertical and horizontal size at the same time.

If you cannot make the image large enough on the CRT

1. If the monitor controls don't let you make the image large enough, try setting Windows for a slower refresh rate at the same resolution. Right-click on an open area of your Desktop, and choose Properties from the shortcut menu.

2. Choose the Settings tab, and then choose the Advanced button.

3. Choose the Adapter tab. ▶

4. In the Refresh Rate drop-down list, choose a different refresh rate, if one is available, and then choose OK and follow the instructions on screen. (These will vary, and may include a requirement to restart your system.) In Windows 2000, choose the List All Modes button and choose a resolution and refresh rate combination.

5. Use the vertical and horizontal size and position controls as described to see if this change lets you adjust the image to fill the screen.

6. If necessary, repeat steps 1 through 5 with different refresh rates, if others are available.

```
S3 ViRGE PCI (325) Properties                          ? X

 General  Adapter  Monitor  Performance  Color Management

        S3 Virge PCI (325)                    [ Change... ]

 ┌ Adapter / Driver information ──────────────────────────┐
 │  Manufacturer:       S3                                 │
 │  Chip type:          ViRGE/DX/GX Rev B                  │
 │  DAC type:           Internal                           │
 │  Memory:             4 MB                               │
 │  Features:           DirectDraw 1.00                    │
 │  Software version:   4.0                                │
 │  Current files:      s3v.drv,*vdd,*vflatd,s3.vxd,S3V.dll│
 └────────────────────────────────────────────────────────┘

 ┌ Refresh rate ──────────────────────────────────────────┐
 │  Adapter default                                    ▼   │
 └────────────────────────────────────────────────────────┘

                        OK        Cancel       Apply
```

> *If this solution didn't solve your problem, go to the next page.*

The image on my screen is too large, too small, or not centered

(continued from page 135)

7. If you still can't make the image large enough, check your graphics adapter documentation to see if the card comes with a utility to set the refresh rate for the card at different resolutions. If so, experiment with different refresh rates for the resolution you want to use.

8. If nothing else works, check your graphics adapter documentation to see if the card comes with a utility to adjust image size and resolution. If it does, try using the utility to adjust the image.

If you have an LCD monitor

1. First, since the monitor bezel (the part of the case that wraps around the front of the screen) may not come up to edge of the LCD panel, you need to get a sense of where the LCD panel ends. Use the horizontal position controls to experiment with moving the image left and right until you're sure you can tell when the edge of the image has reached or gone past the edge of the LCD panel.

2. Use the horizontal position control to move the image to the left so that the left edge of the image just disappears.

3. Move the image back to the right one step at a time until the edge reappears, and then one more step so you have a black line at the edge of the image.

4. Move the image back to the left one step.

5. If the right edge of the image falls short of the right edge of the screen, use the horizontal size control to expand the image to the right until the right edge disappears off the screen.

Tip

As a rule of thumb, you don't want to extend the image out to the very limits of a cathode ray tube (CRT) monitor's bezel (the part of the case that extends over the front edge of the CRT). On many monitors, you'll wind up with a distorted image along the edges. A few monitors offer high quality images edge-to-edge, but if you take advantage of this feature and then view the screen from even a slight angle, one of the edges will disappear under the bezel. A black border of about a quarter-inch all around is about right for most CRT monitors.

On a liquid crystal display (LCD) monitor you can and should extend the image to the very edges of the panel, assuming the monitor offers the appropriate controls. (A digital LCD monitor will not offer these controls, because it doesn't need them.)

6. Shrink the image until the right edge reappears, then shrink it one more step to get a black edge to the right of the image, and confirm that you're really seeing the edge of the image.

7. Expand the image one step. The screen should now be filled edge to edge.

8. Check this by using the horizontal position control. Move it one step to the left, and the left edge of the image should disappear at the same time that a black edge appears at the right side. One step to the right should fill the whole screen again; then one more step to the right should make the right edge disappear, with a black edge showing up along the left side. One step back to the left should fill the whole screen. If you don't get this result, repeat the steps in this section.

9. It's unlikely that an LCD monitor will have any problems with vertical size or position. In fact, LCD monitors often lack a control for vertical size. Should you see a problem, however, you can use the same techniques described here for the horizontal adjustments to adjust the vertical size, position, or both.

Tip

If the image appears to fold over along one edge of your CRT monitor, or you see multiple images on the screen, then the refresh rate is probably wrong. The other likely cause is that the monitor does not support the current resolution.

Try before you buy

There is a great deal of variation in image quality between monitors of the same brand and model, to the point where two monitors coming off the assembly line, one right after the other, can have noticeable differences in image quality. In spite of mass production, monitors are individually hand-tuned at the factory. These settings can require delicate adjustments that are easily ruined by rough handling during shipping.

As a result, we recommend that, if at all possible, you preview the specific monitor you want to buy before you buy it. Not all stores will want to open a new box before you pay for it, but it will probably be easier to talk a sales representative into letting you check the monitor beforehand than to get the store to take back a working monitor after you've paid for it just because you don't like the geometry. It can also save you a trip back to the store. Bring a test image file with you, or use Windows paint. Create a black background with the same number of pixels as the screen resolution, and then, using a 1-pixel-wide line, draw the largest possible box, so you can see what the image quality is like at the edges of the screen. To test the geometry, add circles in different areas of the screen and create a grid.

Circles on my screen aren't round, or lines are bent

Source of the problem

It's remarkable how accurate human perception can be. Ask someone to make a mark halfway down a sheet of paper, then fold it in half to find out where the midpoint really is. You may be amazed to see how close people come to the precise center without using a ruler or compass or anything other than their eyes. (On the other hand, maybe it isn't so remarkable; if people couldn't do that, they probably would have serious problems figuring out where to move their hands to grab something they want to pick up.)

This talent is also a bit of a curse. Most people also quickly notice when something is a bit off on their computer screen's images. If you are fortunate enough to have an LCD monitor, the lines and shapes on the screen should, as a rule, have perfect geometry (with one exception: see the tip on the next page). If you have a traditional CRT monitor, however, there are likely to be some geometry problems with the image on the screen. The larger the screen—especially with the new flat CRT picture tubes—the more likely the image will be deformed on at least some portion of the screen.

Depending on the controls your monitor has, you may be able to make some adjustments that can improve the shape of the images. (See the sidebar on page 140 for a listing of monitor control symbols.)

How to fix it

1. The first step is to identify what kind of image geometry problems you need to deal with. Display an image that puts a grid pattern on the entire screen. Ideally, the pattern should be lines on a black background, with the lines 1-pixel wide. DisplayMate Technologies has a good pattern available for download in a range of resolutions at their Web site—check it out at *www.displaymate.com/patterns.html#mastertp*. If you prefer, you can create your own equivalent image in any reasonably capable graphics program. (See the figure on the facing page.)

2. Check to make sure that the lines are straight at the sides, top, and bottom of the image. Vertical lines should be vertical, not slanted to one side or the other. They should be parallel, not bending toward or away from each other near the top or bottom of the screen. The squares of the grid should be square, and the same size in all regions of the screen. If there are circles in the pattern, make sure that they are round, rather than squashed either vertically or horizontally.

3. If you see any defects, you may be able to correct them—or at least minimize them—depending on the controls your monitor offers. Proceed through the following sections, and skip any that don't apply either because the image doesn't show the problem, or the monitor doesn't have the controls mentioned in that section.

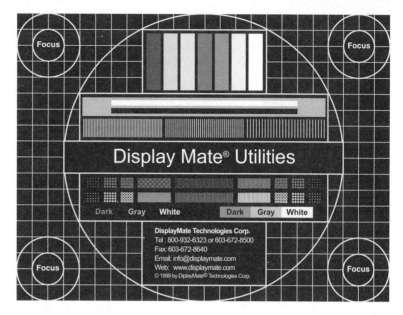

If the lines on the sides are curved

1. Check your monitor's documentation to see if there is a pincushion control. Some monitors will have a dedicated button on the front panel, but usually the control will be available via an onscreen menu.

2. Use the pincushion control to make the lines at the edge of the screen as straight as possible. It may help to sight along the line from above the monitor to avoid being distracted by the curvature of the face of the monitor.

3. If one side remains curved when the other side is straight, check for a control named *pin-balance* or something similar. This will straighten one side—typically the left—without changing the other side.

If the vertical lines are not vertical

1. If the whole image is rotated such that vertical lines aren't vertical and horizontal lines are not horizontal, check your monitor for a rotation control that rotates the entire image.

2. Rotate the image clockwise or counter-clockwise until the horizontal lines are horizontal.

3. If the horizontal lines are horizontal but the vertical lines are not, check your monitor for a parallelogram control. This control adjusts the angle of the vertical lines without changing the angle of the horizontal lines.

4. Adjust the parallelogram control until the vertical lines are vertical.

> *If this solution didn't solve your problem, go to the next page.*

Circles on my screen aren't round or lines are bent

(continued from page 139)

If the lines are not parallel

1. Check your monitor for a trapezoidal control. This control adjusts the width of the top and bottom edges of the image.

2. Adjust the width of the top and bottom edges until they match.

If the squares are not the same size, or circles are squashed

1. Check your monitor for a vertical linearity control. This adjusts the spacing between the horizontal lines, typically for the top portion of the screen.

2. Adjust the vertical linearity so that all the squares in the grid are the same size.

If the geometry is still not correct

1. If your monitor does not have the controls necessary to correct these geometry flaws, or if you are not able to correct them completely even if the controls are present, you might be able to get an improved image by having a repair professional tune the monitor. If this doesn't help, your only choices are to live with the image as is or replace the monitor.

Monitor control symbols

Here are some symbols used to mark different monitor geometry adjustments. Your monitor might use somewhat different icons.

)X(	Pincushion
[X(	Pin-balance
)X(	Rotation
▱	Parallelogram
△	Trapezoid
▤	Vertical linearity

Tip

LCD displays used in notebooks and LCD desktop monitors are just about perfect. Every pixel (short for *picture element*, the smallest element of a picture) created in the graphics adapter corresponds to a single pixel on the screen (actually a single set of red, green, and blue cells), so there is no way for circles to get out of round—at least when you're using the display at its native resolution (defined as the resolution that matches the cells in LCD, pixel for pixel). And in most cases, even when you scale the image up or down to fit the screen's resolution, you still get round circles, because the different resolutions use the same aspect ratio (the ratio of width to height); 1024 by 768, 800 by 600, and 640 by 480 all have a ratio of 4:3 between the horizontal and vertical resolutions.

But then there's the SXGA resolution of 1280 by 1024. Instead of being 4:3, it has a 5:4 aspect ratio. This is fine when you display SXGA images, but if you try to scale one of the other standard resolutions onto an SXGA resolution LCD panel, circles will end up squished. There is nothing to be done about this. You should just be aware of it.

Some desktop LCD monitors have controls that let you adjust the image size, placement, and other settings. Others are like notebook displays, however, and only have a single brightness control. The reason is that these displays rely on a digital interface, as opposed to the analog interface used by most LCD and CRT desktop monitors. You don't get the extra controls because you don't need them. The digital signal lets the display adjust the image by itself.

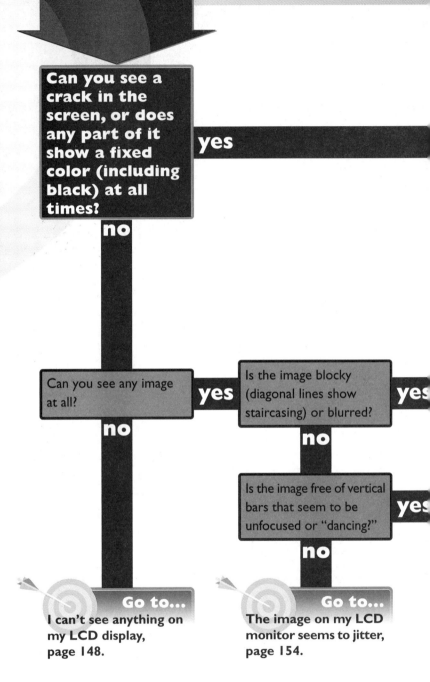

Can you see a crack in the screen, or does any part of it show a fixed color (including black) at all times?

yes

no

Can you see any image at all?

yes

Is the image blocky (diagonal lines show staircasing) or blurred?

yes

no

no

Is the image free of vertical bars that seem to be unfocused or "dancing?"

yes

no

Go to...
I can't see anything on my LCD display, page 148.

Go to...
The image on my LCD monitor seems to jitter, page 154.

Display: LCD

Is there a large block of black or a visibly cracked screen?

yes

Go to...
My LCD screen has black areas, black lines, or cracks, page 144.

no

Quick fix
Your display may have stuck pixels. These can be dark defects that are always black, or bright defects that show as a tiny colored dot. Stuck pixels are fairly common on LCD panels and can't be repaired. Most manufacturers have a policy for how many stuck pixels they consider acceptable. This is not a fixed number, since it depends on where the stuck pixels are and how close together they are. For example, stuck pixels in the center of the screen tend to be more objectionable than stuck pixels near the edges, so a manufacturer's policy may allow few or no stuck pixels near the center of the screen, but several on the outside inch or so. If you find these defects to be objectionable in a new display, complain to the store or manufacturer. Some will make an effort to satisfy you, even though their policies permit the number of defects you see.

Go to...
The image on my LCD looks blocky or blurred, page 146.

Is the problem a visible horizontal line across the screen?

yes

Go to...
There's a horizontal line on my LCD panel, page 152.

no

Go to...
This is probably not an LCD-specific issue. See the other Display chapters.

If your solution isn't here
Check these related chapters:
Computer startup: blank screen, page 68
Display: color and brightness, page 110
Display: quality flaws, page 156
Or see the general troubleshooting tips on page xv.

My LCD screen has black areas, black lines, or cracks

Source of the problem

You can never be too thin or too beautiful seems to be the right motto for the liquid crystal display (LCD). LCD displays (that's liquid crystal display displays, alas alas, but don't blame us; that's what they're called) have been a mainstay of portable computers since the first laptops. They're now showing up on more and more desktops in the form of monitors.

These slender, lightweight wonders not only give you much of your desktop back (the real thing, not the Microsoft Windows desktop), but their images are inherently crisper and cleaner than an image on a standard cathode ray tube (CRT) monitor, which means you don't need as large a screen for the same level of readability.

Despite these advantages, however, LCDs also have drawbacks. They may weigh much less than a standard CRT monitor of similar size, but they are also much more fragile. The LCD panels themselves are sandwiches of liquid crystal material between impossibly thin layers of glass and plastic, which can be damaged relatively easily. Also, there are many more electrical connections in an LCD panel than there are in a CRT, which in turn makes them more vulnerable to damage (not that we would recommend dropping either kind of monitor on the floor). If you manage to harm your LCD panel—whether it's part of your notebook or part of a desktop monitor—we can't recommend that you try to repair it on your own, but we have some suggestions that can help you decide whether it's worth repairing.

How to fix it

If the panel has a visible crack in it

1. A visible crack means you broke something in the panel itself—probably one or more of those thin layers of glass and plastic. And that's only part of the bad news. There is no way to repair a cracked panel; you can only replace it, at a cost that's typically half the original price of the notebook or more. But…read on.

> **Tip**
>
> Most manufacturers exclude a broken LCD panel from their warranty coverage, particularly for laptops, which have a relatively high risk of getting dropped. However, some manufacturers offer a warranty for the LCD at an extra cost.
>
> These warranties often work like contact lens insurance, typically allowing some maximum number of replacements in a year. Given that replacing an LCD can be expensive, an LCD warranty is well worth considering if your notebook manufacturer offers one, particularly if you tend to treat your notebook somewhat roughly.

2. Even if the notebook or monitor is still under warranty, a cracked LCD is probably not covered, since it's a result of abuse rather than defects in materials or workmanship. But don't simply assume it's not covered. Check the warranty information you got with the notebook or monitor, or check with the manufacturer.

3. If you're stuck with paying the bill yourself, the conventional wisdom is that it's probably not worth replacing an LCD panel. If you've had the notebook or monitor for more than a year, you may be able to find a closely equivalent product for about the same amount it would cost to replace the LCD panel in the old one. However, the conventional wisdom assumes you're going to an authorized repair center or the equivalent. There's another way.

4. If you go to your favorite search engine on the Web and search for variations on *LCD replace*, you'll find vendors who can replace LCD panels with surplus or used panels. These are much less expensive than the same panels would cost new. Some of these vendors also sell replacement kits, so you can do the work yourself. *However, we can't recommend trying this yourself. It's too easy to damage a notebook or LCD monitor if you try to take it apart.*

If you see a rectangular black area or black lines

1. A rectangular black area or black vertical or horizontal lines usually mean that your display has a loose connection to the panel. We do not recommend that you try to fix this yourself! Notebook computers and desktop LCD monitors are not designed for their owners to take apart. The pieces are tightly packed inside, and you're likely to do more harm than good by trying this on your own. ▶

2. If the warranty period is still valid, you can probably get this fixed under the warranty. This kind of problem is often covered, because a loose connection can come under the category of a defect in material or workmanship.

3. If the warranty has expired, take the monitor or notebook to a reputable repair service, and have them look first for a loose connection. The fix may be as simple as reseating a connector that has come loose, but it leave it to the professionals to do the job.

Tip

If the black area you see is a black frame around the outside of the image there's probably nothing wrong with your LCD display. Some LCDs deal with low resolutions by using only as much of the screen as they need to display the image, rather than trying to expand it to fill the screen.

The image on my LCD looks blocky or blurred

Source of the problem

Artists and physicists (now there's an odd pairing) know that if you start with the right colors you can use just three *primary colors* to create every other color you need. (If you're not an artist or physicist, think back to using fingerpaints in kindergarten. Mix blue and yellow together, and you get green.) Virtually all monitors (we know of only one exception) use red, green, and blue dots (or the equivalent of dots) as their primary colors and mix them by varying the intensity of each color.

You've probably heard the term *pixel*, which is short for picture element, and is defined as the smallest part of an image. When you talk about using a particular monitor resolution, like 640 by 480 or 800 by 600, the numbers refer to the number of pixels. Liquid crystal display (LCD) panels—unlike cathode ray tubes (CRTs)—are designed to display one pixel for each set of red, green, and blue LCD cells. This means that a panel has a native resolution—namely, the resolution that provides one and only one pixel in the image for each set of cells in the display.

When you try to display an image at something other than the native resolution, you can have problems. The panel has to scale the image to make it larger or smaller, so it will fit on the screen. If the image is a solid area of color, making it larger or smaller is easy. But if the image contains fine lines—such as text characters—decisions about which cells to use for which pixels get much more complicated. In fact, whether you shrink or expand the image, you'll almost certainly wind up with a lower quality image than if you use the LCD's native resolution.

Tip

You can't set your video card to a higher resolution than an LCD's native resolution without losing some information. And whether you shrink the image or expand it, the result will always lose some image quality, though the loss is greater when shrinking the image than when expanding it.

Some LCD displays deal with this issue by not trying. Instead of trying to shrink an image, they simply won't work with anything higher than their native resolution (see "I can't see anything on my LCD display" on page 148), or they won't show the image on screen all at once, forcing you to scroll left, right, up, and down to see the whole image.

Similarly, instead of trying to expand an image that uses a lower resolution than the native resolution, some LCD displays use only as many LCD cells as the image needs. The image is centered in the screen, with a black frame of unused cells around it.

How to fix it

1. Start by determining your panel's native resolution. You should be able to find this information in the display's documentation, in a Specifications section. Be sure to look for the *native* or *physical* resolution, not the *maximum* resolution.

2. Choose Start, Settings, Control Panel, and then Display to open the Display Properties window. Alternatively, you can right-click on any empty part of your Windows desktop and then choose Properties from the short-cut menu.

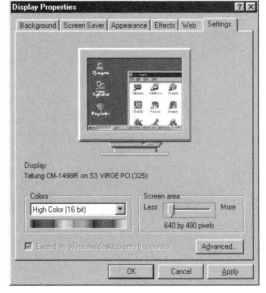

3. Choose the Settings tab.

4. In the Screen Area section of the window, move the slider left or right until it matches the panel's native resolution. ▶

5. Choose OK.

6. You'll see a dialog box saying that Windows is about to resize your desktop. It will also tell you that if Windows does not reappear correctly, you only need to wait 15 seconds for your original settings to be restored. Choose OK.

7. Windows will resize the desktop and show you a dialog box that asks if you want to keep the new setting. You have 15 seconds to choose the Yes button before Windows returns to the original settings.

Tip

You might find it useful to try each of the resolutions the LCD display supports, so you can see if any of the other resolutions will be acceptable for particular circumstances or particular programs. A resolution that's too blocky for word processing, for example, may be acceptable for working on a presentation.

I can't see anything on my LCD display

Source of the problem

Early monochrome LCD displays were so hard to read that the standing joke was, *Is it on yet?* Most of today's displays can give you a bright, crisp, colorful image—at least they can when they're working properly. When they're not working properly, you may see nothing but an empty, dark screen. Sometimes the fix when that happens is as easy as making sure that the controls are adjusted correctly and that the display is receiving a signal that it knows how to display. Other times, the panel may need professional attention. Either way, here are some steps to take when your LCD display leaves you wondering if it's on yet.

How to fix it

Check the controls

1. Check your display's brightness control, contrast control, or both if it has both. You may find, particularly on a notebook, that you've accidentally turned these controls down. Turn the brightness all the way up, and then slowly move the contrast control through its full range of adjustment. If you don't see an image after doing this, leave both the brightness and contrast controls near the middle of their range.

2. If the display is in a notebook computer, make sure you have the computer set to use the LCD display. Most notebooks have an external graphics port for a desktop monitor or a projector. In most cases, you can press a combination of keys to switch the image from the built-in LCD, to the external display, to using both at the same time. Consult your notebook's manual for the keystroke for your system.

3. If your display is part of a desktop monitor and it has more than one signal input, make sure that you have it set to display the image from the input that you have connected.

> **Tip**
>
> For many notebooks, the keystroke for rotating from LCD display to external monitor to both is obvious from looking at the keyboard. Often, you only need hold down the function key, typically labeled *Fn*, and then press another key that has a reasonably intuitive screen icon on it.
>
> If the keystroke for your notebook isn't obvious, and you can't find it in the notebook's manual, check *www.infocus.com/service/tech_library/laptop_chart.asp*. This site offers a chart that lists the right keystrokes for hundreds of popular laptops.

Check the resolution

1. Not being able to see anything on the display is a common problem when first installing an LCD monitor. If your previous monitor used a higher resolution than the LCD display can manage, the LCD monitor won't be able to show you anything at all. This is not the only time you may run into this problem, however. It is possible (although difficult) to set Windows to a higher resolution than the LCD monitor can handle even with the monitor attached. This problem doesn't usually show up with notebooks because the graphics driver for most, if not all, notebooks won't let you set the resolution higher than the built-in LCD can handle.

2. The first step in fixing the problem is to lower the resolution to VGA, which almost all displays will handle. You'll need to be able to see what you're doing, however, which means you'll have to connect another display to your computer and get it working before you can complete these next steps.

3. Turn off your computer, disconnect the LCD monitor, connect the temporary replacement monitor, and then turn your computer and monitor back on.

4. When Windows finishes booting up, you will hopefully be able to see an image on screen. If you're using a CRT-based monitor and the picture is scrambled, you probably have the resolution set higher than the CRT monitor can handle and will need to find another monitor.

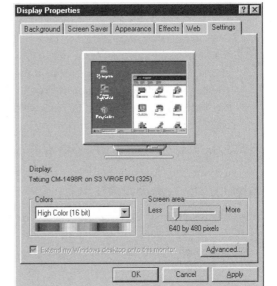

5. Assuming you can see the image, choose Start, Settings, Control Panel, and then Display. (Alternatively, you can right-click on any empty part of your Windows desktop to open a menu, and then choose Properties.)

6. Choose the Settings tab.

7. In the Screen Area section, move the Screen Area slider all the way to the left, to the 640 by 480 pixels setting. ▶

8. Choose OK.

9. You'll see a dialog box saying that Windows is about to resize your desktop. It will also tell you that if Windows does not reappear correctly, you only need wait 15 seconds for your original settings to be restored. Choose OK.

10. Windows will resize the desktop and show you a dialog box that asks if you want to keep the new setting. You have 15 seconds to choose the Yes button before Windows returns to the original settings. Choose Yes, and then shut down Windows.

> **If this solution didn't solve your problem, go to the next page.**

I can't see anything on my LCD display

(continued from page 150)

11. Turn off your computer and monitor.

12. Disconnect the monitor you just used, reconnect your LCD display, and see if the screen now shows an image.

13. If this did not solve the problem, switch back to the second monitor and adjust the refresh rate for the graphics adapter. Again, after Windows boots, choose Start, Settings, Control Panel, and then Display.

14. On the Settings tab, choose the Advanced button, then in the adapter card's Properties dialog box, choose the Adapter tab. ▶

15. Set the refresh rate to 60 Hz if it's available in the drop-down list. If 60 Hz is not a choice, choose the lowest setting available. If the only choices are Default and Optimal, try the Optimal setting. In Windows 2000, choose the Adapter tab and then choose the List All Modes button. In the List All Modes dialog box, set the refresh rate to 60 Hz if it's available.

16. Switch back to your LCD display and see if an image is visible on the screen.

Checking the backlight

1. If you still can't see an image, shine a bright light on the LCD panel and look for an image. If you can see one, however faint, the panel's backlight may have failed. This can be an inexpensive repair—at least when compared with the cost of a new LCD panel—but it must be done professionally.

2. Be aware that some panels are not designed to have the backlight repaired or replaced. In those cases, you'll have to buy an entire display panel, which can be so expensive that, if you've had the monitor for more than a year, a new one may cost only a little more than repairing the old one. However, if you search the web for variations on *LCD replace*, you can find vendors who can replace LCD panels with surplus or used panels that are much less expensive. Some of these vendors also sell replacement kits, so you can do the work yourself. However, we *strongly* recommend against trying this yourself.

There's a horizontal line on my LCD panel

Source of the problem

WARNING: If you *don't* see a thin, horizontal line on your LCD display, *do not* read this section. It may well be there, but be so subtle that you haven't noticed it. If so, you don't want to know about it, because once we've drawn your attention to it, you may not be able to ignore it anymore.

You have been warned. Proceed at your own risk.

A horizontal line is most often the natural consequence of the LCD technology used to create the panel. There are, in fact, different types of LCD display panels, each of which uses a slightly different technology, and each of which has its own characteristics. Some of these features enhance the image quality—letting you see the image when standing off to the side, for example. Other characteristics detract from the image quality, at least for some people. A faint horizontal line across the middle of the image is one of those characteristics that falls into the second category.

How to fix it

1. Actually, fixing it may not be an option. If the line is a faint line exactly in the middle of the display, check your display specifications to see if it is a *dual-scan* design. This technology divides the display into two equal regions—top and bottom—as part of a technique that increases the contrast and brightness. How visible the seam is depends on the particular design, the brightness and contrast settings on the LCD, and your individual sensitivity to the line. Some people don't notice the seam between these two regions. Others see it clearly. In any case, it's an inherent part of the technology. Not only does the LCD not need repair, but the only repair option is to get a different kind of LCD display.

> **Tip**
>
> If there's a solid black line anywhere across the screen, you may have a loose connection or a broken component in the panel. Briefly, the typical notebook LCD panel requires a large number of connections. Should any of these wires become loose, part of the display may not work properly. We do not recommend that you try to fix this type of problem yourself, since it's very easy to damage your display or damage the case if you take the case apart. It's also difficult to put everything back together again. For more details, see the section "If you see a rectangular black area or black lines," on page 145.

The image on my LCD monitor seems to jitter

Source of the problem

A place for everything, and everything in its place. That's good advice for a toddler's toys (even if toddlers tend to ignore it) and even better advice for individual picture elements, or *pixels*, on a screen. A typical CRT-based display is a bit casual about exactly where it puts each pixel for an image. But it doesn't matter much, both because the edges of each pixel aren't all that sharp, and because the pixels can move back and forth in a continuous, rather than jerky, motion. That, in turn means you won't notice if a dot moves a fraction of an inch left or right.

LCDs are much more precise, which is both a Good Thing and a Bad Thing. It's a Good Thing, because it makes LCD images inherently sharper. Each pixel corresponds to a specific set of red, green, and blue LCD cells. Each cell has a sharp edge, which makes LCDs sharper than CRTs and makes the same size text easier to read from an LCD than a CRT. It's a Bad Thing because if the pixel position shifts, it shifts suddenly and by a whole set of cells at a time.

This can be a problem, because when an LCD monitor gets an analog signal, it has to decide which cell is supposed to display a specific pixel. If it can't make up its mind, the pixel will jump back and forth between adjacent sets of cells, creating an annoying jitter in the display. This effect is most obvious in large areas with patterns of fine lines or *dithered* gray (which is a gray created from a mix of black and white sets of cells, rather than from sets of cells that are all the same color gray). This effect can not occur on LCD panels in notebooks or in desktop monitors with digital interfaces. The good news is that analog LCD monitors have built-in controls to help you minimize or eliminate the problem.

How to fix it

1. Display an image on your screen that has large areas of dithered gray or finely detailed patterns.

2. You can download an appropriate test image from the DisplayMate Web site at *www.displaymate.com/ patterns.html#fine.* ▶

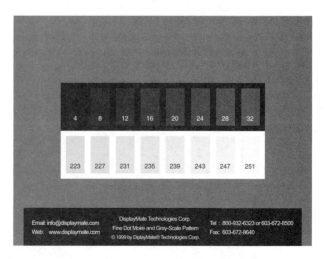

3. The image is available at different resolutions. If one's available at the resolution you use, choose it. If you use a higher resolution than any of the choices on the Web site, pick the highest resolution test image available.

If you need to create your own test image

1. If you need to create your own test image, you can use almost any program that includes a graphics feature that will let you cover all or most of the screen with a pattern. We produced the image on this page, for example, using Microsoft Word's drawing tools. ▶

2. The details for creating the image will depend on the program you use. In general, however, you'll want to create a rectangle that fills most of the screen, and then look for a Fill tool (which usually looks like a paint bucket pouring out a stream of paint) to fill the rectangle.

3. Also look for a way to define the filled area as a pattern rather than a solid color or black. You may need to experiment with different fills to find one that best brings out the jitter.

Adjusting your monitor

1. Start by adjusting the coarse timing for the panel, which should be an available setting in the onscreen display (OSD). Typical names for this feature are *Clock* and *Tuning*, although there are other possibilities. The setting will often be on a sub-menu, which may have a name like *LCD Control*. Consult your display's documentation for the name and how to adjust it.

2. Increase or decrease the setting until you have minimized the number of vertical bars you see in the image.

3. Adjust the fine timing for the panel. Typical names for this adjustment are *Phase* and *Fine Tuning*, although here again there are other possibilities. Once again, consult your display's documentation for the name and how to adjust it.

4. Increase or decrease the setting to minimize the jitter.

5. With a little luck, you'll be able to get rid of the jitter entirely. If you can't, however, you may wind up with only a little jitter in one or two vertical bars. If that happens, you may be able to adjust the position of those bars using the same controls. In general, the jitter will be least distracting if the bars are at the extreme right edge of the display.

6. Keep in mind too that the image you're using to adjust the monitor is designed to make the jitter stand out. When you close the image and return to the programs you normally use, the jitter may not be visible.

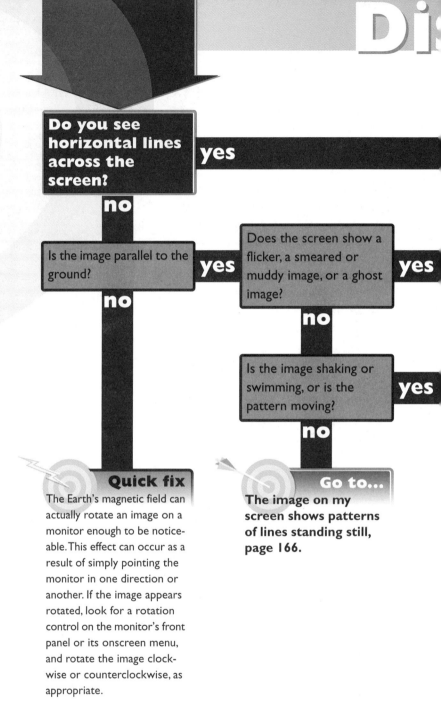

Do you see horizontal lines across the screen?

yes

no

Is the image parallel to the ground?

yes

Does the screen show a flicker, a smeared or muddy image, or a ghost image?

yes

no

no

Is the image shaking or swimming, or is the pattern moving?

yes

no

Quick fix

The Earth's magnetic field can actually rotate an image on a monitor enough to be noticeable. This effect can occur as a result of simply pointing the monitor in one direction or another. If the image appears rotated, look for a rotation control on the monitor's front panel or its onscreen menu, and rotate the image clockwise or counterclockwise, as appropriate.

Go to...

The image on my screen shows patterns of lines standing still, page 166.

Go to...
The image on my screen is flickering, smeared, muddy, or ghosting, page 158.

Go to...
The image on my screen is shaking or shows moving lines, page 164.

Quick fix

If your monitor uses a Trinitron or similar picture tube, you may see a faint horizontal shadow line on smaller models, or two lines on larger models. This is normal; one or two tiny wires inside the tube hold the aperture grill at the right curvature and block the electron beam slightly, causing the faint shadow.

If you have a dual scan passive matrix LCD display, you may notice a faint horizontal seam in the middle of the panel. This is also normal; the panel is divided into top and bottom halves that are driven separately so that the image can be brighter and respond more rapidly.

If your solution isn't here

Check these related chapters:
Computer startup: blank screen, page 68

Display: color and brightness, page 110

Display: flawed images, page 122
Or see the general troubleshooting tips on page xv.

The image on my screen is flickering, smeared, muddy, or ghosting

Source of the problem

Your computer's monitor is in many ways the most critical component of the entire system. It's the part you look at—for hours at a time in many cases—and if it's not performing up to par, you may suffer eyestrain and fatigue. Sometimes the problems are subtle—the letters aren't quite as crisp as they might be. In other cases, the problems can be dramatic, from multiple images to an entirely scrambled image.

These problems cover lots of territory. They can be caused by mismatched monitors and graphics adapters. They can be due to limitations inherent in the actual devices. Some can be corrected by a simple adjustment, and others can be improved only by replacing the monitor completely. So keep your fingers crossed, and dive right in.

How to fix it

If your monitor appears to be flickering

1. There are two very different effects that are both usually described as flicker. With one kind of flicker, the effect is vaguely similar to looking through a rotating fan, with the screen essentially going blank for an instant each time a fan blade passes between your eyes and the screen.

2. The second kind of flicker is perhaps best described as the entire screen jiggling up and down. What's actually happening is that the monitor is drawing each screen in two passes, painting every other line the first time through, then filling in the missing lines the second time through—essentially interlacing two images. This kind of flicker is easiest to see on a screen with thin black text characters on white. If you have a sense that there may be some flicker, look closely at the text. If you see this kind of flickering, it means your monitor is operating in *interlaced mode*.

> **Tip**
> There are no hard and fast rules about settings for getting rid of flicker. Some people are more sensitive to it than others, so two people can be staring at the same screen, and one will see flicker while the other won't. However, it's worth knowing that large monitors are more prone to the problem, because peripheral vision is more sensitive to it and you see more of a large monitor with your peripheral vision than you see of a small monitor. If you think your screen might be flickering, but you're not sure if it's just your imagination, look slightly to the side of the monitor to give your peripheral vision its best look.

3. If you can't decide which kind of flicker you're dealing with, assume it's the first, since that's by far the most common kind of flicker.

If you see the kind of flicker that looks like the screen is repeatedly going blank for an instant

1. Right-click on an open area on your desktop.

2. Choose the Properties option on the shortcut menu.

3. In the Display Properties window, choose the Settings tab.

4. Choose the Advanced button.

5. Choose the Adapter tab. ▶

6. Open the Refresh Rate drop-down list, and choose Optimal.

7. Choose OK, and then choose OK again to close the Display Properties window.

8. Restart your computer if prompted to do so. If the problem is not resolved, continue to the next step.

9. Repeat steps 1 through 5 to return to the graphics adapter Properties dialog box. (Right-click on your desktop, choose Properties, the Settings tab, and then the Advanced button.)

10. Open the Refresh Rate drop-down list and choose the fastest refresh rate offered.

11. Choose OK twice and restart the computer if prompted. If this does not resolve the problem, you may be dealing with the other kind of flicker, and you should continue to the next step.

If you see the kind of flicker that looks like the image jiggles up and down

1. If your monitor is displaying the image in interlaced mode, you should be able to reduce flicker significantly by choosing a noninterlaced mode, which means switching to a lower resolution. To reduce the resolution, start by opening the Display Properties dialog box. (Right-click on your desktop, choose Properties, and then choose the Settings tab, as shown in the graphic on the following page.)

If this solution didn't solve your problem, go to the next page.

The image on my screen is flickering, smeared, muddy, or ghosting

(continued from page 159)

2. Click on the slider in the Screen Area section of the window, and slide it one position to the left. The selected resolution will show below the slider.

3. Choose OK, and restart the computer if prompted. If this does not seem to fix the problem, follow (or repeat) the steps under the previous section, "If you see the kind of flicker that looks like the screen is repeatedly going blank for an instant," on page 154.

If the display looks muddy

1. Start by checking on the cause of the problem. Create a test pattern by opening Microsoft Notepad. Make the window about one-quarter the size of the whole screen.

2. Turn on Caps Lock.

3. Hold down the *M* key until the entire window is filled with rows of capital *M* letters. You may want to save the file at this point in case you want to use it again in the future, although it's easy enough to recreate as needed. ▶

4. Move this window to the four corners of the display. If the letters look fuzzier in some places than others, the problem is most likely that the electron guns are out of focus for portions of the screen. This isn't something you can easily correct on most monitors. However, relatively few monitors provide focus controls, and you should look to see if that's an option for your monitor. If it is, you can try to improve the focus using the Notepad test image to judge the improvement. If your monitor doesn't offer a focus control, you might consider having it repaired, but you will probably need to replace it to correct the problem.

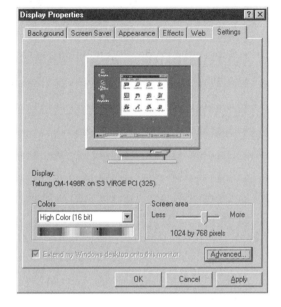

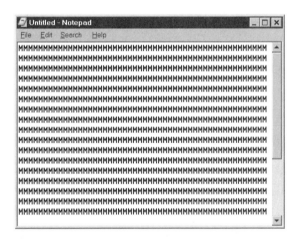

5. If the letters look the same at all locations on the screen but the spaces between the letters are gray instead of white, it could indicate that the monitor has insufficient bandwidth to display images at this resolution and refresh rate—in other words, it's trying to process more information than it can handle. The first step in that case is to lower the refresh rate.

6. Right-click on an open area on your desktop.

7. Choose the Properties option from the shortcut menu.

8. Choose the Settings tab in the Display Properties dialog box.

9. Choose the Advanced button.

10. Choose the Adapter tab.

11. Open the Refresh Rate drop-down list, and choose the slowest refresh rate available. In Microsoft Windows 2000, choose the List All Modes button, choose the slowest refresh rate available in the List All Modes dialog box, and then choose OK.

12. Choose OK twice to close the Display Properties dialog box.

13. Restart your computer if prompted to do so.

14. If this resolves the problem with muddiness, check to see if it's created a problem with flicker. If it has, then repeat steps 6 through 13 and increase the refresh rate by one level at a time until the flicker is eliminated. If you cannot eliminate the gray between the letters, or if you can't eliminate the flicker without making the space between the letters go gray, continue with the next step.

15. Reducing the refresh rate reduces the amount of information sent to the screen in any given amount of time. However, if you didn't find a refresh rate setting that lowered the amount of information to the point that the monitor could handle it adequately, you can try reducing the resolution to reduce the amount of information being sent by even more. To reduce the resolution, start by opening the Display Properties window and choosing the Settings tab. (Right-click on your desktop, choose Properties, and then choose the Settings tab.)

16. Move the slider in the Screen Area section of the window one position to the left. The selected resolution will show below the slider.

17. Choose OK, and restart the computer if prompted. If this does not fix the problem, go back to the beginning of this section and repeat the steps starting with step 1.

18. If none of these steps solves the problem, try using a different cable between the graphics adapter and the monitor to see if the cable is the source of the problem.

19. If you are using a cable extender or switch box for the monitor signal, try connecting the monitor without them and see if that clears up the problem.

If this solution didn't solve your problem, go to the next page.

The image on my screen is flickering, smeared, muddy, or ghosting

(continued from page 161)

The image on the screen is smeared, scrambled, or ghosting

1. If the smearing is so great that the image is hard to read, the resolution is probably set too high. Right-click on an open area on your desktop.

2. Choose the Properties option from the shortcut menu.

3. Choose the Settings tab in the Display Properties window.

4. Click on the slider in the Screen Area section of the window, and slide it one position to the left. The selected resolution will show below the slider.

5. Choose OK, and restart the computer if prompted.

6. If this does not fix the problem, reduce the resolution further. If you reach the VGA resolution setting—640 by 480—the problem is not the resolution. Either the graphics adapter or monitor may have failed. Try the monitor on a different computer that is known to be working correctly, or try a monitor that you know is good on this computer to determine which component may be at fault.

7. If the image is broken into many duplicates, try reducing the refresh rate or lowering the resolution, as described in earlier parts of this section.

Dots enough

Another factor that can cause the image to look muddy is the monitor having insufficiently fine dot pitch (or strip pitch for an aperture grill monitor) to display a given resolution. (Pitch is a measure of distance—between dots or stripes in this case.) It's common for manufacturers to claim support for resolutions that the monitors cannot display well because the phosphor dots are too large.

As a rule of thumb, you don't want a pixel (short for picture element, the smallest element of a picture) to be smaller than 1.3 times the width of the red, green, and blue phosphor dots it would take to make a white pixel. Here are the largest recommended specifications—based on that rule of thumb—for different resolutions and monitor sizes:

Monitor size (viewable diagonal inches)	Maximum recommended *dot pitch* by resolution (in mm)				Maximum recommended *stripe pitch* by resolution (in mm)			
	VGA (640 by 480)	SVGA (800 by 600)	XGA (1024 by 768)	SXGA (1280 by 1024)	VGA (640 by 480)	SVGA (800 by 600)	XGA (1024 by 768)	SXGA (1280 by 1024)
15 inch	0.35 mm	0.28 mm	0.22 mm	0.18 mm	0.31 mm	0.25 mm	0.20 mm	0.16 mm
17 inch	0.44 mm	0.35 mm	0.27 mm	0.22 mm	0.38 mm	0.31 mm	0.24 mm	0.19 mm
19 inch	0.48 mm	0.39 mm	0.30 mm	0.24 mm	0.43 mm	0.43 mm	0.27 mm	0.21 mm

The image on my screen is shaking or shows moving lines

Source of the problem

There are times when you want to have moving images on your monitor—like when you're watching a movie on DVD. But sometimes the picture moves when you don't want it to. The image may sway from side to side or you may see shadowy bands that roll from top to bottom like a television with a vertical hold problem.

Sometimes these problems mean the monitor is poorly designed or on its way to giving up the ghost. But there are also times when these symptoms are caused by external sources, in which case you may be able to either correct or at least minimize the effects.

How to fix it

1. If you have a second monitor (or television) immediately adjacent to the monitor, turn off the second screen and see if the effect stops. If so, you need to move the monitors further apart or erect some sort of barrier—such as a grounded sheet of metal screening—between them. Alternatively, you can replace one or both monitors with models that have their own internal shielding and are designed to be placed next to other monitors.

2. If you have a fluorescent lamp near the monitor, turn it off. If that eliminates the effect, move the monitor and lamp further apart or replace the fluorescent lamp with an incandescent model.

3. Try moving any speakers, motors, or cables away from the monitor to see if that reduces or eliminates the effect.

4. Make sure that the graphics cable is firmly attached at both ends, and that the screws on the connectors are secure, providing a good electrical ground.

5. Make sure that the computer and monitor are plugged into the same electrical circuit.

6. If the problem persists, get a power strip for the computer and monitor that provides shielding from radio-frequency interference that may be traveling along the electrical wiring.

The image on my screen shows patterns of lines standing still

Source of the problem

The human eye and brain love to play connect-the-dots, which often helps you see patterns in partial information—like recognizing someone whose face is partly hidden. Unfortunately, it also helps you see patterns that aren't there. Take a typical hair comb. Look through it. You see a nice, even pattern of lines. Now take a second comb, put it on top of the first, and rotate it slightly so the two combs aren't precisely parallel. You'll see a second pattern of lines emerge. This is an interference pattern caused by the two offset lines of comb teeth producing what's called a *moiré pattern*. ▶

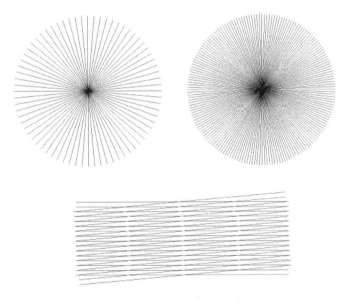

A similar effect can happen with monitors, especially when displaying images that have fine patterns of dots or lines. On monitors that use cathode ray tubes (CRTs), a pattern of pixels (picture elements, the smallest elements of a picture) is projected onto a pattern of phosphor dots, and you can get interference between the two patterns. On a liquid crystal display (LCD) monitor that uses an analog interface, the pattern of pixels generated by the graphics adapter may not be interpreted correctly, so the pixels don't correspond precisely with the pattern of LCD cells that the LCD uses to display them. The good news is that, depending on your monitor, you may be able to reduce or eliminate the moiré pattern.

How to fix it

1. First, confirm that you have a problem worth worrying about. Monitors that rarely show moiré patterns with most application programs will often show moiré with images designed to bring out the problem. For example, if you choose Start, Shut Down, Windows essentially dims the

screen by putting what amounts to a pattern of dots on screen. This pattern might as well have been designed specifically to bring out moiré patterns. It certainly does the job well. If that's the only time you see the moiré pattern, or you have to look carefully to see it at other times, it's probably not worth trying to get rid of it. If the problem shows up clearly in applications and you find it distracting or annoying, it probably is worth the effort.

2. When you adjust your monitor to try to remove the moiré patterns, use an image that helps bring it out. If you don't have a test image designed to do that, close all your programs so you can see the Windows desktop, and choose Start, Shut Down to bring up the Shut Down screen. ▶

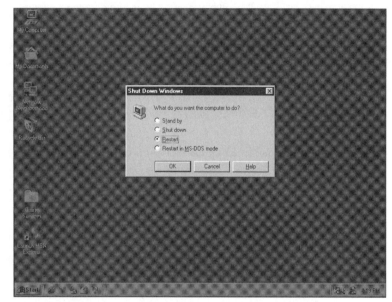

If you have a CRT monitor

1. Moiré patterns on a CRT tends to appear as slightly curved vertical lines, although you may also see a cross-hatch pattern of curved lines that are about 30 degrees off vertical.

2. If you see this on your screen, check first for a moiré adjustment control. This is generally found on higher-performance models, although it's becoming more common on less expensive monitors as well. On older models, it may be available on a dedicated or multifunction button. On newer models, it's typically available though the monitor's onscreen menu.

3. If your monitor has a moiré adjustment control, adjust it to minimize the patterns you see on the screen. If this doesn't help, proceed to the next step.

4. If your monitor doesn't have a moiré adjustment control, look for a focus control. Focus controls are relatively rare, but you can find them on some monitors. Defocusing the image just a touch can help to minimize or eliminate moiré patterns.

5. If your monitor doesn't offer either kind of control, or even if it does, but neither control tones down the moiré pattern sufficiently, try adjusting the size and position of the image by using the horizontal size and position controls. By shifting the image slightly to the left or right, or by making it slightly wider or narrow, you may be able to alleviate the effects somewhat.

> *If this solution didn't solve your problem, go to the next page.*

The image on my screen shows patterns of lines standing still

(continued from page 167)

6. If the effect is still pronounced, the best remaining option is to try a different resolution. A lower resolution will produce larger pixels, which are less likely to create interference patterns with the phosphor dots. To lower the resolution, start by right-clicking on an open area of your Desktop.

7. Choose Properties from the shortcut menu.

8. On the Display Properties window, choose the Settings tab. ▶

9. Move the slider in the Screen Area region one step to the left. The new resolution will be displayed below the slider.

10. Choose OK, and restart your computer if prompted to do so.

11. Check for moiré patterns. If the problem persists, you'll have to decide whether it's bothersome enough to justify replacing the monitor.

If you have an LCD monitor with an analog interface

1. As a rule of thumb, moiré patterns on an LCD tends to be much worse at resolutions other than the *native* resolution—the resolution that has a one-to-one correspondence between each pixel in the image and each set of red, green, and blue cells in the LCD. Because of this (and a long list of other reasons), we recommend using the native resolution in any case—unless you have a compelling reason not to. So your first step in getting rid of moiré patterns on an LCD monitor is to make sure you're using the native resolution.

2. If you have any doubts about the LCD's native resolution, check the monitor's manual to find out what it is.

3. Next, right-click on an open area of your desktop, choose Properties to open the Display Properties dialog box, and then choose the Settings tab.

4. Look in the region labeled Screen Area, and check the resolution as given just below the slider. If it doesn't match the native resolution for the monitor, move the slider left or right, as appropriate, until the resolutions match.

5. Choose OK, and restart your computer if prompted to do so.

6. If your system was already set for the monitor's native resolution, or the monitor still shows moiré after resetting the resolution, you'll need to try to adjust the monitor. Moiré patterns on an LCD tend to show as broad vertical bars that alternate between darker and lighter. To eliminate the moiré pattern, you have to adjust the timing used by the monitor to synchronize with the image signal. Start by checking your monitor's documentation for information on how to access the controls. Typically, there will be a coarse and a fine adjustment. Often they are called *Phase* and *Tracking*, but they may have different names. Some monitors also have an automatic adjustment that's designed to synchronize on the signal and adjust the timing automatically.

7. If there's an automatic adjustment feature available, try that first.

8. If this fails to eliminate the moiré pattern (or if there is no automatic control available), adjust the Phase control—or whatever the coarse timing adjustment is called on your monitor. Increase or decrease the setting so you have the minimum number of vertical bars on the screen. If you can't set it so the screen is more or less uniform across its entire width, choose the setting that produces the lightest image.

9. Next, use the Tracking control—or whatever the fine adjustment is called on your monitor. Try to eliminate all vertical bars, and choose the setting that produces the lightest image. (Also watch for pixel swim and jitter. *Swim* is a slow movement of pixels back and forth across a small area. *Jitter* is the same kind of movement, but with the pixels moving more quickly.) Use the same controls to eliminate these effects as much as possible also.

10. After you have made these adjustments, check the horizontal image size and position. You may need to readjust them after changing the timing settings. If so, go back to the beginning of this section on LCDs and repeat steps 2 through 5 until the timing settings produce an optimum image of the correct size and in the right position on the panel.

Tip

It sounds paradoxical, but there are times when you can set your system to a non-native resolution for the LCD and still be using the LCD's native resolution.

Some LCD drivers—particularly on notebook computers—let you set your system for a higher resolution than the LCD's native resolution, but show you only as much as would normally fit on the screen in native resolution. For example, if the LCD offers 800-by-600 native resolution, it will show you only an 800-by-600 area of a 1024-by-768 image. You can then scroll up, down, left, and right to see more of the image, with the LCD acting as an 800-by-600 pixel window on the larger image.

For lower than native resolutions, some LCDs don't even try to expand the image to fill the screen. Instead, they use just as many LCD cells as needed to maintain the one-to-one correspondence between LCD and image, and leave a large black border around the image. With other LCD monitors, you have the option of expanding the image or not. We recommend choosing not to.

In either of these situations, the LCD is still effectively operating at its native resolution, and changing the system resolution to match the native resolution won't affect the moiré pattern.

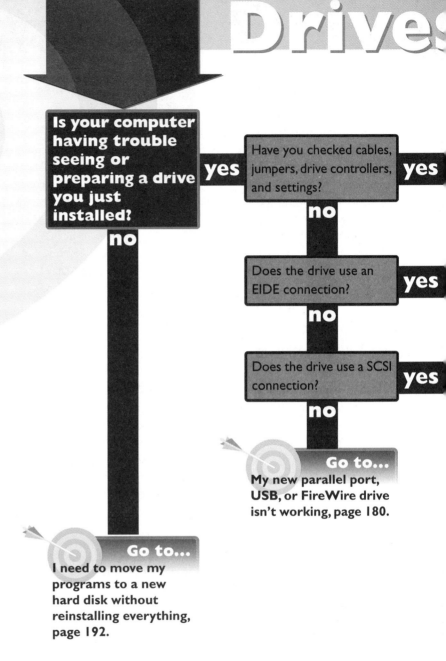

Drive

Is your computer having trouble seeing or preparing a drive you just installed?

yes → Have you checked cables, jumpers, drive controllers, and settings? **yes**

no

Does the drive use an EIDE connection? **yes**

no

Does the drive use a SCSI connection? **yes**

no

Go to...
My new parallel port, USB, or FireWire drive isn't working, page 180.

no

Go to...
I need to move my programs to a new hard disk without reinstalling everything, page 192.

If this is a hard drive, do you know how to partition it, and, if so, have you done it?

yes Go to...
I need to format a drive, page 190.

no

Go to...
My new EIDE hard disk isn't working, page 172.

Go to...
I need to partition a hard disk, page 186.

Go to...
My new SCSI hard disk isn't working, page 176.

If your solution isn't here
Check these related chapters:
Computer startup: won't boot, page 74
Drives: hard disk booting, page 220
Drives: removable disks, page 234
Or see the general troubleshooting tips on page xv.

My new EIDE hard disk isn't working

Source of the problem

Different types of hard disks connect by different types of interfaces. The most common one is called Enhanced Integrated Drive Electronics—EIDE—and you'll find that just about every computer running Microsoft Windows supports this interface.

One reason EIDE is so popular is that it's relatively easy to configure and use. There's a port on a motherboard or expansion card. A ribbon cable attaches to the port and can connect to two drives. Most systems have two EIDE ports, so you can have up to four EIDE devices in one computer. (You can also have more than two EIDE ports, if you get special expansion cards.) About the only tricky part is configuring the hard disks themselves; on a single EIDE channel, you can have one Master device and one Slave. As long as you make the first device on a channel the Master, and never have two Masters or two Slaves on a single channel, everything will usually work without problems. However, some older drives balk at working on the same channel as drives from another manufacturer, and sometimes you can make a mistake with the cables or settings. If you do, fortunately, tracking down the problem is reasonably straightforward.

How to fix it

1. Before you do anything else, if you haven't read our recommendations and warnings in "Working inside your computer" at the beginning of this book, read them now to avoid the risk of doing damage to your computer.

2. Turn off your system and open the computer's case.

3. Turn your system back on, and look for evidence that power is reaching the drive. The drive may have an access light that flashes, you may be able to hear it spinning up to speed, or you may hear the head moving inside the drive. If it's clear that power is reaching the drive, skip ahead to step 9. If you don't see or hear any signs of life, shut down the computer.

4. Disconnect and reconnect the power connector for the drive. The connector has four colored wires, and typically attaches to the drive at one corner using a white plastic connector that has a D-shape at the end so that you can't insert it upside-down.

Warning

You probably don't need this warning, but for obvious reasons, when the power is on with the case off, be careful not to touch anything inside the case. Also be careful not to drop anything—particularly metal objects like screwdrivers or pliers—inside the case. You could short something out and damage something that will be expensive to replace. Always be sure to turn your computer off before you do anything inside the open case.

5. Turn the computer back on. Once again, look for evidence that power is reaching the drive. If you see it, skip ahead to step 9.

6. If you still don't see any evidence that the drive is working, turn the computer off.

7. Remove the power connector and try a different connector. If possible, remove the connector from a drive that you know is working, and plug it into the drive that's giving you a problem.

Bend, but don't break

If you need to work the power connector back and forth to loosen it, move it parallel to the plane of the drive's controller circuit board. If you move it in a perpendicular direction, you may flex the board enough to break something. This rule about the direction of movement for working connectors loose also applies to the ribbon cable connectors on the drive and is a good rule to keep in mind whenever you remove a cable.

Also plug the connector you've been using on the problem drive into the drive that you know is working. This will let you test both the power connector and the drive at the same time.

8. Turn the computer back on. If you now see indications that the problem drive is getting power and the drive that previously worked shows no signs of life, the problem is with the connector, and you should be able to solve it by ignoring the faulty connector and using a different one. Experiment to find working power connectors (being careful to turn off your system each time you change connectors, of course), put your system case back on, and you should be done. If there's still a problem, continue to the next step.

9. Make sure the data ribbon cable is properly connected. It's surprisingly easy to be off by one set of pins, or to be plugged into only one of the two rows. But if you look carefully from various angles with a flashlight, you can usually see if the pins are sticking out along the edge of the connector. If the cable appears to be properly connected, skip to step 14. ▶

10. If you can see that the cable is not properly connected, remove the cable (with the system turned off) and reconnect it; be careful to plug it in using *all* the pins. Don't force it if you meet resistance. If the pins are slightly out of alignment, forcing the connection may bend them severely. Try straightening them using needle-nose pliers or a small, flat-bladed screwdriver to push against them.

> *If this solution didn't solve your problem, go to the next page.*

My new EIDE hard disk isn't working

(continued from page 173)

11. Check the cable again and make sure it's properly plugged in.

12. Turn on your system to see if the problem is solved. If it is, you can turn off your system and put the case back together. If this didn't solve the problem, however, turn off your system and continue with the next step.

13. If the drive still doesn't show any signs that it's getting power, try it in another system that you know works. If the drive doesn't work in the second system, it has probably failed, and needs to be repaired or replaced. If the drive seems to be getting power, but still has a problem, continue to the next step.

14. Check the ribbon cable carefully for any nicks or cuts that might have broken the signal connection. Also check for sharp creases in the cable if it's been folded over. The wires in the cable are delicate and can break. If you have any doubts, replace the cable. You shouldn't have to think about this twice; the cable is one of the least-expensive parts of your computer.

15. Remove and reconnect the ribbon cable for your drive at the motherboard or expansion card. Make sure that the colored edge of the cable attaches to Pin 1 of the connector. Pin 1 may be marked with a silk-screened number; if not, you will have to consult your system documentation or check with the manufacturer's technical support to determine which end is Pin 1. ▶

16. When you reconnect the cable, check to make sure it's connecting to all the pins.

17. Also make sure that the ribbon cable is plugged into the right channel. Keep in mind that the boot drive must be on the Primary EIDE channel. Here again, unless the connectors are identified as Primary and Secondary with silk-screened text, you will have to consult your system documentation or check with your computer's manufacturer.

Warning

A reminder: if you need to work the connector back and forth to loosen it, move it parallel to the plane of the drive's controller circuit board. If you move it in a perpendicular direction, you may flex the board enough to break something.

18. Remove and reconnect the ribbon cable at the drive. Make sure that the colored edge of the cable is attached to Pin 1. If the ribbon cable's connectors are keyed with a physical bump on one side, a solid plug in place, or one pin, the cable will connect to the device in only one way.

19. If the cable is not keyed, you'll need to verify the Pin 1 position. In most cases, this will be the edge of the connector closest to the power connector, but check to make sure. There may be a silk-screened number on or near the connector, markings embossed near the connector, or a label on the hard disk that describes the connections. If you can't confirm the Pin 1 position by these methods, contact the drive manufacturer. ▶

20. Locate the setting for the drive configuration. In general, EIDE drives have three options: Master, Slave, and Cable Select, typically abbreviated as MA, SL, and CS. A few drives have the option Master Without Slave Present for specifying that the drive is the only one on its ribbon cable. The settings are usually controlled by a set of jumpers along the back edge of the drive, often between the data connector for the ribbon cable and the power connector. On some hard disks, however, the jumpers are on the bottom of the hard disk, directly mounted on the controller circuit board. These jumpers may be unmarked, in which case you will need to consult the drive's documentation for the correct settings. ▶

21. If there is a second drive on the cable, check its settings. If the first drive is set to Master, the second drive must be set to Slave. If the first drive is set to Slave, the second one must be set to Master.

22. After checking the settings, turn on your computer and see if the problem has been solved.

23. If the drive still doesn't work, shut down the computer. If there is another device on the same EIDE chain, try changing the Master drive to Slave, and the Slave drive to Master.

24. Once again, turn on your computer and see if the problem has been solved.

25. If the drive still doesn't work, try removing the second drive and continuing with the next step. Keep in mind that if this is to be the boot hard disk, it will have to be on the Primary EIDE channel.

26. If the drive is the only one on the cable, make sure the jumper is set to either Master or, if the drive has a separate setting for it, Master Without Slave Present.

27. Once again, turn on your computer and see if the problem has been solved. If you find that the drive works by itself, but not with the other drive you had on the same ribbon cable, you need to install the two drives on different EIDE channels. If you have more than two drives, you'll have to experiment to see if either or both of the drives you've been working with can be on the same channel as any of the other drives in your system.

28. If the drive still doesn't work, try it in another system that you know works. If the drive doesn't work in the second system, it may well have failed, in which case it needs to be repaired or replaced.

My new SCSI hard disk isn't working

Source of the problem

The Small Computer System Interface (SCSI) offers some advantages over other types of connections: It can work with a wide range of peripherals—hard disks, optical drives, scanners, and more. It's fast, transferring data at up to 40 MB per second depending on the version. It provides something like a local network for the devices, so your computer can just give the SCSI bus a request and go do other work until the answer comes back. And you can have up to either 7 or 15 different devices on a single SCSI chain, depending on the flavor of SCSI. Plus you can have more than one SCSI chain in a computer, so you can attach lots of devices to your computer at one time.

Connecting SCSI devices is a little different from connecting devices with other interfaces, and they have a reputation for being hard to connect. But while it's true that early SCSI devices demanded both patience and luck to get them working, the interface has been refined so that now it's really no harder to set up a SCSI device than an equivalent device using another type of connection. In fact, it's often simpler.

The two issues that can cause problems are termination (or the lack of it) and ID numbers. The chain of SCSI devices must be terminated—which means that a terminator (actually a resistor) has to be included at the connection for the last device at each end of the line. Also, each device (including the interface card itself) must have a unique ID number from 0 to 7 (or 0 to 15 if the SCSI adapter supports it). Most problems are related to one or the other of these issues.

How to fix it

For all devices, internal or external

1. Before you do anything else, whether the drive is internal or external, if you haven't read our recommendations and warnings in "Working inside your computer" at the beginning of this book, read them now.

2. Check the ID assigned to each device on the SCSI chain. Make sure each one has an ID that isn't assigned to any other device on the chain.

3. If that doesn't solve the problem, check the termination at each device along the SCSI chain. Make sure that only the ones at the end are terminated. Many SCSI adapter cards, and some devices, can detect whether there are devices connected on one side of the chain or both, and automatically turn termination on or off as needed. Other adapters and devices use jumpers or

switches to set termination. Consult the documentation for the adapter and each device to confirm that each has the correct termination setting.

4. If the device still does not work, remove it and confirm that the rest of the devices work properly. If they do, double-check the termination and ID settings for the new device. If you're adding the device at the end of the SCSI chain, make sure you disabled termination on the device you attached it to. If the new device still doesn't work, continue with the next sections, "If the device is outside your computer" or "If the device is inside your computer," as appropriate.

If the device is outside your computer

1. Turn off your computer and all external SCSI devices.

2. Disconnect the cable that's attached to device you're having trouble with from the SCSI connector at the *other* end of the cable, and then reconnect it. Make sure the cable is attached securely, with any clamps or screws firmly in place to hold it to the connector.

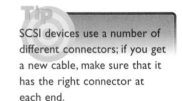

Tip

SCSI devices use a number of different connectors; if you get a new cable, make sure that it has the right connector at each end.

3. Check the cable for kinks or cuts that might indicate damage to the wires inside. If you have any questions about the cable's integrity, have the leads tested for continuity or simply replace it with a new cable.

4. Remove and reconnect the cable at the device. Make sure that it's securely connected to the port. Most devices will have two ports so you can daisy-chain another device to the first. In most cases, it doesn't matter which port you use to connect the device to the interface (or another device), but double-check the device's documentation to make sure that's not an issue.

5. Check the termination again. If the device is the last item in the chain, make sure that it's terminated. If it is *not* the last item in the chain, then make sure it is *not* terminated. Termination can be done in one of three ways. Some devices rely on *external termination*, with a terminator plug connected to the open port on the device. Others rely on *internal termination*, and expect you to set either a jumper or switch to turn termination on and off. Still others offer *automatic termination*. These devices sense whether there's another device connected in each direction on the chain, and set their termination accordingly. Check your product's documentation to see which type of termination the device uses. ▶

If this solution didn't solve your problem, go to the next page.

My new SCSI hard disk isn't working

(continued from page 177)

If the device is inside your computer

1. Turn off the computer.

2. Inspect the ribbon cable for possible damage; a nick or cut can break the connection for a signal. Also check for sharp creases in the cable if it's been folded over. The wires in the cable are delicate and can break. If you have any doubts, replace the cable. Ribbon cables are inexpensive, so you shouldn't have to give this a second thought.

3. Remove and reconnect the ribbon cable from the adapter card (or the motherboard, if the SCSI interface is integrated into the motherboard). One edge of the ribbon cable will be colored. That edge should attach to Pin 1 of the connector. Some SCSI cables are keyed with a bump that fits in a notch on the adapter's connector, so you can only connect it the right way. If the cable connector or adapter connector is not keyed, you'll have to identify Pin 1. It may be marked with a silk-screened number; if not, you will have to consult the SCSI adapter's documentation or check with the manufacturer's technical support to determine which end is Pin 1. ▶

4. Remove and reconnect the ribbon cable at your device. Make sure that the colored edge of the cable is attached to Pin 1. The same advice about keyed connectors and identifying Pin 1 on the SCSI adapter apply to the device end as well.

> **Warning**
>
> A reminder: if you need to work the connector back and forth to loosen it, rock it parallel to the plane of the drive's controller circuit board. If you move it in a perpendicular direction, you may flex the board enough to break something.

If the device still doesn't work

1. If you've gone through all these steps and the device still doesn't work, it may need repair or replacement. You may be able to verify whether or not the device is working properly by setting it up as the only device on the SCSI chain.

My new parallel port, USB, or FireWire drive isn't working

Source of the problem

It used to be easy. Storage devices attached to hard disk controllers or SCSI adapters. Parallel ports were just for printers. Serial ports were suitable for modems and mice and that was it. There were some hassles involved in configuring some of these connections, but the division of labor was straightforward.

Now it's a bit more complex. You can get hard disks and optical drives that are designed to hang off of all sorts of ports. It started with parallel ports; instead of opening your computer, you just plug the device into the familiar and simple parallel port. Then the Universal Serial Bus (USB) came along, providing high-speed access and plug-and-play simplicity. USB is fast, but FireWire is faster. (FireWire is Apple Computer's name for the IEEE 1394 high-speed serial bus, but everyone calls it *FireWire* because that's so much easier to remember than the totally forgettable and unlovely *1394*—which most people probably confuse with the IEEE 1284 parallel port standard anyway).

Alas, there's still trouble in Paradise. Parallel ports remain a part of the standard computer configuration, but they can be set up in a number of different ways—which can have a major effect on how (and whether) devices work when attached to them. USB ports have been a part of computers for years, but only recently have they become reliable partners in peripheral connections. And FireWire is just beginning to have an impact beyond digital video enthusiasts. Here are some of the problems you may encounter, and how to resolve them.

How to fix it

If you're connecting to a parallel port on the motherboard

1. Check the drive documentation to find out what parallel port settings it requires. In most cases, it will be Enhanced Parallel Port (EPP), although Enhanced Capabilities Port (ECP) may also be supported.

2. Boot your system, and enter the CMOS configuration utility. Different systems have different ways to start this program, but in most cases you will see a prompt on the screen before Microsoft Windows starts to load instructing you to press a certain key to enter a setup program. The most common keystrokes for this function are Delete and F2. Some systems do not

have such a feature at boot up; you either have to run a program from a disk or press a key combination after the computer has booted. (For more details on starting the CMOS configuration utility, see "The computer is booting from the wrong disk drive" on page 82.)

3. Find the options for setting the parallel port type. These may be in a section called *Advanced* or *Chipset Features*, and will vary depending on the type and version of BIOS in your system.

4. Find the entry for the onboard parallel port mode. Depending on the features supported by your system's BIOS, you may find up to five different choices:

- Standard or AT
- Bidirectional or PS/2
- EPP
- ECP
- EPP + ECP

5. Choose the setting that best matches the requirements for your drive. (If your computer doesn't provide support for the kind of port you need, you may have to buy an adapter card, but you might as well try the closest match you have available before you buy the card.)

6. Save the changes—if any—exit the utility, let your system reboot, then turn off your computer. Skip to the section "For all parallel ports" on the next page.

Tip

If you have a choice between EPP and ECP settings for your device, try EPP first. ECP requires something called a DMA channel. DMA channels are in limited supply in a computer, so using one could cause conflicts with other devices that also require DMA support. EPP does not require a DMA channel, which makes it less likely to cause a resource conflict.

Tip

The parallel port was originally intended just to send data, and to just one device. Over the years, the capabilities of this lowly port have been expanded to run faster, allow data in both directions at the same speed in each direction, and, to some extent, work with a daisychain of devices.

Call us Luddites, but we remain skeptical about putting multiple devices on a parallel port. Sure, it works. Sometimes. But it often creates problems. A better plan is one device per port; if you need another parallel port, you can add one for $10 to $20. Better yet, use USB instead if it's available on your system. USB was designed from the ground up for multiple devices.

If this solution didn't solve your problem, go to the next page.

My new parallel port, USB, or FireWire drive isn't working

(continued from page 181)

If you're connecting to parallel port on an adapter card

1. Check the documentation for the type of ports the card supports. Make sure that it can provide the parallel port configuration that your drive requires; if it can't you will need to replace the card or add another card, using one that has the proper support.

2. Also check how to set the parallel port type. This will usually involve running a utility or physically setting a switch or moving a jumper—a small plastic piece with metal inside that slips over two pins to tie them together electrically.

3. If you can set the parallel port type though a utility, follow the adapter's instructions to set the port to the appropriate type.

4. If you have to change something physically on the card, shut down Windows and turn off your computer.

5. If you haven't read "Working inside your computer" at the beginning of this book, read it now to avoid risking damage to your computer.

6. Open your computer case.

7. Check the parallel port settings to make sure that it's configured for the correct type of port, as required by your drive.

For all parallel ports

1. After you've verified that the port is configured correctly for the drive's requirements, disconnect any other device from the port so that this drive is the only device attached to it.

2. Make sure you have the correct cable. Different devices use different connectors. Use the cable that came with your drive if there was one. If not, get a cable with the correct connectors and with the correct specifications. Unless your drive requires unusual wiring for the cable, your safest bet is to get a cable that is IEEE 1284 compliant, since it will work with any of the standard types of parallel ports. The connectors on an IEEE 1284 cable look identical to the connectors on standard parallel cable, except that many manufacturers print IEEE 1284 on the cable itself. ▶

3. Remove the cable from the drive end, if it's designed to be removable, and reconnect it. Make sure that the cable is securely fastened at both ends. Use the clips or screws to attach the connector to the port.

4. Turn your computer back on and let it reboot.

5. If the drive now works, you're done. Otherwise, right-click on My Computer, and choose Properties.

6. Choose the Device Manager tab. (In Windows 2000, choose the Hardware tab, and then the Device Manager button.)

7. In the Device Manager window, expand the category Ports (COM & LPT).

8. Find the Printer Port entry that matches the port your drive is plugged into, and select it. (If there is more than one Printer Port entry and you're not sure which one your drive is plugged into, repeat this step and the next one for each printer port.)

9. Choose Remove (or, in Windows 2000: Action, Uninstall, and then OK).

10. After Windows removes the parallel port from the installation, choose Start, Shut Down, Restart, and then OK to let the system reboot.

11. While rebooting, Windows should find the LPT port and install the right driver for its current setting. It may ask you to supply the Windows CD. Put the disc in the CD-ROM drive, or, if you have the Windows CAB files on your hard disk, enter the path to the files tell Windows where to find them.

12. After Windows finishes booting, it should be installed for the right kind of LPT port. You can check to make sure that it recognized the ports by returning to the Device Manager by choosing Start, Settings, Control Panel, System, and then Device Manager in Windows 98, or Hardware and then Device Manager in Windows 2000.

13. If your drive still does not work, check the manufacturer's Web site to make sure that you have the latest version of drivers and other software for the drive itself. Install the updates, if there are any, and test the drive again.

14. If you still have a problem with the drive, try installing it on another system if possible—preferably one that has somewhat different hardware than the first system. If it doesn't work on the second system either, it may well need repair or replacement, or it may have compatibility problems with your hardware (which is why it's best to test it on a system with different hardware). In either case, you should contact the manufacturer.

If this solution didn't solve your problem, go to the next page.

My new parallel port, USB, or FireWire drive isn't working

(continued from page 183)

If you're connecting to a USB port

1. Disconnect all USB devices from your computer (except for a USB keyboard and mouse, if that is what your computer uses).

2. Verify that you have the correct cable for your device. In most cases, a broad, flat connector—called *Type A*—plugs into the port on a hub. (There are some devices called *hubs*, but any device with ports to plug other devices into—including your computer or a USB keyboard for example—is also a hub.) A narrow, square connector—called *Type B*—plugs into the device that connects to a hub (including another hub). However, a few devices use a flat connector for both connections, so check the documentation and ports carefully. ▶

3. Make sure that your version of Windows provides USB support. You must have Windows 95 OEM Service Release 2.1 or later; Windows 98 Second Edition and Windows 2000 provide the most robust support for USB. (Windows Millennium Edition should provide robust support as well.)

4. Make sure that your USB Root Hub is installed correctly and functioning properly. If you have any doubts whether USB is working on your system, see the chapter "Connections," beginning on page 84.

5. If you're sure that USB is working correctly, make sure that you have the latest drivers and software for the drive. Contact the manufacturer or check the company's Web site.

6. Check the documentation for your drive, and reinstall it. Follow the installation instructions precisely: Some USB devices need to have the driver and other software installed *before* you connect the device for the first time. Others need you to connect the device to your system first, and *then* install the drivers and software (if any is needed).

7. If the device is not recognized by Windows, or is recognized but doesn't work, it may not be getting sufficient power. If it has a separate power supply, make sure that it's plugged in.

8. If the device still doesn't work, there may be something wrong with it, or the drivers may have a problem working with your particular hardware. Either way, you'll need to contact the manufacturer to pursue the problem.

9. If the device works now, reconnect the other devices to the USB ports one at a time, and reboot after you reconnect each one. Check after each reboot to make sure that all the devices are working correctly. If you encounter a problem, it may be a driver conflict. Get the latest drivers for the device that caused a problem when you added it to the USB chain. If that doesn't resolve the problem, contact the manufacturers of both devices that are conflicting with each other.

If your device connects using a FireWire port

1. Make sure that you're running Windows 98 Second Edition, Windows 2000, or later versions; earlier versions of Windows do not support FireWire.

2. Disconnect all other devices from the FireWire port.

3. Make sure that the FireWire port is configured correctly in your system. (We don't cover FireWire in this book, but the procedure for making sure it's working in your system is similar to the procedure for USB, which we cover in the chapter "Connections," beginning on page 84.

4. Make sure that you have the correct cable. Some devices require a flat 6-pin connector, called an *A connector*. Others require a square 4-pin connector, called a *B connector*.

5. If your device requires a B connector, it cannot draw power from the FireWire bus. Make sure that its power supply is plugged in and connected correctly to the device.

6. Make sure that the cable is securely connected to your computer and the drive.

7. If the drive still isn't working, check the installation instructions, and reinstall it following the instructions precisely.

8. If the device is now working, reconnect any other FireWire devices you have. If your new device requires an A connector and draws power from the FireWire bus, make sure there are no B connector devices between it and the computer; a device with a B connector cannot pass power along to other devices in the chain.

9. If the device still does not work or is not recognized, it may be in need of repair or replacement. Contact the manufacturer.

I need to partition a hard disk

Source of the problem

You need to prepare your hard disk before you can use it—like a cook preparing a tough steak by tenderizing it. So if you've just installed a hard disk and your system can't see it, the first question you need ask is whether you remembered to prepare it.

In the case of a hard disk, preparing means creating one or more segments, called *partitions*, and then formatting them so Windows can use them. Some of the finer points can get complex, but the fundamental reality is simple; without an active Primary partition, you won't be able to boot. In fact, you won't even be able to format the hard disk.

As it happens, Windows 98 and earlier versions of Windows give you a lot of control over the size and function of your partitions. Windows 2000 does not. We'll focus on Windows 98 first, and then address what you can and can't do in Windows 2000.

How to fix it

If you are running Windows 98

1. Boot to the MS-DOS prompt. If you're set up to boot from the hard disk drive (or another hard disk in the same system), boot to Windows, then choose Start, Shut Down, set the option to Restart In MS-DOS Mode, and then choose OK.

2. Alternatively, if you're booting from the hard disk, reboot and press F8 repeatedly. When the Microsoft Windows 98 Startup menu appears, choose Command Prompt Only from the menu.

3. If you cannot boot from the hard disk, you'll need to boot from a bootable floppy disk that has the program FDISK.EXE on it. If you need details for how to create the disk, see the Appendix.

4. Whether you booted from a hard disk or from a floppy that has the FDISK program on it, type **FDISK** and press Enter. In either case, if the FDISK program fails to start you need to locate a

> **Warning**
>
> The flow chart at the beginning of this chapter assumes that you're having problems using a new hard disk you just installed. If you're following these directions so you can partition a drive that already has data on it, be sure to make a complete backup of any data you need *before* you run FDISK. Deleting a partition will wipe out all the data on that part of the drive.

> **Warning**
>
> If you have more than one hard disk, be careful to make the changes to the right one, since deleting a partition will wipe out everything in that partition. If FDISK finds more than one hard disk, the FDISK Options menu will include the option Change Current Fixed Disk Drive, but keep in mind that FDISK may not be seeing your new hard disk.
>
> To positively identify which hard disk you're working with, choose the Display Partition Information option and compare the information with what you know about the drive or drives on the disk.

copy of the program. If you booted from a hard disk, you may be able to find it in the C:\Windows\Command directory (a directory in MS-DOS is similar to a folder in Windows). Alternatively, you can look for the file in the directory (or folder) by that name on another system that has Windows 98 installed.

5. If your hard disk is larger than 512 MB, you will see a screen with the question Do You Wish To Enable Large Disk Support (Y/N). If you want the option to have a drive defined that's larger than 2 GB, you must choose **Y**, which we recommend doing. This will create a FAT32 partition, as opposed to the less-capable FAT partition. (The FAT and FAT32 partition types get their name from the file allocation table that these types of partitions use.)

6. To create a new partition, you have to remove any partitions that are already using the part of the drive you want to use. So you first need to make sure that at least some of the drive is available. On the FDISK Options Menu, choose Option 4, Display Partition Information. ▼

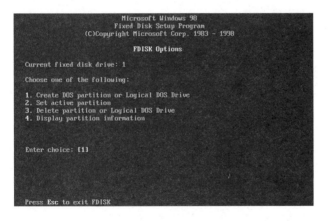

7. If there are no partitions defined on the hard disk, you'll see a message saying so. If there are any partitions, however, you'll see information about both the partitions and the *logical drives*. Windows sees each partition as a logical drive that mimics a physical hard disk. Note the number and type of partitions on the hard disk, if there are any, and logical drives, if there are any.

If this solution didn't solve your problem, go to the next page.

Tip

Why would you carve up your hard disk into logical drives? Depending on how you work, it could be a helpful idea. If you store all your programs and data files on a single, huge Drive C, then you have to search through the entire drive when you're looking for some specific file. Also, it may be hard to find the time to back up the entire drive, which will include any number of program files that don't change.

If you divide the hard disk into more than one logical drive, however, you have more options. You can keep all your programs on Drive C, and all your data files on Drive D. (*D* for Data, get it?) Then all you have to do to safeguard your work is back up Drive D, and backup Drive C only when you add a program or change a configuration setting.

You could also create a Drive E (*E* for Extra?) where you could keep extra copies of your work files or collections of your temporary files that you haven't decided if you'll keep permanently.

Think of logical drives as drawers in a file cabinet; instead of one long drawer, you divide the space into smaller units, which can make it easier to manage their contents.

I need to partition a hard disk

(continued from page 187)

8. If you need to remove one or more partitions, choose option 3, Delete Partition Or Logical DOS Drive. The choices on the menus are straightforward. But if step 7 indicated that there is an extended partition and logical drives, keep in mind that you must delete the logical drives before you can delete the extended partition.

9. After you remove prior partitions, if there were any, choose Option 1 on the FDISK Options menu, Create DOS Partition Or Logical DOS Drive.

10. In most cases, you'll have the option of creating a single partition the size of your hard disk. If that's what you want, type **Y**, when FDISK asks the question, Do You Wish To Use The Maximum Available Size For A Primary DOS Partition And Make The Partition Active?

> **TIP**
>
> If you have more than one hard disk in your system, FDISK will not let you make a partition active unless it recognizes the physical drive as drive 1. For IDE and EIDE drives, this means the drive has to be set as the Master, rather than the Slave. If FDISK won't let you set an active partition, and you need details on Master and Slave settings, go to "My new EIDE hard disk isn't working" on page 172.

11. If you want to create more than one drive, make the primary partition the size you want for the first drive—which will be Drive C if this will be the boot disk—and then make an extended partition with the remaining capacity. Next, use the FDISK menu to create logical drives in the extended partition, dividing the capacity however you choose.

12. If you create more than one partition and this is the hard disk you want to boot from, you'll also need to set a partition as active. From the FDISK Options menu, choose Option 2 and follow the instructions on screen to set the Primary partition as the active partition.

13. Once you have created the partitions you want, as well as any logical drives within the extended partition, don't forget to format the drives. See "I need to format a drive" on page 190.

If you cannot make the whole disk one partition

1. If FDISK won't let you create a partition larger than 504 MB, your system may not support a feature called Logical Block Addressing (LBA). You'll need to check your computer's CMOS configuration settings to see if you have the option of enabling this feature in the BIOS.

2. To start the CMOS configuration utility, reboot the system. In most cases, you'll see a message early in the boot process telling you which key to press—often Delete or F2—to start the utility. If your computer doesn't show you the key to press, and neither of these choices works, see "The computer is booting from the wrong disk drive" on page 82 for more details about starting the CMOS utility.

3. Look through the screens of the CMOS setup utility for an option to enable LBA. If you can't find one, you may need to buy an expansion card that provides LBA support.

4. If you cannot create a partition larger than 2 GB, you are either using FAT16 (the standard FAT) instead of the FAT32 used by Windows 98 with the Large Disk Support, or your computer's BIOS is limited to a 2-GB maximum. To rule out the first possibility, go back to the beginning of this section and run through the steps again, answering **Y** to the question Do You Wish To Enable Large Disk Support (Y/N)?

5. If you cannot create a partition larger than 7.8 GB, the problem is that your system does not support the Interrupt 13 (INT13) extensions. You may be able to add support for this feature by upgrading your system's BIOS—contact your motherboard manufacturer for details—or you may have to replace your system, or add an adapter card.

6. If you find some other limit on drive size, the problem is likely caused by an arbitrary limit defined in your system's BIOS. The limit was probably more than adequate when the BIOS was designed, but has been overtaken by the relentless growth in drive capacity. Here again, you may be able to add support for larger drives by upgrading your system's BIOS—contact your motherboard manufacturer for details—or you may have to replace your system or add an appropriate adapter card. As a last resort—which we do not recommend—you may have to rely on utilities that add the support as software that installs on the drive's boot sector.

If you have Windows 2000

1. Windows 2000 does not have a separate partition utility, but instead makes all the partitioning decisions for you when you first install Windows on your hard disk. When you run the Windows 2000 Setup routine, it gives you a choice of file systems to use on the disk. If you are not going to use the system on a network, or if you are going to use it on a network with only Windows 2000 and Windows NT systems, you may want to choose the NTFS option. If you plan to share files with Windows 98 systems on a network, however, choose the FAT32 option. The installation routine gives you the option of defining multiple logical drives on a single hard disk similar to the way you can with FDISK in Windows 98.

Tip

If you see an error message when you leave FDISK that indicates the changes weren't written to your hard disk, you probably have your system set to prevent writing to your disk's boot sector. Start the CMOS configuration utility, as described in step 2, and look for an option—usually under a Security section—to set the hard disk boot sector to normal rather than write protected.

Warning

Some large hard drives come with utility software that adds LBA support or other support for large drives by way of an overlay that installs on the drive's boot sector. In general, we recommend that you rely on hardware to add support for large hard disks. The software may work perfectly well, but if you run into problems—or need to move the hard disk to another computer—this approach can create extra work and problems. It's best to avoid the issue and upgrade your hardware instead.

I need to format a drive

Source of the problem

If you got here by following the flowchart you've already established that you have a partition on your hard disk, but you still can't use it. Before you format, a partition on your hard disk is like a blank sheet of paper. Actually, it's like cartons and cartons of blank sheets of paper. And your computer is like a child who knows how to write but needs lined paper to keep all the words in place. Formatting the hard disk is the equivalent of drawing guidelines on a blank sheet. It gives the computer a way to know where a given piece of data is stored, so it can find it as quickly and reliably as possible.

How to fix it

1. Double-click on the My Computer icon.

2. Find the icon for the hard disk drive you want to format.

3. Right-click on the icon, and choose Format from the shortcut menu that appears to open the Format dialog box.

4. In the Format dialog box, you can choose a Quick or Full format type and specify a Volume Label for the drive. If you want to make the drive bootable, look in the Other Options section, and make sure that the Copy System Files box is checked. (If you have Windows 2000, the Format Window will look a little different, with additional choices and with only a Quick Format check box in a Format Options section. If this box is not checked, you get a Full Format. There is no option for System Files in the Windows 2000 Format window.) ▶

5. If you have a check in the Display Summary When Finished check box, then Windows will show the capacity and other details of the drive when the format process is complete. (Windows 2000 does not offer this option and does not do this.) If the Format utility doesn't report any errors, you're finished formatting.

6. If the format process does not complete or won't even start, make sure that the hard disk is partitioned properly. See "I need to partition a hard disk" on page 186.

If the format utility reports an error

1. Double-click on My Computer.

2. In the My Computer window, right click on the icon for the drive you formatted.

3. Choose Properties from the shortcut menu that pops up.

4. Choose the Tools tab.

5. In the Error-Checking area, choose the Check Now button.

6. If you have Windows 98, the ScanDisk window will open. In the Type Of Test area, make sure it's set for Thorough. Then choose Start. ▶

7. If you have Windows 2000, the Check Disk window will open. Make sure there is a check in the Scan For And Attempt Recovery Of Bad Sectors check box. Then choose Start. ▶

8. If your disk has just a few bad sectors reported, then it is probably OK—though you should repeat the Error Checking at least once a month to make sure that the number of bad sectors doesn't increase over time. If a lot of bad sectors are reported, or you notice a steady increase in the count whenever you use the Error Checking feature, it's likely an early warning that your disk is going to fail catastrophically. Keep thorough backups of any programs or data stored on that disk, and start thinking about replacing it now, rather than waiting until it fails.

Tip

Although the Format window allows spaces in the Label text box (the Volume Label text box in Windows 2000), avoid spaces in the volume names. Some programs have difficulty finding drives—especially on a network—if the volume name contains spaces. To be safe, use an underscore character instead of a space. For example, **DRIVE_D** instead of **DRIVE D**.

I need to move my programs to a new hard disk without reinstalling everything

Source of the problem

Running low on hard drive storage space? No problem. Hard disks are cheaper than they've ever been—you can add more capacity for less than $10 per gigabyte. (Or maybe less by the time you read this. That's a penny per megabyte. And it's been only seven years since manufactures were trying hard to break the magic figure of a dollar per megabyte.)

Oh. And did we mention that the new hard disk you buy today will probably be faster than your current one?

But there's a problem. What do you do about all the programs you already have installed on your system? Many applications make changes to the Windows Registry when they are installed, so you can't just install Windows on the new hard disk, copy the program files to the disk, and expect everything to work correctly. If you're using Windows 98, the good news is that you can copy all the files over from the old disk to the new one and safely move everything. But there is a trick to it.

How to fix it

In Windows 98

1. Before you do anything else, if you haven't read our recommendations and warnings in "Working inside your computer," at the beginning of this book, read them now.

2. If you already have the new hard disk installed as the boot drive, and the old hard disk as an additional drive, skip to the next step. Otherwise, turn off your computer and open the case. Reinstall the old hard disk if necessary, or simply change the drive settings. If you have EIDE drives, set the Master and Slave settings so that the new hard disk is the boot drive. (If both drives are on the

Warning

We assume you already have the new hard disk installed and working (or you would have wound up elsewhere in this chapter if you followed the flowchart).

We also assume that to get this far, if you're using EIDE drives you know about Primary and Secondary channels (the drive needs to be on the Primary channel to boot) and about Master and Slave settings and how to change them. (The Master drive on the Primary channel is the boot drive.) For SCSI drives, we assume you know how to set one drive or the other as the boot drive—typically by changing the SCSI IDs for one or both drives, but in some cases by changing a setting in the SCSI adapter card, telling it which ID to boot from.

If these assumptions are wrong, you may need to first work your way though the appropriate section on connections and cabling for EIDE or SCSI hard disks ("My new EIDE hard disk isn't working" on page 172, or "My new SCSI hard disk isn't working" on page 176).

Primary channel, the Master is the boot drive.) If you have a SCSI drive, change the SCSI ID settings so the new hard disk is the boot drive. (With most SCSI adapter cards, the drive with the lowest ID number is the boot drive.)

3. If you worked your way through the flowchart, the new hard disk should be partitioned and formatted correctly and working. If it isn't, set it up properly before continuing. If necessary, go back to the flowchart at the beginning of this chapter and work though it for help on steps you don't already know how to do.

4. Since the presumption is that you're working with a brand new hard disk, you shouldn't have any data on it yet, but if you do, move it elsewhere; copy it to the old hard disk or archive it on any handy alternative, such as a Zip drive or even a floppy. You can put it back on whatever drive you like when you're done.

5. Install Windows on the new hard disk, using the same version of Windows as on your old hard disk. (Strictly speaking, this step shouldn't be necessary, but in practice, it often prevents problems.) Don't worry about the options you choose. You'll be deleting this installation of Windows when you're done. You just want to ensure that the disk has a bootable installation of Windows on it.

6. When Windows Setup finishes, reboot to confirm that you can boot from the new hard disk.

7. Turn off your computer, and reset whatever jumpers or switches are necessary so the system will boot up from the old hard disk but still see the new one. (With EIDE drives, this generally means making the old hard disk the Master and the new hard disk the Slave. With SCSI drives, it generally means changing the SCSI IDs)

8. Turn on your computer and let it boot from the old hard disk.

9. You need to know the designation for the first logical drive on the new hard disk—the one that will become your new C drive when you're finished. (A physical hard disk is divided into one or more segments known as *partitions*. Windows sees each partition as a logical drive that mimics a physical hard disk.) In most cases, the first logical drive will be drive D at this point. Whether it actually is, however, depends on what other physical drives are in the system, as well as those drives' cabling and settings.

Warning

If you used FDISK to partition your new hard disk when the drive was set up as something other than the boot drive, it probably won't boot when you change its designation to be the boot drive. That's because your system needs to see a partition designated as Active to know where to boot from, and FDISK won't let you designate an active partition except on the boot drive (the Master drive on the Primary channel, for EIDE).

To designate a partition on the new hard disk as active, first make sure you have a bootable floppy with FDISK on it. (If you need details for how to create the disk, see the Appendix.) Boot from the floppy, load FDISK, choose the option Set Active Partition, and follow the instructions on screen to set the partition as Active. If you need more details about using FDISK, see "I need to partition a hard disk" on page 186.

10. Since you just installed Windows on the logical drive you need to identify, and since you know there should be nothing else on that drive, you should be able to easily determine which drive it is. Open Windows Explorer by choosing Start, Programs, and then Windows Explorer). Look at Drive D first, but if it has either more or less than it should have on it, navigate to the each of the other drives until you find the right drive.

11. When you find the right drive, right-click on the drive icon and choose Properties to open the drive's Properties dialog box with the General tab chosen.

12. Also right-click on the C drive icon and choose Properties to open its Properties dialog box. ▶

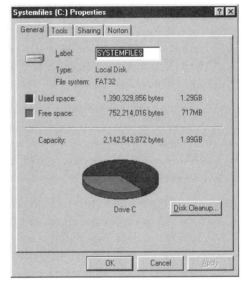

13. Compare the amount of used space on drive C with the amount of free space on the drive you need to copy to, and make sure there's enough room to copy the entire contents of drive C.

14. Next, use Windows Explorer to delete the entire Windows folder structure that's on the new hard disk: right-click on the folder, and choose Delete.

15. When Windows Explorer finishes the deletion, open an MS-DOS window by choosing Start, Programs, and then MS-DOS.

16. At the command prompt (which will look similar to c:\> or c:\windows>), type **xcopy c:*.* d: /c/h/e/k/r<Enter>** where *d* is the drive that's slated to become your new drive C, and <*Enter*> represents the Enter key.

17. When the copying finishes, turn off your computer and change whatever jumpers or switches you need to reset so that the system will boot up from the new hard disk. You can either leave the old hard disk in the system, or remove it.

18. Restart your computer. The new hard disk should have Windows and all existing applications that were on the original C drive installed and available.

Warning

Do not try to copy by rebooting in MS-DOS mode and entering this XCOPY command. In MS-DOS mode XCOPY won't recognize most of the switches (the /c,/ h,/e,/k, and /r). And even if it did, the copying would take much longer.

19. If you have additional logical drives on the old hard disk, including some with programs on them, you can now repeat the steps of opening an MS-DOS or Command Prompt windows and using the XCOPY command to copy the files from the old hard disk to the appropriate logical drive on the new hard disk.

Drives: CD,

Floppy disks and hard drives rely on magnetism to store data and then read it back again. CD-ROM drives, audio CD players, CD-R and CD-RW drives, DVD-ROM drives, DVD movie players, and DVD-RAM drives don't use magnetism; they use light. Tiny laser beams reflect off the shiny surface of the discs, bouncing off microscopic spots that register as the 1s and 0s of digital data.

The reflected light is then captured by a series of lenses and brought to sensors. The fact that these drives use light and lenses instead of magnets is why they are sometimes called optical drives. In this chapter, we use the term optical drive or optical disc drive as shorthand to refer to all these drives as a group.

Does the drive door open without problems? yes

Can you hear music from audio CDs? yes

no

Go to... My optical drive doesn't play audio CDs, page 198.

no

Go to... My optical drive tray won't open, page 211.

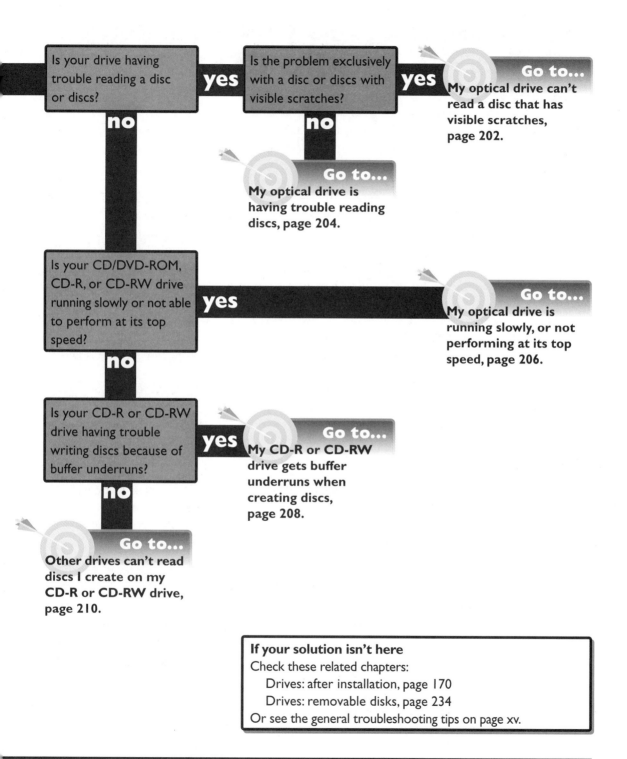

Is your drive having trouble reading a disc or discs?

yes — Is the problem exclusively with a disc or discs with visible scratches?

yes — Go to... **My optical drive can't read a disc that has visible scratches, page 202.**

no — Go to... **My optical drive is having trouble reading discs, page 204.**

no

Is your CD/DVD-ROM, CD-R, or CD-RW drive running slowly or not able to perform at its top speed?

yes — Go to... **My optical drive is running slowly, or not performing at its top speed, page 206.**

no

Is your CD-R or CD-RW drive having trouble writing discs because of buffer underruns?

yes — Go to... **My CD-R or CD-RW drive gets buffer underruns when creating discs, page 208.**

no — Go to... **Other drives can't read discs I create on my CD-R or CD-RW drive, page 210.**

If your solution isn't here
Check these related chapters:
    Drives: after installation, page 170
    Drives: removable disks, page 234
Or see the general troubleshooting tips on page xv.

My optical drive doesn't play audio CDs

Source of the problem

Optical disc drives have revolutionized personal computers. First CDs, and now DVDs, put enormous quantities of data on a slender, 120-millimeter (about 4.75-inch) plastic platter. Instead of installing software from a small mountain of floppy disks, you can pop in a CD and install operating systems or programs in a single easy step. (Well...sometimes it takes a couple or three CDs, and two or three steps, but think about how many floppy disks would be involved.)

However, we all know what happens to Jack on a steady diet of all work and no play. There are times when whistling a happy tune can make your workload seem lighter, and if you can't whistle, then your optical disc drive can also double as an entertainment device that will play your favorite audio CD through your computer's sound system. Whether you have a CD-ROM, CD-R, CD-RW, DVD-ROM, or DVD-RAM drive—in short, any of the common optical drives—it has the circuitry inside that's needed to decipher the music on your CD. If all goes well, the output goes directly to your sound card, and you hear music.

Or at least you should hear music. Sometimes all does not go well. When it doesn't, here are the steps to make the music go 'round and 'round, and come out here—or, more precisely, come out *there*, with *there* defined as your computer's speakers.

How to fix it

1. Start by verifying that your optical disc drive can play the audio CD, if you can. Most (but not all) offer an audio jack on the front of the drive, along with a thumb-wheel for volume control. Assuming your drive offers this feature, get a pair of stereo headphones with an appropriate plug. You may already have appropriate headphones for a portable radio or CD player.

2. Before you plug the headphones in, set the volume control to a middle position, so it's at neither the minimum volume setting, where you won't hear anything, or the maximum, which could damage your hearing.

3. Load the CD Player accessory: on most systems, you'll find this by choosing Start, Programs, Accessories, Entertainment, and then CD Player. The CD Player will have a very different look in Microsoft Windows 98, which uses a classic ▶

Windows-style dialog box, than in Windows 2000, which has a much more 3-D look to it. ▶

4. In Windows 98, look at the entry in the Artist box and make sure it's set for your optical disc drive. (In Windows 2000, choose Options, Preferences, and then Advanced Audio to see the drive setting.) If CD Player isn't set correctly, pick the right drive from the drop-down list. (If you have only one optical disc drive in your system, it should be the only one listed, but it doesn't hurt to check.)

5. Insert an audio CD that you know is readable in a CD player or a CD-ROM drive.

6. After Windows does its initial read of the disc, the status text in CD Player should should change from *Data or no disc loaded* (in Windows 98) or *No Disc Loaded* (in Windows 2000) to either *New Artist* or information specific to your audio CD. If this does not happen, the drive may be having a problem reading the disc. Try another audio CD in the drive. If the second one isn't recognized either, return to the flowchart at the beginning of this chapter and follow the tree from the question "Is your drive having trouble reading a disc or discs?"

7. After the disc is recognized by Windows, if it doesn't start playing automatically, click on the Play button in the CD Player window. The icon is a triangle pointing to the right.

8. The drive access light should go on, and you should see the counter advancing in the large window in CD Player. If this doesn't happen, there may be a problem reading the CD. Click on the Next Track button—the icon is a pair of triangles pointing to a vertical line at the right—and see if the next track will play. If not, there may be a problem reading the particular CD. Try another CD that you know is readable in a CD player or a CD-ROM drive. If the second one doesn't work, return to the flowchart at the beginning of this chapter, and follow it starting with the question "Is your drive having trouble reading a disc or discs?"

9. If the counter is advancing, listen to the headphones. Bring them near your ears slowly; the volume can get loud enough to damage your hearing.

10. If you cannot hear sound in the headphones, move the volume control back and forth to its limits. If you still hear nothing—and you know that the headphones are functioning correctly—your drive may have a problem. It is possible for it to read data discs with no problem, but not decipher audio CDs. If that's happening, it needs either professional repair or replacement.

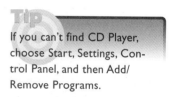

Tip

If you can't find CD Player, choose Start, Settings, Control Panel, and then Add/Remove Programs.

In Windows 98, choose the Windows Setup tab, then scroll down to Multimedia, select it, choose Details, make sure there's a check in the CD Player check box, and choose OK. Then step through the rest of the Wizard screens to install the CD Player.

> *If this solution didn't solve your problem, go to the next page.*

My optical drive doesn't play audio CDs

(continued from page 199)

11. If you hear the audio CD in the headphones, you know that the drive is reading the disc and deciphering its information correctly. Click on the Stop button in the CD Player window. The icon on this button is a solid black square.

12. Next, you need to make sure that the computer is set to play the CD Audio channel. In most cases, you will see a volume control icon—in the form of a stylized speaker—in the System Tray at the right side of your Windows taskbar. Right-click on the volume control icon and choose Open Volume Controls from the menu. If you don't see this icon, you can open the Volume Control dialog box by choosing Start, Programs, Accessories, Entertainment, and then Volume Control. ▶

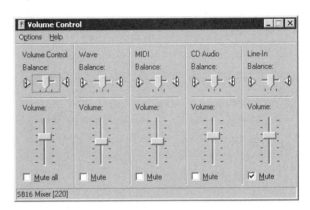

13. Note that your volume controls may include more or fewer options than the example above. The differences aren't important. If you see a column for CD Audio Balance, skip to step 17. Otherwise, choose Options and then Properties.

14. Look at the Adjust Volume For area and make sure that the Playback button is selected. ▶

15. Scroll through the list in the area marked Show The Following Volume Controls, and make sure there's a check in the CD Audio check box.

16. Choose OK.

17. Find the column marked CD Audio Balance. Make sure that the Balance slider is in the middle, that the Volume slider is all the way to the top of its range, and that the Mute check box is not checked.

18. In the Volume Control column at the far left, also make sure that that the Balance slider is in the middle, that the Volume slider is all the way to the top of its range, and that there is no check in the Mute All check box.

19. If your speakers have a power switch, make sure it's turned on. If they have a volume control, adjust it to about the middle of its range.

20. Start playing the audio CD again by clicking on the Play button—the one with the triangle pointed to the right. If you don't hear any sound, adjust the volume setting for CD Audio Balance, slowly moving it all the way to top volume. If your speakers also have a volume control, adjust that control next.

21. If you now hear the audio CD playing through your speakers, you can adjust the volume to taste and stop here. If you still can't hear the CD, proceed to the next step.

22. At this point, you need to open the computer to check on the cabling between the drive and your sound card. If you haven't read it yet, be sure to read the section "Working inside your computer" at the beginning of this book before you go on. Then turn off your computer and remove the cover from the case.

23. Find the back of your optical drive. You should see three cables attached to it. The power cable is a group of four colored wires that meet in a single, white connector. The data cable is a ribbon cable—typically gray—that ends in a wide connector that's typically black. The third cable is the stereo audio cable. It carries the audio signal from the drive to the sound card. It is typically a thin, round cable that ends in a small plastic connector that is often either black or white. ▶

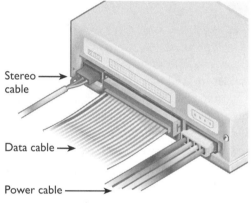

Stereo cable

Data cable →

Power cable →

24. If there is no stereo cable, you will need to get one. Make note of the specific make and model of your optical drive and your sound card, then contact a company that supplies cables for personal computers. The makes and models are important because there are a number of different connectors available for both optical drives and sound cards, and you need to make sure you get a cable with the right connector on each end.

25. If there is a cable attached, disconnect and reconnect the cable at the drive to make sure that it is seated securely.

26. Follow the cable to the sound card and disconnect and reconnect the cable there as well.

27. Turn your computer back on.

28. When it finishes booting, start the CD Player program again, and click on the Play button. If the problem is solved, you can stop here.

29. If you still don't hear the audio CD, the problem is almost certainly either the stereo cable or the sound card. Replace the cable first, if possible, because it's the less expensive choice.

30. If a new cable doesn't solve the problem, you probably need to replace the sound card. It is possible for a sound card to fail in one channel—such as the CD Audio feature—and still work fine for WAV and MIDI files.

My optical drive can't read a disc that has visible scratches

Source of the problem

Admit it: you know that you're supposed to treat your optical discs—meaning all variations on CD discs and DVD discs—with care. You know you should always store them in their cases or protective sleeves when they're not in a drive. But sometimes you get too rushed to actually do it. If you have discs that you trade off—switching between a disc that you need for the immediate moment, say, and a disc with reference material that you plan to put right back in your drive—sometimes you don't put the discs in a case or protective sleeve. Sometimes you just put them on any handy flat surface. Which means that sometimes the disc will get scratched. And that can sometimes create a problem.

Optical drives—including CD-ROM, CD-R, CD-RW, DVD-ROM, and DVD-RAM drives, as well as audio CD players—read discs by shining a laser on the disc and then measuring the amount of light that gets reflected back. This is why the bottom surface of a CD or DVD is made of clear plastic. Much of the time, a small scratch on the bottom surface won't matter. The effect is the same as looking through a window with a window screen. The mesh of the screen is out of focus—and effectively invisible—because you're focusing on the distant scene. Most scratches don't interfere with reading a disc for the same reason; the scratches are out of focus and, effectively invisible, because the lensing system in the drive is focused on the far surface of the disc.

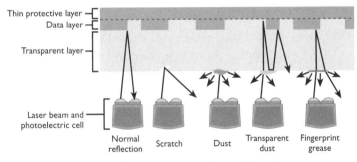

Alas, some scratches are big enough to make themselves known, like a broad streak of paint across a window. These scratches can interfere with the light and disrupt the reading of the data. The bad news is that some scratches can't be repaired, so you'll have to buy a new disc. The good news is that some can be repaired. Here's how.

How to fix it

If the scratches are on the label side of a single-sided disc

1. The actual data layer of an optical disc sits just beneath the label of a single-sided disc, such as a typical audio CD. This layer is then coated with a thin layer of lacquer, and the label is printed

on top of that. Almost any scratch that's noticeable on the label side will be deep enough to damage this data layer. If the damage occurs where data is stored, then at least that portion of the disc will be rendered useless.

2. You can test for label-side damage by holding the disc up to a bright light, with the label side toward the light. If you see pinholes or lines of light

Get professional help

There are services that will take CDs and DVDs with scratches on their clear plastic sides and polish them away. You can find some of these companies on the Web by searching for *CD and repair and service* with your favorite search engine, using whatever word or symbol the search engine uses for *and*. You should turn up a number of services, including AuralTech (888-454-3223, *www.auraltech.com*), Compact Disc Repairman (888-FIX-DISC, *www.cdrepairman.com*), and Madman CD Repair (*www.madmancdrepair.com*).

Plan on spending from $2 to $6 per disc, plus shipping, to have them repaired. You can also find accessories and supplies, including polishing kits and protective layers for the label side of single-sided discs.

through the CD, the data layer has been damaged. Depending on the extent of the damage, it's possible that the disc won't work at all and will have to be replaced.

If the damage is on the clear plastic side

1. In the spirit of doing no harm, make sure you don't damage the sensitive label side of a disc while trying to fix problems on the clear plastic side. Whenever you are working on the clear plastic side of a single-sided disc, lay the disc on a soft towel on a clean, flat surface. If you have to apply pressure to the disc, the soft layer underneath it will help to protect the other side from damage.

2. It's possible that the disc is only dirty rather than scratched. Mix a mild detergent—such as dishwashing soap—in warm water, and use a soft cloth to gently clean the clear plastic surface.

3. Rinse and dry the disc, then try it in the optical drive again. (Make sure it's fully dry before putting it in the drive.)

4. If visible scratches remain, try polishing them with a mild abrasive—such as toothpaste—using a soft cloth.

5. If the scratches are too deep or large for the toothpaste to be effective, try rubbing them first with a standard pencil eraser. This will make the surface of the disk cloudy, but you can then polish it to a clear surface again with the toothpaste.

6. After you have polished the scratches to make them as clear as possible, buff the surface with a clean, dry, coarse cloth—such as a piece of denim—to polish the surface even more.

7. Try the disc in the drive again. If your system still can't read it reliably, you may need to replace it.

My optical drive is having trouble reading discs

Source of the problem

You put a disc in your optical disc drive (meaning any drive in the CD or DVD family) and close the drawer. The access light goes on, the drive starts to spin, and...spin, and...spin some more. Then the light goes out and the drive stops. And your computer doesn't think there's a disc in the drive. What happened?

There are a lot of possible explanations, ranging from a dirty disc drive to a broken drive. If your drive can't read discs that don't have any obvious scratches or a dirty surface, and the same discs work in other drives, read on to find out how to determine the cause, and in some cases, fix the problem.

How to fix it

If your drive won't read *any* CD-ROM or audio CD disc

1. Make sure that the disc can be read in another drive or CD player, just to make sure that the surface isn't damaged somehow. If the disc works in another device, proceed to the next step.

2. Make sure that the optical drive doesn't have a disc in it.

3. Blow clean, dry air into the drive to remove any dust or debris that may have accumulated on the read head. You can get a can of compressed air at most photographic supply stores. If this does not help, proceed to the next step.

4. Clean the optical drive. You can use a standard audio CD player cleaning kit available at most music and electronics stores. In general, this requires placing the kit's cleaning solution—usually alcohol—on a special disc with brushes on the bottom side, and inserting the disc into the drive. The drive will spin and the brushes will clean off the read head lens. If this does not solve the problem, proceed to the next step.

5. If the drive still doesn't work, it may require repair or replacement. Keep in mind that a new, high-speed IDE CD-ROM drive costs less than $50, so it may not be worth repairing an older model.

> **Tip**
>
> Whether or not you have problems with your optical drive, it's a good idea to clean it at least once a year using a cleaning kit like the one described here. This helps remove any accumulated dust or grime before it becomes a problem—and before it gets more difficult to remove.

If your optical drive can't read a CD-R disc

1. Try the cleaning steps described in the previous section.

2. If that does not resolve the problem, try using a different type of disc when you burn your CD-R discs. CD-R media comes in different types based on the color of the light-sensitive dye and the reflective layer. There are two dyes—a blue dye and a dye that's more or less clear. There are also two kinds of reflective layers—gold and silver. These yield four possible combinations for CD-Rs: green/gold, blue/silver, gold, and silver. Some of these combinations have lower reflectivity, so that older optical drives may have difficulty reading them. You may need to try samples of all four types to find the one that works best with your drive.

3. If your drive can read CD-ROM and audio CD discs, but not any type of CD-R discs, it may need to be repaired or replaced.

If your optical drive can't read a CD-RW disc

1. If your optical drive is not a CD-RW drive, you need to check its specifications. CD-RW discs have lower reflectivity than CD-ROM and CD-R disks. As a result, older models may not be able to read the CD-RW discs. Check to see if your drive is rated as *MultiRead compatible*, which is a specification that indicates that the drive can read all CD formats, including CD-RW discs.

2. Your system must also be able to decipher the data that is stored on the disc. CD-RW discs can be recorded as if they were CD-R discs, in which case any MultiRead drive should be able to read them. However, CD-RW discs can also be recorded using something called *packet writing*, which does not require the separate recording sessions used by CD-R disc formats. Windows 98 has support for the Universal Disc Format (UDF) packet writing standard 1.02, but this is the format used for DVD discs. In order to read (or write) CD-RW discs, your system must support UDF 1.5. Windows 2000 includes read-only support for UDF 1.5. Windows 98 does not; it requires additional software. You can download UDF Reader—a free program for reading CD-RW discs on a MultiRead drive with Windows 95, 98, or NT—from the Adaptec site at *www.adaptec.com/support/advisor/cdrupdates/udfreaders.html*.

Tip

The MultiRead2 specification relates to DVD drives. Older DVD-ROM drives cannot read the newer DVD-RAM rewritable discs. Some new DVD-ROM drives and DVD players are rated as compatible with the *MultiRead2* specification, which means these devices can read DVD-RAM discs. This feature will make it practical to record movies on your own DVD discs, and to create data discs that other computers can read using DVD-ROM drives.

My optical drive is running slowly, or not performing at its top speed

Source of the problem

Your CD-ROM drive says that it is rated at 32x, which sounds pretty fast. But then you play some computer game, and at a crucial moment, just when the alien bad guys are about to come bursting through the air lock, your screen freezes. Then you hear a siren sound coming from your CD drive, and after it warbles high and low a few times, the image on your monitor comes unstuck and the bad guys blast you into the next galaxy. What happened?

The fact is that some performance problems are inherent in the CD drive itself. High-speed drives power down when not in use—to save wear and tear on the motor, but also to be quiet—and then they take a noticeable length of time to get back up to speed. Also, most are variable speed and have to speed up or slow down depending on what part of the disc they are trying to read. Finally, their speed rating is almost always a maximum that's achieved only on a CD that's loaded to maximum capacity, and even then only on the outermost edge of the disc. On the inside tracks, where the data is written first, a typical 24x CD-ROM drive performs at 12x speed or slower.

Still, there are some things you can do to maximize the performance of your optical drives.

How to fix it

1. Make sure that the disc you are trying to read is clean, clear of scratches, and free of other defects.

2. Clean your optical drive using a CD player cleaning kit that you can buy at most music or electronics stores.

Check the CD cache size (Windows 98 only)

1. Right-click on My Computer and then choose Properties.

2. Choose the Performance tab.

3. Choose the File System Properties button to open the File System Properties window.

4. Choose the CD-ROM tab.

5. Move the slide for Supplemental Cache Size all the way to the Large end of the scale. This will reserve the maximum amount of your computer's system memory for caching reads from your optical disk, but it will still be a relatively small amount compared to the total memory installed in your system. ▶

6. If you have an optical drive rated at 4x or faster (and almost all drives on recent systems are rated faster than this), choose Quad-Speed Or Higher in the Optimize Access Pattern For drop-down list.

7. Choose OK, and then OK again to close the File System Properties and System Properties dialog boxes.

Setting the DMA option correctly (Windows 98 only)

1. Consult your optical drive's documentation, and find out whether it supports Direct Memory Access (DMA). If Windows is configured for the wrong setting, the drive may perform much more slowly than it should.

2. Right-click on My Computer.

3. Choose Properties from the shortcut menu.

4. Choose the Device Manager tab.

5. Expand the category that includes your optical drive, usually CD-ROM Drives.

6. Select your optical drive.

7. Choose the Properties button to open the Properties window for your drive.

8. Choose the Settings tab.

9. If your optical drive supports DMA, make sure that there is a check in the DMA check box in the Options section. If your drive does not support DMA, make sure there is not a check in the check box.

10. Choose OK to close the drive's Properties window.

11. Choose OK to close the System Properties window.

My CD-R or CD-RW drive gets buffer underruns when creating discs

Source of the problem

If you have a CD-R or CD-RW drive, you'll learn to dreaded *buffer underrun* error messages—unless, of course, you *like* turning your CD-R discs into coasters because they've become quite useless as CDs. The problem grows from the way optical drives store data.

When you create a file on a hard disk, the data gets broken up into little chunks, with each chunk written any place where there is room. When you record a CD on a CD-R or CD-RW drive, the data is written in one long sequential chunk—actually a continuous spiral on the disc. If the flow of data is interrupted, a blank space appears in the continuous spiral, and when a drive tries to read the disc, it loses its place when it hits the blank spot. In short, a break in the data ruins the disc.

To keep the data flowing smoothly to the drive during the write process, CD-R and CD-RW drives have memory added to act as a buffer. Think of a bucket with a small hole at the bottom. The computer dumps lots of data into the bucket, and then the data trickles out the hole to provide a steady flow of data to write to the CD. As long as the computer comes back with more data before the bucket runs dry, the flow to the disc will be uninterrupted. If the computer doesn't refill the bucket in time, however, the stream stops and you get a buffer underrun error. And another coaster for your coffee table.

As drive write speeds have increased—effectively making the hole in the bucket larger—manufacturers have increased the size of the buffer, so the bucket can hold more data. You can still get buffer underrun errors, however. The causes include the computer being busy with other tasks and slow hard drive or CD drive performance. Here's how to identify the problem and—with a little luck—solve it.

How to fix it

1. Close all other programs while you are writing to a CD-R or CD-RW drive; the programs can steal processing time or need hard disk access, either of which can interrupt the flow of data

Tip

If you're copying audio tracks directly from one CD drive to a CD-R or CD-RW drive and you get static and pops in the new disc, the problem may be slow data transfer that's not slow enough to cause an error but that still creates flaws.

If both drives are Integrated Drive Electronics (IDE) drives, try installing them on separate IDE channels. If that doesn't help, try creating an image of the CD on your hard disk as an intermediate step in writing the CD. Your only other choices are using a different interface for one of the drives—such as Small Computer System Interface (SCSI) or Universal Serial Bus (USB)—or getting a newer CD-R or CD-RW drive with a larger buffer.

to the CD-R or CD-RW drive. In addition to closing any open applications, you can also close most of the programs that place icons in the System Tray on your taskbar; right-click on each, and choose Exit or Close or a similar option if one is available. If you still can't write a disc without a buffer underrun, even with all programs closed, proceed to the next step.

2. Write your discs at a slower rate. Most CD-R and CD-RW drives are rated at multiples of the standard audio CD playback speed. Your CD-writing software should let you pick different writing speeds; start with the slowest, which should be the standard audio CD speed, or *1x*. If this does not produce buffer underruns, you can try increasing the speed, one step at a time, until you determine the fastest speed that will reliably write discs without causing buffer underruns.

3. If slowing down the write speed doesn't help, or you want to take advantage of faster speeds, and you are trying to write data that is read directly from another CD drive, try creating an image of the CD you wish to create and storing it on your hard drive temporarily. Most CD-writing programs support this procedure; check the program's documentation for details. If you still get buffer underruns when using an image stored on the hard disk, you should defragment your hard disk.

To defragment your hard disk

1. Double-click on My Computer to open the My Computer window.

2. Select the hard disk where you want to store the CD image before writing it to the CD.

3. Right-click on that disk's icon.

4. Choose Properties from the shortcut menu.

5. In the drive's Properties window, choose the Tools tab. ▶

6. Choose the Defragment Now button.

7. Windows will defragment your hard disk, which means that it will place all the pieces of different files adjacent to each other on the drive. This will let the hard disk access the data more quickly.

8. If none of these solutions work, you may need to replace the CD-R or CD-RW drive with a model that has a larger buffer.

Other drives can't read discs I create on my CD-R or CD-RW drive

Source of the problem

CD-R or CD-RW drives sometimes have problems creating discs that other drives can read, for reasons that range from a dirty drive head to the wrong choice in the type of disc you use. If you've confirmed that the problem isn't in the playback drive, you have to look at the drive that's creating the discs.

How to fix it

1. Check the settings in the CD creation software you're using. Make sure the software is closing the session. If the session isn't closed, most drives won't be able to read the disc.

2. Try to read the disc in the same drive that created it. If it doesn't work, skip to the next step. If it works, try the disc in the drive that you want to use to play it. If that drive has a problem with the disc, see "My optical drive is having trouble reading discs" on page 204.

3. Make sure that your CD-R or CD-RW drive does not have a disc in it. Then use compressed air—available at photography supply shops—to blow clean, dry air into the drive to remove dust or debris that may be on the head. If this does not help, proceed to the next step.

4. Use a standard audio CD player cleaning kit to clean the drive's head. You can get a kit at most music and electronics stores. Follow the instructions that come with the kit to clean the drive head. If this does not solve the problem, proceed to the next step.

5. Try recording at a slower speed. Newer drives are able to record at multiples of the standard audio CD playback speed, such as eight (8x) or twelve (12x) times the standard speed. Use your recording software to record a short disc at the standard (1x) speed. If this resolves the problem, try recording at each faster speed to find the fastest speed that reliably records discs that your other drives can read.

6. Try different types of blank disc. Discs vary in quality and are rated for different recording speeds. Try different brands and speed ratings to see if one will provide more reliable results.

My optical drive tray won't open

Source of the problem

It may be apocryphal, but there's a classic story about the call received by a support technician at a major desktop computer maker. The customer complained, "My cup holder broke. I need a new one." Cup holder? The technician was puzzled and asked for details. "Yes, the cup holder," explained the frustrated customer. "You know, you push a button on the front of the computer, and a cup holder comes out. Now it won't go back in!"

Of course, the customer was talking about the tray in his CD-ROM drive, which has a familiar, round hole in the middle. And hanging a heavy cup of French roast in this delicate mechanism is definitely not recommended procedure.

Unfortunately, there may be times when you can't get your cup holder—er—CD or DVD tray—to eject, due to a mechanical problem such as a drive failure, an electrical problem that prevents the drive from getting the signal, or software that disables the mechanical switch in favor of a software command. Here's how to check out the problem.

How to fix it

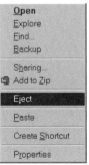

1. When the computer is on, hold down the eject button on the front of the drive to confirm that it doesn't work. (You've probably already done this step.)

2. Double-click on My Computer to open the My Computer window.

3. Find the icon for your optical drive. Right-click on the icon to open the shortcut menu, and select the Eject option. ▶

4. If the tray ejects, the mechanism works. Either the eject button on the drive is defective—in which case the drive needs to be repaired or replaced—or some program has disabled the button. To find out whether it's a mechanical problem, choose Start, Shut Down, Restart In MS-DOS Mode, and then OK. (If you're running Windows 2000, boot with a bootable Windows 98 floppy disk.)

5. After rebooting, press the eject button on the drive. If it works, you don't have a hardware problem.

6. If the tray does not eject, open the case—be sure read our advice in "Working inside your computer" at the beginning of this book, first. Check to make sure that the data and power cables are firmly attached to the optical drive. If they are, and the drive still doesn't eject, it probably needs to be repaired or replaced.

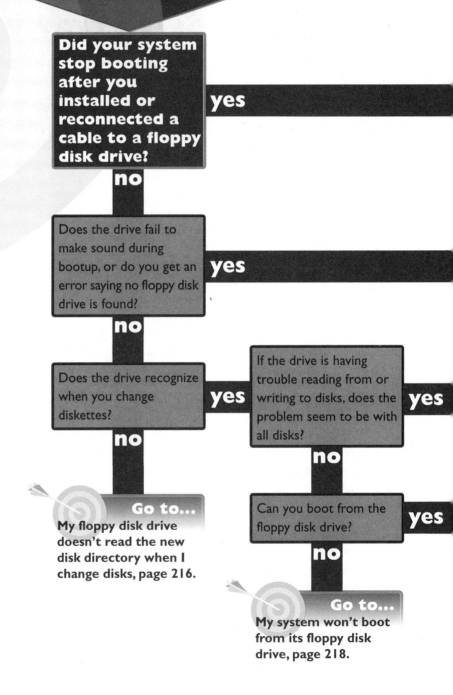

Drives

Did your system stop booting after you installed or reconnected a cable to a floppy disk drive?

yes

no

Does the drive fail to make sound during bootup, or do you get an error saying no floppy disk drive is found?

yes

no

Does the drive recognize when you change diskettes?

yes

If the drive is having trouble reading from or writing to disks, does the problem seem to be with all disks?

yes

no

no

Go to...
My floppy disk drive doesn't read the new disk directory when I change disks, page 216.

Can you boot from the floppy disk drive?

yes

no

Go to...
My system won't boot from its floppy disk drive, page 218.

floppy disk drives

Go to...

My computer doesn't find its floppy disk drive during bootup, page 214.

Go to...

My floppy disk drive doesn't seem to read any disks, page 219.

Go to...

Drives: removable disks, page 234.

Quick fix

The most common cause for this problem is that something is wrong with the floppy data cable.

1. Make sure that the colored edge of the ribbon cable is connected to Pin 1 of the floppy disk drive. This is usually the pin closest to the power connector.

2. If this doesn't solve the problem, inspect the ribbon cable carefully for any nicks or cuts. If you find any, replace the cable.

If the problem persists, see "Computer startup: blank screen" on page 68.

If your solution isn't here

Check these related chapters:

   Computer startup: blank screen, page 68

   Drives: removable disks, page 234

Or see the general troubleshooting tips on page xv.

My computer doesn't find its floppy disk drive during bootup

Source of the problem

On the original IBM PC, the only way to boot up was by using a floppy disk. But PC's have come a long way since then. Now there are all sorts of devices you can boot from: hard disk, CD-ROM, other optical drives, and proprietary removable disk drives such as an LS-120 or ZIP drive. And, of course, you can still boot from a floppy disk. Or maybe not.

The floppy disk drive's days seem to be numbered. Microsoft Windows 2000 can't boot from a floppy disk, and the current draft of the PC 2001 system recommendations—created by Microsoft and Intel with contributions from Compaq, Dell, Gateway, and Hewlett-Packard—calls for the elimination of the floppy disk controller entirely, although Integrated Drive Electronics (IDE) and universal serial bus (USB) floppy disk drives will be supported).

Even so, there are millions of floppy disk drives out there. And for Windows 95 and Windows 98 installations, the floppy disk drive can be an indispensable adjunct. But although floppy disk drives are relatively simple and remarkably reliable, there are occasions when the floppy disk drive doesn't answer the call when the power goes on—typically because the system BIOS (Basic Input/Output System) is not set correctly or there's a physical problem such as a reversed cable or loose connection. Here's how to fix the most common problems.

How to fix it

1. Turn on your computer, and enter the system's CMOS configuration utility, which lets you change settings for the BIOS. Check your computer's documentation, or check the screen for a prompt on how to start this function—sometimes named Setup. The Delete and F2 keys are the most common choices. If neither of these keys work, and your screen doesn't show you the key to press, see "The computer is booting from the wrong disk drive" on page 82 for more details about starting the CMOS utility.

2. Check the standard CMOS settings to see if the floppy disk drive is configured properly. Most current systems have a 3.5-inch floppy disk drive with a 1.44-MB capacity.

Tip

Just because you don't hear your floppy disk drive grind away when you turn on the computer's power doesn't necessarily mean that something is wrong with the drive. Some computer BIOS versions have configuration settings that let you disable the power-on self test check for the floppy disk drive. Choose this option, and the drive will sit silently during bootup. If you think this might be the case, check your system documentation or the CMOS configuration utility to see if your computer has such a setting.

3. Also check for a boot sequence item. Some systems can boot from the floppy disk drive, one or more hard disks, a CD-ROM or other optical drive, or even some proprietary devices. If you want to be able to boot from the floppy disk drive, make sure that it's listed first.

4. Check for other floppy-disk-drive-related settings. Some BIOS versions have support for features such as disabling the floppy disk drive or designating it as read-only. Make sure the floppy disk drive is set for normal operation; if you are not sure what a setting does, consult your computer's manual or contact the manufacturer.

5. Reboot your system. If the problem has not been resolved, continue to the next step.

6. Turn off the computer and open the case. But first, be sure you've read our recommendations in "Working inside your computer" at the beginning of this book.

7. Remove and reconnect the ribbon data cable from the floppy disk drive. Make sure that the colored edge of the cable connects to Pin 1 on the drive. In many cases, Pin 1 is closest to the power connector. ▶

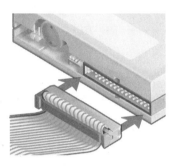

8. Remove and reconnect the ribbon cable from the floppy disk drive controller or motherboard port. Again, make sure that the colored edge of the cable connects to Pin 1. Pin 1 may be marked with a silk-screened label on the motherboard or card; if not, you will have to consult your manuals or contact the manufacturer to make sure of its position.

9. Remove and reconnect the power connector from the drive. A 3.5-inch floppy disk drive will usually have a small power connector with four colored wires. A 5.25-inch floppy disk drive uses a larger power connector with four colored wires; this is the same type of connector used for hard disks and optical drives such as CD-ROM and DVD-ROM drives. ▶

10. If the floppy disk drive still does not work on bootup, try using a different power connector from the computer's power supply, if one is available.

11. If the drive still doesn't work, try it in another computer in place of that computer's floppy disk drive, or take a floppy disk drive that you know works out of another computer and try it in the first computer, or try both tests. If the problem moves with the floppy disk drive, the drive may be in need of repair or replacement. If the drive works in the second machine, or a drive that you know is good doesn't work in the original system, the problem may be with the original system's floppy disk drive controller.

My floppy disk drive doesn't read the new disk directory when I change disks

Source of the problem

Life is full of imponderables. How do monarch butterflies migrate thousands of miles to a place that they've never been before? Why does toast always land with the buttered side down? And how can a floppy disk drive tell one disk from another?

We can't explain the first two—at least, we won't try here—but there is an answer for the last one. Inside each floppy disk drive there is a tiny switch that detects whether there is a disk in the drive. The computer tracks the status of this switch, using a signal called the *change line*. If the computer detects that the disk has been removed and reinserted, it reads the directory again in case the disk is different from the one that was removed.

If the switch is broken or its signal can't get to the computer, the computer won't know that the disk has been changed. So if your floppy disk drive doesn't read the new directory when you change disks, you need to find out why the computer isn't getting the signal and then fix the break in communications, or repair or replace the drive.

How to fix it

1. Turn off your computer and open the case. (Before you do, be sure to read our recommendations in "Working inside your computer" at the beginning of this book.)

2. Disconnect and reconnect the ribbon cable from the floppy disk drive and its controller or motherboard port. Be sure to reconnect it in the same position, so that the colored stripe is connected to Pin 1 on the connectors. ▶

3. Turn the computer on, let it boot, and test the floppy disk drive. If it works, you're done. If it doesn't, turn the system off and continue with the next step.

4. Inspect the ribbon cable carefully for any nicks, cuts, or sharp bends. These could indicate a broken lead. Pay special attention to the edge that is *not* colored. If there is any evidence of damage, replace the cable. Even if there's no evidence of damage, if you have another cable available that you know works, it's a good idea to swap out the cable as a way to definitively rule the cable in or out as the source of the problem.

5. Once again, turn the computer on, let it boot, and test the floppy disk drive. If it works, you're done. If it doesn't work, turn the system off and continue with the next step.

6. If the ribbon cable has two connectors that fit your floppy disk drive, try attaching the drive to the other connector.

7. Run the test again: turn the computer on, let it boot, and test the floppy disk drive. If the problem still isn't fixed, continue with the next step.

8. If you have another computer available and know that the floppy disk drive in the second computer is working properly when you change disks, try swapping floppy disk drives between the two computers. If you do this, be careful to note how the power cables and ribbon cables are connected to the drives before you unplug any cables. Not only do you want to make sure that you plug the cables in correctly when you swap the drives, you also want to make sure, as much as possible, that you're using the same cables and connectors as you were using before the swap. Ideally, the drives themselves should be the only thing that's changed.

9. What you need to determine is whether the problem goes with the drive or stays with the computer. If the problem goes with the drive, which will usually be the case, the drive itself is the culprit. If it stays with the computer, and you've already ruled out the cable as the source of the problem, your prime suspect is the floppy disk drive controller, which may be integrated into the system motherboard.

10. If the drive is malfunctioning, the micro switch in the drive may be broken or there may be a problem with its electrical connections. In either case, you may be able to have it repaired. Keep in mind, however, that a new floppy disk drive can cost less than $20, so it may not be worth the time or expense to salvage the old one.

11. If the problem lies with the floppy disk drive controller, you'll need to buy a new controller. If the current controller is on the motherboard, you'll have to disable it.

12. To disable an integrated floppy disk controller on the motherboard, turn on your computer and enter the system's CMOS configuration utility. Check your computer's documentation or check the screen for a prompt saying how to start this function; the Delete or F2 keys are the most common choices. If neither works and your screen doesn't show you the key to press, see "The computer is booting from the wrong disk drive" on page 82 for more details about starting the CMOS utility.

13. Once you've started the setup utility, look for a setting for the integrated floppy disk drive controller and disable it. Then close the utility.

Warning

In rare cases, changing which connector your floppy disk drive is plugged into may cause your system to change drive letter assignments—changing the floppy disk drive from Drive A to Drive B, for example. If this happens, go ahead and test the drive using its new drive letter.

If the drive works with the new drive designation, the most likely source of the problem is the ribbon cable or the connector on the cable. So if you want to use the drive designation you're used to, you will need to get a new cable. However, there is no reason you can't use the new drive designation, at least as a workaround, until you get the new cable.

My system won't boot from its floppy disk drive

Source of the problem

In the early days of personal computing, floppy disk drives were the drives you booted from. Today, the poor little floppy disk drive can get lost in the shuffle, so you can't boot from it on those few occasions when you want to. The culprit is often incorrect BIOS (Basic Input/Output System) settings or problems with the boot floppy disk. If you're having problems booting from your floppy disk drive, here's what to look for.

How to fix it

1. First confirm that the drive is making a sound when your system boots. If it isn't, start with "My computer doesn't find its floppy disk drive during bootup" on page 214.

2. Make sure the disk itself is bootable by booting from it on a different computer.

3. If the disk checks out OK and you have more than one floppy disk drive in your system, confirm that you've had the bootable disk in Drive A when you've tried booting from it.

4. If you're sure the disk was in Drive A, the next step is to confirm that your system can read the disk. Boot from your hard disk, insert the floppy disk in the floppy disk drive, and use Windows Explorer to view the contents of the disk. If you get an error or can't read the disk, proceed with the next step. If you can read the disk, skip to step 6.

5. Create a new bootable floppy disk using the same drive you're trying to boot from. Start with a full format. (See the Appendix, on page 337, for more details.) If the new bootable floppy disk doesn't work, proceed to the next step.

6. Restart your computer, and enter the CMOS configuration utility for your system. You can often enter the utility by pressing F2 or Delete during startup. If neither of these keys work and your screen doesn't show you the key to press, see "The computer is booting from the wrong disk drive" on page 82 for more details about starting the CMOS utility.

7. Check the boot sequence settings, which will probably be under the Advanced settings. Choose an option that lists Drive A as the first choice in the boot sequence.

8. Place the bootable floppy disk in Drive A, and exit the configuration utility, saving the changes. Your system will reboot, and it should boot from the floppy disk drive.

My floppy disk drive doesn't seem to read any disks

Source of the problem

If your system recognizes your floppy disk drive but can't read or write floppy disks reliably, it may be time for a new drive. Fortunately, a new drive costs only about $20. But spending even $20 is a waste if you don't have to spend it, so it's still worth making sure that the drive actually needs to be replaced.

How to fix it

1. If you're having trouble reading floppy disks, see if the drive can format one. Insert a disk in the drive, using a disk with the right capacity for the drive and that doesn't have data you need. Right-click on My Computer, and choose Explore to open Windows Explorer.

2. Right-click on the drive's icon in Windows Explorer, and choose Format.

3. In Windows 98, choose the Full option. (In Windows 2000, make sure that the Quick Format option check box is not checked.) Then choose Start to format the disk.

4. If the format fails, try formatting the disk on another computer to confirm that the disk is not the problem. If the drive can't format a disk that another drive can format, the drive may need to be repaired or replaced. Skip to step 7.

5. If the format succeeds, copy a small (under 100-kilobyte) data file to the disk using Windows Explorer. Then try to open the copy on the floppy disk. If the drive can't read the file, the drive probably needs to be repaired or replaced. Skip to step 7.

6. If the drive can read the file it copied, try reading the disk on another computer. If the second computer can't read the file, one of the drives is probably out of alignment and should be replaced. Try reading the disk on at least one other computer to confirm which drive is the problem.

7. Before you replace a questionable drive, try it in another system, if one's available, to rule out a problem with the floppy controller. If the original drive works in the new system, the controller is likely the problem. If the drive does not work in the new system, the drive is the likely source of the problem. For details about how to swap floppy disk drives between two computers, see "My floppy disk drive doesn't read the new disk directory when I change disks" on page 216.

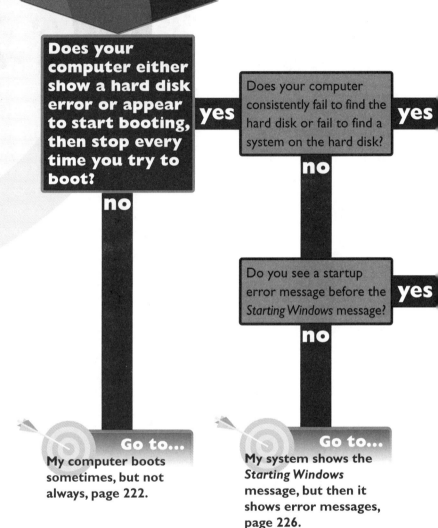

When you boot your computer, you may see an image of the computer manufacturer's logo or the Windows "cloud" screen at various stages. These screens can obscure helpful information that is being written to your screen.

Pressing the Escape key will get rid of the extraneous screens and reveal the text messages that may be hidden beneath them.

Does your computer either show a hard disk error or appear to start booting, then stop every time you try to boot? **yes**

no

Does your computer consistently fail to find the hard disk or fail to find a system on the hard disk? **yes**

no

Do you see a startup error message before the *Starting Windows* message? **yes**

no

Go to...
My computer boots sometimes, but not always, page 222.

Go to...
My system shows the *Starting Windows* message, but then it shows error messages, page 226.

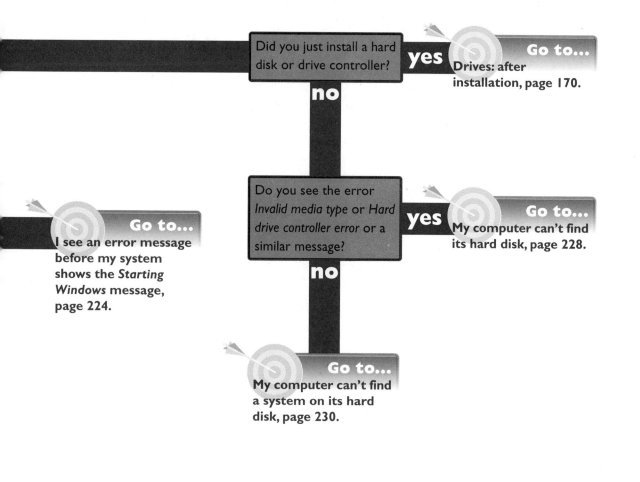

Did you just install a hard disk or drive controller?

yes Go to... **Drives: after installation, page 170.**

no

Do you see the error *Invalid media type* or *Hard drive controller error* or a similar message?

yes Go to... **My computer can't find its hard disk, page 228.**

Go to... **I see an error message before my system shows the *Starting Windows* message, page 224.**

no

Go to... **My computer can't find a system on its hard disk, page 230.**

If your solution isn't here
Check these related chapters:
Computer startup: won't boot, page 74
Drives: after installation, page 170
Drives: removable disks, page 234
Or see the general troubleshooting tips on page xv.

My computer boots sometimes, but not always

Source of the problem

As we've stated elsewhere in this book, intermittent problems are the most vexing problems of all. If you can't make the problem happen consistently, it's hard to pin down the source, and even harder to know when you've solved the problem. Whenever the problem goes away, the question remains whether you actually fixed it, or just got rid of it for the moment.

Fortunately for your sanity, intermittent problems with hard disks are usually physical. Often they are caused by a loose connection, which is relatively easy to fix. Alas, those that aren't caused by loose connections are often caused by a failing hard disk that should be replaced.

How to fix it

If the problem happens when you first turn on the computer

1. Problems that turn up when the system is cold are usually mechanical. Shut down the computer, and open the case. (Be sure to check our suggestions first in "Working inside your computer" at the beginning of this book.)

2. Remove and reconnect the power connector to the hard disk. This is usually a white connector with four colored wires. If you have to work the connector back and forth to loosen it, be sure to move it in the same plane as its long edge.

3. Remove and reconnect the data ribbon cable that's connected to the hard disk. Make sure that you reconnect the cable in the same orientation that you found it. If the drive works sometimes, the cable is oriented correctly. Be careful not to reverse it by accident. Make sure that the colored edge of the cable is attached to Pin 1 on the hard disk.

4. Remove and reconnect the data ribbon cable from the hard disk controller. The connector may be on the motherboard or on a separate expansion card.

5. If the hard disk controller is a separate expansion card, remove the card and reseat it in its expansion slot.

> **Tip**
>
> Here's a rule of thumb for intermittent computer problems in general: If the problem happens while the system is cold—such as when you first turn it on—the problem is most likely mechanical, such as a loose connection. On the other hand, if the problem occurs when the system is hot—after it has been running for a while—it is probably caused by a semiconductor component that is close to failure.

6. You may have to use the computer for a while to find out if the problem is gone. If it isn't, you'll need to run a surface scan of the hard disk to make sure that there are no defects on its surface.

7. Open My Computer, right-click the drive icon, and choose Properties.

8. Choose the Tools tab. ▶

9. In the Error Checking Status area (the Error Checking area in Microsoft Windows 2000), choose Check Now.

10. In Windows 98, under Type Of Test choose Thorough, and then the Start button. (In Windows 2000, check the Scan For And Attempt Recovery Of Bad Sectors check box, and then choose the Start button.)

11. If this doesn't resolve the problem, try installing the hard disk in another computer and see if it will boot reliably, or try a different hard disk in this system. If the problem goes with the hard disk, you're well advised to replace it before it fails. If the problem stays with the original system, you probably need to replace the hard disk controller.

If the problem happens only when rebooting after running for a while

1. Shut down the computer and open the case. (Be sure to check our suggestions first in "Working inside your computer" at the beginning of this book.)

2. Make sure that the airflow around the hard disk and the hard disk controller isn't obstructed. Reroute the ribbon and power cables if necessary to improve the flow of air.

3. If this doesn't solve the problem, move the hard disk to a different drive bay so it will have an open bay next to it, if that's possible. You may be able to add auxiliary fans to the empty bay to increase airflow.

4. If the hard disk controller is a separate expansion card, move it to a different slot if one is available. Try to arrange your system with empty slots next to the card so it gets more air.

5. If the problem still shows up, try a different hard disk. If the problem then goes away, consider replacing the original hard disk permanently, before it fails. If the problem remains, you probably need to replace the hard disk controller.

I see an error message before my system shows the *Starting Windows* message

Source of the problem

If you've reached this solution by going through the flowchart at the start of this chapter, you're getting an error message before your system indicates that it's starting to load Windows but the error message does not appear to involve the hard disk. (If the error message does refer to the hard disk or a missing operating system or something similar, go back to the flowchart and choose *Yes* in response to the question "Does your computer consistently fail to find the hard disk or fail to find a system on the hard disk?")

If your system recognizes the hard disk and starts to load, but it doesn't get as far as showing the *Starting Windows* message, and you're sure that Windows is installed properly, there are two likely causes. Either the system is trying to boot from the wrong disk, or there is a problem with the boot file configuration. Note that except for the first step, these comments do not apply to Windows 2000.

How to fix it

1. Check your floppy disk drive and any other removable media drives—such as CD-ROM and Zip drives—and remove any discs you find in these drives. If you find any, reboot the computer. If this fixes the problem, you may want to check "The computer is booting from the wrong disk drive" on page 82.) If this does not solve the problem and you are not using Windows 2000, proceed to the next section.

If an error message mentions Himem.sys

1. If Windows can't find Himem.sys or finds a corrupted version of the file, you should see an error message saying so, and possibly showing the location where it expected to find the file. If the error message shows a location, write it down. Otherwise you can safely assume that Windows expects to find Himem.sys in the Windows folder. In either case, you need to put a

> **Tip**
> If you have access to another computer that's running *exactly* the same version of Windows, the easiest way to put a new copy of Himem.sys on your computer is to copy the file to a floppy disk on the other computer, then boot from the floppy disk drive on your computer and copy the file from the floppy disk to the Windows folder of your hard disk.

new copy of Himem.sys in the appropriate folder. To do this, you first need a bootable floppy disk that will let your system recognize your CD-ROM drive. If you don't already have one, you'll need to create one on another system. (For details on how to create a bootable floppy disk, see the Appendix on page 337.)

2. Boot with the floppy disk.

3. Put your Windows 98 CD in your CD-ROM drive.

4. At the command line, type:

d:\win98\extract d:\win98\base5.cab himem.sys /l c:\windows

and press Enter to create a new copy of Himem.sys in your Windows folder.

5. Remove the floppy disk from the floppy disk drive.

6. Reboot your computer. The problem should be solved.

7. You should check the hard disk, since it may have been the source of the problem. Open My Computer, right-click the drive icon, and choose Properties and then the Tools tab.

8. In the Error Checking Status area, choose Check Now. Then, under Type Of Test, choose Thorough and then the Start button.

If the error message refers to other files

1. Boot with a floppy disk to the command prompt.

2. Change to the hard disk by typing **c:** and pressing Enter.

3. Make sure that you're at the root directory by typing **cd ** and pressing Enter.

4. Type **rename config.sys config.old** and press Enter.

5. Type **rename autoexec.bat autoexec.old** and press Enter.

6. Remove the floppy disk from the floppy disk drive.

7. Reboot your system. If this solves the problem, you will need to check the contents of your Config.sys and Autoexec.bat files to determine which line is causing the problem. You can use Microsoft Notepad to recreate each file a few lines at a time until you find the culprit.

Tip

For these instructions, we assume that the floppy disk drive is Drive A, your hard disk drive is Drive C, and the CD drive is Drive D. If the drive assignments are different on your system, you'll need to make the appropriate changes in the commands. We also assume that your system is looking for Himem.sys in the Windows folder. If the error message shows a different location, you'll need to substitute that location for the Windows folder in the appropriate commands.

My system shows the *Starting Windows* message, but then shows error messages

Source of the problem

You say that Windows starts to load, but then you get a blue screen with an error message warning that Windows can't find a certain file?

Don't panic. This is a software problem, and all it means is that Windows couldn't find a file that it's been told to find. We're covering it here because sometimes a hardware problem is the reason the file's gone AWOL. In any case, the error message screen also includes an instruction to press a key to continue. When you follow that instruction, there are two possible outcomes: either Windows will continue to load normally and then will run reliably, or it won't. If Windows loads and runs, the likely cause of the error message is the incomplete deletion of software associated with a piece of hardware or a program. If Windows runs, but something that used to work stops working, a critical file is either missing or damaged. And that could be caused by a failing hard disk. Alas, if Windows won't run at all, you may need to reinstall it.

How to fix it

If Windows continues to load and runs normally

1. Write down the name of the file that's missing. (If you see error messages indicating that there is more than one missing file, write all the names down and repeat these steps for each one.)

2. Choose Start, choose Run, type **regedit** in the Open text box, and then choose OK.

3. Choose Edit, choose Find, and type the name of the missing file in the Find What text box. (The Keys, Values, and Data check

Warning

This solution involves editing with the Registry Editor, which you should approach with caution. Any changes you make are immediate, there is no undo feature, and you don't get the option to save or cancel your changes at the end. So be careful. And make detailed notes about anything you change or delete so you can return everything to its original state if necessary. (Note too that there are Registry editors and utilities available as commercial programs, shareware, and freeware. You may find these safer and easier to use than the Windows Regedit program.)

boxes should all be checked, and the Match Whole String Only check box should not be checked.) Choose the Find Next button. ▶

4. If Regedit finds an entry for the file, look at the full entry for clues about the program or hardware it's associated with. If it's related to something you're still using, close Regedit without making any changes (choose Registry, Exit), and reinstall the software for that program or device. This should solve the problem.

5. If you determine that the Registry entry is associated with something you have deleted or removed from the system, you'll need to delete the key that mentions that file. (Don't forget to write it down first, so you can recreate it if necessary.) Then press F3 to find the next instance of the file name in the Registry, and delete that key as well. Continue until you have deleted all references to the file, and then choose Registry, Exit to exit the program.

6. Restart your computer. If a new problem shows up, restore the registry entries using a backup or your notes on the entries you deleted.

If Windows loads but does not run correctly

1. You first need to find out if the hard disk is damaged or failing: Open My Computer, right-click the hard disk's icon, and choose Properties.

2. Choose the Tools tab, and, in the Error Checking Status area (the Error Checking area in Windows 2000), choose Check Now.

3. In Windows 98, under Type Of Test, choose Thorough and then the Start button. (In Windows 2000, check the Scan For And Attempt Recovery Of Bad Sectors check box, and then choose the Start button.) (The rest of this section applies to Windows 98 only.)

4. If the utility doesn't find any errors on the hard disk, close the open windows and choose Start, Programs, Accessories, System Tools, and then System Information.

5. Choose Tools, System File Checker.

6. Select the Scan For Altered Files option and choose Start.

7. This program will check all your Windows system files and replace any changed files with fresh copies from your original Windows CD.

My computer can't find its hard disk

Source of the problem

Before your computer can boot from your hard disk, it first has to find it. If there is something wrong with it—it's not getting power, there's a hardware failure, or some other issue—the hard disk won't answer the call from your system. Problems finding the hard disk fall into two main categories. If the hard disk isn't spinning at all, you've got one set of causes to consider, ranging from a loose power connection to a dead hard disk. If the disk is spinning, you have a wholly different set of issues to consider, including a loose data cable and the wrong configuration in your computer's settings.

How to fix it

1. Determine whether your hard disk is spinning. The platters are sealed inside the drive, so you can't see any movement, but you may be able to hear them spinning up to speed when you turn on the computer. Many drives are very quiet, however, and you may need to take the cover off your computer to hear them. (Be sure to review our suggestions first in "Working inside your computer" at the beginning of this book.)

2. If you still can't hear the platters spinning, rest your fingers lightly on the drive as you turn on the computer. You should be able to feel the vibration as the platters spin up to speed.

3. If resting your fingers on the drive leaves you with doubts about whether the platters are spinning, use this old car mechanic's trick: Take a short wooden or hard plastic stick—such as a ruler or a chopstick—and place one end against the hard disk and the other end against (not in!) your ear. Then turn on the computer. (You may need another person's help with this step.) The stick will transmit the vibrations from the drive. If the platters are spinning, you should be able to hear the sound clearly.

If the platters are not spinning

1. With the case still open, shut down the computer.

2. Check the power connector on the hard disk. The connector is generally white with four colored wires attached. Unplug and reconnect it to make sure that it is securely seated. Then turn on the computer again and see if the disk spins. If you have to work the connector back and forth to loosen it, be sure to move it in the same plane as its long edge as shown on the following page.

3. If the hard disk still does not spin, turn off the system and try using a different power connector. It's possible that the one you are using has a broken connection.

4. If changing the power connector doesn't help (or if you don't have another power connector available inside your computer to test with the drive), try connecting the drive in another computer, if you have one available. If the drive spins up in the new computer, there may be something wrong with your power supply; see "I need to replace my power supply" on page 72. If the drive does not spin up on the other system, the most likely cause is that there is something wrong with it, and it needs to be replaced.

If the platters are spinning

1. Shut down your computer and open the case, if it isn't open already.

2. Remove the ribbon cable from the hard disk, and reconnect it. Make sure that the colored edge of the cable is connected to Pin 1 on the hard disk drive. Pin 1 should be marked on or near the connector. If it isn't marked, check the documentation for your system to find the correct way to orient the cable. ▶

3. If the hard disk uses an Enhanced Integrated Drive Electronics (EIDE) interface, rather than a Small Computer System Interface (SCSI) interface, start your computer and enter the Basic Input/ Output System (BIOS) configuration utility. Your computer may provide an onscreen prompt during the boot process to press a certain key to enter Setup. The most common choices are Del and F2. If there is no prompt and neither of these keystrokes work, check your documentation or check with the manufacturer to find the correct keystroke. (For more details about starting the setup utility, see "The computer is booting from the wrong disk drive" on page 82.)

4. If the BIOS configuration utility has a hard disk autodetect feature (most do), use it to find and identify the hard disk. If it cannot find the hard disk or identify it correctly, there may be a problem with the hard disk itself, and you should skip to step 6.

5. If there is no autodetect hard disk feature in the BIOS configuration utility, check your system documentation or check with the manufacturer to determine what the correct settings should be, and then set them manually in the configuration utility.

6. If the hard disk still doesn't work, or if it's a SCSI drive, go to the chapter "Drives: after installation" on page 170 for troubleshooting suggestions for EIDE and SCSI hard disks.

My computer can't find a system on its hard disk

Source of the problem

If your computer fails to find a bootable disk when it starts up, you can get all sorts of different error messages. The messages are generated by the system's Basic Input/Output System (BIOS) program, and vary from computer to computer. One thing can be said for sure; it is going to sound scary. Here are some of the possibilities:

- Missing operating system
- NO ROM BASIC
- Nonsystem disk or disk error
- Boot error

All of these mean essentially the same thing: your computer can't find a disk with the operating system. The causes range from the system looking at the wrong disk to a problem with the operating system on the disk.

How to fix it

If you are running Windows 98

1. Boot to the command prompt from a write-protected, bootable floppy disk that has FDISK.EXE and SYS.COM on it. Make sure that the floppy disk was created using the same version of Windows that is installed on your hard disk. For more details on creating a boot floppy disk, see the Appendix on page 337. If you have problems booting from the floppy disk drive, see "The computer is booting from the wrong disk drive" on page 82.

2. Scan your hard disk using a good virus checking utility to make sure that your boot sector has not been infected with a virus. If it has been infected, follow the instructions in the anti-virus program to deal with the problem. If it hasn't been infected, continue with the following steps.

Tip

What is ROM BASIC and why does your computer keep trying to find it?

The answer is a bit obscure, but contains a bit of interesting PC history. The original IBM PC was designed so it could operate without any disk drives at all. A simple version of the BASIC programming language was a permanent part of the system's BIOS. If no operating system was loaded during the boot process, this version of BASIC would load. You couldn't store your programs to floppy disk, because the disk operating system wasn't loaded, so this feature had only limited practical value.

When other companies created their own PC-compatible BIOS versions, they left out the BASIC language, but to maintain compatibility with the original, some kept the feature that tried to load it. The result is that even today you get the error message *NO ROM BASIC* on some computers.

3. Make a backup of any important files on your hard disk. Then try to restore the Master Boot Record on the hard disk. At the command prompt, type **fdisk /mbr** and press Enter.

4. Try to boot from the hard disk. If it does not boot, refresh the boot files. At the command prompt, type **sys c:** and press Enter.

If you are running Windows 2000

1. Format a floppy disk on another computer running Windows 2000.

2. Copy Boot.ini, Ntldr, and Ntdetect.com to the floppy disk. (Boot.ini, Ntldr, and Ntdetect.com are hidden system files.)

3. Use Notepad to open the Boot.ini file on the floppy disk. It should look similar to the following:
```
[boot loader]
timeout=30
default=multi(0)disk(0)rdisk(0)partition(1)\WINNT
[operating systems]
multi(0)disk(0)rdisk(0)partition(1)
\WINNT="Microsoft Windows 2000 Server" /fastdetect
```

4. If you installed Windows 2000 to a directory other than the default, \WINNT, change \WINNT in lines 3 and 6 to the correct path. For example, if you installed Windows 2000 to C:\Win2K, the Boot.ini file should look like the following:
```
[boot loader]
timeout=30
default=multi(0)disk(0)rdisk(0)partition(1)\Win2K
[operating systems]
multi(0)disk(0)rdisk(0)partition(1)
\Win2K="Microsoft Windows 2000 Server" /fastdetect
```

5. If your computer boots from an IDE, EIDE, or ESDI hard drive, or if your computer boots from the first or second SCSI drive, skip to step 6. Otherwise replace each occurrence of *multi(0)* with *scsi(0)* in Boot.ini, and copy the correct device driver for your SCSI controller to the floppy disk and rename the driver as Ntbootdd.sys.

6. Save your changes and close Notepad.

7. Put the floppy disk in your computer's A drive.

8. Turn on your computer. If your computer still doesn't boot correctly, skip to step 11.

9. Copy Boot.ini, Ntldr, and Ntdetect.com from the floppy disk to the root directory of your hard disk.

10. Remove the floppy disk from Drive A and restart your computer. If your computer boots correctly into Windows 2000, stop here; otherwise proceed to step 11.

> *If this solution didn't solve your problem, go to the next page.*

My computer can't find
a system on its hard disk

(continued from page 231)

11. If your system can boot from a CD or if you have your Windows 2000 Setup boot disks, skip to step 15; otherwise you'll need to make Windows 2000 Setup boot disks. You'll need four blank, formatted floppy disks.

12. Put the Windows 2000 CD-ROM in the CD-ROM drive of another computer running Windows.

13. Click Start, and then click Run.

14. In the Open box, type **drive:\bootdisk\makeboot a:** (where *drive* is the drive letter of the CD-ROM drive) and then press Enter. Follow the onscreen instructions to create the Windows 2000 Setup boot disks.

15. Boot your computer from either the Windows 2000 CD-ROM or the Windows 2000 Setup boot disks.

16. Press R when Setup asks you whether you want to set up Windows 2000, repair a Windows 2000 installation, or quit.

17. Press R when Setup asks you whether you want to use the recovery console or the emergency repair process.

18. Press F to select the Fast Repair option.

19. Press L to have Setup manually find your Windows 2000 installation.

20. Be sure your Windows 2000 CD is in your CD-ROM drive, and then press Enter to repair your Windows 2000 installation.

21. When Setup is finished, it will wait 15 seconds and then reboot your computer. If you have a floppy disk in Drive A or a CD-ROM in your CD-ROM drive, be sure to remove them before your computer reboots.

Your computer should now boot correctly into Windows 2000. If not, you might be able to find more information by searching the Microsoft Knowledge Base at *search.support.microsoft.com/ kb/c.asp*. (It's a good idea to search this database even if your computer is now working correctly; there are many good articles on how to back up your system files and install and use the Windows 2000 recovery console.)

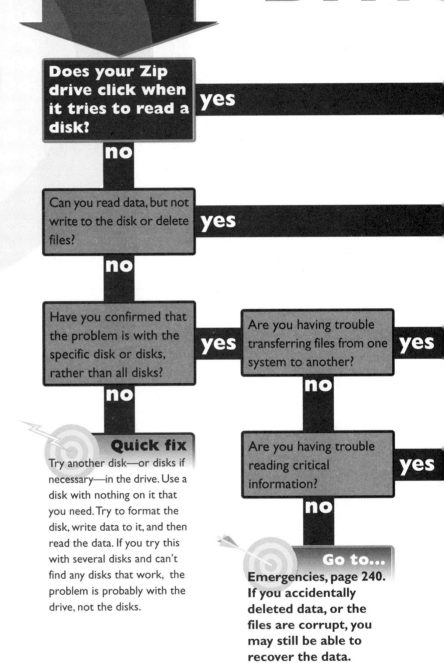

Drive

Make fresh copies of the data saved on removable disks at least every two years. Verify that you can read the data reliably when you make the copy.

Not only does this give you some assurance that the data is still safe, it also reminds you to create new copies in different formats as you change your equipment. For example, you would be able to move your data from 5.25-inch disks to 3.5-inch disks while you still have a system that can read the larger disks. The same issues apply to changes in operating systems over time, or to other disk formats such as LS-120 or Zip.

Does your Zip drive click when it tries to read a disk?   **yes**

no

Can you read data, but not write to the disk or delete files?   **yes**

no

Have you confirmed that the problem is with the specific disk or disks, rather than all disks?   **yes**

Are you having trouble transferring files from one system to another?   **yes**

no

no

Quick fix

Try another disk—or disks if necessary—in the drive. Use a disk with nothing on it that you need. Try to format the disk, write data to it, and then read the data. If you try this with several disks and can't find any disks that work, the problem is probably with the drive, not the disks.

Are you having trouble reading critical information?   **yes**

no

Go to...

Emergencies, page 240. If you accidentally deleted data, or the files are corrupt, you may still be able to recover the data.

: removable disks

Go to...

I hear clicking from my Zip drive (aka *The Click of Death*), page 236.

Go to...

I can read from a disk, but I can't write to it or delete from it, page 238.

Quick fix

If your system can't read files you're trying to transfer from another computer, the drives on one or both systems may be misaligned or the disk may have been formatted originally on a third system that is out of alignment with the system you're trying to transfer files to. You can often get around this problem.

1. Format an appropriate disk in the machine you're trying to transfer files to.

2. Put the disk in the system you're trying to tranfer files from.

3. Copy the files to the disk. If you can successfully copy the files to the disk, you should be able to read those files in the machine you're trying to transfer files to.

4. Move the disk to the system you're trying to transfer the files to and copy the files to the hard disk.

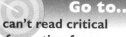
Go to...

I can't read critical information from a removeable disk, page 239.

If your solution isn't here

Check these related chapters:

Computer hardware and Windows, page 22

Drives: CD, CD-R, CD-RW, DVD, page 196

Or see the general troubleshooting tips on page xv.

I hear clicking from my Zip drive (aka *The Click of Death*)

Source of the problem

Disk drives occasionally die. When Iomega's Zip (and Jaz) drives die, they often start making a clicking noise, which has earned such charming names as *Click Death*, *The Click of Death*, and *COD*.

The clicking sound indicates that the read/write head is having trouble finding data on the disk. And if the head can't find the right place to read data from, it cycles over and over again, clicking each time. This repetitive clicking is *not* a normal sound. Sometimes it simply means that it's time to retire the disk cartridge, but in many Click of Death events, the drive itself is damaged. In some cases, a damaged drive can damage disks that were doing just fine until you put them in the drive. And according to reports, there are some very rare cases—for Zip drives only—in which the disk can be damaged in a way that will damage another drive. The only practical fix when this happens is to replace the drive. But even so, there are few issues you should know about, and a few additional points you should keep in mind.

How to fix it

1. If you hear even an occasional clicking from a Zip or Jaz drive, the drive or disk may be on its way to failure. Make sure you have a copy of any data on that cartridge, and keep that backup current if you continue to use the disk and drive. Also consider retiring that particular disk cartridge.

2. If the drive fails, you *may* be able to read the cartridge's data on another drive, but remember that there is a small risk that the cartridge may be damaged in a way that can damage the other drive as well. So understand that you are taking a risk, however small, if you insert the cartridge in another drive.

3. If you insert a disk cartridge from one drive that has been clicking and is unable to read the cartridge and find that the new drive cannot read it either and also starts clicking, this does not necessarily mean you've damaged the second drive. The disk cartridge itself may be damaged, or the first drive may have

> **Tip**
>
> You may be able to diagnose a potential problem with a Zip drive or cartridge using a free utility from Steve Gibson Research Corporation. Trouble in Paradise is a Windows program that tests Iomega Zip and Jaz drives and cartridges for possible damage and may be able to warn of problems before they become fatal to either your drive or your data. Check *www.grc.com/clickdeath.htm* for more information on this program.

written data on the disk in a way that makes it impossible for the second drive to find it. And if the second drive can't find the data, it will produce the clicking sound. Try a cartridge in the second drive that has never been in a damaged drive. The drive should be able to read the cartridge without a problem. However, if you suspect that the cartridge may have damaged the second drive, don't even consider placing the cartridge in a third drive.

So many drives, so many Click Deaths

The best description we've ever heard of the lottery is that it's a tax imposed on people who don't understand statistics. The Click of Death is pretty much in the same category: there are a lot of dead Zip drives out there, but that doesn't necessarily mean there's anything wrong with the design or manufacture of the drives. It may only mean that Iomega has sold a lot of drives. (We will deal only with Zip drives in this discussion, but the same concepts apply to all disk drives.)

A typical mean time between failure (MTBF) for drives is 100,000 to 300,000 hours. Iomega claims 100,000 hours for the Zip drive. Contrary to what most people think, a 100,000 MTBF does *not* mean that the drive is supposed to last 100,000 hours—which would be about 11.4 years of uninterrupted operation. In fact, the design lifetime for drives is typically five years. What the MTBF tells you is that if you ignore the infant mortality rate (drives that die in the first two to three weeks) and you replace drives when they reach the end of their design lifetime (typically every five years), then for every 100,000 drives you have operating, one drive will die *every hour*.

A reasonable assumption is that Zip drives average 8 hours of operation per day, so that for every 100,000 Zip drives, 8 will die every day.

And for every 1,000,000 Zip drives, 80 will die. *Every day.*

As of this writing, Iomega's latest published number of Zip drives shipped is 32,000,000 (yes, 32 *million*), all in the first five years of the Zip drive's existence. If only half of those are still being used, then the 100,000 MTBF figure means that 16 times 80, or 1280 drives, will die every day. If we assume that they are being used 5 days a week, 50 weeks a year, or 250 days per year, we would expect 320,000 drives to die every year. If there are more drives still in use, and if they are used more hours per day on average, or more days per week, the number quickly goes higher. But even 320,000 is a lot of dead drives in a year. And 320,000 is a conservative number based on the claimed MTBF and the number of drives sold. Add a few more drives for infant mortality, and some more for people who run the drive past its design lifetime—at which point its failure rate goes way up.

So are there a lot of dead Zip drives out there?

You betcha.

Does it indicate that there is anything wrong with the design or manufacture?

Nope. Or, at the very least, *not necessarily.* Lacking the complete statistics on the number of dead Zip drives, we can't give a definitive answer. We can only point out that given the stated mean time between failure, we expect to see a lot of dead Zip drives. And we're not surprised that lots of people with dead Zip drives have found each other and established Web sites to complain to each other about how many Zip drives have died.

I can read from a disk, but I can't write to it or delete from it

Source of the problem

The disk is in the drive, and you can read files from it, but you can't delete files or save new files. What's wrong? Chances are that there's a simple answer to the problem. The disk's write-protect feature may be turned on, preventing you from deleting or overwriting the data on the disk. Similarly, you may simply have run out of space on the disk, or you may have too many files in the root directory. Here's how to check the problem out.

How to fix it

1. Remove the disk from the drive.

2. Look for a write-protect or write-enable tab on the disk cartridge. For example, 3.5-inch floppy disks have a small plastic slider that can cover a hole in one corner of the disk. If the slider covers the hole, you can only read data from the disk. With 5.25-inch drives, the equivalent notch has to be uncovered to let you write data to the disk or delete files.

3. If the disk is not write-protected and you cannot write any data to the disk, put the disk in the drive and open Windows Explorer.

4. Right-click on the drive's icon, and choose Properties.

5. Check to see if there is free space on the disk. Also, choose the Tools tab and run the error-checking feature to make sure that there aren't any lost file fragments taking up space.

6. If there is sufficient free space on the disk and you are trying to save a file to the root directory, use Windows Explorer to look at the contents of the root directory. If there are 512 files and folders in the root (or 224 on a 3.5-inch floppy disk), you will need to delete some files or move them.

> **Tip**
>
> Never take a removable disk out of its drive while the activity light is on. (Most drives have an activity light; some have a power light as well.) If you remove the disk while the drive is writing, you could lose some or all of the data on the disk. If you can eject the disk using a command from the computer this will assure that all write operations finish before the disk is ejected.

I can't read critical information from a removable disk

Source of the problem

On occasion, we have been known to describe a product as a "write-only backup device." Our not-so-subtle implication is that the storage device is so unreliable that you can't count on it to read the backed up data when you need it. Unfortunately, Murphy's Law dictates that you won't find out about a problem with your backed up data—or critical files such as drivers on a distribution disk—until you need it. If you go to recover some valuable data from a removable disk and your computer chokes, don't panic. Very often, the problem is simply that you can't read the particular disk with the particular drive, typically because the drive is out of alignment with the drive that originally created the disk. If that's the case, it isn't hard to get the data back.

How to fix it

1. Try to read the disk in another drive. If the drive is on another computer and you can read the data, copy it to the second computer's hard disk. You might want to create a temporary folder first, and copy the files to the temporary folder.

2. Take a new disk and format it on the first computer.

3. Take the newly formatted disk to the second computer. In most cases, you'll be able to copy the recovered files successfully from the hard disk to the new disk.

4. If you can copy the files to the new disk, bring it back to the original computer. You should have no problem copying the files to the computer's hard disk.

5. If using the newly formatted removable disk doesn't let you transfer the files for any reason, look for other approaches to moving files between the two computers. You may be able to send them from one computer to the other as e-mail attachments, by way of a local area network, or by using a file transfer utility.

6. If you can't find a computer that can read the data from the original disk and the data is critical, consider using a professional data recovery service. These services can be expensive, but they use sophisticated techniques and equipment that often succeed where normal methods fail.

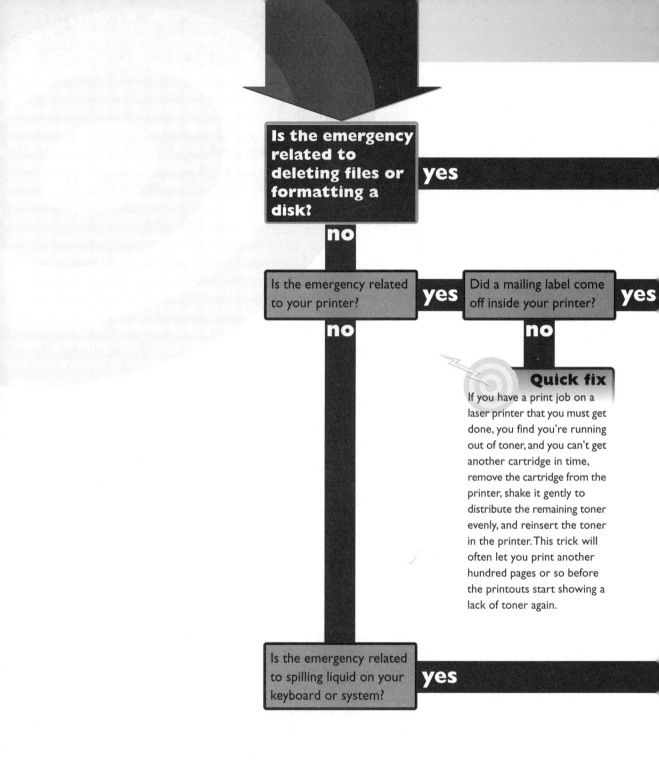

Is the emergency related to deleting files or formatting a disk?

yes

no

Is the emergency related to your printer?

yes

Did a mailing label come off inside your printer?

yes

no

no

Quick fix

If you have a print job on a laser printer that you must get done, you find you're running out of toner, and you can't get another cartridge in time, remove the cartridge from the printer, shake it gently to distribute the remaining toner evenly, and reinsert the toner in the printer. This trick will often let you print another hundred pages or so before the printouts start showing a lack of toner again.

Is the emergency related to spilling liquid on your keyboard or system?

yes

Emergencies

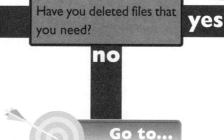

Have you deleted files that you need?

yes — Go to... **I've deleted files that I need, page 242.**

no

Quick fix

If you can reach the label, peel off as much as you can and then remove the adhesive with some light machine oil or salad oil. Be sure to remove all of the label and adhesive residue or else paper may not feed reliably. Also be sure to clean off all the oil residue when you finish, and be careful not to use so much that you drip any inside the printer.

Go to... **I've formatted a disk or drive that has files I need, page 244.**

Go to... **I spilled something on my keyboard or computer, page 246.**

If your solution isn't here
Check these related chapters:
Computer hardware and Windows, page 22
Computer startup: blank screen, page 68
Computer startup: won't boot, page 74
Or see the general troubleshooting tips on page xv.

I've deleted files that I need

Source of the problem

It happens so quickly—most often late at night when you're exhausted from having pushed yourself to finish some work that *must* be done by morning. You select a file or two in Microsoft Windows Explorer. Maybe you hold down a key too long, or the mouse slips, and you select some extra files or a folder. Then you press the Delete key or Shift+Delete, and automatically confirm your action. Boom—the files are gone—usually just as you realize that you're deleting one or more of the wrong files.

Have they disappeared into the ether? Can you entice them to rise, phoenix-like, from the digital ashes? The answer is a definite maybe, depending on how you deleted them, and what happened on your system between the time you deleted them and decided you want them back. Recovery can range from free and easy to difficult and expensive. Keep your fingers crossed, and read on.

How to fix it

If you just deleted a file by sending it to the Recycle Bin

1. First, you need to check your Recycle Bin; if the file is there—which will normally be the case if you deleted it recently and deleted with a Delete command, rather than Shift+Delete—you'll be able to restore it easily.

2. To open the Recycle Bin, double-click on the Recycle Bin icon on your desktop. (Depending on how your options are set, you may see a column in the Recycle Bin window to the left of the file list, as shown in the figure.) ▶

3. If you want to restore one or more files, select the file or files in the file list and choose File, Restore. Windows will restore any selected files to their original locations.

If the file's not in the Recycle Bin

1. If you've just deleted a file in a way that bypasses the Recycle Bin—by using Shift+Delete instead of Delete by itself for example—you can still recover the file easily. However, there are no appropriate utilities included in Windows, which means you need a commercial utility to do the job. In any case, the first, and most important, step is to refrain from doing anything that will write new data to the disk and possibly overwrite the data you need to recover.

2. If you don't already have an appropriate utility on hand, you should ideally turn off your system immediately, without saving any files you have open, if that's an option, and without shutting Windows down normally, which would write data to the disk. Just turn off the power switch, and go buy the utility. Note that you need a utility with an "emergency undelete" feature—which typically means the ability to boot from and run from a provided floppy disk or CD without having to install something on your system first. (We've found Symantec's The Norton Utilities to be a good choice.) In any case, once you have an appropriate utility in hand, put the disk or disc in the appropriate drive, turn your system on, and follow the instructions that came with the utility for undeleting the files.

3. If you already have an appropriate utility on hand, the same rules apply, except that instead of turning your system off, you can put the disk or disc in the appropriate drive and use your computer's reset button to reboot. Here again, don't save any open files if you can avoid it, and do not shut down Windows normally before rebooting.

4. If the file proves unrecoverable or if the lost data is so valuable that you don't want to risk further damage to it by trying to recover it, you may want to contact a company that provides a professional data recovery service. These companies use sophisticated software and hardware tools to locate and recover lost data. In some cases, they can even recover data from deleted files that have been overwritten. These services can be expensive, however, so you can justify the expense only if the data is extremely valuable. One data-recovery company is Ontrack Data International (800-872-2599, *www.ontrack.com*). Ontrack also provides tools that may be able to recover your data using an Internet connection, so you may not have to send them your hardware.

Tip
Although the Recycle Bin is part of Windows, there are some utility programs that replace it with their own features for retrieving deleted files. These utilities offer a better chance of getting your work back. But you'll have to read the documentation that came with the utility to find out how to use them.

Tip
If you have emptied your Recycle Bin since sending the file to the Recycle Bin, or it you deleted the file awhile ago, you may still be able to retrieve it with a commercial utility. However, the more data that has been written to disk since you deleted the file, the lower the odds of being able to restore the file.

I've formatted a disk or drive that has files I need

Source of the problem

"WARNING: Formatting will erase ALL data on this disk." The warning message you see when you're about to reformat a disk may sound ominous, but it's not entirely accurate. When you format a disk, the original data is left intact. The reason you can't access the data is that formatting erases the table that keeps track of the various parts of the files. If you had a way to recreate the table of information, you could recover your data.

Earlier versions of MS-DOS included a utility that let you reverse the format process, but this fell by the wayside with the introduction of Windows 95, and—up to now, at least—has not been resurrected. Fortunately, there are some commercial programs that perform similar magic.

How to fix it

1. The most important first step is to *do nothing!* Any software that you install on the freshly formatted disk will overwrite original data, and you will not be able to recover the lost information easily, if at all.

2. Get a commercial recovery utility, such as EasyRecovery from Ontrack Data International (800-872-2599, *www.ontrack.com*). These programs are able to recover most of the data from a re-formatted disk.

3. One limitation of unformat utilities is that they cannot recover the names of folders from the root directory, even though they can recover the folders and their contents. As a result, you will have to go back after running the recovery software and rename the folders.

> **Tip**
> It should go without saying, but most data loss problems would not be problems if you had a backup on hand. Before you reformat a disk—for whatever reason—consider making a backup of its contents first. If you need to recover some or all of the original files later, the task will be far easier if you can restore from a backup.

4. If you cannot recover all the missing data, or if the data is so critical that you don't want to risk losing it, you may want to consider using a professional recovery service. This can be expensive and may require that you send your disk to the service for the recovery process, but it will give you the best chance of retrieving data that you may not be able to get back on your own. There are many companies that provide data recovery services, including Ontrack Data International.

I spilled something on my keyboard or computer

Source of the problem

There was a time when using a computer meant working in a controlled environment, where all hazards were carefully excluded.

Those days are long gone, and we now emphasize the *personal* in *personal computer*. We have all sorts of accessories and aids designed to make computer use more comfortable and friendly. We think nothing of having food and drink close at hand as we work at our keyboards—even to the point of giving free reign to the peanut-butter-and-jelly set. And we have grown accustomed to taking our laptop computers into all sorts of settings.

All of which means that computers today occasionally suffer from an unwanted dousing of anything from water to hot coffee to sugary soft drinks. The problems that each of these liquids can cause range from the inconvenient to the potentially damaging. And different procedures are required depending on where the liquid lands, and where it winds up.

How to fix it

If you spill liquid on the keyboard

1. First, if the keyboard in question is on your notebook computer and the spill appears to be confined to the keyboard, you may be able to treat the problem the same way as for liquid spilled on a desktop keyboard. But if the liquid has reached the interior of the notebook case, you'll need to treat the problem the same way as if you spilled liquid directly inside the case. And rule one when you've spilled liquid inside a notebook's case is *don't try to open it yourself*. Notebook interiors are best left to professionals.

2. For a desktop keyboard, you also need to ask whether the liquid has gotten inside the keyboard case or is only on the keys themselves and the surface of the keyboard, just beneath the key caps. If the liquid is inside the case, here again you'll need to treat the problem the same way as if you spilled liquid inside a computer case. With a keyboard, however, unlike a notebook computer, you can probably successfully open up the keyboard yourself and then put it back together. And if you find that you can't put it back together, it won't cost much to buy a new keyboard.

> **Tip**
> Before you spend a lot of time trying to resurrect a flooded keyboard (or a keyboard with some other problem, for that matter) consider the fact that replacement keyboards don't cost much. Good quality keyboards are priced between $10 and $30, so spending the time fixing one may not be worth the effort.

3. If the liquid is water, and has not gotten inside the case, try turning the keyboard upside down and letting it dry for a while—at least 24 hours. You can also dry it with the cool setting from a hair dryer, but don't let any part of the keyboard get hotter than merely warm to the touch.

4. After the keyboard is thoroughly dried, plug it in and test all the keys. Your computer may have come with a diagnostic program that makes it easy to check each key. If you don't have a test program handy, you can check the keys by opening programs that use those keys, and then trying to use them.

5. If all the keys work, you're done. If some or all don't work, consider having the keyboard fixed professionally. Alternatively, just replace it, which will likely be the less expensive choice.

6. If you spill a soft drink or other liquid that will leave a residue when it dries, you'll need to clean both the key caps and the surface of the keyboard itself (meaning the part of the keyboard normally hidden by the key caps). That means you'll need to pry off the key caps. Before you start, make sure you know where to put them back when you're done. If you don't have the layout available in the system manual, a digital camera picture of the layout (or a film-based picture with an instant camera) can be invaluable as a reference later. Make sure you can read the words on the keys in the picture.

7. To pry off the keys, place the blade of a small, flat-bladed screwdriver under each key cap and use it as a lever to pop the key cap off. Do not remove the Space Bar, Enter key, Shift keys, or other large key caps. These often have springs or other supports that can be extremely difficult to put back in place. ▶

8. Clean the key caps and the surface of the keyboard. Do not put any liquid on the keyboard's surface to clean it. Rather, wet a cotton swab and then use it to clean the surface. Be careful not to wet it enough to risk liquid coming out of the swab and going inside the case. If you must use soapy water to clean the surface, follow up with fresh water to rinse the surface before reassembly. Also, when cleaning the key caps, be careful not to scrub the legends off the top of the key caps.

9. Put all the key caps back in place.

10. Plug the keyboard in and test all the keys. Your computer may have come with a diagnostic program that makes it easy to check each key. If you don't have a test program handy, you can check each key using any program that uses that key.

11. If all the keys work, you're done. If some or all don't work, consider having the keyboard fixed professionally or simply replace it, which will likely be the less expensive choice.

> *If this solution didn't solve your problem, go to the next page.*

I spilled something on my keyboard or computer

(continued from page 247)

If you spill liquid inside your computer's case

1. First turn off the system and unplug it. The liquid could cause an electrical short leading to permanent damage.

2. While you're deciding what to do next, position the case so that, as much as possible, the motherboard is arranged vertically, and any liquid dripping down inside the case will not touch any disk drives, the power supply, or other components. Keep in mind that the most valuable thing in the computer is almost certainly the data on the hard disk, so if you have to choose between water getting near the hard disk and getting near almost anything else, protect the hard disk.

3. If the system is a notebook, remove the battery; arrange to have the system inspected and—if necessary—cleaned by a professional repair service. Even if all you spilled was water, it may have collected inside the case where it can cause damage. If you spilled something other than water, it will likely leave a residue of sugar or some other substance when it dries. Either way, the system has to be cleaned to avoid possible corrosion. As a general rule, notebook cases are not designed to be opened by end users, so turn this job over to a professional.

4. If the system is a desktop computer and the spilled substance is water, open the case and inspect the inside to see where the water went and how much went where. (Before you open the case, be sure to read "Working inside your computer" at the beginning of this book.) Here again, as much as possible, position the case to keep the water from dripping into important components.

5. You may want to pat down (*not rub*) wet areas with a clean, dry, untreated cloth to soak up as much water as possible. You can also blow warm air with a hair dryer set to its cool setting. Be careful not to let any part of the computer get hotter than warm to the touch.

6. After the case is thoroughly dried out, you can plug everything in and see if it works correctly. If so, you're done (and very lucky). If not, seek professional repair assistance.

7. If the substance spilled inside the case is a soft drink or other substance that is likely to leave a residue, you'll need to get professional help to clean it out. Some substances can promote corrosion, which could damage expensive components or even destroy your motherboard.

> **Tip**
>
> An ounce of prevention is worth a pound of cure, or in this case, a gallon of cleaning solution. Avoid damage from spills in the first place by keeping drinks and other liquids well away from the computer and its components. Set up a separate snack table to hold your coffee next to your workspace, and always put the cup back there when you're not drinking from it. If you keep a houseplant on your desk, move it to a temporary spot when you water it. A good rule too is to keep liquids on a desk or table that's lower than any of your system components. That way, if you spill something, it's less likely to fall on the system.

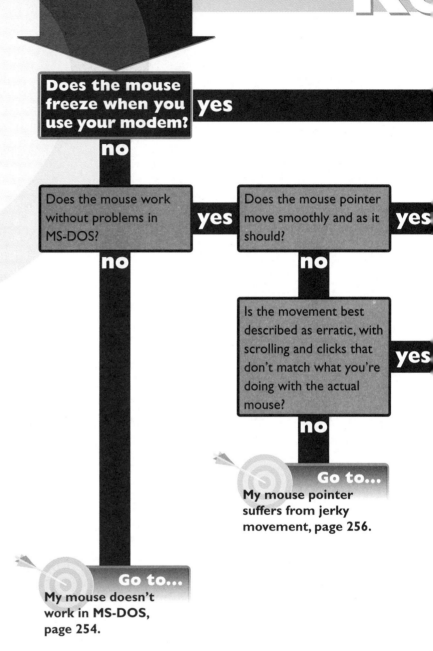

If your notebook computer has both a pointing stick and a touchpad, and you want to use only one of them, you can probably disable one or both through the BIOS configuration settings or through a Windows utility. Check your system's documentation for details.

Ke

Does the mouse freeze when you use your modem? **yes**

no

Does the mouse work without problems in MS-DOS? **yes**

no

Does the mouse pointer move smoothly and as it should? **yes**

no

Is the movement best described as erratic, with scrolling and clicks that don't match what you're doing with the actual mouse? **yes**

no

Go to...
My mouse pointer suffers from jerky movement, page 256.

Go to...
My mouse doesn't work in MS-DOS, page 254.

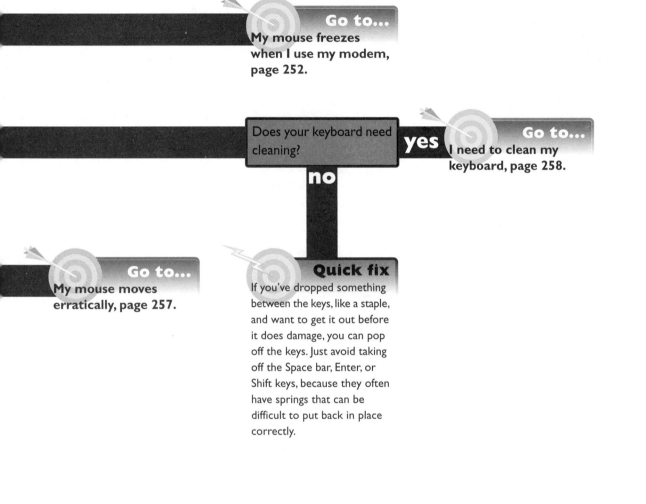

Go to...
My mouse freezes
when I use my modem,
page 252.

Does your keyboard need cleaning?

yes

Go to...
I need to clean my
keyboard, page 258.

no

Go to...
My mouse moves
erratically, page 257.

Quick fix
If you've dropped something
between the keys, like a staple,
and want to get it out before
it does damage, you can pop
off the keys. Just avoid taking
off the Space bar, Enter, or
Shift keys, because they often
have springs that can be
difficult to put back in place
correctly.

If your solution isn't here
Check these related chapters:
Computer hardware and Windows, page 22
Connections, page 84
Emergencies, page 240
Or see the general troubleshooting tips on page xv.

My mouse freezes when I use my modem

Source of the problem

Sometimes it's easy to see how things connect to each other. And sometimes it's not so easy. One of the classic problems with computers, for example, is with a mouse and modem that don't get along. What's the connection between them? Well, since you ask: the problem is almost always a resource conflict, with both devices trying to use the same interrupt. Here's how to track down and fix the problem.

How to fix it

1. Right-click on My Computer, and choose Properties.

2. Choose the Device Manager tab. (With Microsoft Windows 2000, choose the Hardware tab and then choose the Device Manager button.)

3. Check for a yellow circle with an exclamation mark next to any device line. If you find one, go to "Windows says some hardware isn't working properly" on page 26.

4. If you don't see the yellow circle and exclamation mark, expand the Modem option. Select your modem, and choose Properties. (Choose Action, Properties in Windows 2000.)

5. Choose the Modem tab, note which Port the modem is using, and choose Cancel.

6. Expand the Ports (COM & LPT) option, select the port used by the modem, and then choose Properties. (Choose Action, Properties in Windows 2000.)

7. Choose the Resources tab, note the interrupt request channel being used, and choose Cancel.

8. Expand the Mouse option (or the Mice And Other Pointing Devices option in Windows 2000).

9. Select your mouse, and choose Properties (Choose Action, Properties in Windows 2000.)

10. If there is a Resources tab, choose it. If the mouse uses the same interrupt request channel as the modem, reconfigure one or the other to use a different channel. See "Windows says some hardware isn't working properly," on page 26 for details.

11. If the mouse Properties dialog box does not have a Resources tab, the mouse is probably plugged into a COM port. The General tab will indicate which port. Repeat steps 6 and 7 to confirm that the mouse is using the same interrupt request channel as the modem, and then reconfigure one or the other to use a different channel.

My mouse doesn't work in MS-DOS

Source of the problem

Without software, hardware is useless. (Well, some hardware can make a good doorstop, but that's about it.) In order for a device to work with your computer, you have to load a driver that lets that device work with the rest of the system. Windows makes this easy. It automatically finds many—if not all—of your computer's components and loads all the drivers you need for them to work. If you open an MS-DOS window, those same drivers are still active in most cases, and you can still use the various devices. Reboot in MS-DOS mode, however, and all bets are off. If you don't load the drivers needed for some devices, they flat out won't work. Your mouse is a prime example of the kind of hardware that can have this problem. (Note that Windows 2000 does not have an MS-DOS mode, so this solution—as well as the problem—applies only to Windows 98.)

How to fix it

Make sure you have an MS-DOS driver for your mouse

1. Current versions of Windows do not include a generic MS-DOS driver for a mouse, so if you didn't get one bundled with your mouse, you'll need to get it from the manufacturer. Start with the company's web site, which may have the driver available for downloading. If that doesn't work, try technical support.

If the driver has a file extension of either .EXE or .COM

1. An .EXE or .COM file extension indicates that the file is an executable program. All you need to do is run the program after you restart in MS-DOS mode, and your mouse should work.

> **Tip**
>
> If you can't locate a driver for your mouse, you can download one for the Microsoft Basic Mouse from the Microsoft Web site. The driver works with most, but not all, mice.
>
> At this writing, the driver is available at: *download.microsoft.com/download/mouse/utility/1/win98/EN-US/msmouse.exe*. If it's been moved from that location, start at *www.microsoft.com* and work your way through the menu system to find it, starting with choices for downloads or support.

If the driver has a file extension of .SYS

1. A .SYS file extension on a driver tells you that you need to add a line to the CONFIG.SYS file used in MS-DOS mode. First copy the driver file to the root directory of your C drive.

2. Open Windows Explorer, navigate to the Windows folder, and find the Exit To DOS file.

3. Right-click on the file, and choose Properties to open the Exit To DOS Properties dialog box.

4. Choose the Program tab. ▶

5. Choose the Advanced button to open the Advanced Program Settings dialog box.

6. If it is not selected, select Specify A New MS-DOS Configuration. ▼

7. In the CONFIG.SYS for MS-DOS Mode box, type the following line:

Device = C:\MOUSE.SYS

where *MOUSE.SYS* is the actual name of the file, whatever it happens to be.

8. Choose OK to close the Advanced Program Settings dialog box.

9. Choose OK to close the Exit To DOS Properties dialog box.

10. To test the driver, choose Start, Shutdown, Restart In MS-DOS Mode. After the system reboots in MS-DOS mode, load an MS-DOS program that can take advantage of a mouse and test the mouse to see if it works.

My mouse pointer suffers from jerky movement

Source of the problem

A clean mouse is a happy mouse.

If your mouse gets dirty inside, the dirt can affect reliability and performance. The mouse ball can pick up dirt and debris that can be transferred to the sensor rollers inside the mouse case. Prevention can help, but sooner or later you're going to have to operate on your mouse to get it working smoothly again.

Note that the suggestions offered here will work equally well with trackballs, which are really just mice flipped over on their backs. Also, be aware that not all mice are mechanical; some rely on optical sensors instead. For those mice, all you can do is make sure that the sensors are clean and that you are using the mouse on a suitable surface. The latest generation of optical mice can work on a wide range of surfaces, but older optical mice require special reflective pads.

How to fix it

1. Turn the mouse over, and look for markings on the hatch that surrounds the ball. In most cases, there will be arrows indicating which way to turn it to remove the hatch.

2. Turn the hatch and remove it.

3. Remove the ball, and wash it with a gentle soap, then rinse it thoroughly and dry it.

4. If the rubber surface has become hard and slippery, and the washing does not soften it, wipe it with denatured alcohol.

5. Look inside the mouse case, where you will find a number of rollers. (Most mice have three.) Remove any debris that has become wrapped around the rollers.

6. Clean any grime from the rollers with a cotton swab and denatured alcohol.

7. Make sure that the rollers turn smoothly. If they don't, double check to make sure that you've removed all the dirt. You can also add a small drop of light machine oil on the roller shafts.

8. Reassemble the ball and hatch, and test the mouse.

> **Tip**
> In addition to cleaning your mouse, clean your mouse pad on a regular basis. Use mild soap and water, and be sure to rinse and dry it thoroughly before rolling the mouse over it again.

My mouse moves erratically

Source of the problem

Does your mouse pointer flick around the screen uncontrollably? Do pages scroll up or down unbidden when you surf the web? Well, your mouse may be possessed, but don't call for an exorcist yet. The more likely problem is a resource conflict or a conflict with the driver for your graphics adapter.

How to fix it

1. Make sure the mouse is working correctly and doesn't have any resource conflicts with other devices. See "Windows says some hardware isn't working properly" on page 26.

2. Check the manufacturer's web site or technical support for the latest mouse driver.

3. If you still have a problem, test to see if it's caused by your graphics adapter driver. Start by right-clicking on the Windows desktop and choosing Properties. In the Properties dialog box, choose the Settings tab, then the Advanced button, and then the Adapter tab.

If you use Windows 98	If you use Windows 2000
4. Choose the Change button to open the Update Driver Wizard.	Choose the Properties button, the Driver tab, and then Update Driver.
5. Choose Next, select the option that starts Display A List Of All The Drivers In A Specific Location, then choose Next.	Choose Next, select the option that starts Display A List Of The Known Drivers For This Device, and then choose Next.
6. Select Show All Hardware.	Select Show All Hardware Of This Device Class.
7. In the Manufacturer's list, select the entry (Standard Display Types).	Choose the chipset manufacturer for your graphics adapter.
8. Choose an appropriate driver, such as Standard PCI Graphics Adapter (XGA).	Choose another driver for your graphics chip, if there is one available.

9. Choose Next twice, and then Finish. If this solves the problem, check with your graphics adapter manufacturer for an updated driver that doesn't conflict with your mouse driver.

I need to clean my keyboard

Source of the problem

The computer equivalent of ring around the collar is the grime that accumulates on top of and around the edges of computer keyboards and mice. We deal with mice elsewhere in this chapter. Cleaning a keyboard is quite a different matter, and a bit more involved. Believe it or not, Ripley, you'll need a small, flat-bladed screwdriver, some cotton swabs, some soapy water, a vacuum cleaner, and, if you have one, a digital camera or an instant film camera. Got your cleaning kit ready? OK, here we go...

How to fix it

1. First make sure you know how the keys are arranged on the keyboard so that you can replace them correctly later. If your computer documentation does not include a diagram, consider taking a digital photo or instant film picture of the layout. Make sure you can read the legends on the keys.

2. In general, we recommend that you don't try to remove the larger key caps, including the Space Bar, Shift, and Enter key caps. These often have springs or small metal bars under them that can make them difficult to reassemble correctly.

3. Remove all other key caps using a small, flat-bladed screwdriver as a kind of tiny crowbar. Place the blade under a key cap, and lift up slowly. In some cases, you may need to pry it up from one side, then the other. ▶

4. After the cap pops loose, remove it from the keyboard.

5. After you have removed all the key caps (except for the large keys), wash them gently in warm, soapy water. Be careful not to scrub the tops too hard, or you may remove the printed legends.

6. Use a cotton swab with the soapy solution to wash the larger keycaps in place. Don't put the soapy solution directly on the keys. Rather, dampen the cotton swab, and use it to clean the key cap. Be careful not to wet the swab so much that it's in danger of letting the soapy water come out and flow into the keyboard case.

7. After you wash all the key caps, rinse them thoroughly; any remaining soap residue can attract more dirt. Here again, for the large key caps that you've left on the keyboard, use the cotton swabs and fresh water to rinse the key caps.

8. While you have all the key caps off, and after the larger key caps still on the keyboard have had a chance to dry, use a vacuum cleaner to remove any dust, hair, and other debris that has accumulated under the key caps on the top surface of the keyboard.

9. If you don't have ready access to a vacuum cleaner, but have canned air, take the keyboard outside and use the canned air to blow the dust off the keyboard. (Quite a lot of dust and debris can accumulate on a keyboard, which is why we recommend doing this step outdoors.) Do not simply blow on the keyboard. Human saliva is corrosive, and you're all but guaranteed to wind up with some on the keyboard if you try blowing the dust away.

10. Gently replace all the key caps in their proper positions. Press on each one in turn, until it snaps in place. Check each one for its full range of movement, and to make sure that the caps are not binding anywhere.

11. When you finish cleaning a keyboard, it's a good idea to check it to make sure everything still works. Plug it in, and turn on your computer. Some systems come with a diagnostic program that makes it easy to check all the keys by confirming each key press. If you don't have such a program on hand, you can test each key with any program that supports that key.

Tip

It's also a good idea to clean the outside of the keyboard case itself. Wiping the keyboard off with a clean rag once a week or so can do wonders for keeping both the keyboard case and the key caps clean, and avoiding the kind of caked-on dirt that takes real effort to clean off. For best results, make sure the system is off, so you can wipe with abandon, without having to worry about giving unintended commands to a program that's running. While you're at it, dust the outside of your computer case and your mouse at the same time. Keep in mind too that if your system is in a dirty environment—with lots of dust, or a smoker nearby, or in a house with cat or dog hair flying around—it will get dirty more quickly, and you should clean it more frequently.

Whether your printer currently has a problem printing or not, you should check out whether it has enough memory. Some printers process print jobs on your computer, so they need little or no on-board memory. But if your printer processes the print job in the printer, it needs memory. Make sure you know how much memory it already has, whether it can accept additional memory, and, if so, what the additional memory will do. It may provide higher resolution, faster printing, or additional features.

Have you run the printer self test (to confirm that the printer itself is working) and found that the printer passed the test?

yes

no

Is the printer connected directly to your system, rather than another parallel port or USB device?

yes

no

Quick fix

Remove the intermediate devices. If the printer then works, check with the printer and device manufacturers to see if either can suggest settings to change. Otherwise, get a separate port for each device. If the printer still doesn't work after removing the other devices, run though all the tests to get the printer working before you plug other devices back in.

Have you run the printer self test?

yes

no

Go to...
My printer fails its self test, page 264.

Go to...
I need to run my printer's self test, page 262.

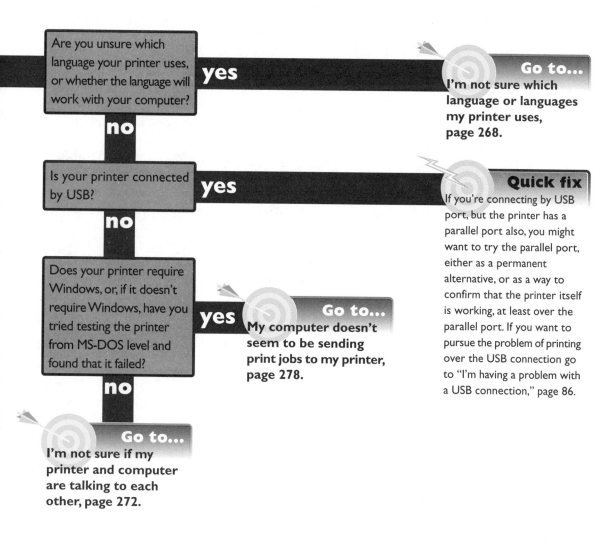

Are you unsure which language your printer uses, or whether the language will work with your computer?

yes → **Go to...** I'm not sure which language or languages my printer uses, page 268.

no

Is your printer connected by USB?

yes → **Quick fix** If you're connecting by USB port, but the printer has a parallel port also, you might want to try the parallel port, either as a permanent alternative, or as a way to confirm that the printer itself is working, at least over the parallel port. If you want to pursue the problem of printing over the USB connection go to "I'm having a problem with a USB connection," page 86.

no

Does your printer require Windows, or, if it doesn't require Windows, have you tried testing the printer from MS-DOS level and found that it failed?

yes → **Go to...** My computer doesn't seem to be sending print jobs to my printer, page 278.

no

Go to... I'm not sure if my printer and computer are talking to each other, page 272.

If your solution isn't here
Check these related chapters:
Connections, page 84
Printer software basics, page 268
Or see the general troubleshooting tips on page xv.

I need to run my printer's self test

Source of the problem

Maybe you just got your hands on a new printer, or maybe your old printer is suddenly refusing to print. Either way, you have no idea what the problem is, no idea where to look for a solution, and no idea what to do next.

Well, a good place to start is with the printer. Virtually any printer (with the exception of Windows printers) will include a self-test feature—and sometimes more than one choice of self-test pages. The point of a self test is that it tests everything within the printer itself—except the connection to the outside world. If it works, it proves that the printer is able to print, that it has ink or toner, and that the problem lies somewhere other than the print engine. If it doesn't work, it proves that there's a problem in the printer itself. Either way, it tells you where to concentrate your efforts to find and fix the problem.

How to fix it

If you have a printer without a built-in menu

1. For printers without a built-in menu system—which includes almost all ink jets—the commands to start a self test are often obscure and hard to remember. Your first line of defense is to check the manual if you have one. If you don't have the manual, check with the manufacturer.

2. If all else fails—or while you're waiting for a response from the manufacturer's technical support staff—you can try experimenting to see if you can find the right command. For most ink jet printers, the command for starting the self test involves holding down one or more buttons while turning on the printer, and then continuing to hold down the button for a few seconds until a light stops flashing or a light starts to flash, or the printer starts printing. Since most ink jet printers have only a few buttons on the front or top panel, it won't take long to try this with each one. The worst that will happen is that you accidentally start some other printer routine, such as cleaning the print nozzles. This might waste some ink, but will otherwise do no harm.

Tip

Whether you find the self-test command immediately in the manual, get it from the manufacturer's Web site, or find it by trial and error, write it down for future reference. This is a critical piece of information that you don't want to risk losing. And keep in mind that manuals often get lost. Your best bet: write the instructions on a small piece of paper and tape the paper securely to the printer, where it will always be handy. If you have aesthetic objections to taping the paper to the side or top of the printer, tape it to the bottom, or even inside. Just be careful not to cover any air vents.

If you have a printer with a built-in menu

1. Most printers with a built-in menu system make it relatively easy to print their self test or tests. You may have to hunt through the menus to find an appropriate option, but you should be able to find it somewhere in the menus. Some offer a self-test option on the first level menu. Others have a Print menu or Help Pages menu that includes a list of various pages you can print.

2. If you can't find an option called Self Test, any other page built into the printer will do. Printing the Menu, Menu Settings, Start Page, Configuration, Demo, Fonts, or even a Consumable Status page will tell you whether the printer can print.

What the self test tells you

1. In a very real sense, the medium in this test is the message. You wanted to know if the printer could print. If it did, you have proof positive that the printer is properly set up physically, that it has toner or ink, that it can move paper though the paper path, and so on. And you can look elsewhere for the source of the problem. However, the test may tell you more as well.

2. Exactly what the test can tell you depends on the particular test. For some ink jets, for example, the self test is actually a nozzle check that tests each nozzle in the print head to let you see if the head needs cleaning. (These tests typically consist of a set of lines. If each line is solid, the nozzles don't need cleaning. If there's a gap anywhere in the lines, there's a clogged nozzle.) For many laser printers, the test may print the alphabet in each of the fonts stored in the printer, which can be useful information. Or it may print out the menu structure. Whatever the test consists of, don't simply ignore it. Make a mental note of it. You may need the information at some other time. And for certain kinds of information—like a menu structure—you may want to keep the output handy for later reference.

3. If your printer couldn't print the self test, you have an answer too. Go to "My printer fails its self test" on page 264.

Tip

If you succeed in printing any of the printer's built-in pages, be sure to print all pages that may help you track down and fix whatever problem you're running into. A Settings or Configuration page will come in handy in later steps, when you're trying to pinpoint the problem or find a setting to change. Similarly, a menu page will help you navigate through the menus to find any printer menu setting you need to change.

Tip

We assume that you're using a laser or ink jet printer because those are the most common choices. However, all of the steps we cover would be essentially the same for any printer using any technology. Just follow the steps for the closest match (dot matrix printers have much in common with ink jets, for example), and substitute the equivalent features of the printer as appropriate (ribbon instead of ink or toner, for example).

My printer fails its self test

Source of the problem

When your printer can't print its own self test, you know that there's a problem in the printer itself. But where? Something could have broken, but the problem could also be as simple as the printer being out of ink or toner. In between these extremes are any number of potential problems that you can also easily fix. Here's a step-by-step checklist for what to look at before you take the printer in for professional repair.

How to fix it

1. If the printer that's not printing is just out of the box brand new, don't do anything else until you take another look inside the printer for packing material such as a piece of tape or a shipping restraint. It's not all that hard to miss a plastic or cardboard piece when you're unpacking a printer. Sometimes a quick-start guide will miss a detail or two, and anything left inside the case can cause a problem. Open each door and cover, and take a careful look for anything that might be packing material. Then reread the setup instructions to see if they tell you anything useful. If you see something that looks like it may be packing material, but aren't sure whether it should come out of the printer, contact the manufacturer.

2. If your printer fed a page correctly without printing anything on it when you ran the self test, skip to the section "The paper feeds, but the self test doesn't print" on page 267. Otherwise, remove the paper from the paper drawers or input trays, and continue to the next step.

If the printer uses a paper drawer

1. Paper drawers typically include a flat plate that's meant to push up against the paper to help the paper feed. In some cases, the plate is spring loaded. In others, the plate moves freely and a mechanism inside the printer pushes against the plate. You should be able to find the plate without too much trouble. Some plates lock in the down position. ▶

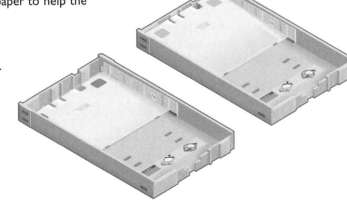

2. If the plate is not locked down, and it's not spring loaded, you'll typically be able to move it freely up and down with no resistance. If it is spring loaded, and is not locked down, it will typically be in its extreme up position immediately after you've pulled the drawer out of the printer. If the plate does lock down, it should unload when you insert the drawer in the printer. ▶

3. If you think you may have pushed the plate back into locked position when you removed the paper, but you aren't sure, slide the drawer back into the printer and then pull it out to see if that releases it from the locked position.

4. If the plate doesn't move freely and still isn't in the up position, and you've installed the printer without ever successfully printing, look for a shipping restraint that's holding the plate down. Even if you removed the restraint earlier, a piece may have been left behind.

5. If you don't find anything holding the plate down, the paper drawer may be designed to automatically lock the plate down when the drawer isn't in the printer or you may have a defective drawer. The only way to test for that is with another drawer that you know works. If you have one available, you'll want to try it. Otherwise, try the other steps we suggest below to find out if the paper feeds from the drawer.

If the printer uses a paper tray

1. Paper input trays sometimes include levers that you have to flip open to insert the paper correctly, then flip closed to make sure the paper feeds correctly. If you have a paper tray, look for the lever, and make sure you know how to use it correctly if it is present. If you've just set up the printer and have never successfully printed from it, take the time to read the manual. Even if loading the paper seems easy, you may be overlooking a simple step.

Check for errors

1. Turn the printer off, wait a moment, and turn it back on. Give it enough time to run through its entire power-up cycle, which should include a power on self-test routine. Then check the printer's liquid crystal display (LCD) or status lights to see if the printer is reporting an error.

2. If the LCD or status lights report an error and the error is informative (like Paper Jam), do whatever the obvious solution seems to be. (If the obvious solution doesn't work, you may find the problem is covered elsewhere in this book.) If the error is not informative and is not explained in the manual, you'll need to contact the manufacturer to decode it. If the error says something like Printer Requires Service, you'll need to take the printer in for professional repair. If the printer doesn't report an error, continue with the next step.

> *If this solution didn't solve your problem, go to the next page.*

My printer fails its self test

(continued from page 265)

Check whether you can feed a page through the printer without printing

1. Most ink jet printers have some way to feed a page without actually printing. Typically this requires pressing a control button labeled Form Feed. Check your manual if necessary to find the command for your printer.

2. Laser and equivalent printers typically do not have any way to feed a sheet without printing something. Some offer a form feed button, but that works only if there is a partial page already sitting in the printer memory. However, some lasers, particularly older models, offer a button—often recessed and typically hidden in the back or side—that lets you run an engine test (the engine being the part of the printer that actually puts toner on paper). If there's an engine test button available, it may not be labeled, so check the manual before you decide the printer doesn't have one. ▶

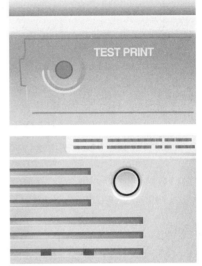

3. If there isn't an engine test button, see if the printer has a setting to print a start page when you turn it on. Check the manual or look through the menus for a Start Page setting. If you find one, make sure the feature is turned on.

4. The point of this exercise is to involve as little of the printer as possible in this test beyond the actual paper feed mechanism. If your printer lacks any way to feed a page without running a self test, you'll have to run the self test.

Test the paper path

1. Load about ten sheets of paper in the printer. If at all possible, use paper from a freshly opened ream.

2. Use one of these methods to test whether you can feed a page through the printer:

   - **If you have an ink jet printer** with a form feed button or the equivalent, give the command for feeding a page through the printer.

   - **If you have a laser printer with an engine test button**, press the test button.

   - **If you have a laser printer with a Start Page feature turned on**, turn the printer off, wait a moment, and turn it back on.

   - **If your only choice is to run the printer's self test,** run the test.

3. With any of these variations, if the page fed correctly, you've proven that the paper can feed through the printer without problems. The earlier problem may have been because of packing

material that you've since removed, or you may have loaded too much paper into the printer's paper tray or drawer. Fill the tray or drawer again, this time being careful not to overfill it. (Look for a line that indicates the maximum paper level, and be sure to stay below that level.) Then rerun the self test to see if it now works. If it does, you're finished. Otherwise, you may have to experiment with different amounts of paper in the drawer or tray to find the right amount. If the problem reappears, but seems to come and go randomly, you can try running through these steps again to try to track down the problem, but you probably need to repair or replace the printer

4. If the paper didn't feed through the printer, first check the printer's LCD or status lights to see if the printer is reporting an error. If it is, it may give you a clue about the problem, or it may tell you that the printer needs service.

5. Look to see if the paper fed from the input tray or drawer at all, and, if so, how far it got before it jammed. Open whatever paper drawers, covers, or doors are necessary to see the paper path. What you're looking for is the leading edge of the paper. Its position should tell you where the problem lies. If you then examine that area, you may find a fix. For example, you may find a small piece of paper stuck in a slit that the page has to feed through. If you can't determine the problem or how to solve it, you'll have to get the printer repaired or replaced.

The paper feeds, but the self test doesn't print

1. If the paper feeds, without the self test printing, the most likely problem is a lack of ink or toner. If you just installed the printer, reread the instructions and make sure you installed the toner or ink cartridge correctly. This is especially important if this is the first time you've installed this particular model of toner or ink cartridge.

2. Check the consumable levels if you can. Some printers have a built-in option for showing the consumable levels. Others will give you this information through the driver. If the information is available, it will tell you how much ink or toner the printer thinks it has.

3. **For ink jets only:** If the cartridge has been in the printer for weeks or months without being used, the nozzles may be clogged. Follow the printer's cleaning routine, and try printing the self test again.

4. **For ink jets only:** If you're new to this model of cartridge, check the cartridges. Some installation directions are confusing enough that if you're new to the printer, it's not unusual to wind up peeling off the electrical contacts on the cartridge when you follow the instructions to take off the shipping tape. Make sure the cartridges have the tape off, but the electrical contacts still on. The printer documentation may warn against removing the cartridges, but so long as you're careful not to touch the electrical contacts or the ink jets, you should be OK. And in the unlikely event that a cartridge is damaged by handling, the next step is to replace it anyway, so there's little risk.

5. As a last step, replace the toner or ink cartridge. It may be empty or defective. Then try the self test again. If the self test still doesn't work with the new cartridge, the printer probably needs to be repaired or replaced.

I'm not sure which language or languages my printer uses

Source of the problem

When Gene Roddenbery created Star Trek, he had to find a way to let Captain Kirk and crew talk to aliens they had never met. And he had to do that without spending three-quarters of every show having the crew learn a new language. Roddenbery neatly solved that problem by inventing a Universal Translator. The Translator took care of this detail automatically and never failed (unless, of course, the plot needed it to).

Computer programs have pretty much the same problem talking to printers. There are any number of printer languages—with a few major families, and lots of variations. In the bad old days, you either had to find a printer driver for each program you used—so the driver could translate the print commands for the printer, or you had to find some workaround that might not let you use all the features in your printer. Then came Windows, in its role as Universal Translator. As long as the printer comes with a Windows driver or uses one that ships with Windows, you're all set. Your programs only have to know how to talk to Windows, which provides the translation by way of each printer's driver.

Even with Windows, however, there are times when you need to know which languages your printer understands. Sometimes knowing the printer's language will tell you everything you need to know—like what driver to use. Sometimes it will tell you enough to let you run troubleshooting tests. Here's how to find out what language your printer speaks.

How to fix it

If you have the manual

1. The first place to look to find out the language your printer uses is the obvious one: check in the printer's manual, if you have one. With a little luck, it will be listed under *printer specifications*. It may be listed as *printer language*, *printer control mode*, *printer emulation,* or some other variation, so read carefully. You can also try getting the information from the manufacturer.

Tip

When you're trying to figure out what language a given printer uses, it's helpful to know that, although there are lots of printer languages, the vast majority of printers use one or more of the major ones.

For most desktop lasers and for Hewlett-Packard (HP) ink jets, the most likely language is *PCL*, which HP originated.

For lasers and ink jets aimed at graphic artists or desktop publishing users, *PostScript* is the most likely possibility.

For ink jets from companies other than HP, the most popular languages are *Epson* and *IBM*, which are similar to each other.

2. Don't assume the manual (or the manufacturer's tech support) will tell you everything. Some printers can print in more than one language, and the manual won't necessarily list all the languages the printer uses. In particular, many ink jet printers today function as GDI printers in Windows—which means that they print directly from something called the Windows Graphics Device Interface. However, these same printers often include a printer language as well, so they can print from MS-DOS if necessary. The manuals may tell you about one of these modes without telling you about the other.

If the printer driver is installed

1. If you have the printer driver installed, it may tell you the language it's using. Choose Start, Settings, Printers to open the Printers window.

2. Right-click on the printer icon and choose Properties to open the printer's Properties dialog box. ▼

3. Browse through the dialog box. It may have something that's a dead giveaway about the printer language, such as a tab labeled PostScript. Also be sure to choose the About button, if there is one, to see if there are any clues there about the language. Keep in mind that having one driver installed doesn't necessarily mean that the printer understands only one language. Some printers—particularly those that come with both Printer Control Language (PCL) and PostScript—come with a driver for each language, but you can install either one without the other. Others come with only one driver, even though they have more than one language.

Tip

GDI isn't really a language. It refers to printers that use the Windows Graphics Device Interface (GDI) directly, instead of their drivers first translating the information to a printer language and then printing using the printer language commands.

True GDI printers are sometimes called Windows printers, because you have to load Windows in order to use them. And if you're trying to print from an MS-DOS program, knowing that you have a GDI printer may explain why you're having a problem printing. Some GDI printers can print from a program running in an MS-DOS window. Others can't. None can print if you boot up in MS-DOS mode.

It's important to know also that just because a printer acts as a GDI printer in Windows doesn't mean that it doesn't understand a language also. In particular, many ink jet printers function as GDI printers in Windows, but also understand one or more common printer languages—typically some variation of Epson or IBM. Knowing about the additional language can be important if you need to print from MS-DOS programs or run troubleshooting tests that require being at MS-DOS level.

If this solution didn't solve your problem, go to the next page.

I'm not sure which language or languages my printer uses

(continued from page 269)

If the printer has a built-in menu

1. If the printer has an LCD-based menu system, it probably includes information on the language or languages it follows. You can search through the menus for the language information. While you do, also keep an eye out for the option to print various types of Help pages. A Status or Configuration page may tell you the language the printer is using. A Menu or Menu Settings page may tell you the language, any other choices in language, and also the menu structure, so you can find the language setting in the menus themselves.

If the printer is working at all

1. If all else fails—including trying to contact the manufacturer—and the printer is printing anything at all when you try printing to it, including garbage characters, you may be able to track down the language through brute force trial and error. You can install drivers in Windows, one at a time, and test each to see if it works with the printer. The trick here is to try a highest-common-denominator driver for each language—one that should work with any printer that uses any version of the particular language.

2. For laser printers, a good place to start is with a Hewlett-Packard LaserJet III driver to test for PCL. Start by choosing Start, Settings, and then Printers to open the Printers window.

3. Choose Add Printer to start the Add Printer Wizard.

4. Choose Next at the first screen, and then Local Printer. (Windows 2000 includes the check box Automatically Detect And Install My Plug And Play Printer. Remove the check from the check box, if necessary.) Choose Next.

5. The Add Printer Wizard has a list of manufacturers to pick from on the left side of the dialog box. Scroll down the list and select HP. ▶

6. The right side of the dialog box shows a list of printers from the manufacturer you select on the left side. Select HP as the manufacturer, and then scroll down the

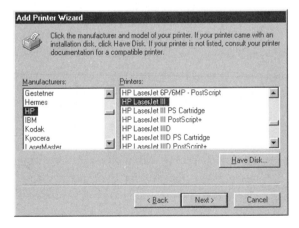

printer list and select HP LaserJet III. (Note that LaserJet III comes after higher numbers on the list, because Windows sorts the Roman numeral as a letter rather than a number.) Choose Next.

7. On the next screen, select the port the printer is connected to—usually LPT1—and choose Next.

8. Continue through the rest of the Wizard, following any additional onscreen instructions and answering Yes to the question Would You Like To Print A Test Page? Windows may ask you to insert your Windows disc in your CD-ROM drive.

9. When Windows finishes installing the driver, it will print a test page, then ask whether it printed correctly. Answer Yes whether it printed correctly or not.

10. Repeat these steps for each driver you want to test with the printer. For Hewlett-Packard ink jets, try an HP DeskJet 500 driver to test for PCL.

11. For both lasers and ink jets, try the Apple LaserWriter driver to test for PostScript.

12. For printers that don't work with any of these choices, try drivers for other models from the same manufacturer. Your best bet is with models with similar names or model numbers.

13. If you've succeeded in tracking down the language the printer uses, you may want to continue testing, using the same approach, to find a driver that lets you take better advantage of the printer.

If your printer offers more than one language

1. If your printer understands more than one printer language, it may or may not be able to switch between the languages automatically. In general, automatic switching is more likely in laser and equivalent printers than in ink jets, and in newer printers rather than older printers.

2. If the printer doesn't offer automatic switching, you'll need to set a physical switch in the printer or change a setting in a built-in menu to pick one language or the other. Even if a printer has an automatic switching mode, it may be set to use only one language, so that you need to manually switch it to the other (or to automatic) if the other language is the one you want to use.

3. If the printer has a built-in LCD-based menu, it will almost certainly let you choose between one language and another, or turn on the automatic mode if it has one, through the menu system. Look for the information in the printer manual, or look through the menus for the command. If you find an option to print the menu, take advantage of it. It will help you find the commands you need.

4. If the printer uses a switch to change languages, you should find instructions for how to set it in the manual. If you don't have a manual, check the manufacturer's Web site for documentation, or get in touch with the printer manufacturer.

Tip

The Windows 2000 Add Printer Wizard asks you to select the port first (step 7), then pick a manufacturer and model (steps 5 and 6). Otherwise, the steps are the same.

Tip

The automatic switching features on today's printers work impressively well. They let the printer look at the incoming print job, figure out what printer language it's using, and pick the right language. This was not always so. If you have an older printer with an automatic mode, you may find that if you turn the feature on, it will guess wrong often enough to waste large amounts of paper. Should that happen, simply ignore the automatic mode and set it for one language or the other manually.

I'm not sure if my printer and computer are talking to each other

Source of the problem

Printing problems can be hard to track down and fix, mostly because there are so many different things that can go wrong. Some possible problems are strictly hardware issues, like whether the cable has a broken wire or is even connected properly. But most are software issues, including whether you have the printer driver installed properly, whether it's printing to the port the printer is actually connected to, whether its other settings are correct, whether any of the printer driver files are corrupted, and even whether you have the right driver installed in the first place.

Still others fall somewhere in between hardware and software, like whether you've set the parallel port on your computer to match the kind of parallel port the printer needs to plug into. (This assumes, of course, that you're connecting the printer through the parallel port, as does this entire section. If you're using a USB port, go to "I'm having a problem with a USB connection" on page 86.)

In general, you should make sure the printer and computer are talking to each other on a hardware level first. The easiest way to do that is to strip away as much software as you can when you test the printer, which means testing it at an MS-DOS level if at all possible. Here's how to run that test, find out if your computer and printer are communicating, and confirm that your hardware is properly set up— or that it's not.

How to fix it

1. Before you can test the connection between your computer and printer, you have to know what language or languages your printer speaks. For purposes of this discussion, there are three basic types of printers: Windows printers, PostScript printers, and everything else.

Tip

There are some dead giveaways that can help you figure out what language your printer speaks. If the manual for your printer talks about the printer being a Windows printer, host-based printer, or GDI printer, it's a Windows printer, which means it works only in Windows and processes the print jobs on the computer (the host) directly from the Windows graphics device interface (GDI). There's also a rarely used language called PrintGear that falls in this category.

If it's a PostScript printer, you should find some mention of PostScript in the printer driver.

If it has more than one built-in language, you may find multiple drivers. If you're still not sure what language or languages your printer speaks, see "I'm not sure which language or languages my printer uses" on page 268.

2. If a printer has more than one of these categories of languages built in, your first choice for confirming that the hardware is set up correctly is any language in the Everything Else category. Your second best choice is PostScript. Try to avoid the Windows printer choice. If that's the only choice, however, go to "My computer doesn't seem to be sending print jobs to my printer" on page 278.

If you have a printer in the Everything Else or PostScript category

1. To eliminate as many complications as possible, you'll want to run these tests from MS-DOS level. Starting with your computer on and Windows running (using Windows 98 or Windows 95), choose Start, Shut Down, and then Restart In MS-DOS Mode. Then skip to the section "The basic test for an Everything Else or PostScript printer" on page 275.

2. If you have one of the new "innovative" PCs, Restart In MS-DOS Mode may not be an option in the Shut Down dialog box. In that case, choose Start, Shut Down, Restart, and then repeatedly tap F8.

A failure to communicate

In truth, we oversimplify a bit by dividing printers into Windows printers, PostScript printers, and Everything Else. Our real definition of the Everything Else category is any printer that you can print text on simply by sending individual characters to it in the code that all PCs use. (That code is American Standard Code for Information Interchange, or ASCII).

Probably better than 99 percent of the printers people try to attach to PCs fall into either this category or the PostScript or Windows printer categories. However, there are a few printers floating around that fall into a fourth category that might be named, *Don't try to use this printer with a PC.*

One type of Don't Try To Use printer that springs to mind is any non-PostScript printer for the Apple Macintosh. Just as some printers are Windows printers, so too are some printers Macintosh printers. Sometimes they are the same printers with different drivers—one for the Macintosh operating system and one for Windows. But many Macintosh printers don't come with Windows drivers, won't work on the PC, and certainly won't work like printers in our Everything Else category.

You should also keep in mind that some printers don't understand ASCII because they use a different code. These printers are generally attached to corporate mainframe computers, but we've seen PC users wind up with them when a corporation upgrades and lets employees take old equipment home with them. As with Macintosh printers, these printers simply will not work with a PC. If you've wound up with a secondhand printer from your company and you're having trouble getting it working, check with your company's support staff to make sure the printer understands ASCII.

If this solution didn't solve your problem, go to the next page.

I'm not sure if my printer and computer are talking to each other

(continued from page 273)

3. This may take a few tries, but eventually, you should see the Windows 98 Startup Menu, which includes the option Command Prompt Only. Choose this option by entering the number next to the line or using the arrow keys to select the line. Then press Enter to boot the system in MS-DOS mode. Skip ahead to the next section, "The basic test for an Everything Else or PostScript printer."

4. If you use Windows 2000, rebooting in MS-DOS mode is not an option. (You can boot up using the option Safe Mode With Command Prompt, but our instructions for testing the printer won't work.) If necessary, you can run the tests we describe below by choosing Start, Programs, Accessories, and then Command Prompt to open a Command Prompt window. However, the preferred approach in this case is to create a bootable floppy disk on another system that is running Windows 98, Windows 95, or even MS-DOS.

5. If you have access to a system running Windows 98, Windows 95 or MS-DOS, create the bootable floppy by putting a floppy disk with nothing on it that you need in the A drive on that system. In Windows 95 or 98, open an MS-DOS window by choosing Start, Programs, and then MS-DOS prompt.

6. Type
format a: /s and then press the Enter key and follow the instructions from the Format program to begin formatting the disk.

7. Windows or MS-DOS will format the disk and put the files on it that you need to boot into MS-DOS mode (for Windows) or MS-DOS itself. When it gives you the option to enter a Volume Label, press Enter to skip the label. ▶

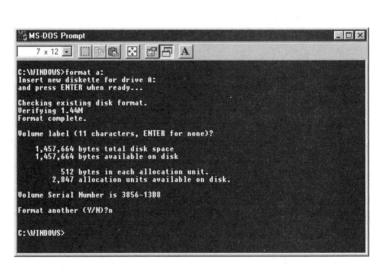

8. When you see the option to format another disk, press N and then press Enter to answer No.

9. You should now be able to use the bootable disk you just created on your Windows 2000 system to boot into MS-DOS or MS-DOS mode. Simply put the floppy disk in the A drive and reboot. (If the system ignores the A drive and boots directly from the hard disk instead, see "The computer is booting from the wrong disk drive" on page 82.)

The basic test for an Everything Else or PostScript printer

1. You need to create a file that will tell your printer to feed a page. The basic test you'll then run, after checking each possible source of a problem, is to send the file to the printer with an MS-DOS–level Copy command. This will tell you at each step whether the hardware side of the connection is set up properly. This section will explain how to create that file and send it to the printer.

2. At this point, you should have just booted up your system in MS-DOS or MS-DOS mode or just opened a Command Prompt window in Windows 2000. (We will refer to all of these possibilities simply as MS-DOS for the rest of this discussion.) The prompt you're most likely to see will be

A:\>

Don't worry if the prompt looks somewhat different, however. All that matters is that it's the prompt you see when you first boot up in MS-DOS or first open the Command Prompt window. You'll be typing commands at the command line.

3. At the MS-DOS command line, type **copy con testfile** and then press Enter.

4. The screen will advance one line, with the cursor now at the extreme left of the line.

If you have a printer in the Everything Else category, hold down the Control key and then press the L key. This will show on screen as

^L

If you have a PostScript printer, type **showpage**

5. Press Enter to advance to the next line.

6. Hold down the Control key, and then press the Z key. This will show on screen as

^Z

7. Press Enter.

8. If you did everything right, you'll see the message *1 File(s) Copied*, you will now have a file named *Testfile* on your hard disk, and the file will have the right command in it to tell your printer to feed a page. To confirm that the file was created, type **dir testfile** and then press Enter.

9. MS-DOS will respond by showing the file name, file size, and the date and time the file was created, confirming that the file actually exists.

If this solution didn't solve your problem, go to the next page.

I'm not sure if my printer and computer are talking to each other

(continued from page 275)

10. In order to use this file to test your connection, you have to know which port your printer is connected to. Most PCs have only one parallel printer port, which MS-DOS calls LPT1. Some PCs have two or even three parallel ports, adding LPT2 and LPT3. The following instructions assume the printer is plugged into LPT1. If your printer is plugged into, say LPT2, you'll need to substitute LPT2 for LPT1. If your system offers more than one parallel port and you're not sure which one your printer is plugged into, you'll need to take a brute force approach and run each of the tests for each parallel port designation. (See the sidebar on the facing page.)

11. There are two other things you need to know before you run this test: how the printer indicates when it's receiving data, and how it indicates when it's holding data in memory that it isn't printing yet. You should be able to find this information in the printer manual.

12. To send the file to the printer, type **copy testfile lpt1** and then press Enter.

13. If the printer feeds a blank page after you copy the file to the printer, you've established that all the hardware is set up correctly and you can look to software issues as the source of your problem. Go to "Printer software basics" on page 286.

14. If the printer reacts by making noise that sounds like it might be coming from the page feed mechanism but it doesn't feed a page, copy the file to the printer a second time. With some ink jets, sending this file to a printer that doesn't have a page loaded in a ready-to-print position will load the page without feeding it through the printer. If the page feeds after the second time you send the file, here again you've established that all the hardware is set up correctly. Go to "Printer software basics" on page 286.

15. If the printer doesn't feed the page but indicates that it has received some data, you may have made a mistake in creating the file, you may not have properly identified your printer's language, or the data may be getting garbled on the way to the printer.

> **Tip**
>
> If you can't find the manual, it's helpful to know the most common ways that printers indicate that they're receiving data. Odds are that your printer falls into one of the following three categories.
>
> Many printers include a Ready status light that blinks when the printer receives data.
>
> Printers with LCD-based menus often use the LCD to indicate that they are receiving data, typically with a message such as *Receiving Data*.
>
> In general, if you see the status lights change in any way when you copy the file to the printer, the change indicates that the printer is receiving data.

16. If you have access to another system with a printer that's in the same category as yours, the second printer is attached to an LPT port, and you know the second printer works, you can test the test file: Copy it to a floppy disk, take it to the other system, reboot the other system in MS-DOS, and then copy the file to the printer using the previous instructions. If it works on the second system, the file is OK and you should go to

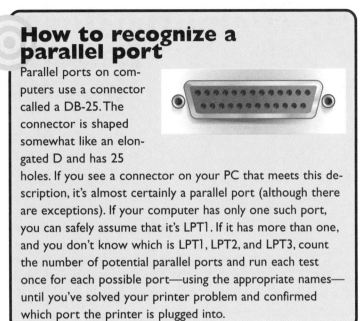

How to recognize a parallel port

Parallel ports on computers use a connector called a DB-25. The connector is shaped somewhat like an elongated D and has 25 holes. If you see a connector on your PC that meets this description, it's almost certainly a parallel port (although there are exceptions). If your computer has only one such port, you can safely assume that it's LPT1. If it has more than one, and you don't know which is LPT1, LPT2, and LPT3, count the number of potential parallel ports and run each test once for each possible port—using the appropriate names—until you've solved your printer problem and confirmed which port the printer is plugged into.

"My computer doesn't seem to be sending print jobs to my printer" on page 278. If the file doesn't work on the second system, create a new file on that system following the instructions from the beginning of this section, confirm that it works there, copy it to a floppy disk, bring it back to your original system, and then go back to step 12 and try the test again.

17. If you don't have access to another system, go back to step 1 and try recreating the file.

18. If the printer still indicates that it's getting data but doesn't print anything, go back to step 1 and try creating a file for the category of printer you didn't use the first time—PostScript instead of Everything Else, or vice versa. If the printer still doesn't feed a page, go to "My computer doesn't seem to be sending print jobs to my printer" on page 278.

19. If MS-DOS responds with an error message that it can't find the LPT port (which Windows 2000 will refer to as not being able to find a file) and you're sure that you're copying to the correct LPT port, you should suspect a problem with your LPT port. Go to "My computer doesn't seem to be sending print jobs to my printer" and look for the section "Check your parallel port" on page 282.

My computer doesn't seem to be sending print jobs to my printer

Source of the problem

You say that you know that your printer works because it passes its self test? But you can't get anything to print? Well then, odds are good that the problem lies in the communications between the two—think digital cell phone with a flaky connection. Or perhaps you have a Windows printer with no self test available, in which case communication issues are a good place to start looking.

If you've worked your way through the flowchart and have a printer that doesn't require Windows to print, you should have created the test described in "I'm not sure if my printer and computer are talking to each other" on page 272. If you haven't been though that section, you should go through it now, unless you have a Windows printer. The steps in this section for non-Windows printers will ask you to run that test at various points to find out if you've fixed the problem. If you have a Windows printer, you'll have to load Windows and try to print something each time you need to test the printer.

As we said in the previous section, in general, you should make sure the printer and computer are talking to each other on a hardware level before you worry about software issues—like whether the problem lies in the Windows printer driver. Once you know the hardware is connected and working, you can go on to worry about software, which we will cover in "Printer software basics" on page 286. This section covers what you need to know to test and fix the hardware side of the equation.

How to fix it

Check your cable

1. If your computer and printer are on, turn them off.

2. Take a look at the back of your computer. The cable coming from your printer will be plugged into a parallel port, which uses a connector called a DB-25. When you remove the cable, you'll see a connector shaped like an elongated D, with 25 holes. (Don't confuse this with a male DB-25 connector with 25 pins. The version with pins is a serial port.) If there is more than one female DB-25 connector on the back of the computer, make a note identifying which one you're using or mark the connector in some way so that you can be sure to plug it back into the same place later. ▶

3. Remove the cable from both the printer and the computer.

4. There are two common kinds of parallel cables. Both have a male DB-25 connector at one end, with 25 individual pins. The connector on the other end depends on the connector that's on your printer. The most common type is most widely known as a Centronics connector and is about 2 inches wide. The less common version is a Half Pitch Centronics connector and is about 1 inch wide. Both types have a plastic support for the pins running down the center of the connector, so it's almost impossible to bend the pins in a Centronics connector. Note which kind of connector your printer uses. You'll need to know this for later steps that involve replacing the cable. ▼

5. Take a careful look at the pins on the DB-25 connector. If any of the pins are bent, carefully straighten them using needle-nose pliers, tweezers, or a small flat-bladed screwdriver. (If you need more details about how to straighten a bent pin, see "If the pins in the connector are bent" on page 104.)

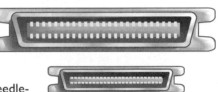

6. Once you're satisfied that the pins in the connector are straight, plug the cable back into both the printer and computer. If you meet any resistance, don't force the connector. That's how pins get severely bent. Remove the connector and take a closer look at the pins to see if any are even slightly out of alignment. You should be able to attach the connector so it's fully seated with only a gentle push. When you plug the connectors back in, make sure the clips or screws are in place to hold the connectors firmly attached.

7. Turn your printer and computer on. Try to print a test page.

- **If you have a Windows printer:**

    1. Choose Start, Settings, Printers, right-click on the printer, choose Properties, then the Print Test Page button.
    2. If the printer prints a page, you're done. If it doesn't, go on to the next step.

- **If you have a non-Windows printer:**

    1. Reboot in MS-DOS mode, using the techniques we described in the section "I'm not sure if my printer and computer are talking to each other" on page 272. (In most cases, this means choosing Start, Shut Down, Restart in MS-DOS mode, and then OK. For Windows 2000 systems, it means booting from a bootable floppy disk created on a Windows 98 or an MS-DOS system.)

> *If this solution didn't solve your problem, go to the next page.*

Tip

With Windows printers, you can't run tests in MS-DOS to eliminate the complicating factors of having Windows loaded. Still, the same hardware issues apply—like needing to check your cabling. In this section, we suggest printing from MS-DOS for non-Windows printers as the best way to simplify your system. For Windows printers, you'll have to load Windows. To eliminate at least one layer of software, however, we'll give you instructions for printing the Windows test page each time rather than printing from another program.

My computer doesn't seem to be sending print jobs to my printer

(continued from page 279)

2. Next you need to copy the file *Testfile* to your printer. (You should have created this file already. If you haven't, you'll find the instructions for creating it in "The basic test for an Everything Else or PostScript printer" on page 275.) Assuming you have created the file, copy it by typing the following copy command at the MS-DOS command line: **testfile lpt1** and press Enter.

3. If your printer feeds a page, you've proven that the hardware is all connected properly and working. Reboot into Windows and see if the printer works now. If it does, you're done. Otherwise, go to "Printer software basics" on page 286.

8. If your printer doesn't feed (or print) a page, try replacing the cable with one that you know is working and is appropriate for the printer. A very few printers require specially wired cables. (If you're not sure whether your printer does, check with the manufacturer.) For printers that use standard cables, you should be using an IEEE 1284 cable, which will also work with printers designed for cables that predate the IEEE 1284 standard.

9. To replace the cable, first turn off your printer and computer. Then remove the current cable, and plug in the replacement cable, being careful not to force the connectors. Once again make sure the clips or screws are in place to hold the connectors firmly attached.

10. After you replace the cable, turn your computer and printer back on, reboot in MS-DOS mode for a non-Windows printer or in Windows for a Windows printer.

11. **If you have a non-Windows printer**, copy the test file to the printer again, using the command **copy testfile lpt1** and press Enter.

12. **If you have a Windows printer,** choose Start, Settings, Printers, right-click on the printer, choose Properties, and then choose the Print Test Page button.

Tip

There's no hard and fast rule that says a printer cable longer than 10 feet won't work. In fact, sometimes it will. More precisely, you can create a short cable that is badly shielded or grounded improperly and, as a result, can't handle a parallel signal reliably even over 10 feet. On the other hand, you can create a long cable with excellent signal isolation that can handle signals over distances much greater than 10 feet. A cable as long as 25 feet is not unreasonable. So if you need a cable longer than 10 feet, it pays to spend extra to get a high-quality cable.

13. If your printer feeds (or prints) a page, you've proven that you need to replace your cable.

14. If your printer doesn't feed a page, look at the cable length. The rule of thumb is that the cable shouldn't be longer than ten feet. If the replacement cable was longer than ten feet, turn off your computer and printer, replace the cable with a shorter one, and try testing the printer connection again.

15. If your printer feeds (or prints) a page, you've proven that the problem is in your cable and that you need to replace your cable with a shorter one, or else get a higher-quality cable.

Check your printer and computer

1. Once you've ruled out the cable as the problem, you should ideally find out whether the printer works with another computer and whether the computer will print to another printer plugged into the same parallel port.

2. To test the computer's parallel port, you'll need another printer. For simplicity's sake, we recommend using a non-Windows printer. If the printer you've been having problems with is a Windows printer, you'll need to create a test file for the replacement printer, a process we describe in the section "The basic test for an Everything Else or PostScript printer" on page 275. If the printer you've been having problems with is a non-Windows printer, try to use a printer that uses the same category of language as your printer.

3. Connect the second printer and try to print. If it uses the same category of language as your printer, you can copy the same Testfile, using the same copy command. Simply reboot in MS-DOS mode and type the command **copy testfile lpt1** and press Enter. If it uses a different category of language, you'll have to create a new test file for that type of printer. (For details go to "The basic test for an Everything Else or PostScript printer" on page 275.)

4. If your computer successfully prints using the second printer, you've just proven that there is nothing wrong with the computer's LPT port. It's possible that you misidentified the printer language for the original printer and are using an inappropriate test file. But if you're sure you have the right test file, you most likely need to replace the printer or have it repaired professionally.

5. If the computer did not print to the second printer, skip to "Check your parallel port" on page 282.

6. To test a non-Windows printer on another system, first copy the test file you created earlier to a floppy disk.

If this solution didn't solve your problem, go to the next page.

My computer doesn't seem to be sending print jobs to my printer

(continued from page 281)

7. Plug the printer into a computer with a parallel port that you know is working using an IEEE 1284 cable (or a specially wired cable if your printer requires one) that you know is good. Then turn on both the printer and the computer

8. Boot up the computer in MS-DOS mode, put the floppy disk with Testfile on it in the floppy disk drive, and copy the file to the printer, using the command **copy a:\testfile lpt1** and press Enter. (This assumes, of course, that the parallel port on the second computer is LPT1. If it has a different designation, such as LPT2, be sure to use the appropriate designation.)

9. If the printer feeds a page, you've proven that the printer works and that the problem is almost certainly related to your computer's parallel port. Skip to "Check your parallel port."

10. If the printer doesn't feed a page, the problem may be that you misidentified the printer language and are using an inappropriate test file. If you're sure you have the right test file, you most likely need to replace the printer or have it repaired professionally.

11. If you have a Windows printer, there is little point in testing it on another system. Whether it works or not, you'll have to go through the same tests after this one, starting with the steps under "Check your parallel port."

Check your parallel port

1. Before you run these tests, you need to know how many parallel ports your computer has and whether the electronics for those ports are integrated into the motherboard or were added with an adapter card. You may be able to get this information simply by looking at the back of the case. Keep in mind that you're looking for DB-25 connectors with holes. If you see any with pins, ignore them.

> **Warning**
>
> Not every female DB-25 connector is a parallel port. Some devices—typically scanners and external drives—that use a SCSI interface come with dedicated adapter cards that use a DB-25 connector instead of the usual connectors for SCSI. If you know the history of your system, you will probably know whether a given card falls into this category. Otherwise, you'll have to do some detective work to find out what each card is. This may include removing the card from your system until you solve your printing problem, and then putting it back in later. ▼

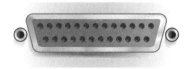

2. If you see just one parallel port, which is the most likely possibility, it's a good bet that it's integrated into the motherboard unless your system is several years old.

3. If you see a female DB-25 connector in a cutout that defines the position for an adapter card, it's on a card. If you also see additional parallel ports in other cutouts, they may or may not be associated with the adapter card.

Common keys to get into CMOS Setup

Some of these keys and key combinations are more widely used than others to get into CMOS Setup, but all are used widely enough to be worth trying if you can't find the answer from your computer manufacturer:

Delete	Ctrl+S	Ctrl+Alt+Enter
F1	Ctrl+Alt+Esc	Ctrl+Alt+I
F2	Ctrl+Alt+Ins	Ctrl+Alt+R
F10	Ctrl+Alt+"+"	Ctrl+Alt+F1
Esc	Ctrl+Alt+"-"	Ctrl+Alt+Q

4. If you have any doubts about how many parallel ports you have, or whether they are on the motherboard, you can find out more by opening the case. (Before you do, be sure to read "Working inside your computer" at the beginning of this book. Find the parallel ports and see what they are attached to, either directly or through a cable. If you find some attached to the motherboard and some not, and you don't know why your system is set up that way or which connector is assigned as which LPT port, try to simplify the system by removing the adapter card with the extra port or ports. This may not be possible if the same adapter card serves other purposes. If you can't remove the card, at least try to find some information on it in whatever manuals you have. Ideally, you'll find instructions that tell you how to set the connector to be inactive or not, and, if active, how to set it as LPT1, LPT2, or LPT3.

5. In the vast majority of cases, you'll have either one or two parallel ports, with at least one on the motherboard, and you'll be able to remove any card that includes an additional port. Put your system case back on, if necessary, and turn on your computer.

6. If all your computer's parallel ports are integrated into the motherboard, you'll need to start your CMOS Setup utility. Most computers will put a message on screen during boot up telling you what key to press to start the utility—often F2 or Delete. If your system hides this information behind a manufacturer's logo, press Escape to clear the logo. If you still can't start the CMOS Setup utility, see our discussion of how to start the utility in "The computer is booting from the wrong disk drive" on page 82.

If this solution didn't solve your problem, go to the next page.

My computer doesn't seem to be sending print jobs to my printer

(continued from page 283)

7. Once you start the CMOS utility, browse though the options, looking for anything relating to the LPT port or parallel port (two names for the same thing). The number of LPT ports you find mentioned should at least equal the number that you found on the motherboard. If the setup screen refers to more LPT ports than are physically on the motherboard, the additional ports should be disabled in the Setup screens.

8. If all your system's parallel ports are on a separate card, the manual or other documentation for the card will tell you how to change the settings on the card. (You may need to contact the manufacturer or vendor to get this information.) Changing the settings may involve moving a small jumper—a plastic piece with metal inside—to tie two pins together, changing switches, or running a utility program, or they may be changed automatically through Plug and Play. In rare cases, they may be set permanently. ▶

9. Whether the parallel ports are on the mother-board or a separate card, before you make any changes, write down the current settings for the LPT ports and put the information where you won't lose it.

10. You will probably see two different kinds of settings. One is for the mode or type of parallel port. This will usually include choices for Standard, Bidirectional, ECP, and EPP—or some variation on this list. (For example, some systems use *AT* or *Unidirectional* instead of *Standard*, and *PS/2* instead of *Bidirectional*. Others offer only ECP or only EPP rather than both, and some offer a choice called *Enhanced*, which usually means ECP, but could mean EPP.) This setting refers to the type of parallel port, and can be the same or different for the different parallel ports in a given system.

11. The second kind of setting will list the LPT designation (LPT1, LPT2, or LPT3), a memory address in a form similar to 378H or 278H, and an IRQ setting. (Don't worry about what an IRQ is; just note that LPT1 is normally set to IRQ 7 and LPT2 is normally set to IRQ 5.) Each parallel port in your system must have a unique setting for each of these items.

12. For simplicity's sake, we strongly recommend that for these tests you do not use a Windows printer. If the printer you've been having problems with is a Windows printer, you'll need to create a test file for the replacement printer, a process we describe in the section "The basic test for an Everything Else or PostScript printer" on page 275.

13. For each parallel port, take the brute force approach of trying each available setting (other than Disabled). Choose a setting. Then reboot into MS-DOS mode, and copy the test file to the printer using the command **copy testfile lpt1** and press Enter to see if a page feeds.

14. If you still can't get the page to feed and you've previously tested the printer and cable to confirm that they work, the problem may be that you misidentified the printer language and are using an inappropriate test file. If you're sure you have the right test file, however, you most likely need to replace the parallel port in your system. If you have more ports than you need, try simply putting the printer on a different port. If you don't have extra ports and the port that's apparently not working is on the motherboard, set the port as disabled, and buy a separate adapter card. If the nonworking port is on an adapter card, you can simply replace the card.

15. If, at any point, the page feeds, you've solved the problem—at least to the point of proving the hardware is connected properly. If you still have trouble printing in Windows, go to "Printer software basics" on page 286.

16. If you took a card out of the computer earlier, you can turn off your system and plug the card back in. Follow the instructions for the card to set it use different settings than the LPT port or ports on the motherboard.

17. To confirm everything still works, test the printer again after you plug the adapter card back in. You should also attach the printer cable to the card and rerun the printer test (copying to the appropriate LPT port) to confirm that the port on the card works also. If the port on your motherboard stops working after plugging the card back in, take a careful look at the settings for the LPT ports; they are probably conflicting with each other.

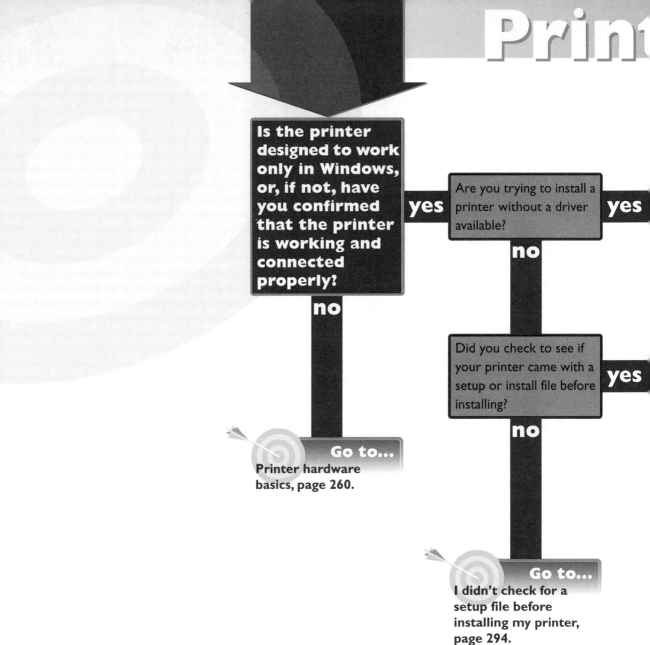

Is the printer designed to work only in Windows, or, if not, have you confirmed that the printer is working and connected properly?

yes → Are you trying to install a printer without a driver available? → **yes**

no

Did you check to see if your printer came with a setup or install file before installing? → **yes**

no

Go to...
Printer hardware basics, page 260.

Go to...
I didn't check for a setup file before installing my printer, page 294.

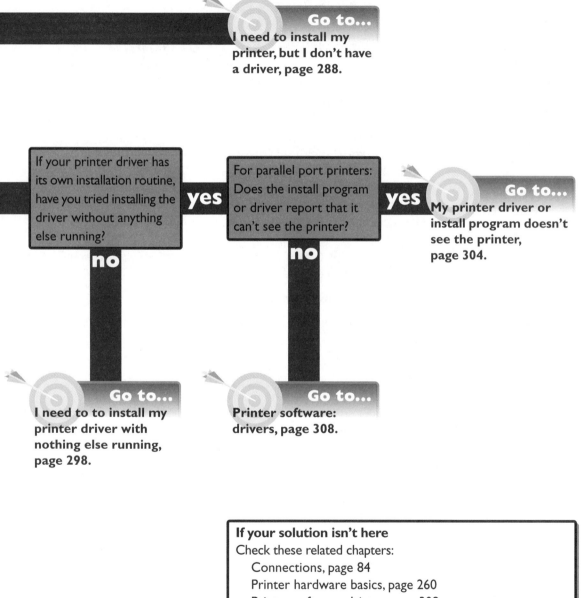

Go to...
I need to install my printer, but I don't have a driver, page 288.

If your printer driver has its own installation routine, have you tried installing the driver without anything else running?

yes

For parallel port printers: Does the install program or driver report that it can't see the printer?

yes

Go to...
My printer driver or install program doesn't see the printer, page 304.

no

no

Go to...
I need to to install my printer driver with nothing else running, page 298.

Go to...
Printer software: drivers, page 308.

If your solution isn't here
Check these related chapters:
Connections, page 84
Printer hardware basics, page 260
Printer software drivers, page 308
Or see the general troubleshooting tips on page xv.

I need to install my printer, but I don't have a driver

Source of the problem

Having a printer without a driver—that critical piece of software that tells Microsoft Windows how to print to the printer—is a little like being all dressed up with no place to go. You may have everything all put together, but what are you going to do with it?

Maybe you've just inherited a printer from someone who upgraded to a new one or bought an old printer at a computer fair. Or maybe you've just upgraded your system or reformatted your disk, and you can't find your printer driver disk. Or maybe you have an old printer that's qualified as obsolete for years but refuses to stop working, even though Microsoft has long since stopped providing a driver for it in the Windows Add Printer Wizard.

The good news is that you can probably get the printer working anyway. There are some exceptions, however. The key ones that you need to know about are as follows:

- Most Apple Macintosh printers—other than PostScript printers—can't work with Windows.

- Neither can printers designed to work with mainframe computers that use a different code for representing characters than the American Standard Code for Information Interchange (ASCII) that all PCs use.

- Windows printers, which require printer-specific drivers, won't work without those drivers.

For all other printers, you may not be able to take advantage of all the printer's features, but you can almost certainly get it printing. Here's how.

How to fix it

1. First check to see if there is, in fact, a printer-specific driver provided in the Windows Add Printer Wizard. Choose Start, Settings, Printers, then Add Printer to open the wizard.
2. Follow the instructions on the wizard's dialog boxes until you reach the one that shows a list of manufacturers on the left side. Look for the printer manufacturer in that list, and select the manufacturer name if you find it. Then look for the printer model in the Printers list on the right. If you find an entry that matches the model you have, select it, choose Next, and continue

through the Wizard, following the instructions on screen. If you find your printer in the list and install the driver, your printer should work. ▶

Add Printer Wizard

Click the manufacturer and model of your printer. If your printer came with an installation disk, click Have Disk. If your printer is not listed, consult your printer documentation for a compatible printer.

Manufacturers:
- Gestetner
- Hermes
- HP
- IBM
- Kodak
- Kyocera
- LaserMaster

Printers:
- HP LaserJet 6P/6MP - PostScript
- HP LaserJet III
- HP LaserJet III PS Cartridge
- HP LaserJet III PostScript+
- HP LaserJet IIID
- HP LaserJet IIID PS Cartridge
- HP LaserJet IIID PostScript+

Have Disk...

< Back   Next >   Cancel

Check with the manufacturer

1. If Windows doesn't offer a suitable driver, check the manufacturer's Web site for a driver for your version of Windows, or contact the company's technical support. Some manufacturers are better than others about supporting old printers, and some manufacturers may be out of business. But even if the manufacturer doesn't have a driver designed for both your model printer and your version of Windows, it may be able to tell you of another driver that will work. There are also Web sites—such as *www.driverguide.com*—that have drivers for all sorts of hardware.

If you find a similar printer model in the Add Printer Wizard

1. If the Add Printer Wizard doesn't show your printer as a choice and checking with the manufacturer doesn't help, try a later model in the same line from the same manufacturer. For example, you won't find the venerable Xerox Diablo 630 daisywheel in the Add Printer Wizard, but you will find the HP LaserJet III. We haven't tried this particular driver with either of these models, so we can't guarantee that it will work. But it's

If this solution didn't solve your problem, go to the next page.

I need to install my printer, but I don't have a driver

(continued from page 289)

worth trying, and it will likely work for most print jobs. Keep in mind, however, that the complication of using a driver designed for another printer is that you may not be able to use some of your printer's features, and the driver may offer some features that your printer can't take advantage of. Watch out for features that don't match between printer and driver.

2. If the driver for the later model turns out to cause too many problems, look for a similar model that may offer a subset of the commands in the printer you have. The LaserJet and LaserJet II, for example, should work with drivers for monochrome Hewlett-Packard DeskJet printers, which use a lower level of the Printer Control Language (PCL) (although this is another mix we haven't tried and can't guarantee will work).

3. Also look for drivers for compatible models. If your printer uses PCL, try one or more of the HP LaserJet drivers. (Hewlett Packard created PCL.) If you have a PostScript printer, try the Apple LaserWriter driver.

If all else fails

1. If you can't find a driver that's designed for your printer, install the Generic/Text Only driver. Choose Start, Settings, Printers, and then the Add Printer Wizard. Step through the Wizard, and when you reach the screen with the Manufacturers list, choose Generic in the list. Then, in the Printers list, choose Generic/Text Only. ▶

2. If you're using Windows 2000, you'll find additional printer choices in the generic category: Generic IBM Graphics 9Pin, Generic IBM Graphics 9Pin Wide, MS Publisher Color Printer, and MS Publisher Imagesetter. The IBM Graphics choices should work with most IBM and Epson printers, and with any printer that uses the IBM or Epson printer codes. If you use Windows 2000, you may want to investigate these choices.

3. The Generic choice provides a kind of highest common denominator that should work with any printer that uses ASCII. It also lets you modify the driver for the specific printer. To make the modifications, first find a list of your printer's control codes. The older the printer, the more likely you are to find these codes in the printer manual.

4. After you install the driver, choose Start, Settings, and then Printers to open the Printers window, right-click on the Generic/Text Only printer, and then choose Properties.

If you use Windows 98	If you use Windows 2000
5. Choose the Paper tab, and then set the paper size.	Choose the Device Settings Tab and set the paper size for each of the three choices in paper types: Cut Sheet, Cont. Feed - No Break, (*Cont. Feed* is an abbreviation for *continuous feed*), and Cont. Feed - With Break.
6. You can also set the type of paper in the box labeled Paper Source. Use Cut Sheet if the printer uses individual sheets, or use one of the continuous feed choices if the printer uses tractor feed paper. With tractor feed paper, you may need to experiment to choose between the Continuous - Page Break and the Continuous - No Page Break settings.	To set the type of paper, choose the General tab, then the Printing Preferences button to open the Printing Preferences dialog box, then the Paper/Quality tab, and, in the box labeled Paper Source, pick the type of paper: Cut Sheet, Cont. Feed - No Break, or Cont. Feed - With Break. With tractor feed paper, you may need to experiment to choose between the two continuous feed choices.

7. You can also define the areas of the page where the printer can't print. Virtually all printers have some unprintable area when printing on cut sheet paper, because they have to hold on to the sheet of paper when printing. If you enter the right numbers, you'll find that programs will do a better job of matching their pagination on screen to what actually prints.

If you use Windows 98	If you use Windows 2000
8. Choose the Unprintable Area button. You can define the Left, Right, Top, and Bottom areas of dead space in thousandths of an inch or hundredths of a millimeter.	Choose the Printer Commands tab. You can define the Left, Right, Top, and Bottom areas of dead space in hundredths of an inch or tenths of a millimeter.
9. Choose the Fonts tab. If your printer offers command codes for setting the font to 10, 12, and 17 characters per inch, double wide, underlined, or bold (often called *emphasized*), you can type those commands here.	Choose the Font Selection tab. If your printer offers command codes for setting the font to 10, 12, and 17 characters per inch, underlined, or bold (often called *emphasized*), you can type those commands here.

> *If this solution didn't solve your problem, go to the next page.*

I need to install my printer, but I don't have a driver

(continued from page 291)

10. Fill in each of the text boxes that matches a control code available on your printer. Many printer control codes start with an Escape character. To enter the character, press the Escape key, which Windows will enter as <ESC>. ▶

11. Choose the Device Options tab (the Printer Commands tab in Windows 2000). If your printer needs special command codes to set paper size, paper source (called Paper Feed Selection in Windows 2000), or the beginning or end of a print job, type them in the appropriate text boxes.

12. If the printer has a reset command, it's a good idea to type it in the Begin Print Job text box. Windows will send the command at the beginning of each print job, which will ensure that the printer is set to its default settings. Similarly, you may want to add a command to feed a page in the End Print Job text box.

13. You should also investigate the other settings in the driver. Any given setting may or may not apply to your particular printer. For example, you'll find a character translation feature in Windows 98 (but not in Windows 2000) that will let you map a daisywheel printer's special characters to specific Windows characters so that you can get symbols such as trademark or copyright symbols to print correctly for your printer.

I didn't check for a setup file before installing my printer

Source of the problem

One of the biggest strengths of Windows over earlier operating systems on the PC (which mostly means MS-DOS) is that it has standard ways of doing things—like installing printers. Before Windows, you had to install a printer driver in every program, and the installation was different in each case. If you bought a new printer, you had to go through a different install routine for each program.

Windows changed that. With Windows, you not only install your printer just once, but you have a standard way to install printers. Once you know how to use the Add Printer Wizard, you know how to install any printer.

Except, of course, for printers that won' t install that way. Printer manufacturers keep thinking they have a better idea, and they keep coming up with supposed improvements on the Windows install feature. However, if you already know the standard installation routine, you may have used it without checking whether the printer came with one of its own. In too many cases, the printers will *seem* to install with the Add Printer Wizard but refuse to work. And even if the printer works, you may miss options to install online help files or utilities such as a status monitor, which pops up to tell you things like when the printer is out of paper. If you just installed a printer with the Add Printer Wizard and found that it's not working or that you're missing some features, here's how to backtrack and fix the problem.

How to fix it

1. If you followed the flowchart steps to reach this discussion, you should have already confirmed that the printer hardware is connected properly. If you haven't, first go to "Printer hardware basics" on page 260, to see if the hardware is the problem.

Tip

Since we mentioned the Add Printer Wizard, it's only fair to explain how to use it. Choose Start, Settings, and then Printers to open the Printers dialog box; choose Add Printer; and then work your way through the Add Printer Wizard. As one of the steps in the wizard, you have to either pick a driver from a list or tell the wizard that you have a disk with the driver on it. Windows will generally have the drivers on the Windows CD printer models that are older than your version of Windows.

For models that shipped after your version of Windows, you should have received a driver disk with the printer. You need to put the disk in an appropriate drive and tell the wizard where to find the files. Once Windows finds them, everything else is pretty much automatic, but with some printer drivers everything will seem to go well without the driver actually being installed properly.

2. Once you've ruled out a hardware problem as best you can, check any manuals or quick start guides that came with the printer to see if they mention running a setup or install program. If you don' t have any manuals, check the distribution disk or CD that came with the printer to see if there's a program with either name. Also check for README.TXT files that may contain installation instructions.

3. If there's no mention of any kind of setup or install program, return to the flowchart on page 287, and go to the question, "If your printer driver has its own installation routine, have you tried installing the driver without anything else running?"

If you found a setup or install file and your printer is working

1. If you found an installation program, run it, following whatever instructions you found in the manual or quick start guide.

2. The installation program will most likely start with a menu of options that includes installing the printer. It may also include choices to install help files, a status monitor, or even applications, assuming your printer comes bundled with application programs. ▶

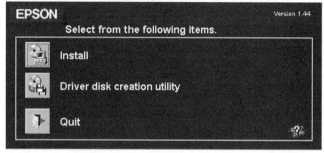

3. Ignore the choice to install the printer. The install routine for many printers is meant as an alternative to, rather than a replacement for, the Add Printer Wizard. In fact, the install program for many printers simply calls up the Add Printer Wizard, so if your printer is working, there is no need to reinstall it. However, you should take the time to investigate the other choices on the installation menu. Ideally, you should back up your system before installing any of them, so you can easily return your system to a working state if something goes wrong during the installation.

If you found a setup or install file and your printer is not working

1. If your printer isn't working, try choosing the install option and working your way through the entire installation. If that solves the problem, you're done, except for exploring any other choices on the installation menu. Keep in mind that you should back up your system before installing anything, so that you can easily restore your system to a working state if the installation causes a problem.

2. If reinstalling the printer driver doesn't work, and you have a backup of your system from before installing the driver the first time, the simplest solution will likely be to restore your system to a working state from the backup (details will depend on your backup program), and then reinstall the printer, this time using the printer's own install program.

> *If this solution didn't solve your problem, go to the next page.*

I didn't check for a setup file before installing my printer

(continued from page 295)

3. If you didn't back up your system just before installing the printer driver, look for a way to uninstall the printer so that you can reinstall it from scratch. Start by looking for an uninstall option on the first screen of the printer's installation program. If you find one, run it to uninstall the printer file.

4. If you couldn't find an uninstall option in the printer's installation program, look for one in the Start menus. Choose Start, Programs, and look for a new entry for the printer anywhere in the menu. If you see an appropriate submenu, open it to see if there is an uninstall option. If there is, run the uninstall routine.

5. If you don't see an uninstall option for the printer files in the Start menu, see if one has been added to the Windows Add/Remove Programs Control Panel item. Choose Start, Settings, Control Panel, and then Add/Remove Programs to open the Add/Remove Programs Properties dialog box with the Install/Uninstall tab selected. (The same commands in Windows 2000 open the Add/Remove Programs window, with the Change Or Remove Programs button selected.)

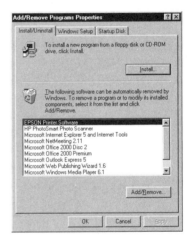

6. Scroll through the list of software that can be removed by Windows, and select the appropriate printer files if you find them. Then choose Add/Remove (or Change/Remove in Windows 2000), and follow any instructions you see on screen. ▶

7. Whether you found an uninstall option or not, choose Start, Settings, and then Printers to open the Printers window and see if the printer is still listed as installed. If it is, right-click on the printer icon, and choose Delete from the pop-up menu to delete the printer files. Follow the instructions on screen. If you see a message asking permission to delete files that are no longer being used, give Windows permission to delete those files.

8. Chose Start, Shut Down, and then Restart to reboot your system.

9. If you have a simple way to back up your system, do so now, before installing any further programs. (For tips on backing up your system, see "Troubleshooting tips" on page xv.)

10. Run the installation routine that comes with the printer. Follow any special instructions in the printer's manual or quick start guide, and follow the instructions on the screen.

11. If the printer still won't print, return to the flowchart on page 286. This time answer Yes to the question, Did you check to see if your printer came with a setup or install file before installing?

I need to install my printer driver with nothing else running

Source of the problem

One of the (many) things Windows does on your system is act like a traffic cop. You may be running umpteen different programs at once, some of them actually trying to do things at the same time—like several million people trying to drive into New York City during morning rush hour. Like any good traffic cop, Windows' job is to help keep things moving and keep them from crashing into each other.

For the most part, Windows does its job reasonably well. But it's not perfect. There are times when a program—or your entire system—will crash. And there are times when everything seems to muddle through, but there's just enough conflict between programs to keep them from working right—as when a printer driver that comes with its own installation routine won't install properly, for example.

One thing to try when you're having trouble installing a printer driver (or any other software for that matter) is to simplify your system as much as possible. If you close any and all programs that aren't absolutely essential, there's that much less for the installation program to conflict with. But getting all programs out of your system's memory may take a little more work than you think. Here are the steps you need to follow.

How to fix it

1. Most people run more programs than they realize when they start their computers. To find out what loads on your system when it starts, choose Start, Shut Down, Restart, and then OK.

If you use Windows 98	If you use Windows 2000
2. When your system finishes booting, press Ctrl+Alt+Delete (that's the Ctrl key, plus the Alt key, plus the Delete key all at the same time) to bring up the Close Program dialog box.	When your system finishes booting, press Ctrl+Alt+Delete (that's the Ctrl key, plus the Alt key, plus the Delete key all at the same time) to bring up the Windows Security dialog box, and then choose Task Manager to open the Windows Task Manager window.

If you use Windows 98

3. If the list in the Close Program dialog box includes anything in addition to Explorer and Systray, you have programs loaded that are probably not necessary to just run your system. Getting rid of them temporarily will generally take several steps. ▼

```
Close Program                                    ×
┌──────────────────────────────────────────────┐
│ Explorer                                    ▲ │
│ Rnaapp                                        │
│ Realplay                                      │
│ Mrtmngr                                       │
│ Qagent                                        │
│ Qbdagent                                      │
│ Ixapplet                                      │
│ Hpsplmwa                                      │
│ Wcescomm                                      │
│ Stimon                                      ▼ │
│ ◄                                           ► │
└──────────────────────────────────────────────┘
WARNING: Pressing CTRL+ALT+DEL again will restart your
computer. You will lose unsaved information in all programs that
are running.

  [ End Task ]   [ Shut Down ]   [ Cancel ]
```

Warning

Be careful not to accidentally choose the Shut Down button or press Ctrl+Alt+Delete again with the Close Programs dialog box open. Either one will reboot your system.

4. Right-click on any empty part of the Windows Taskbar (the bar normally at the bottom of the Windows screen).

If you use Windows 2000

Choose the Applications tab. There should be no programs listed. Then choose the Processes tab. You should see a list of 13 processes:

System Idle Process	lsass.exe
System	svchost.exe
smss.exe	regsvc.exe
winlogon.exe	MSTask.exe
csrss.exe	Explorer.exe
services.exe	taskmgr.exe
spoolsv.exe	

Some of these may show up more than once, but if you see anything else in this list or on the Applications tab, you have programs loaded that are unnecessary. You'll need to get rid of them temporarily. ▼

```
Windows Task Manager                        _ □ ×
File  Options  View  Help
┌Applications┐ Processes ┌Performance┐

  Image Name    PID  CPU  CPU Time  Mem Us...
  System Idle Pr...  0   95   0:02:10    16 K
  System             8   00   0:00:07    76 K
  smss.exe         120   00   0:00:01    72 K
  winlogon.exe     144   00   0:00:06   456 K
  csrss.exe        148   00   0:00:01   424 K
  services.exe     196   00   0:00:03  2,108 K
  lsass.exe        208   00   0:00:01  1,072 K
  svchost.exe      384   00   0:00:00   844 K
  spoolsv.exe      416   01   0:00:00  1,084 K
  svchost.exe      460   00   0:00:01  3,228 K
  regsvc.exe       508   00   0:00:00    60 K
  MSTask.exe       528   00   0:00:00   196 K
  WinMgmt.exe      600   00   0:00:13   180 K
  Explorer.exe     792   01   0:00:07  1,632 K
  mspaint.exe      894   00   0:00:00  1,204 K
  taskmgr.exe      920   03   0:00:00  1,668 K

                              [ End Process ]
Processes: 16    CPU Usage: 5%   Mem Usage: 45460K / 700C
```

Right-click on any empty part of the Windows Taskbar (the bar normally at the bottom of the Windows screen).

If this solution didn't solve your problem, go to the next page.

I need to install my printer driver with nothing else running

(continued from page 299)

If you use Windows 98

5. In the menu that pops up, choose Properties to open the Taskbar Properties dialog box. Then choose the Start Menu Programs tab, and then the Advanced button to open Windows Explorer with the Start Menu folder selected.

If you use Windows 2000

In the menu that pops up, choose Properties to open the Taskbar And Start Menu Properties dialog box. Then choose the Advanced tab, and then the Advanced button to open Windows Explorer with the Start Menu folder selected.

6. Starting from the Start Menu folder, navigate to the Start Menu\Programs\StartUp folder. Any files in this folder load every time you start Windows. If you see files in this folder, you'll need to move them temporarily; you can move them back later, after you've installed the printer driver. ▶

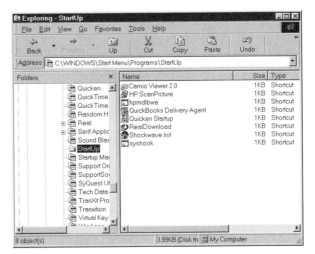

7. Press the Backspace key to back up one level to the Start Menu\Programs folder.

8. Choose File, New, Folder, and enter an appropriate name for the new folder. We'll call it ParkFilesHere.

9. Return to the Start Menu\Programs\StartUp folder, and select all the file names in the folder.

10. Choose Edit, and then choose Cut.

11. Navigate to the Start Menu\Programs\ParkFilesHere folder.

12. Choose Edit, and then choose Paste. This will move all the files from the StartUp folder to the ParkFilesHere folder.

13. Close the Windows Explorer window.

14. Reboot your computer by choosing Start, Shut Down, selecting Restart, and then choosing OK.

15. After your system reboots, press the Ctrl+Alt+Delete combination to bring up the Close Program dialog box in Windows 98. (In Windows 2000, press Ctrl+Alt+Delete, choose Task Manager, and then the Applications tab and Processes tab in turn.) You should see fewer programs listed, but you still may see more than the minimum number you need to run Windows. If so, see if there are any whose names you recognize as programs with options that let you change settings. A fax program for example, may be set to load a piece of the program when starting Windows, but if you load the program directly, you will usually find a setting somewhere in the menus that lets you set it to always receive incoming calls (which means loading the program at system startup) or not (which means not loading the program on startup).

16. Make a list of the names you recognize; it will serve as a checklist in the next step, since you'll have to look for settings to change in each program. Having the list handy will also make it easier to reset the programs back to their original settings later, after you've finished installing the printer driver.

17. For each program you recognize, load the program, set the appropriate option to tell the program not to load when you boot Windows, and then close the program.

18. Reboot your computer by choosing Start, Shut Down, selecting Restart, and then choosing OK.

If you use Windows 98

19. After your system reboots, press the Ctrl+Alt+Delete combination to bring up the Close Program dialog box. If you still see more than Explorer and Systray in the list, you can close the programs through the dialog box.

If you use Windows 2000

After your system reboots, press the Ctrl+Alt+Delete combination, and then choose the Task Manager button to open the Task Manager window. If you still see any programs when you choose the Applications tab, or if you see more items than the core set mentioned above when you choose the Processes tab, you can close each item through the window.

If this solution didn't solve your problem, go to the next page.

I need to install my printer driver with nothing else running

(continued from page 301)

If you use Windows 98

20. For each program you need to close, highlight the program in the list and choose End Task. Then press Ctrl+Alt+Delete again to re-open the dialog box.

21. Most programs will simply stop running when you choose End Task. In some cases, however, you'll see this message: This Program Is Not Responding. It May Be Busy, Waiting For A Response From You, Or It May Have Stopped Running. Click Cancel To Ignore And Return To Windows. To Close This Program Immediately, Click End Task. If you see this message, press the Enter key to end the task. Then press Ctrl+Alt+Delete again to reopen the dialog box.

If you use Windows 2000

For each program or process you need to close, highlight the item and choose the End Task button if you're working with applications, or choose the End Process button if you're working with processes.

When you choose the End Process button you'll usually see this warning: Terminating A Process Can Cause Undesired Results Including Loss Of Data And System Instability. You can safely ignore this warning and choose Yes to terminate the process. If terminating the process winds up causing a problem, simply reboot, go back to step 19 to start again, and don't terminate that particular process this time. If you pick a critical process to terminate, Windows 2000 will simply tell you that it can't terminate the process.

22. With either Windows 98 or Windows 2000, once you've pared the list down to the minimum number of programs (or processes) running, try installing your printer driver again, following whatever instructions came with the installation disk.

23. If the printer doesn't print, return to the flowchart on page 286, and this time answer Yes to the question "If your printer driver has its own installation routine, have you tried installing the driver without anything else running?"

24. If the printer now prints, reboot to make sure it will print with all the programs that are currently set to load on system startup. Then go through the list of any programs you previously set not to load on system startup and reset them to load automatically. You might want to reboot after each one and test the printer to make sure it still works. If it turns out that you have a conflict between the printer software and some other program, contact the printer manufacturer to determine whether this is a known problem with a known fix.

Warning

Anti-virus programs can be helpful for obvious reasons, but they are also notorious for interfering with installation programs. Don't be tempted to play it safe by leaving your anti-virus program running. If there is any one program that rates as the major suspect for interfering with installing your new printer driver, your anti-virus program is it.

My printer driver or install program doesn't see the printer

Source of the problem

There was a time when the conversation between computers and printers was pretty much a monologue. Computers sent the print job to the printer and didn't need anything back other than a request to stop every so often to give the printer a chance to catch up. Cables and parallel ports were designed with this unidirectional flow in mind, and all was well.

Then printer manufacturers came up an idea: Wouldn't it be nice to send messages *back* to the computer? Messages like: *Paper Jam*, or *Tray Empty*, or even the current levels of ink or toner? And while they were at it, they also added things like printer settings for speed, font, paper type, network settings, and whatnot.

Well, sure it would be nice, but that requires a cable and parallel port designed for two-way communication. The problem, unfortunately, is that various manufacturers then proceeded to create different variations on two-way communication before the industry settled on the IEEE 1284 specification as a standard. Today, there are still a lot of older, but still serviceable, cables and computers floating around from before the current standard. And even new computers generally let you set their parallel ports for unidirectional flow, for those printers that need it. The bottom line is that if you don't have the right combination of cable and parallel port setting for your printer, you will (not may) have a problem, with your installation program or printer driver not being able to see the printer. Here's what you can do about it.

How to fix it

Preliminary steps

1. If you followed the flowchart to reach this section, you should already have made sure you have the right cable. If you skipped that, however, do it now. Very few printers need special wiring for their cables. Unless yours is one of those, you should have an

> **Tip**
>
> Broadly speaking, there are three kinds of parallel cables: unidirectional, bidirectional, and IEEE 1284 (which is also bidirectional). Unless your printer needs a specially wired cable, you should be using an IEEE 1284 cable, which incorporates all earlier standards.
>
> You can't tell one kind of parallel cable from another just by looking at it, but some cable manufacturers are kind enough to print *IEEE 1284* on the cable itself. That's something you might want to check when you buy a cable, so that once it's out of its bubble pack, it will be easy to pick out from older cables that aren't IEEE 1284 compliant. If you get an IEEE 1284 cable that doesn't have an identification printed on it, paste your own label on the cable, so in the future you won't have to wonder what kind of parallel cable it is.

IEEE 1284–compliant cable. If you're not sure whether you have one, it's worth the small investment to buy one. Make sure you get one with connectors that match the connectors on your computer and printer. (If you need more details about the cables or connectors, you can find them in "My computer doesn't seem to be sending print jobs to my printer" on page xxx.

2. Don't overlook the obvious. Make sure the printer is plugged into the same parallel port you're trying to print to. If your computer has more than one parallel port, and you have any doubts about whether the printer is plugged into the right one, be sure to try it with each parallel port, even if it means running through all the testing steps for each port.

3. You also need to ensure that both Windows and the computer's parallel port are set to the right kind of parallel port for your printer. Once again, if you followed the flowchart to reach this point, you should already have set the parallel port in your computer. If you skipped that, you should do so now. Check with the manufacturer to find out what kind of parallel ports the printer works with; you need to know all the possible choices, because your system may or may not offer the printer's preferred choice. If you can't get this information, you'll have to take the brute force approach of setting your system and Windows to each kind of parallel port your system supports, testing the printer, and moving on to the next choice if the printer doesn't work. The details for how to set the parallel port to the right type of port are in "My computer doesn't seem to be sending print jobs to my printer" on page 278.

Make sure Windows is set correctly

1. After you set your computer to the right kind of port, you need to set Windows to match. The easiest way is to delete the current port in Windows and let Windows install the new, correct port. As always when making software changes to your system, it's best to back up the system before making the changes, to make it easy to return to a working system if something goes wrong.

2. Choose Start, Settings, Control Panel, and then System to open the System Properties dialog box.

3. Choose the Device Manager tab (or, in Windows 2000, the Hardware tab and then the Device Manager button).

4. With Device Manager set to View Devices By Type, scroll down if necessary to find the entry Ports (COM & LPT). ▶

System Properties

General | Device Manager | Hardware Profiles | Performance

View devices by type
View devices by connection

- Computer
  - CDROM
  - Disk drives
  - Display adapters
  - Floppy disk controllers
  - Hard disk controllers
  - Imaging Device
  - Keyboard
  - Modem
  - Monitors
  - Mouse
  - Network adapters
  - Ports (COM & LPT)
  - SCSI controllers
  - Sound, video and game controllers
  - System devices
  - Universal serial bus controller

Properties | Refresh | Remove | Print...

OK | Cancel

If this solution didn't solve your problem, go to the next page.

My printer driver or install program doesn't see the printer

(continued from page 305)

5. Expand the Ports item if necessary to see the Printer Port entry (or Printer Ports entries if there are more than one).

6. Highlight the Printer Port entry you want to change, and choose Remove. (Or, in Windows 2000, choose Action, Uninstall, and then OK.) ▶

7. After Windows removes the parallel port from the installation, choose Start, Shut Down, Restart, and then OK to let the system reboot.

8. While rebooting, Windows should find the LPT port and install the right driver for its current setting. It may ask you to supply the Windows CD. Put the disc in the CD-ROM drive, or, if you have the Windows CAB files on your hard disk, enter the path to the files to tell Windows where to find them.

9. After Windows finishes booting, the driver should be installed for the right kind of LPT port. You can check to make sure that it recognized the ports by returning to the Device Manager. Choose Start, Settings, Control Panel, and then System; then choose Device Manager in Windows 98, or Hardware and then Device Manager in Windows 2000.

10. If your earlier problem was with the printer driver installation program, try rerunning the installation. If you set the ports properly, the installation program should now see the printer. If the problem was with the driver not being able to see the printer for issues such as current settings for the printer, check the driver again. It should now be able to see the printer.

If the printer still doesn't work

1. ...and you have any doubts about which parallel port your printer is plugged into, repeat the previous steps for each parallel port in the system.

2. ...and you haven't been able to confirm the right type of port setting to use, repeat these steps with each type of port setting available on your computer. If it still doesn't work, and your system doesn't have an ECP or EPP option, you may have to buy a parallel port adapter card.

3. ...and you skipped over the suggestion in the "Printer software basics" flowchart to work through the "Printer hardware basics" flowchart first, go to "Printer hardware basics" on page 260.

If everything seems set up right, but your printer still doesn't work, or doesn't work well, focus your attention on the printer's driver—and on the settings in the driver that tell your printer how to print.

Have you confirmed that you have the most current version of your printer driver?

yes

Have you already documented the current settings in your printer driver?

yes

no

no

Go to...
I need to document my printer driver settings before I change them, page 311.

Go to...
I need to make sure I have the most current version of my printer driver, page 310.

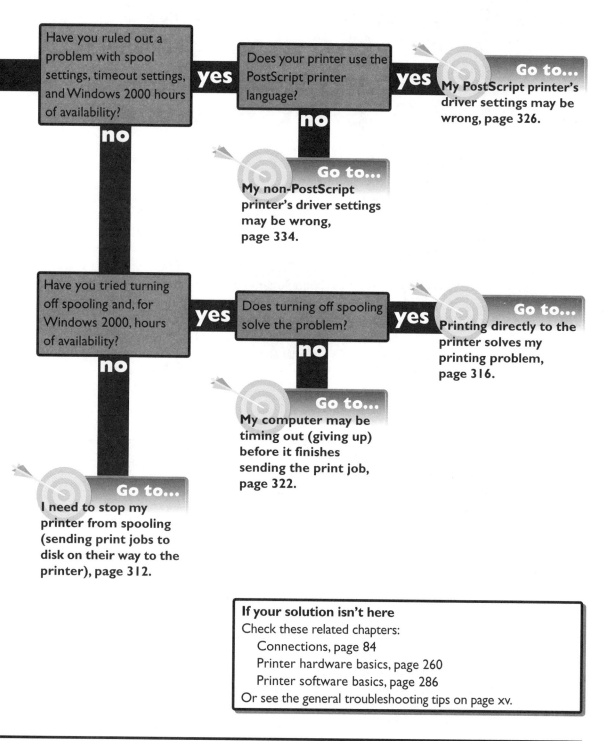

Have you ruled out a problem with spool settings, timeout settings, and Windows 2000 hours of availability?

yes Does your printer use the PostScript printer language?

yes **Go to...** My PostScript printer's driver settings may be wrong, page 326.

no

no **Go to...** My non-PostScript printer's driver settings may be wrong, page 334.

Have you tried turning off spooling and, for Windows 2000, hours of availability?

yes Does turning off spooling solve the problem?

yes **Go to...** Printing directly to the printer solves my printing problem, page 316.

no

no **Go to...** My computer may be timing out (giving up) before it finishes sending the print job, page 322.

Go to... I need to stop my printer from spooling (sending print jobs to disk on their way to the printer), page 312.

If your solution isn't here
Check these related chapters:
   Connections, page 84
   Printer hardware basics, page 260
   Printer software basics, page 286
Or see the general troubleshooting tips on page xv.

I need to make sure I have the most current version of my printer driver

Source of the problem

Most printer drivers are reasonably reliable, but some include bugs that show up only with certain programs or unusual circumstances. Competition in the marketplace is fierce. And it can be more important to get there first than to get it right. The rise of the Web has made the *ship-it-now-fix-it-later* mentality even more prevalent, and, thankfully, easier to live with. If a manufacturer isn't finished stamping out bugs in the driver by the time the printer is supposed to ship, it's increasingly common to ship the printer as is, then make the updated driver available on a Web site. And it's only fair to point out also that some don't turn up until after the manufacturer gets feedback from early buyers.

In any case, if you've established that your hardware works—the printer passes its self test, the cable is good, and the printer port works—and that the basic Microsoft Windows setup is right, the driver should be the next thing on your list to look at.

How to fix it

1. The first rule for any kind of suspected driver problem—whether it's a printer driver or anything else—is to make sure you have the latest version of the driver. This holds true even if you just bought the printer, especially if it's a relatively new model. If you have an older printer and you installed it using a driver that came with Windows, look for a driver on a disc or disk that came with the printer. Assuming the driver on the disc or disk is for your version of Windows, try installing it instead of the driver that came with Windows.

2. Whether you installed a driver that came with Windows or one that came with the printer, check with the manufacturer to make sure there isn't a later version of the driver. Very often, you'll find one on the manufacturer's Web site. If there's one there, ignore the one you have in hand, download the new version, and install it, following the manufacturer's instructions. That by itself may be enough to solve your problem.

Tip

When you check for a newer driver at the printer manufacturer's Web site, also take a few minutes to see what other kinds of support the manufacturer provides. Very often, you'll find a searchable database of known bugs and common problems that people run into with the printer. If you take a moment to look around, you may even find information that tells you how to solve your specific problem.

I need to document my printer driver settings before I change them

Source of the problem

Experimenting with your printer driver means changing settings. With luck, you'll find that changing one or two settings will solve your printing problem. But once you find the right setting to change—or decide there is none—you'll probably want to return the rest of the options back to their original settings. To do that, you need to know what they are.

You can, of course, document the settings simply by writing them all down. However, it's easier to capture an image, paste it into a program, and save it as a file.

How to fix it

1. To capture an image of any window, including a driver's dialog box, first open the window and make sure it's active by clicking anywhere on it. (But be careful not to click on an option that will change a setting.)

2. Next, press Alt+Print Screen (that's the Alt key plus the Print Screen key) to store an image of the dialog box in the Windows clipboard.

3. Open or switch to any program that will let you paste images into a file. (To open Microsoft WordPad, for example, choose Start, Programs, Accessories, and then WordPad.) ▶

4. Choose Edit, Paste to paste the image into the file, then File, Save. Depending on the program you're using, you may have to save a separate file for each capture, or you may be able to put all the captures into the same file (as with WordPad).

I need to stop my printer from spooling (sending print jobs to disk on their way to the printer)

Source of the problem

Spooling is a feature that uses your hard disk as a kind of staging area for your print jobs. When you print, the spooler sends the print job to a file on the hard disk, and then moves the data from the hard disk to your printer.

Although this takes an extra step—one that can slow down the overall print time—it has some notable advantages. As a general rule, if you print directly to the printer, your computer will be tied up longer and will tend to be sluggish responding to your mouse and keyboard. If you spool to disk, however, the program you're working in will finish printing much faster (because the hard disk can accept data much faster than a printer can print it). And you'll be able to continue using your computer while the spooler works in the background to send the data to the printer.

Clearly, if all goes well, spooling is usually worth having. But it also adds another level of complication. So when you're trying to track down a printing problem, it's a good idea to turn spooling off (at least temporarily) and find out if that's what's causing your problem.

How to fix it

If you have Windows 98

1. Open the printer driver by choosing Start, Settings, Printers, selecting the printer, and then choosing File, Properties.

2. Choose the Details tab, which follows a standard Windows layout and should be similar for all printers. ▶

3. Choose the Spool Settings button to open the Spool Settings dialog box shown at the top of the following page.

4. Document the current settings by writing them down or capturing an image of the dialog box as described in the section "I need to document my printer driver settings before I change them" on page 311. (Briefly: With the Spool Settings dialog box active, press Alt+Print Screen to store an image of the dialog box in the clipboard. Then open a program such as WordPad, and use the Edit, Paste command to paste the image into a document.)

5. The driver will probably have the spooling option set to Spool Print Jobs So Program Finishes Printing Faster. If so, choose Print Directly To The Printer, and continue with the next step. If the driver is already set to Print Directly To The Printer, you're finished with this section, and should go to "My computer may be timing out (giving up) before it finishes sending the print job" on page 322.

6. Choose OK to close the Spool Settings dialog box, and then OK again to close the printer's Properties dialog box.

7. Test the printer to see if the problem is fixed. If it is, you've established that the problem is related to the spool settings and you should go to "Printing directly to the printer solves my printing problem" on page 316.

8. If the problem isn't solved, go to "My computer may be timing out (giving up) before my it finishes sending the print job" on page 322. Do not turn the spool feature back on.

If you have Windows 2000

1. Open the printer driver by choosing Start, Settings, and then Printers, selecting the printer and choosing File, Properties.

2. Choose the Advanced tab

3. Document the current settings by writing them down or capturing an image of the dialog box as described in the section "I need to document my printer driver settings before I change them" on page 311. (Briefly: With the dialog box active, press Alt+Print Screen to store an image of the dialog box in the clipboard. Then open a program such as WordPad, and use the Edit, Paste command to paste the image into a document.)

Warning

If the problem was that the printer wouldn't work at all, you can print a test page from the printer's Properties dialog box by choosing the General tab and then choosing the Print Test Page button. However, be sure to close the dialog box first and then reopen it to make sure you're running the test with the new settings.

If the printer was already able to print, but had either problems with specific files or intermittent problems, testing it may involve printing a file that you know the printer was having problems with or printing an assortment of files to test for intermittent errors.

> *If this solution didn't solve your problem, go to the next page.*

I need to stop my printer from spooling (sending print jobs to disk on their way to the printer)

(continued from page 313)

4. If the printer is already set to Always Available, skip ahead to step 9. If the Always Available choice isn't selected, choose it now and then choose OK to close the dialog box. ▶

5. Test the printer.

6. If this procedure solved the problem, you're basically done. If you don't want the printer to be always available, however, you should return to the driver and adjust the times the printer is available to better match your needs.

7. If changing the printer availability didn't solve the problem, reopen the printer driver. The Printers window should still be open. Select the printer and choose File, Properties to open the printer's Properties dialog box.

8. Choose the Advanced tab. Leave the printer set to Always Available.

9. Check the spooler: The driver will probably have the option selected to Spool Print Documents So Program Finishes Printing Faster. If so, choose Print Directly To The Printer and continue to the next step. If the driver is already set to Print Directly To The Printer, you're finished with this section, and should go to "My computer may be timing out (giving up) before it finishes sending the print job" on page 322.

10. Choose OK to close the printer's Properties dialog box.

11. Test the printer to see if the problem is fixed. If it is, you've established that the problem is related to the spool settings and you should go to "Printing directly to the printer solves my printing problem" on page 316.

12. If the problem isn't solved, go to "My computer may be timing out (giving up) before my it finishes sending the print job" on page 322. Do not turn the spooling feature back on.

Tip

Windows 2000's security features can affect whether you can print, since you have to be logged in as someone who has permission to print. The security features are a little too far afield from hardware to cover here, but as a Windows 2000 user, you should learn how they work and make sure you have permission to print.

Printing directly to the printer solves my printing problem

Source of the problem

If printing directly to the printer solved your printing problem, the problem is related to spooling—the feature that saves a print job to disk and then sends it to the printer in the background, while you keep working. But turning off spooling altogether is a drastic solution.

If you have the choice, it's generally better to keep spooling on. (This is not strictly true under all conditions, but if your printer is attached directly to your system, it's true the vast majority of the time.) With spooling off, you may not be able to use your keyboard or mouse effectively until the print job finishes. And since spooling is a useful feature, you'll probably want to experiment with the spool settings to see if there's a way to keep spooling on and still be able to print. Besides, a problem with spooling can be related to having too many temporary files on your hard disk or not enough room on your hard disk, so the fix can be as simple as cleaning up your hard disk.

How to fix it

If you have Windows 98

1. To clean out temporary files you no longer need, start by rebooting in MS-DOS mode. Choose Start, Shut Down, the Restart In MS-DOS mode option, and then OK.

2. If you have one of the new "innovative" PCs, you may not have Restart In MS-DOS Mode as an option. If that's the case, choose Start, Shut Down, Restart and then repeatedly tap F8.

3. This may take a few tries, but eventually, you should see the Windows 98 Startup Menu, which includes the option Command Prompt Only. Choose this option by entering the number next to the option or by using the arrow keys to select the line. Then press Enter to boot the system in MS-DOS mode.

4. When your system boots up, it should be in MS-DOS mode, with a command line prompt similar to

   C:\>

   To confirm where your temporary files are stored, type **set<Enter>** where <Enter> represents pressing the Enter key.

> **Warning**
>
> "Reboot" means reboot. Really. Don't use an MS-DOS window for cleaning out the temp directory. If you try this from an MS-DOS window, Windows may have one of the fields in the directory open, which will complicate matters.

5. Look for a line that reads

　　temp=DriveAndPath

where DriveAndPath will usually be C:\windows\temp. For the rest of this discussion, we'll assume that's the correct path. If your system uses a different path, substitute that path whenever we use \windows\temp.

6. At the command line, type **cd \windows\temp<Enter>**

7. The command line prompt should now read

　　C:\WINDOWS\TEMP>

If it doesn't, you need to confirm that this is the right directory (a directory in MS-DOS is similar to a folder in Windows). Type **prompt pg<Enter>**. If the command line prompt still isn't correct, back up one step and type the **cd \windows\temp** command again.

8. Once you're sure you're logged into the right directory, delete all the files in the directory by typing **del *.*<Enter>** and then answer Y when MS-DOS asks, Are You Sure (Y/N)?

9. Next, you need to delete any leftover spool files. To switch to the spool directory type **cd \windows\spool\printers<Enter>**. The command line prompt should now read

　　C:\WINDOWS\SPOOL\PRINTERS>

If it doesn't, repeat the command.

10. To delete any leftover spool files, type **del *.spl<enter>**

11. Press Ctrl+Alt+Delete to reboot.

12. After Windows reboots, you'll need to find out how much free space you have on the drive that includes the spool files and temp files—typically Drive C. Double-click on My Computer, right-click on the drive icon, and then choose Properties to open the Properties dialog box for the appropriate drive. This should open with the General tab chosen. ▶

13. Take a look at the amount of free space available. There is no hard and fast rule saying how much is enough, but as a rule of thumb, if there's less than 200 MB free, there's a good chance that you're running out of disk space when you print and create a spool file for a large or complex document.

14. If your drive has less than 200 MB free space, free up additional space by deleting, moving, or archiving some files.

If this solution didn't solve your problem, go to the next page.

Printing directly to the printer solves my printing problem

(continued from page 317)

15. Once you've freed up some space, turn the spooling feature back on: Choose Start, Settings, Printers, select your printer, choose File, Properties, then Details, and then Spool Settings. Select the Spool Print Jobs So Program Finishes Printing Faster option. To finish, choose OK and then OK again to close the printer's Properties dialog box.

16. Test the printer to see if it will now print reliably with its original settings for spooling. If it does, you're done.

17. If the printer still doesn't print with its original spool settings, try changing the spool settings without turning off spooling. The Printers window should still be open. Select the appropriate printer, and choose File, Properties, and then Spool Settings. If you have any kind of printer other than a PostScript printer, you will typically have two choices for Spool Data Format: RAW and EMF (PostScript and a few other printers offer RAW only). If the data format is currently set to EMF, try RAW instead. Choose OK, and then OK again to close the dialog box. ▶

Warning

Delete with care. One of the steps here is to delete, move, or archive files to free up space on your hard disk. Old data files are the safest choice to remove from your hard disk. Second best is to uninstall programs that you don't need. If you choose to uninstall a program, be sure to follow the program's instructions for uninstalling. Ideally you should also back up your system first, in case something goes wrong during the uninstall. Do not move or delete any files in the Windows folders or in any program folders unless you're absolutely sure you know what you're doing.

18. Test the printer to see if it will print reliably with spooling using the RAW setting. If it does, you're done. If not, select the appropriate printer in the Printers window again, choose File, Properties, and then Spool Settings, and then choose the option Print Directly To The Printer. You should contact the manufacturer to see if it can help you track down the problem, but until you do, this setting will let you print.

If you have Windows 2000

1. To clean out temporary files you no longer need, choose Start, Programs, Accessories, System Tools, and then Disk Cleanup to start the disk cleanup utility. You may then see a dialog box that asks you to select the drive you want. Pick the appropriate drive and choose OK to open the Disk Cleanup dialog box. (If you have more than one hard disk drive on your system, it's a good idea to go through these steps for each drive, picking a different drive in this step each time.)

2. Choose the Disk Cleanup tab, if it isn't already selected. ▶

3. Scroll though the different types of files that Windows identifies as candidates for deleting. Make sure you put a check in the check box for Temporary Files. You can check any other options you care to as well.

4. Choose OK to tell Windows to delete the files, and then Yes, to confirm the deletion.

5. After Windows finishes deleting the files, you'll need to find out how much free space you have on the drive Windows is installed on—typically Drive C. Double-click on My Computer, and then right-click on the drive icon and choose Properties to open the Properties dialog box for the appropriate drive. This dialog box should open to the General tab.

6. Take a look at the amount of free space available. There is no hard and fast rule saying how much space is enough, but as a rule of thumb, if there's less than 200 MB free, there's a good chance that you're running out of disk space when you print and create a spool file for a large or complex document. ▶

7. If your drive has less than 200 MB free space, free up additional space by deleting, moving, or archiving some files.

8. Turn the spooling feature back on: Choose Start, Settings, and then Printers, select your printer, and choose File, Properties, and then the Advanced tab.

9. Select the Spool Print Jobs So Program Finishes Printing Faster option. To finish, choose OK to close the printer's Properties dialog box.

10. Test the printer to see if it will now print reliably with its original settings for spooling. If it does, you're done.

11. If the printer still doesn't print with its original spool settings, try changing the spool settings without turning off spooling. The Printers window should still be open. Select the appropriate printer, choose File, Properties, and then choose the Advanced tab.

If this solution didn't solve your problem, go to the next page.

Printing directly to the printer solves my printing problem

(continued from page 319)

12. There are four check boxes below the area that turns spooling on or off. Clear any that are checked.

13. Choose OK to close the printer's Properties dialog box.

14. Test the printer again to see if the problem is fixed. If it isn't, skip to step 17.

15. If the problem is fixed, you've established that it's related to one of the check box features. If you removed more than one check, return to the printer's Properties dialog box by selecting the printer in the Printers window and choosing File, Properties, and then the Advanced tab. Add back one of the checks, choose OK to close the dialog box, and then test the printer. Repeat this as many times as necessary, testing only one check box option at a time, until you find which one or which ones cause the problem.

16. When you've pinpointed which check box item or items cause the problem, set the rest of the check boxes back to their original settings. Test the printer to confirm that it's still working, and you're done.

17. Check your print processor settings: If the printer still doesn't print, there's one setting left to check. The Printers window should still be open. Select the appropriate printer, and choose File, Properties, the Advanced tab, and then the Print Processor button to open the Print Processor dialog box. ▶

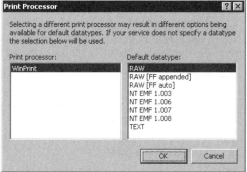

18. Normally, you'll see only one item in the Print Processor list. (If you see more than one, you'll need to find out what it is, how it got there, and under what conditions you should use it. If someone else set up your system—including the computer vendor—you should ask him or her about it.) The default datatype (which will affect only some programs) will typically be set to RAW. If it is set to any other datatype, document the current setting, and change it to RAW. Then choose OK twice to close the Printer Processor and Properties dialog boxes.

19. Test the printer to see if it changing the default datatype fixed the problem. If it did, you're done. If not, select the appropriate printer in the Printers window again, choose File, Properties, the Advanced button, and then the Print Processor button, and change the default datatype back to its original setting. Then choose OK, and choose the Print Directly To The Printer option. You should contact the manufacturer to see if it can help you track down the problem, but until you track it down, this setting will let you print.

My computer may be timing out (giving up) before it finishes sending the print job

Source of the problem

If you're a football or basketball fan, a timeout is short pause in the game called by one team or the other, usually to give it a chance to regroup or make a plan; if you're a parent or young child, a timeout means someone has gotten too rambunctious and Dad or Mom thinks it's time to calm down a bit. If you're a computer, however, a timeout means that means that something has run out of time, and you're not going to wait for it any longer.

Computers use all sorts of timeout settings. What these settings all have in common is that they provide a way to keep the computer from trying to do something forever (literally—computers are nothing if not patient), and let it move on to something else. Timeout settings can be quite useful, particularly if you're not sitting next to the computer so you can see what's going on and call a halt to it yourself. But if the timeout setting is too low for the job at hand, the computer will quit before the job's done. And if that job happens to be a print job, you'll have problems printing. What you need to do is to set the timeout to a higher number. Sometimes a much higher number.

How to fix it

If you have Windows 98

1. Open the printer driver by choosing Start, Settings, and then Printers, selecting the printer, and then choosing File, Properties.

2. Choose the Details tab. ▶

3. Document the current settings by writing them down or capturing an image of the dialog box as described in the section "I need to document my printer driver settings before I change them" on page 311. (Briefly: With the dialog box active, press Alt+Print Screen to store an image of the dialog box in the clipboard. Then open a program such as WordPad, and use the Edit, Paste command to paste the image into a document.)

4. You'll find two items in the Timeout Settings area of the dialog box. The Not Selected option will usually be set for 15 seconds, which should be adequate for any printer. Transmission Retry will usually be set to 45 seconds. This is not enough for many printers, especially if you print large files with, for example, high resolution 8-by-10-inch photos. Set this for a much longer length of time—600 seconds (ten minutes) will usually be enough. If your problem has been that the printer generally prints, except for complex pages or pages with high-resolution images, this may well solve the problem. Even if that hasn't been the problem, it's usually a good idea to set this to a higher number than the default in any case.

5. Choose OK to close the printer's Properties dialog box. If the problem was related to certain pages only, test the printer by printing one of those pages to see if the problem is fixed. Then if it's fixed continue with the next step. If you're still having a problem printing to to step 8.

6. If the printing problem is gone, select the printer in the Printers window and choose File, Properties, the Details tab, and then the Spool Settings button. Return the spool settings to their original values, using your documentation of those settings as a guide. Choose OK to close the Spool Settings dialog box, and then OK again to close the printer's Properties dialog box.

7. Test the printer. If there's still no problem, you're done. If another problem appears after you restore your printer's spool settings to their original values, go to "Printing directly to the printer solves my printing problems" on page 316.

8. If you still have a problem printing and you have a non-PostScript Printer, go to "My non-PostScript printer driver's settings may be wrong" on page 334.

9. If you still have a problem printing and you have a PostScript Printer, the Printers window should still be open. Select the printer in the Printers window, and choose File, Properties, then the PostScript tab. ▶

10. Document the current settings by writing them down or by capturing the image and saving it in a file.

11. You'll see a Job Timeout setting and a Wait Timeout setting. Job Timeout should be set to 0 seconds (at least, that's the default setting). This tells the printer to wait as long as it takes for any given print job to reach the printer.

12. Wait Timeout is typically set to 240 seconds, which may be too short for complex print jobs. Set Wait Timeout to 600 seconds, which should be enough for even long print jobs (although you may conceivably have to set it even higher).

13. Choose OK to close the printer's Properties dialog box. If the problem was related to certain pages only, print one of those pages to see if the problem is fixed.

If this solution didn't solve your problem, go to the next page.

My computer may be timing out (giving up) before it finishes sending the print job

(continued from page 323)

14. If you can now print, you're done.

15. If you still have a problem, go to "My PostScript printer's driver settings may be wrong" on page 326.

If you have Windows 2000

1. Select the printer in the Printers window, and choose File, Properties to open the printer's Properties dialog box.

2. Choose the Ports tab, select the port the printer is attached to (this will have a check in its accompanying check box), and choose Configure Port to open the Configure LPT Port dialog box.

3. Document the current setting by writing it down or capturing an image of the dialog box as described in the section "I need to document my printer driver settings before I change them" on page 311. (Briefly: With the dialog box active, press Alt+Print Screen to store an image of the dialog box in the clipboard. Then open a program such as WordPad, and use the Edit, Paste command to paste the image into a document.)

4. The Transmission Retry setting in the Configure LPT Port dialog box tells your system how long to wait for your printer before it gives up. This is usually set to 90 seconds. However, 90 seconds is not enough for many printers, especially if you print large files with, for example, high resolution 8-by-10-inch photos. Set this for a much longer length of time—600 seconds (ten minutes) will usually be enough. If your problem has been that the printer generally prints, except for complex pages or pages with high-resolution images, this may well solve the problem. Even if that hasn't been the problem, it's usually a good idea to set this to a higher number than the default in any case. ▶

5. Choose OK to close the Configure LPT port dialog box.

6. If your printer does not use PostScript, choose OK to close the printer's Properties dialog box. If the problem was related to certain pages only, print one of those pages to see if the problem is fixed. Then skip to step 12 or to step 13, as appropriate.

warning

As we pointed out in an earlier section, if the problem was that the printer wouldn't work at all, you can print a test page from the printer's Properties dialog box. (Choose the General tab, and then the Print Test Page button.) But be sure to close the dialog box first and then reopen it.

If the printing problem was with specific files or was intermittent, be sure to test with a file that you know the printer was having problems with or print an assortment of files to test for intermittent errors.

7. If your printer uses PostScript, choose the Device Settings tab and browse through the choices, looking for additional timeout settings.

8. Document the current settings, either by writing them down or by capturing the image and saving it in a file. (Briefly: With the dialog box active, press Alt+Print Screen to store an image of the dialog box in the clipboard. Then open a program such as WordPad, and use the Edit, Paste command to paste the image into a document.)

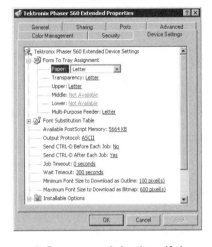

9. You should find a Job Timeout setting and a Wait Timeout setting. Job Timeout should be set to 0 seconds (the default setting). This tells the computer to wait as long as it takes for any given print job to reach the printer. It will wait forever, if that's what it takes.

10. Wait Timeout is typically set to 300 seconds, which may be too short for complex print jobs. Set Wait Timeout to 600 seconds, which should be enough for even long print jobs (although you may conceivably have to set it even higher). ▶

Tip

There's nothing magic in the default timeout settings for printers, and also nothing magic in the 600 seconds suggested here. If you find that your printer works for some pages, but not for others, set the timeout settings for an extremely large number, like 10,000, and see if that solves the problem. If it does, you might then halve the number to see if that, works, then halve it again, and so on, until you find a number that's too low for the problematical file to work. You can then bracket the number, until you find a timeout setting that lets you print your most complex print job without setting the timeout to an unreasonably large number.

11. Choose OK to close the printer's Properties dialog box. If the problem was related to certain pages only, print one of those pages to see if the problem is fixed.

12. If you still have a problem printing and you have a PostScript printer, go to "My PostScript printer's driver settings may be wrong" on page 316. If you have a non-PostScript printer, go to "My non-PostScript printer driver's settings may be wrong" on page 334.

13. If the printing problem is gone, select the printer in the Printers window, choose File, Properties, and then the Advanced tab, and return all other options (with the possible exception of the Available From and To options) to their original settings. Then choose OK to close the printer's Properties dialog box.

14. Test the printer. If there's still no problem, you're done. If another problem appears after you restore your printer's other options to their original settings, go to "Printing directly to the printer solves my printing problems" on page 316.

My PostScript printer's driver settings may be wrong

Source of the problem

PostScript is a standard printer language that any number of printers use. Unfortunately, like most so-called standards in the computer world, it's subject to variations, thanks largely to the fact that there are different levels of PostScript and different ways to set up a PostScript printer. As a result, different PostScript printers need different settings in their drivers.

To make matters worse, some PostScript printers (fortunately, not many, and mostly older models) install with default settings that don't match what the printer needs. So the printer won't work reliably until you make changes. And, of course if you accidentally make changes you shouldn't have made, you risk making the printer unusable, even if the default settings were right.

All of which means that if you're having a problem printing with a PostScript printer, you need to check the PostScript settings. Here are the settings you need to check.

How to fix it

If you have Windows 98

1. Open the printer driver by choosing Start, Settings, Printers, selecting the printer, and then choosing File, Properties.

2. Choose the PostScript tab. ▶

3. The layout and available options for PostScript may vary somewhat, depending on the particular version of PostScript driver you have. However, even if your driver doesn't exactly match the driver shown on the next page as a model, it should have essentially the same settings available. If your driver looks like the one shown on the next page, choose the Advanced button to open the Advanced PostScript Options dialog box. If necessary, explore the options to find where the driver hides the equivalent settings.

4. Document the current settings by writing them down or capturing an image of the dialog box as described in the section "I need to document my printer driver settings before I change them" on page 311. (Briefly: With the dialog box active, press Alt+Print Screen to store an image of the dialog box in the clipboard. Then open a program such as WordPad, and use the Edit, Paste command to paste the image into a document.)

Advanced PostScript Options

These settings have been chosen to optimize printer performance. You should not change them unless you have specific reasons to do so.

PostScript language level
- ○ Use PostScript Level 1 features
- ● Use PostScript Level 2 features

Bitmap compression
- ● Compress bitmap images
- ○ No bitmap compression

Data format
- ● ASCII data
- ○ Binary communications protocol
- ○ Tagged binary communications protocol
- ○ Pure binary data
- ☐ Send CTRL+D before job
- ☑ Send CTRL+D after job

[Send Mode]

[OK] [Cancel] [Restore Defaults]

5. The PostScript settings you're concerned with fall into two categories: Those that will help simplify your testing because one of the settings should work with any PostScript printer, and those that you have to test both ways, because any given printer may need one setting or the another. In the first category are PostScript Language Level and Bitmap Compression (available in the Advanced PostScript Options dialog box shown on this page), and PostScript Output Format (available on the PostScript tab shown on this page). Find these settings first.

6. For most printing, the PostScript Output Format option should be set to PostScript (Optimize For Speed). Make sure it's set that way. (If you select the current setting for PostScript Output Format and then press F1, you should see some pointers explaining when you might want to use one of the other settings.)

7. If you didn't need to change the PostScript Output Format setting, skip to step 12.

8. If you had to change the setting, choose OK to close each dialog box, test the printer, and continue to the next step.

9. If the new setting solves the problem, select the printer in the Printers window and choose File, Properties, the Details tab, and then the Spool Settings button. Return the spool settings to their original values, using your documentation of those settings as a guide. Choose OK to close the Spool Settings dialog box, and then OK again to close the printer's Properties dialog box.

10. Test the printer. If there's still no problem, you're done. If another problem appears after you restore your printer's spool settings to their original values, go to "Printing directly to the printer solves my printing problems" on page 316.

11. If the new setting doesn't solve the problem, go to the Printers window, select your printer, and choose File, Properties. Then choose the PostScript tab, then the Advanced button, and continue to the next step.

> *If this solution didn't solve your problem, go to the next page.*

My PostScript printer's driver settings may be wrong

(continued from page 327)

12. For PostScript Language level, choose the lowest level available, which should be Use PostScript Level 1 Features.

13. For Bitmap Compression, choose No Bitmap Compression.

14. Also make sure that the Print PostScript Error Information check box is checked. The printouts of error messages that may result from this setting may not tell you anything, but if you ultimately have to call for technical support, they can provide critical information that will help your printer manufacturer's tech support staff solve the problem much more quickly.

15. After making these settings, save them by choosing OK to close each dialog box, and then test the printer. If changing the Bitmap Compression and Language Level options didn't help, skip to step 19.

16. If it the printer works now, you should experiment with the PostScript Language Level and Bitmap Compression settings to see if either one alone makes the difference between printing and not printing. If only one of these settings makes the difference, set the other back to its original setting.

17. After you finish experimenting with these two settings, select the printer in the Printers window, choose File, Properties, the Details tab, and then the Spool Settings button. Return the spool settings to their original values, using your documentation of those settings as a guide. Choose OK to close the Spool Settings dialog box, and then OK again to close the printer's Properties dialog box.

18. Test the printer. If there's still no problem, you're done. If another problem appears after you restore your printer's spool settings to their original values, go to "Printing directly to the printer solves my printing problems" on page 316.

19. The remaining PostScript settings require brute force methodical testing. The driver should let you choose both a data format and whether to send a Ctrl+D before each print job, after each print job, or not at all. (You should be able to set it to send Ctrl+D both before and after each print job, also, but that choice should never be necessary.)

20. Any given combination of these options may be the right one for your printer. You'll have to pick a Ctrl+D setting (or combination of settings), test it with each Data Format setting, and then repeat the cycle for each Ctrl+D setting. ▶

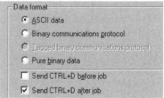

21. If you don't find any combination of settings that solve the problem, you'll have to contact the manufacturer for help. There isn't any more you can reasonably do on your own.

22. If you find settings that solve the problem, return to the driver and set the PostScript Language Level and Bitmap Compression options back to their original settings.

23. Test the printer to see if the problem is still solved. If it is, go to the next step. If the printer stops working at this point, experiment with the PostScript Language Level and Bitmap Compression settings to see if either one alone makes the difference between printing and not printing. If only one of these settings makes the difference, leave the other option at its original setting. Confirm that the printer still works, and then go to the next step.

24. Select the printer in the Printers window, choose File, Properties, the Details tab, and then the Spool Settings button. Return the spool settings to their original values, using your documentation of those settings as a guide. Choose OK to close the Spool Settings dialog box, and then OK again to close the printer's Properties dialog box.

25. Test the printer. If there's still no problem, you're done. If another problem appears after you restore your printer's spool settings to their original values, go to "Printing directly to the printer solves my printing problems" on page 316.

If you have Windows 2000

1. Open the printer driver by choosing Start, Settings, Printers, selecting the printer, and then choosing File, Properties.

2. Choose the Advanced tab, the Printing Defaults button, and then the Advanced button to open the printer's Advanced Options dialog box.

3. The available options for PostScript, their locations, and the order they are listed in will vary somewhat, depending on the particular version of PostScript driver you have. However, even if your driver doesn't exactly match the driver shown here as a model, it should have essentially the same PostScript settings available. Browse through the advanced options, expanding the sections as necessary, looking for a section called PostScript Options. This should be under a section called Document Options. When you find it, select it and press the plus sign on your numeric keypad to expand the options. ▶

If this solution didn't solve your problem, go to the next page.

My PostScript printer's driver settings may be wrong

(continued from page 329)

4. Document the current settings by writing them down or capturing an image of the dialog box as described in the section "I need to document my printer driver settings before I change them" on page 311. (Briefly: With the dialog box active, press Alt+Print Screen to store an image of the dialog box in the clipboard. Then open a program such as WordPad, and use the Edit, Paste command to paste the image into a document.)

5. The PostScript settings you're concerned with in the Advanced Options dialog box all fall in the category of settings that will help simplify your testing, because if you pick the right setting, they should work with any PostScript printer. The settings that you will likely find here will have names similar to PostScript Output Option, PostScript Language Level, Send PostScript Error Handler, and Compress Bitmap. Note that you may not find all of these settings (a driver for a PostScript Level 1 printer, for example, won't offer a choice of language levels), and you may find them with slightly different names. If you don't find them all in this dialog box, however, you should search through the driver for any missing choices, to make sure they don't exist elsewhere in the driver.

6. For most printing, the PostScript Output Option should be set to PostScript (Optimize For Speed). Make sure it's set that way. (If you select the current setting for PostScript Output Option and then press F1, you should see some pointers explaining when you might want to use one of the other settings.)

7. If you didn't have to change the PostScript Output Option setting, skip to step 12.

8. If you had to change the PostScript Output Option setting, choose OK to close each dialog box and then test the printer.

9. If the new setting solves the printing problem, select the printer in the Printers window, choose File, Properties, and then the Advanced tab, and return the spool settings to their original values, using your documentation of those settings as a guide. Then choose OK to close the printer's Properties dialog box.

10. Test the printer. If there's still no problem, you're done (with the possible exception of adjusting the Available From and To settings). If another problem appears after you restore your printer's spool settings to their original values, go to "Printing directly to the printer solves my printing problems" on page 316.

11. If the new setting doesn't solve the problem, go to the Printers window, select your printer, and choose File, Properties. Choose the Advanced tab, the Printing Defaults button, and then the Advanced button to open the Advanced Options dialog box. Find the PostScript Options section

again, and expand it to show the individual options. (Keep in mind that some of the options mentioned in the following steps may not be available.) ▼

12. Set PostScript Language Level to the lowest level available, which should be 1.

13. Set Compress Bitmaps to No.

14. Also make sure that the Send PostScript Error Handler option is set to Yes. This tells your printer to print any PostScript error messages that crop up. The printouts that may result from this setting may not tell you anything, but if you ultimately have to call for technical support, they can provide critical information that will help your printer manufacturer's tech support staff solve the problem much more quickly.

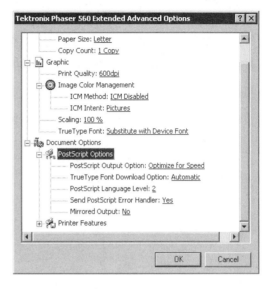

15. After changing these settings, save them by choosing OK to close each dialog box, and then test the printer. If changing the Compress Bitmaps and PostScript Language Level options didn't help, skip to step 19.

16. If it the printer prints now, you should experiment with the PostScript Language Level and Bitmap Compression settings to see if either one alone makes the difference between printing and not printing. If only one of these settings makes the difference, set the other back to its original setting. Confirm that the printer works, and continue on to the next step.

17. After you finish experimenting with these two settings, select the printer in the Printers window, choose File, Properties, and then the Advanced tab, and return the spool settings to their original values, using your documentation of those settings as a guide. Choose OK to close the printer's Properties dialog box.

18. Test the printer. If there's still no problem, you're done. If another problem appears after you restore your printer's spool settings to their original values, go to "Printing directly to the printer solves my printing problems" on page 316.

19. The remaining PostScript settings require brute force methodical testing. Go to the Printers window, select the printer, and choose File, Properties, and then the Device Settings tab.

20. Scroll through the list of device settings, looking for settings with names similar to Output Protocol (the current setting will most often be ASCII or some variation on Binary), Send CTRL+D Before Each Job, and Send CTRL+D After Each Job. Note that between them, the two Ctrl+D settings let you choose whether to send a Ctrl+D before each print job, after each print job, or not at all. (Sending Ctrl+D both before and after should never be necessary.)

> *If this solution didn't solve your problem, go to the next page.*

My PostScript printer's driver settings may be wrong

(continued from page 331)

21. Any given combination of the Output Protocol may be the right one for your printer. You'll have to pick a Ctrl+D setting (or combination of settings), test it with each Data Format setting, and then repeat the cycle for each Ctrl+D setting. ▼

22. If you don't find any combination of settings that solve the problem, you'll have to contact the manufacturer for help. There isn't any more you can reasonably do on your own.

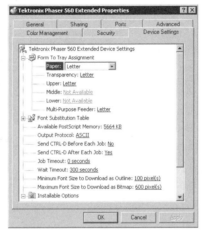

23. If you find settings that solve the problem, return to the driver and set the PostScript Language Level and Bitmap Compression levels back to their original settings.

24. Test to see if the problem is still solved. If it is, go to the next step. If the printer stops working at this point, experiment with the PostScript Language Level and Bitmap Compression settings to see if either one alone makes the difference between printing and not printing. If only one of these settings makes the difference, leave the other option at its original setting. Confirm that the printer still works, and then go to the next step.

25. Select the printer in the Printers window, choose File, Properties, and then the Advanced tab, and then return the spool settings to their original values. Then choose OK to close the printer's Properties dialog box.

26. Test the printer. If there's still no problem, you're done. If another problem appears after you restore your printer's spool settings to their original values, go to "Printing directly to the printer solves my printing problems" on page 316.

Tip

The surest way to guarantee that you won't have to go through these steps more than once for any given printer is to document all the settings once you have the printer up and running. The easiest way to do this is with the technique referred to throughout this chapter and described in "I need to document my printer driver settings before I change them" on page 311— using Alt+Print Screen to copy the active window to the clipboard, and then pasting it into a WordPad document or some other program.

If you have both the printer's Properties dialog box and WordPad (or any equivalent program) open, you can repeat this capture and paste technique for each tab in the printer's Properties dialog box and each additional window that opens in response to a button. Simply capture an image with Alt+Print screen, use Alt+Tab to switch back to WordPad, paste the image in, add a paragraph return or two, switch back to the printer's Properties dialog box, move on to the next tab, and so on.

Repeat these steps as many times as necessary to document all the driver settings. Then save the file you pasted the images in, and print it. Keep the printed version with your manuals and other documentation for your computer system. And don't delete the file. You'll need it if you misplace the printed version.

My non-PostScript printer's driver settings may be wrong

Source of the problem

There are more variations on non-PostScript printers than you can shake an ink cartridge at (which is probably not a good thing to do, because you might splatter ink all over the place). That means there are any number of driver settings that can potentially create problems for printing, but because they depend on the particular printer driver, we can't cover all the possible details here. What we can offer, however, is a strategy that will help you find the settings you should consider suspect and then test to find them guilty or innocent. (This is a little like throwing a suspected witch into a nearby river to see if she's a witch. But in this case, the innocent won't drown.)

How to fix it

1. There's no getting around a brute force approach. You'll need to examine the choices in the driver, one by one, try to identify the settings that may be causing a problem, and then experiment with changing those settings and trying to print.

2. First identify settings that may cause problems, and disable them if possible. If that's not possible, try changing the suspect settings to alternative settings one at a time and then testing whether the new setting solves the problem printing.

3. Features that affect memory use or disk use may be responsible for problems.

4. Features that affect output quality or speed are not likely to keep the printer from printing, except to the extent that increased quality may require more memory—or disk space for printers that process their print jobs at the computer.

5. If you've tested all the settings, and still haven't solved the problem, it's time to call the manufacturer for help. You may even have a broken printer.

Tip
You can find out what most settings in a printer driver are meant for by selecting the option and pressing the F1 key. Windows will pop up a message explaining the setting and usually explaining the differences between the choices. Unfortunately, the explanations can sometimes be confusing or even dead wrong (usually because they were written in another language originally and translated badly). If an explanation is confusing, or if you're convinced it's wrong after trying to modify the setting, contact the printer manufacturer to find out what the setting does.

When you have to reinstall Windows

Source of the problem

This is a book about fixing problems with PC hardware, not with software such as the Microsoft Windows operating system. The fact is, however, that some problems—hardware and software—may require that you install a fresh copy of Windows. And in order to install a fresh copy of Windows, there are times when you need to make some preparations, such as creating a way to boot your system so that you can then perform the rest of the steps.

There are times when some of those preparatory steps can be useful in solving other problems. For example, we have referred to this section frequently throughout the book when you need to have a bootable floppy disk in order to perform some diagnostic steps.

This appendix is not comprehensive when it comes to reinstalling Windows; for that, we recommend that you get a good book on the subject (such as *Troubleshooting Microsoft Windows* by Steve Sagman (Microsoft Press, 2001), or *Troubleshooting Microsoft Windows 2000 Professional* by Jerry Joyce and Marianne Moon (Microsoft Press, 2001). We will give you enough help here to make a fresh start.

If you are running Windows 2000

The first and most important consideration about installing Windows 2000 is how you're going to get at the source files. If you are going to have to wipe out your hard disk so that it is no longer bootable, there are just two ways that you can reinstall the software from the original CD.

If your computer can be made to boot from its optical drive (its CD or DVD drive), you're all set. Change your BIOS configuration settings to boot from the optical drive—see "The computer is booting from the wrong disk drive" on page 82 for more details on how to do this. When you boot from the Windows 2000 CD, you will be given the choice of installing Windows 2000 or repairing an existing installation.

If your computer cannot boot from the optical drive, your other choice is to boot from a floppy disk. If you have a working Windows 2000 installation, you can use the MAKEBOOT utility program to create a set of four boot disks that will let you access the optical drive and install Windows 2000 or repair the Windows 2000 installation on your hard disk. See "My computer can't find a system on its hard disk" on page 230 for more details.

If your installation of Windows 2000 is not working, you will either have to create the boot disk set on another computer that's running Windows 2000, or use a boot floppy created on a computer running Windows 98 (or earlier) using the technique described in the next section. This will give you access to your optical drive, and you will then be able to access the Windows 2000 setup utility from there.

If you are running Windows 98

The same initial choices exist for Windows 98 as for Windows 2000. If you can reset your system to boot from the optical drive, you can boot straight to the Windows 98 CD and access the utilities and setup programs you need to reinstall Windows on a hard disk. If your system cannot be set to boot from the optical drive, you'll need to create a bootable floppy disk. The key to the floppy disk is that you will want to make sure that it has all the programs on it that you'll need, and then test it to make sure it works before you make major changes to your hard disk.

Creating a bootable floppy

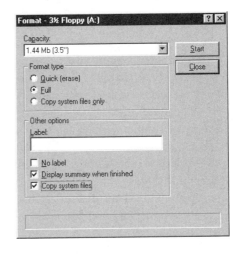

1. Insert a floppy disk in your computer's floppy drive. The disk does not need to be blank, but you will lose any data on it.

2. Double-click on My Computer to open it.

3. Right-click on the icon for the floppy disk drive, and choose Format from the menu.

4. Select the Full option under Format Type, and make sure that there are checks in the Display Summary When Finished and Copy System Files check boxes. ▶

5. Choose Start.

6. When the formatting is complete, you'll see a summary window. If the summary reports any bytes in bad sectors, this means that there are flaws on the floppy disk. We recommend that you do not use this disk, as there's a chance that it may not work when you need it to boot your computer system. Since you'll be stuck if your boot disk doesn't work, don't take a chance on a flawed disk. Chuck this one in the trash and start over with another floppy disk. ▶

7. The next step is to make sure that the files you'll need are on the bootable floppy disk. In order to partition your hard disk, you'll need the FDISK.EXE utility. To format the disk, you'll need the FORMAT.COM program. These two files are located in the Windows\Command folder. Open Windows Explorer, and navigate to this folder. Select these two files, and drag copies of them to the floppy disk drive icon.

8. The next problem is that you'll need to access your optical drive. This requires that two files be on your boot floppy disk. One of these files must be a "real mode" (or MS-DOS) driver for your optical drive. This is a file that ends with a .SYS extension, and it may have been provided with the drive. If not, check the drive manufacturer's Web site to see if there is a version of the file that you can download. If you can't locate a driver from the manufacturer and your optical drive was included as part of a prepackaged computer system, contact the system manufacturer's technical support to see if they have the file. Once you have obtained the driver, place a copy on your boot floppy disk.

> ## Boot floppy disk files
>
> There are other files that you might want to add to this boot floppy disk, to make it more useful for emergencies. For example, consider adding the following files:
>
> - A computer virus scanner, so that you can perform a clean boot from a disk that you know is not infected, and then scan the hard disk of a system that you think might be infected
>
> - SCANDISK.EXE (from the \Windows\Command folder), to scan hard disks that may have errors or flaws
>
> - SYS.COM, so that you can transfer or refresh the boot files for a hard disk
>
> - ATTRIB.EXE, which lets you change the attributes of files, so that you can see hidden files or modify files that are marked as read only

9. The other file that you'll need is a program designed to let a computer read an optical drive under MS-DOS. The program is named MSCDEX.EXE (for Microsoft CD Extensions) and is available in the \Windows\Command folder on your hard disk. Using Windows Explorer, select the file and copy it to the floppy disk.

10. Next, you must configure the boot floppy disk to load these files. Choose Start, Programs, Accessories, and then Microsoft Notepad.

11. The driver is loaded by a file named CONFIG.SYS. The actual details of the line will vary, so you will need to get the required information from the source where you got your copy of the optical disk's MS-DOS driver. In most cases, it will be something similar to the following:

> **DEVICE=driver.sys /D:msc001**

where you should replace *driver.sys* with the actual name of your device driver file. You may also be asked to use some other settings in addition to the /D: in this example. You also may be given some parameter after the /D: that is different from the *msc001* in this example; use the *msc001* instead of a different drive name parameter that the manufacturer might suggest. Type this line in the Notepad window.

12. Choose File, Save, and then type
A:\CONFIG.SYS in the File Name box. ▶

13. Choose Save to save the file.

14. Choose File New to start a new file in
Notepad.

15. Type **MSCDEX /D:msc001** and make certain that the parameter after /D: matches the
driver name parameter from the line in the
CONFIG.SYS file in step 11.

16. Choose Save and then type
A:\AUTOEXEC.BAT in the File Name Box.

17. Choose Save to save the file.

18. Now comes the most important step of all; you must test the boot floppy disk to make sure
that it works correctly. Start by making certain that your system is set to boot from the floppy
disk drive. (See "The computer is booting from the wrong disk drive" on page 82 if you need
help on checking this feature.)

19. Place the floppy disk in the drive.

20. Shut down your computer, and turn off the power.

21. Turn the computer on.

22. Watch the screen while the system is booting. If it boots from the floppy disk as desired, watch
for possible error messages about trying to load the driver for the optical drive. If you see any
errors, you will have to reboot without the floppy disk and use Notepad to review the contents
of the CONFIG.SYS and AUTOEXEC.BAT files as described in steps 11 and 15.

23. If the floppy disk boots successfully, you will see an MS-DOS prompt, A:\>, on the screen. Place
the Windows CD in the optical disk drive.

24. Type **DIR D:** and press Enter. This should read the contents of the CD in the optical disk drive.
If it does not, try a different drive letter. If your hard disk could not be found, the optical drive
may be Drive C. If your hard disk has more than one logical drive, the optical drive may have a
letter higher than D, such as E or F.

25. If you are able to access your optical drive after booting with the boot floppy disk, you may
want to make absolutely sure that the floppy disk works correctly. Power off your computer
(there is no need to shut down from the MS-DOS prompt the way you have to do under
Windows), and disconnect the power to your hard disk drive.

26. Turn on the power with the boot floppy disk in the floppy disk drive. If this time you can boot
the computer to the MS-DOS prompt and access the contents of the Windows CD-ROM in the
optical drive, you know you can erase the contents of your hard disk and still access the system
to partition and format the hard disk, so that you can reinstall Windows.

Index

Italicized page numbers refer to figures or tables.

Autoexec.bat file
  files loaded by, 301
  hard disk boot failure and, 225
  reinstalling Windows and, 340
AVI files, 66

backing up
  data files, 13, 52, 64, 244
  system, 10, 20–21
  Windows, 10, 24
backlight, failed LCD monitor, 150
Basic Input/Output System. *See* BIOS (Basic Input/
    Output System)
BASIC language, 230
battery, replacing, 56–57
beep codes, 78–79
  AMI BIOS, *78*
  IBM BIOS, *79*
  Phoenix BIOS, *79*
beeping instead of booting, 78–79
benchmarking programs, testing graphics
    cards with, 66
Benchmarq, 57
BIOS (Basic Input/Output System). *See also* CMOS
    configuration utility
  adapter card recognition by, 33, 39
  beep codes for select, *78, 79*
  failure to find floppy disk during boot and, 214
  flashing, 39
  hard disk autodetect feature, 229
  system failure to boot from floppy disk drive and,
    218
  upgrading, 33
  USB support and, 91
Bitmap Compression setting, 327, 328, 329, 331,
    332
black areas or lines on LCD displays, 145
black frame on LCD displays, 145
blackouts, 19

blank screen after bootup, 98–109
  failure to display image, 106–9
  failure to turn on, 100–101
  flowchart, *98–99*
  video cable operation, 102–5
blank screen at startup, 68–73
  flowchart, *68–69*
  installation errors, 70–71
  power supply failure, 72–73
  quick fixes, 68, 69
blue circle with white lowercase *i* icon, 26
blue screen of death, 24
booting. *See also* rebooting
  blank screen after. *See* blank screen after bootup
  creating bootable floppy disks, 20, 92, 108, 232,
    274, 338–40
  failure. *See* booting failure
  failure to find floppy disk drive, 214–15
  hard disk. *See* hard disk booting
  missing DLL files and blue screen, 24–25
  modem auto answering and, 45
  noises during, 52
  slowness, 58–59
booting failure, 74–83
  beeping sounds and, 78–79
  booting from wrong disk drive, 82–83, 224
  CMOS error message, 80, 81, 83
  flowchart, *74–75*
  intermittent hard disk, 222–23
  memory self-test failure, 76–77
  password request, 80–81
  system failure to boot from floppy disk drive, 218
booting sequence settings, 82–83, 215, 218
Boot.ini file, 231
brightness. *See also* color and brightness problems
  dark and empty LCD displays and, 148
  dark and washed out screen colors and, 120–21
  missing image and, 107
buffer underruns when creating discs, 208–9
built-in menu system in printers
  determining printer languages using, 270
  running self-test using, 263
bus-powered (passive) USB hub, 86

cables
    blank screen at startup and, 68
    EIDE drive, 173–75
    FireWire port, 185
    floppy disk drive, 213, 215, 216, 217
    monitor video, 102–5, 112–14
    optical disc drive, 201
    parallel port, 182, 304
    power. *See* power cables
    printer, 278–81, 304–5
    sound card, 201
    speaker, 48–49
    USB connections and, 86–87, 184
Cable Select (CS) drive configuration, 175
cache size, CD, 206–7
calibrating game controllers, 97
captive graphics cable, 103
captive monitor power cable, 100–101
cards. *See* adapter cards; expansion cards; graphics
        adapter cards; sound cards
carpeting, static electricity buildup and, 4, 5
case, computer
    color of bezel, 110
    crashes caused by touching, 4–5
    electrical shock when touching, 18
    extending image to monitor bezel of, 136
    liquid spills inside, 248
    motherboards and, 72–73
    opening and working in, 6–8, 172
cathode ray tube monitors. *See* CRT (cathode ray
        tube) monitors; monitors
CD Audio Balance, 200, 201
CD cache size, 206–7
CD Player accessory, *198*, 199
CD players. *See* optical disc drives
CD-R and CD-RW discs, failure to read, 204–5
CD-R and CD-RW drives. *See also* optical
        disc drives
    buffer underruns when creating discs, 208–9
    other drives' failure to read disc created by, 210

CD-ROM discs, optical drive failure to read, 204–5
CD-ROM drives. *See* optical disc drives
CDs (compact discs)
    failure of optical drive to read, 198–205
    failure of optical drive tray to open, 211
    repairing scratched, 203
change line, 216
Check Disk, *191*
checking. *See also* testing
    boot file configuration, 224–25
    computer-printer communication, 281–82
    Device Manager recognition of cards, 32–33
    for errors in hard disk drive and file system, 65
    for errors in printer, 265
    for free space on removable disks, 238
    hard disk drive for bad sectors, 191, 227
    input/output or memory ranges, 37
    LCD monitor backlight, 150
    monitor power cord, 100–101. *See also* power
        cables
    parallel ports, 282–85
    printer cables, 278–81
    printer errors, 265
    printer page feed and paper path, 266
    resolution of LCD displays, 146–47, 149–50
    resource conflicts, 29, 35–37
    USB connections, 88, 89, 90–91
    video cable operation, 102–5
    for viruses, 230–31
    Window's recognition of devices, 28–29
chips containing clock, CMOS memory, and
        battery, 57
circle images, distortions of, 138–40
cleaning
    computer case, 248
    computer interior, 7–8, 77
    discs, 203
    keyboards, 247, 258–59
    mouse, 256
    optical disc drive, 204
clearing logo and Windows cloud screen, 74, 220
clicking sounds
    in monitor, 51
    in Zip drives, 236–37

Close Program dialog box, 298–302
closing programs, 298–302
CMOS configuration utility
  clearing settings, 80–81
  connecting parallel ports and, 180–81, 282–85
  disabling floppy disk drive controller, 217
  error message, 80, 81
  failure to find floppy disk drive at boot and, 214–15
  freeing IRQs with, 35
  hard drive partitioning and, 188–89
  keys and key combinations into, *82, 83, 283*
  Plug and Play cards and, 38–39
  replacing battery and saving settings, 56–57
  trying to boot from floppy disk and, 83
  USB support, 91
CMOS Setup. *See* CMOS configuration utility
color and brightness problems, 110–21
  changes in colors, 118–19
  dark and washed out colors, 120–21
  discolored screen spotches, 116
  flowchart, *110–11*
  misconvergence and wrong lines of colors, 111
  shift toward specific color, 112–14
colors
  and brightness. *See* color and brightness problems
  depth settings, 118, 119
  fixed, or cracks on LCD displays, 144–45
  gradients, 118–19
  improving performance by reducing number of, 67
  memory requirements for higher resolution or
     increased number of, 125
  monitor, 112
  monitor controls, 114
  primary, and display images, 146
color signal, missing, 112–14
COM files, mouse drivers in, 254
compact discs. *See* CDs (compact discs)
COM ports, freeing IRQs by disabling, 35
Compress Bitmap setting, 331, 332
compressed air, removing dust with, 7–8, 77
Computer Properties
  adding IRQ and DMA channels, *36, 37*
  checking input/output and memory range, *39*
  recognizing Plug and Play card, *39*

computers
  best ambient temperature for, 6
  booting. *See* booting; booting failure; hard disk
     booting; rebooting
  clock, 56–57
  color of case bezel, 110
  connections. *See* connections
  crashes. *See* crashes
  displays. *See* displays; monitors
  drives. *See* drives; floppy disk drives; hard disk
     drives; optical disc drives; removable disks
  electrical shock when touching, 18
  emergencies affecting, 240–48, *240–41*
  grounding, 5
  hardware. *See* hardware; hardware problems
  input. *See* joysticks; keyboards; mouse
  liquid spills inside, 246, 248
  making filters for vents of, 8
  noises. *See* noises
  notebook. *See* notebook computers
  opening and working in, 6–8, 172
  performance. *See* performance
  printers. *See* printers; printing
  proper air flow and cover of, 7
  removing dust from interior of, 7–8, 77
  screen image extended to case bezel, 136
  software. *See* software
  startup with blank screen, 68–73, *68–69. See also*
     startup
  system. *See* system
  timeout settings, 322–25
  tips on reassembling, 21
  troubleshooting. *See* troubleshooting PCs
  unblocking and cleaning vents of, 6, 7, 8
Config.sys file
  files loaded by, 301
  hard disk boot failure and, 225
  mouse function and, 255
  reinstalling Windows and, 339–40
configuration information
  CMOS. *See* CMOS configuration utility
  editing system, 58, 59
  hard disk booting problems and, 224, 225
  monitor, 126

ink jet printers
  determining language of, 268–71
  failure of self test, 264–67
  as GDI printers, 269
  running self test, 262, 263
input and output
  checking for adapter card, 37
  joysticks, 84, 92–97
  keyboards, 246–47, 251, 258–59
  monitors. *See* displays; monitors
  mouse, 252, 254–57
  printers. *See* printers
install file (Setup) for printer
  failure to check for, 294–96
  printer not recognized by, 304–6
installing. *See also* reinstalling; uninstalling
  blank screen due to errors in, 69, 70–71
  changes in Registry after, 12–13
  drive problems after. *See* drive problems after
    installation
  hardware or software and crashes after, 10–13
  memory, 62
  printer and failure to check for setup file, 294–96
  printer with missing driver, 288–92
  printer driver, closing programs for, 298–302
  Resource Meter, 16–17
  System Monitor, 61, *61*
  USB devices on second computer, 89
  Windows. *See* reinstalling Windows
interlaced resolution
  noninterlaced resolution vs., 125
  eliminating flicker when switching to
    noninterlaced mode from, 159–60
Interrupt Request. *See* IRQ (Interrupt Request)
Iomega Zip drives, 236, 237
IRQ (Interrupt Request)
  DMA conflicts for resources with, 26, 31–32
  editing, 32
  freeing, 35, 36
  two devices using one, 39
IRQ Holder for PCI Steering technology, 39

Jaz Zip drives, 236
jittery images, 154–55
Job Timeout, 323, 325
joysticks
  calibrating, 97
  fixing nonfunctioning, 92–97
  quick fix, 84

keyboards. *See also* keys and key combinations
  beep codes and, *78–79*
  cleaning, 247, 258–59
  liquid spills on, 246–48
  removing keys, 251, 258
  replacement, 246
keys and key combinations
  booting while pressing Spacebar, 83
  bringing up Close Program, 298, 299, 301–2
  clearing logo during booting, 74
  finding printer driver settings, 334
  getting into CMOS Setup, *82, 283*
  switching between monitors, 113, 148
  switching between MS-DOS and Windows, 51, 60

languages, printer, 268–71
  built-in menu for determining, 270
  printer driver for determining, 269
  searching printer manual to determine, 268–69
  switching between multiple, 271
  trial-and-error determination of, 270–71
  versions of, 289
laptop computers. *See* notebook computers

laser printers
  determining language of, 268–71
  failure of self-test, 264–67
  low supplies of toner, 240
  running self test, 262, 263
LCD (liquid crystal display) display problems,
      142–55. *See also* LCD (liquid crystal display)
      monitors
  blank screen and resolution capability, 149–50
  connections, 145, 152
  correcting image size and position, 136–37
  correcting moiré patterns, 168–69
  damaged monitors, 144–45
  extending image to monitor edge, 136
  flowchart, *142–43*
  horizontal lines, 152
  matching computer to native resolution, 146–47
  resolution changes, 130
  stuck pixels, 143
LCD (liquid crystal display) monitors
  brightness and contrast controls, 121
  digital, 142
  display image accuracy and, 140
  display problems. *See* LCD (liquid crystal display)
      display problems
  horizontal lines on, 157
  non-native resolution settings, 169
legacy devices, recognizing, 34–37
lights
  power problems and dimming, 18–19
  screen brightness and colors and ambient, 121
line conditioners, 19
lines
  distorted, 138–40
  horizontal, on LCD, 152, 157
  on LCD, 144–45
  moiré patterns, 166–69
  moving, 164
liquid crystal displays. *See* LCD (liquid crystal
      display) monitors
liquid spills in computer or keyboard, 246–48
Logical Block Addressing (LBA), 188–89
logical drives, 187–88
Lose Your Mind Development, 17
LPT1, LPT2, and LPT3. *See* printer ports

Macintosh printers, 273, 288
magnetic fields
  rotated images caused by, 156
  screen splotches caused by, 116
mailing label stuck in printer, 241
MAKEBOOT utility, 227
managing power, computer crashes due to problems
      in, 14–15
manual, finding printer languages in, 268–69
Master (MA) settings, 175, 188, 192
memory. *See also* resources
  checking memory range for adapter card, 37
  computer crashes due to insufficient, 16–17
  finding leaks in, 17
  for more colors or higher resolution, 125
  swap files and virtual, 60–62
  for True Color settings, 119
memory modules
  blank screen at incorrect installation of, 71
  correct seating and cleaning of, 76–77
  failure of self test of, 76–77
  installing, 62
  swapping, 77
memory self test. *See* power-on self test
Microsoft Basic Mouse, downloading, 254
Microsoft Diagnostic (MSD) program
  diagnosis of game port and joystick failure, 93–94
  starting, 92–93, *93*
Microsoft MS-DOS
  fixing resolution problems in, 132–33
  mouse driver files in, 254–55
  switching between Windows and, 51
  testing monitors and, 107–8
  testing printer-computer communication and,
      273–77, 279
Microsoft Notepad, 160
Microsoft Windows. *See also* Microsoft Windows
      98; Microsoft Windows 2000
  Add Printer Wizard, 270, 271
  Advanced Power Management, *14, 15*

printer software drivers, *continued*

  stopping print spooling, 312–14

  timing out of computer before finishing print job, 322–25

printer software problems, 286–306

  closing programs for printer driver installation, 298–302

  drivers. *See* printer software drivers

  failure of printer driver or install program to see printer, 304–6

  failure to check for setup file before installing printer, 294–96

  flowchart, *286–87*

  printer installation and problem of missing driver, 288–92

PrintGear printer language, 272

printing. *See also* printers

  CMOS settings, 81

  unwanted speaker noises while, 49

Print Processor, 320

professional data recovery, 239, 243, 244

programs. *See also* software

  closing, for printer driver installation, 298–302

  computer crashes following installation of, 10, 12–13

  enlarging text in, 129

  insufficient memory for, 16–17

  missing DLL files and deleted, 24–25

  moving, to hard disk without reinstalling, 192–94

  slow performance when switching between, 60–62

quality flaws. *See* display quality flaws

RAW Spool Data Format, 318, 320

reassembling computers, tips for, 21

rebooting. *See also* booting

  holding down Spacebar while, 83

  spontaneous, 18

recognizing

  of adapter cards by BIOS, 33, 39

  of adapter cards by Device Manager, 32–33

  of devices by Device Manager, 28–29, *28, 35,* 39, 252

  of devices by Windows, 28–29

  of legacy devices, 34–37

  non–Plug and Play adapter cards, 34–37

  Plug and Play adapter cards, 38–39

  parallel ports, 277, *277*

  of printer by install file, 304–6

recovery. *See* data recovery

Recycle Bin

  recovering accidentally deleted files from, 242

  recovering files not in, 243

red *X* icon, 26, 29

reformatting hard disk drive, 21. *See also* formatting

Refresh Rate

  displaying resolutions, 133

  eliminating flicker, 159

  eliminating muddy images, 161

  enlarging images on CRT, 135

  image distortions due to, 137

Registry

  editing, 25, 226–27, 301

  effect of moving programs on, 192

  reducing slowness by cleaning out, 59

  software installation and changes in, 12–13, 301

Registry Editor, 25, *25,* 226, *227*

reinstalling. *See also* installing; uninstalling

  adapter cards, 28–33

  moving programs to new hard drive without, 192–94

  printer, 295–96

  solving blank screen problems by, 69, 70–71

  software, 13

  Windows. *See* reinstalling Windows

reinstalling Windows

  after crashes, 13, 21

  Windows 98, 338–40

  Windows 2000, 337

WINNT directory, 231
wiring, electrical, 5, 18
WordPad. *See* Microsoft WordPad
write-protected disks, 238
writing to removable disks, problems with, 238

XCOPY command, 194

yellow circle with exclamation point icon, 11, 26, 29, 252

ZDNet Software Library, 17
Zip drives
  clicking noise in, 236–27
  failure rates, 237
Zoom feature, enlarging text with, 129

About the authors

M. David Stone is an award-winning freelance writer and computer industry consultant with special areas of expertise in storage, displays, printers, scanners, digital cameras, and word processing. His 25 years of experience in writing about science and technology includes a nearly 20-year concentration on PC hardware and software. He also has a proven track record of making technical issues easy for nontechnical readers to understand, while holding the interest of more knowledgeable readers. Writing credits include seven computer-related books, major contributions to four others, and more than 2,000 articles in national and worldwide computer and general interest publications. Much of Mr. Stone's current writing is for *PC Magazine*, where he has been a frequent contributor since 1983 and a contributing editor since 1987. His work includes feature articles, special projects, reviews, and both hardware and software solutions for *PC Magazine's* Solutions column. He is also a regular contributor to *Computer Shopper*, primarily for hardware buying guides, and has extensive experience writing for a more general audience. As Computers Editor at *Science Digest* from 1984 until the magazine stopped publication, he wrote both a monthly column and additional articles. His newspaper column on computers appeared in the *Newark Star Ledger* from 1995 through 1997.

Mr. Stone's non-computer-related work includes the *Project Data Book* for NASA's Upper Atmosphere Research Satellite, and magazine articles and multimedia productions on subjects ranging from cosmology to ape language experiments. He also develops and writes testing scripts for leading computer magazines, including *PC Magazine's* PC Labs. His scripts have covered a wide range of subjects, including computers, scanners, printers, modems, word processors, fax modems, and communications software. He lives just outside of New York City and considers himself a New Yorker at heart.

Alfred Poor is one of the most widely read experts on computer troubleshooting and upgrades, with monthly readership in magazines and on the Web measured in the millions. He is an independent technology industry analyst and freelance writer, specializing in PC-compatible microcomputer hardware and software products. He brings to his work strong communication skills, a broad background covering a wide range of products, more than 19 years of experience with the microcomputer market, and the ability to make complex computer concepts accessible to nontechnical people, especially business professionals.

Mr. Poor has written feature articles and reviews for *PC Magazine* since 1983 and has been a contributing editor since 1989. He also contributes to the magazine's Solutions column. He is a columnist with *Computer Shopper* magazine, where he has written Alfred Poor's Computer Cures since 1994. In addition, he was the author of the Help section for *Family PC* from 1996 to 1999. He has had reviews and articles published in *PC Week, PC Sources, Windows Sources,* and *Computer Life* magazines.

Mr. Poor is a member of the Society for Information Display, and is a founding member of the international *Display of the Year Award Committee* for that organization, serving as the committee chair 1999 through 2001. He is a contributing editor for the organizations magazine *Information Display.* He has been a frequent guest on computer radio shows, including *The Personal Computer Show* on WBAI in New York and *The Compududes* on WHYY in Philadelphia. He lives in bucolic Bucks County, Pennsylvania.

The manuscript for this book was prepared and galleyed using Microsoft Word 2000. Pages were composed using Adobe PageMaker 6.52 for Windows, with text in ACaslon Regular and display type in Gill Sans. Composed pages were delivered to the printer as electronic prepress files.

Cover designer

Landor Associates

Interior graphic designer

James D. Kramer

Principal compositor

Dan Latimer

Principal graphic artist

Rob Nance

Manuscript editor

Cheryl Penner

Copy editor

Lisa Pawlewicz

Indexer

Shane-Armstrong Information Systems

Target your
solution and fix it
yourself—fast!

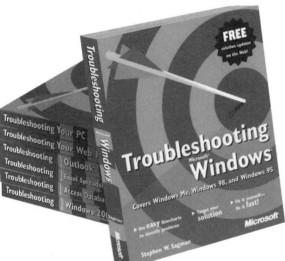

When you're stuck with a computer problem, you need answers right now. *Troubleshooting* books can help. They'll guide you to the source of the problem and show you how to solve it right away. Use easy diagnostic flowcharts to identify problems. Get ready solutions with clear, step-by-step instructions. Go to quick-access charts with *Top 20 Problems* and *Prevention Tips*. Find even more solutions with handy *Tips* and *Quick Fixes*. Walk through the remedy with plenty of screen shots to keep you on track. Find what you need fast with the extensive, easy-reference index. And keep trouble at bay with the Troubleshooting Web site—updated every month with new FREE problem-solving information. Get the answers you need to get back to business fast with *Troubleshooting* books.

Troubleshooting Microsoft® Access Databases
(Covers Access 97 and Access 2000)
ISBN 0-7356-1160-2
U.S.A. $19.99
U.K. £14.99
Canada $28.99

Troubleshooting Microsoft Excel Spreadsheets
(Covers Excel 97 and Excel 2000)
ISBN 0-7356-1161-0
U.S.A. $19.99
U.K. £14.99
Canada $28.99

Troubleshooting Microsoft® Outlook®
(Covers Microsoft Outlook 2000 and Outlook Express)
ISBN 0-7356-1162-9
U.S.A. $19.99
U.K. £14.99
Canada $28.99

Troubleshooting Microsoft Windows®
(Covers Windows Me, Windows 98, and Windows 95)
ISBN 0-7356-1166-1
U.S.A. $19.99
U.K. £14.99
Canada $28.99

Troubleshooting Microsoft Windows 2000 Professional
ISBN 0-7356-1165-3
U.S.A. $19.99
U.K. £14.99
Canada $28.99

Troubleshooting Your Web Page
(Covers Microsoft FrontPage® 2000)
ISBN 0-7356-1164-5
U.S.A. $19.99
U.K. £14.99
Canada $28.99

Troubleshooting Your PC
ISBN 0-7356-1163-7
U.S.A. $19.99
U.K. £14.99
Canada $28.99

Microsoft Press® products are available worldwide wherever quality computer books are sold. For more information, contact your book or computer retailer, software reseller, or local Microsoft Sales Office, or visit our Web site at mspress.microsoft.com. To locate your nearest source for Microsoft Press products, or to order directly, call 1-800-MSPRESS in the U.S. (in Canada, call 1-800-268-2222).

Prices and availability dates are subject to change.

mspress.microsoft.com

Target your
solution
and fix it
yourself—
fast!

U.S.A. **$19.99**
U.K.   £14.99
Canada $28.99
ISBN: 0-7356-1160-2

Trouble with your database? TROUBLESHOOTING MICROSOFT® ACCESS DATABASES can help you fix it. This plain-language book will guide you to the source of your problem—and show you how to solve it. Use easy flowcharts to identify your database problems. Get ready solutions full of clear, step-by-step instructions. Go to the quick-access chart for *Top 20 Problems*. Discover even more solutions with handy *Tips* and *Quick Fixes*. Walk through the remedy with plenty of screen shots. Find what you need fast with the extensive, easy-reference index. And keep trouble at bay with the Troubleshooting Web site—updated every month with new FREE solutions.

mspress.microsoft.com

Proof of Purchase

0-7356-1163-7

Do not send this card with your registration.
Use this card as proof of purchase if participating in a promotion or
rebate offer on *Troubleshooting Your PC*. Card must be used in conjunction with
other proof(s) of payment such as your dated sales receipt—see offer details.

Troubleshooting Your PC

WHERE DID YOU PURCHASE THIS PRODUCT?

CUSTOMER NAME

mspress.microsoft.com

Microsoft Press, PO Box 97017, Redmond, WA 98073-9830

OWNER REGISTRATION CARD

Register Today!

0-7356-1163-7

Return the bottom portion of this card to register today.

Troubleshooting Your PC

FIRST NAME   MIDDLE INITIAL   LAST NAME

INSTITUTION OR COMPANY NAME

ADDRESS

CITY   STATE   ZIP

(   )

E-MAIL ADDRESS   PHONE NUMBER

U.S. and Canada addresses only. Fill in information above and mail postage-free.
Please mail only the bottom half of this page.

**For information about Microsoft Press®
products, visit our Web site at
mspress.microsoft.com**